MOBILE MILLIONAIRE

Making The Most From Digital Marketing Using Mobile Tools

STEPHEN AKINTAYO

Disclaimer

This book is not intended for use as a source of legal, business, accounting or financial advice. All readers are advised to seek he services of competent professionals in legal, business, accounting and finance fields.

Table of Contents

CHAPTER ONE

THE POWER OF THE MOBILE

"What new technology does is to create new opportunities to do a job that customers wantdone faster and more efficient."

-Tim O'reilly

The number of unique mobile subscribers around the world will surpass 5 billion later this year, according to a new GSMA study. Mobile technology (and devices) form a critical part of innovation technology, which in the 21st century is referred to as the "Third Platform." Mobile (or Smart) devices — portable tools that connect to the internet — have become a part of our lives. In the last quarter of 2010, sales of smart phones outpaced those of PCs for the first time, according to data from IDC. By 2014, more smart devices could be used to access the internet than traditional computers. There is an obvious move to an increasingly mobile world, and this is creating new players and new opportunities for a variety of industries. According to Hindustantimes.com

With populations in Asia, and notably India, on the rise, the number, which stood at 4.8 billion a year ago, should mushroomto 5.7 billion, or three quarters of the world's population, by 2020.

Asia will account for around half total growth, according to GSMA's 'Mobile Economy' report with India alone adding some 310 million new subscribers in the coming three years.

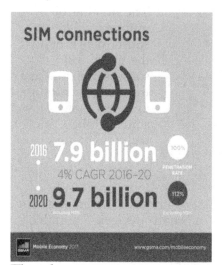

The study also showed a trend towards mobile broadband networks and smartphones, said the study, which highlighted the mobile industry's growing contribution to economic activity and social development.

The telecoms sector account for a 4.4 percent share of world GDP worth $3.3 trillion dollars last year, rising to a 4.9percent share by 2020, for economic value equivalent to $4.2 trillion.

The report said the mobile ecosystem last year employed 28.5 million people directly or indirectly, however, this figure would rise to 30.9 million by 2020.

It added the sector would contribute $500 billion in tax receipts by 2020, up from $450 billion last year, not including revenue from spectrum auctions, worth almost $19 billion in 2016.

Operators are forecast to invest a further $700 billion by 2020 when 5G connectivity is set to bring ever faster data connection.

Ahead of 5G – forecast to enable subscribers to download a full HD film in less than one second – 4G has been steadily becoming the norm, rising from current market penetration of 21 percent to 41 percent by 2020. GSMA said '2016 saw 580 4G networks launched in 188 countries covering 60% of the World population.

The organization added 55 percent of overall connections were now running on mobile broadband (3G/4G) networks, which are forecast to account for almost three-quarters of connections by 2020.Emerging markets will also create plenty of opportunities related to smart technology, and this will not be limited to for-profit enterprises.

As smart devices become increasingly accepted, companies are also moving into adjacent markets to exploit new revenue models such as mobile commerce (m-commerce) and mobile payment systems. It should be noted that a number of data and tech giants are already jockeying for position in this area.

This growth is mirrored by strong mobile connections growth, to almost 7 billion connections, as many consumers have multiple devices or use multiple SIM cards to access the best tariffs, while firms in many industry sectors roll out M2M applications to boost their own productivity and tap into new markets. Despite challenging economic headwinds in many regions, the market is expected to grow even more strongly on the dimension of connections over the next five years, with 3 billion additional connections expected to be added between 2012 and 2017, a growth rate of 7.6% p.a.

Benefits of the Mobile Technology

 In the past few years technology has drastically changed the way business is conducted. Not only has the internet empowered the consumer, but it has also given new powers to sales reps. Equipped with smartphones, tablets, and an arsenal of

applications and software to interpret loads of data, the savvy salesperson must remain "in-the-know" with today's technological trends.

"Social media" "4G" "apps" and a plethora of other mobile technologies have already become indispensable for many businesses. One poll conducted by AT&T found that 98% of small businesses use wireless technologies in their operations, with two-thirds (66%) indicating they could not survive- without them.

1. Access

Access is the primary benefit of mobile technology. And what's even better is that there are thousands of applications and programs that can help you stay informed and relevant to your precious customers. For example, marketing automation and CRM coupled with mobile tech can tell you every detail

 regarding a lead anywhere at any time. When your prospects are ready to take action, mobile technology enables you to seize the moment making it easier to close a deal. Internet technology lets you

strike while the iron is hot.

2. Higher Efficiency

Whether you own a smartphone, tablet, computer or other technological contraption, you are using a device that has been designed to help you become more productive and efficient.

3. Reduced Cost of Operations

At a glance, it could seem that the cost of expanding technologies may cause a deficit in the company's expenses. However, the increased productivity can easily outweigh the minimal cost and effort it would take to implement a new technology. For example, if your company has 10 employees and each employee saves 1 hour or 60 minutes per week by implementing a new technology, you've just lowered your staff cost by over 500 hours per year. The potential savings could be amazing with the right software and the right equipment for your company.

4. Endless Possibilities

Though its capabilities are already vast, mobile technology is growing rapidly. There is ample room for improvement and innovation to help you better serve your customers. As a forward-thinking leader, push the envelope of the sales industry and embrace every opportunity to expand your levels of efficiency and productivity through technology.

Facts About Mobile Devices

Mobile Device Online Dominance:

Mobile devices are the new primary design point for end-user access

➤ Soaring Sales Rates in Mobile Devices: Mobile devices arethe new primary design point for end-user access. Participating across the full spectrum of mobile devices (smart phones, mini tablets, full-size tablets, PC/tablet hybrids, etc.) and aligning with mobile platforms that win the battle for developers and apps is the essential recipe for end user device manufacturers; seeing these as whollydistinct markets is an obsolete vision.

➤ Mobile Application Platforms (App):
Mobile platformsthat, by the end of 2013, fail to crack the 50% barrier of developers that are "very interested" in developing apps for them will be on a gradual track to demise. The real "PC versus mobile device" battle is between PCsoftware platforms (especially Windows) and the leading mobile device platforms (iOS and Android). And the market power of these competing platforms iOS, Android, Windows, and other mobile software platforms will depend completely on the ability of each platform to attract large numbers of app developers.

➤ Strategic Customer Communities:
In 2013, the accelerating shift to the 3rd platform (of which mobile devices is chief) will continue to raise the profile of key customer communities that are driving industry growth and redefining the design points of successful offerings. Worldwide IT spending will grow by 5.7%, thanks largely to mobile devices

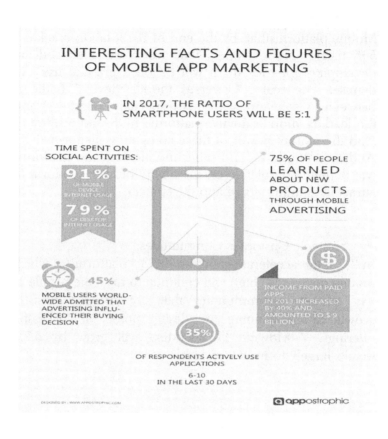

INTERESTING FACTS AND FIGURES
OF MOBILE APP MARKETING

{ IN 2017, THE RATIO OF
SMARTPHONE USERS WILL BE 5:1 }

TIME SPENT ON
SOICIAL ACTIVITIES:

91%
OF MOBILE
DEVICE
INTERNET USAGE

79%
OF DESKTOP
INTERNET USAGE

75% OF PEOPLE
LEARNED
ABOUT NEW
PRODUCTS
THROUGH MOBILE
ADVERTISING

45%
MOBILE USERS WORLD-
WIDE ADMITTED THAT
ADVERTISING INFLU-
ENCED THEIR BUYING
DECISION

INCOME FROM PAID
APPS
IN 2013 INCREASED
BY 40% AND
AMOUNTED TO $ 9
BILLION

35%
OF RESPONDENTS ACTIVELY USE
APPLICATIONS
6-10
IN THE LAST 30 DAYS

DESIGNED BY : WWW.APPOSTROPHIC.COM

appostrophic

Hindrances To Being Connected To The Mobile Web

There are still many adults and young people who
would appreciate the social and economic benefits of
mobile technology but are unable to access it,

16

highlighting a huge opportunity for future growth and a challenge to all players in the industry ecosystem to expand the scope

of products and services to tap this demand. Some of the easily identified challenges being:

- Expensive devices:
In many developing countries, due to high poverty rate, some of the population considers these devices as too expensive. *But this isquickly changing.*

- Expensive service plans:
For some others, the service plans are simply too expensive.

Mobile Is The Future. And There's No Such Thing As Communication Overload.

Eric Schmidt
Google

- Poor mobile network: Mobile network is usually better in the city centers. At the suburbs, there are simply no mobile networks to connect to.

- Content is not always available in the local language.
- Awareness of the value of internet is limited.
- Availability of power sources is limited.
- Networks can't support large amounts of data.

CHAPTER TWO

THE HISTORY OF MOBILE TECHNOLOGY

"MOBILE IS THE PERFECT EXAMPLE OF WHAT IS ENABLING ECONOMIC GROWTH IN THE TECHNOLOGY SECTOR."

MAX LEVCHIN

Mobile phones have come a long way in the last 70 years, so be thankful yours fits in your pocket. Maybe one day it will even be able to bend like a piece of thin plastic (*there are rumorsof a flexible phone already*). Maybe youwon't even have to touch it, doing all of your multitasking from cellular implants. But 70 years ago, you'd be lugging a 25-pound 'portable' phone on your back, with a very limited 5-mile range.

A Brief History of the Mobile

1938

Not quite what you would consider a mobile phone,

the SCR-194 and 195 were the first portable AM radios, produced by the U.S. Army Signal Corps Engineering Laboratories in Fort Monmouth, New Jersey. Considered the first "walkie talkie," these devices weighed roughly 25 pounds and had a 5 - mile range. They were widely used for infantry battalion and company intercommunication during World War II.

1940

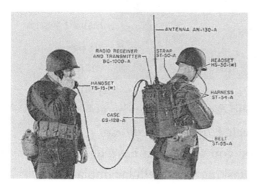

Next came the SCR-300 radio transceiver, developed for the U.S. Military by Motorola. This time a portable FM radio, it weighed anywhere from 32 to 38 pounds with a 3-mile range. It replaced the SCR-194 and 195 with nearly 50,000 units used in World War II by Allied Forces.

1942

Motorola produced the first handy "walkie talkie" for the U.S., labelled SCR-536. 130,000 units were manufactured and used during the war. Back toAM, this handheld version shedthe fat off the previous two transceivers, weighing only 5 pounds. But its land range was only 1-mile (3 miles over water). Moving away from military-grade portable radios, we get to the mobile radio telephones

1946

Bell System introduced the first commercial mobile telephone service, called theMobile Telephone System (MTS). The original equipmentwas large, weighing 80 pounds (not quite what you would call mobile) with limited calling bands available from AT&T. The service wasn't cheap either— costing $30 a month (roughly $330 today) with additional per call charges. Not really intended for regular Joe Blows, these devices were used by utilities, truck fleet operators, and reporters.

The telephones used were not particularly portable and used a half-duplex "press to speak" system where the caller would have to release the button to hear the other person. That very same year two BellLabs engineers proposed the foundations for the modern cellular network. At the time, the plans were daring, and it took until the 1960s for the plans to be implemented and even longer to come to market.

1960

Ericsson's Mobile System A (MSA) was the first partly automatic mobile system for automobiles. First used by Sweden, the unit weighed a whopping 88 pounds. Again, "mobile" is kind of a misnomer, considering it is equivalent to almost 300 iPhones!

1964

With the adaption of Bell's newer pre-cellularImproved Mobile Telephone Service (IMTS), auto owners saw lighter, more advanced mobile car phones with push buttons. This one by Motorola weighed 40 pounds, half as much of the original units from the '40s. Overthe years, they managed to get down into the 20-pound range. But they never managed to get into the hands of Joe Blow, with a still-hefty price and rationed service throughout the nation.

With a prototype of the DynaTAC(Dynamic Adaptive Total Area Coverage) portable phone, former Motorola Vice President Martin Cooper made the first private, practical mobile phone call in a non-vehicle setting. Who would he call? His rival at Bell Labs, Joel S. Engel.

1982

With the impressive size of the DynaTAC prototype, it's disappointing to see Nokia's Mobira Senator weighing in at 22 pounds. It launched during the world's first fully automatic international cellular service—NMT—the first-generation (1G) of mobile communications.

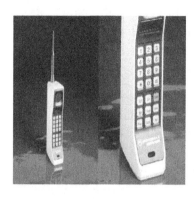

1983

10 years later after the prototype, Motorola's DynaTAC cellular phone was made available to the public, weighing under 2 pounds, but costing nearly $4,000 (almost $9,000 today)— which is why it was strictly for the Gordon Gekkos of the world. It worked on AMPS, North America's first 1G analog service, launched first by Ameritech in Chicago.

1984

Back to larger mobile devices, the Mobira Talkman brought longer talk time at cheaper costs. The DynaTAC could only manage 60 minutes of talk time, but this miniature beast gave hours or voice-to-voice communication

1989

Next up was Motorola's MicroTAC, which introduced the first flip phone design. The hardware was place in a hinged section of the phone, reducing the phone's size when not in use. It was truly the world's first pocket phone.

1992

The Motorola International 3200 became the first hand-sized digital mobile phone that used 2G digitally encrypted technology (unveiled in 1991 as GSM).

1993

Perhaps the world's first smartphone, IBM Simon was a mobile phone, pager, fax machine and PDA, all rolled into one. It included a calendar, address book, clock, calculator, notepad, email, gamers and a touchscreen with QWERTY keyboard. It originally sold for

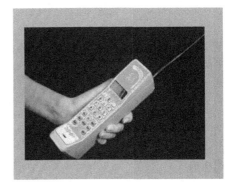

$899, which would be just over $1,300 nowadays. You may remember Simon from Sandra Bullock'sThe Net.

1 9 9 4

Car phones remained popular, despite their smaller pocket-sized versions, but Motorola's Bag Phone (2900) was the car phone to have due to its long talk time, great battery life and superior signal range. They first worked with 1G networks, but eventually crossed over into 2G territory.

1996

Still shrinking the line of TACs, Motorola unveiled the first clamshell mobile phone with StarTAC. It improved the folding feature by collapsing in half, which is why it's called "clamshell"— because it resembles a clam opening and closing shut. It ran on 1G networks, but eventually crossed over into the world of 2G. It's said to be inspired by the communicator from the original Star Trek series.

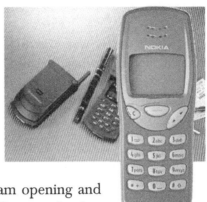

1997

The Simon was good, but the Nokia 9000 Communicator was what really brought on the smartphone era. It was the first cell phone that could also be called a mini-computer (though it had limited web access). When opened, the long ways clamshell design revealed an LCD screen and full QWERTY keyboard— the first on a mobile phone.

1998

The Nokia 8810 was the first cell phone without an external antenna whip or stub -antenna, possibly paving the way for iPhones and DROIDs. It also made mobile phones more aesthetically pleasing, with its sliding keypad cover.

1999

One of the most popular mobile phones in history was the Nokia 3210, with over 160 million sold. It was one of the first to allow picture messages, but only preinstalled ones like "Happy Birthday" and was one of the first to be marketing toward young people.

1999

Nokia's 7110 was the first cell phone to incorporate Wireless Application Protocol (WAP), which gave mobile users web access for simple devices—a stripped-down, mostly text version, but a revolutionary step for mobile internet.

1999

GeoSentric was responsible for the world's first mobile phone and a GPS navigator integrated in one product—the Benefon Esc! It was splash proof, greyscale, and allowed users to load maps to trace position and movement.

1999

In Japan, Kyocera's Visual Phone (VP-201) was the first to have a built-in camera, but it was designed primarily38as a peer -to-peer video phone, as opposed to Sharp's the next year...

2000

Sharp was first to the
camera phone m
market with their J-
SH04 (J- Phone),
released by J-Mobile in
Japan. It offered a mere
0.1 megapixel
resolution.

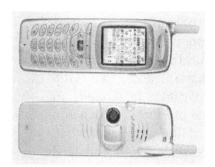

Some like to give credit to Olympus for being the first
camera to transmit digital images over a cellular network
with their Deltis VC-1 100. Others prefer Philippe Kahn's
story of rigging up a camera to a cellphone with wires to
send images of his new born baby. But the J -SH04 was
the first commercially available cell phone to have an
integrated CCD sensor, with the Sha- Mail (Picture-Mail)
infrastructure. This was the start of what we know as
MMS.

2002

Not too far from the J-
Phone, the Sanyo 5300
from Sprint was the first
camera phone sold in

North America.

2002

RIM's BlackBerry 5810 was not the first BlackBerry device, but it was the first to incorporate a mobile phone into their popular brand of data-only devices. Professionals who needed immediate access to their emails and schedules were the main target for RIM, but the built-in phone made it appealing to everyone. The downside? No speaker or microphone.

2002

One of the first phones to equip a fully functional web experience and integrate an instant messaging client (AIM) was the Danger Hiptop in 2002, later re-branded the T - Mobile Sidekick.

It's messaging features and keyboard made it one of the best-selling phones in the deaf community. Also new was an LCD screen that rotated and flipped to reveal a large QWERTY keyboard.

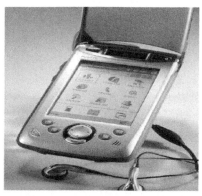

2002

Perhaps surpassing the BlackBerry achievements, Microsoft's Pocket PC Phone Edition started spreading across PDAs like wildfire, including the HP Jornada 928 Wireless Digital Assistant, combining the best of the PDA with integrated wireless voice and data capabilities.

It was a nice addition to the older Windows Mobile Classic devices, which essential ran a mini-version of Windows XP.

2002

Another PDA adding phone support was Palm's Treo 180 by Handspring, running the Palm OS.

2 0 0 4

The next highly popular device was a camera phone called the Motorola RAZR, which was first marketed as a "fashion" phone in 2004, selling 50 million units by mid-2006.

It helped give cell phones a new look, which were getting stale with the same ol' boring designs. Though nothing revolutionary, its looks did more than impress.

2005

The first Palm smartphone to operate outside of the Palm OS was the Treo 700w, powered by Windows Mobile. It was a great alternative for users who needed access to Microsoft software on the go.

2005

Believe it or not, the iPhone was not the first cell phone to haveApple's iTunes music player integrated. Itwas the Motorola ROKRE1, but it only could manage 100 songs at a time—not quite then same as an iPhone.

2007

In 2007, Steve Jobs introduced the Apple iPhone,   a revolutionary touchscreen smartphone. It wasn't the first smartphone, but it was the first to get the user interface

right, eventually adapting 3G technology (which was already available since 2001).

2008

The first smartphone to run Google's Android OS was the HTC Dream slider smartphone. It featured a QWERTY keyboard, full HTML web browser, Gmail, YouTube and more, and paved the way for phones like the Nexus One and Motorola DROID.

2010

The HTC EVO 4G from Sprint was the first cellular phone to meet 4G standards, running on the WiMAX network. It was sold powered by Android 2.1 and had one of the largest touchscreen displays, an 8MP camera, HD video capture, HDMI output, Mobile Hotspot capability and HTC Sense.

THE HISTORY OF **MOBILE PHONES**

1973 1989 1992 1993 1998 1999 2000 2002 2004 2007 2008 2010 2014

first flip phone

Thought of as the world's first smart phone

"Merry Christmas"

Wireless Application Protocol (WAP)

integrate a mobile phone into the previously data-only device

The first Apple iPhone

The HTC EVO 4G was the first mobile phone to meet 4G standards

Android holds
67%
of the worldwide mobile phone market share

with iPhone holding
27%

Weight: 2 pounds

The first Android smartphone

SOURCES: http://www.businessinsider.com.au/complete-visual-history-of-cell-phones-2011-9?op=1#/#!/1-24
http://www.diymaclehistory.com/news/evolving-cell-phone-1973-2014/
http://cbs.net/i_ima.com/timeslineigallery/0,28227,1636864_1318481,00.htm
http://www.gizmodo.com.au/2014/09/android-continues-to-gain-market-share-over-apple-ios-in-australia/

SIGNET

36

CHAPTER THREE

MOST COMMONLY USED APPS ON MOBILE DEVICES

To make money online, it is important that you know where your market is. Then you can craft your marketing activities to reach your potential customers. It should be known that marketing is a game of numbers. The more your reach, the more your response rate (provided you get your homework right).

I think the biggest change, and one that we're already starting to see take shape, is that globally the majority of internet usage will be done via a mobile device and for most people the mobile web will be their primary – if not their only – way of experiencing the internet.

Over the past few years, the demand for smartphones has grown exponentially as companies develop increasingly advanced software and features. Popular mobile phone apps have truly revolutionized theentire mobile phone industry.

Smartphones are defined as mobile telephone devices boasting PC-like functionality and featuring powerful processors, open operating systems, vast memory capabilities, and the ability to interface with built-in features such as miniature QWERTY keyboards, touch screens, cameras, contact management programs, GPS or navigation hardware,media software for playing or storing music, videos, pictures, etc., and internet connectivity.

The first mobile device categorized as a "smartphone" appeared on the market in 1993, as a product called Simon, designed

While these programs would seem simple by today's standards, Simon was certainly the first phone of its kind, and set the precedent for phones such as the BlackBerry, released in 2001 and the iPhone, released in 2007.

Popular mobile phone apps (an abbreviation for 'applications') have become the next craze amongst smartphone users. Mobile service providers now offer a vast array of applications that can be downloaded directly onto smartphones. The Google Play Store, launched by Google Inc., has become the most widely recognized application service, offering both free and paid applications that can be downloaded directly to phones running on the Android OS.

by IBM and carried by Bell South. Simon featured an on - screen keyboard, a calendar, world clock, calculator, address book, email and facsimile capabilities and games.

Curious about applications for Smartphones? Begin by browsing Apple's App Store, or the Google Play Store. Here is a list of the most popular mobile phone apps and mobile phone app categories.

Distribution of time spent on apps on mobile devices in the United States in June 2015, by category

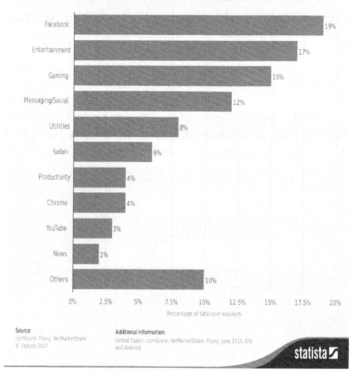

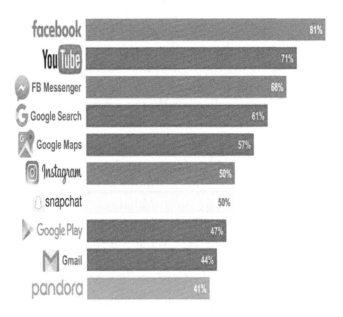

Top 10 Mobile Apps by Penetration of App Audience
Source: comScore Mobile Metrix, U.S., Age 18+, June 2017

facebook	81%
YouTube	71%
FB Messenger	68%
Google Search	61%
Google Maps	57%
Instagram	50%
snapchat	50%
Google Play	47%
Gmail	44%
pandora	41%

Top Ten Most Popular Mobile Phone Apps Categories

1. Voice Command/Voice-Control – Avariety of popular mobile apps for smart-phones have made it easier to use voice commands to look up contacts, dial phone calls by voice command, dictate e-mail or text messages, select music, or even browse websites or television stations by voice control, without pressing any buttons.

2.   MobiTV – This application offers bothtelevision and digital radio stations to mobile phones. MobiTV stations includeMSNBC,ABC News, ESPN, CNN, CSPAN, the Weather Channel, The Discovery Channel, etc.

3.   WhatsApp – Anyone interested in savingcell phone credits or reducing the cost of international phone calls is sure to praiseWhatsApp, a high quality application for free long distance calls over Wi-Fi or mobile data.

4.   Games - have ranked as some of the mostpopular applications offered through Apple's App Store and Google Play Store. Some of the most popular paid games in 2017 in App Store are; Minecraft: Pocket Edition, *Heads Up!*, Grand Theft Auto: San Andreas, Goat Simulator and NBA 2K17. While on Google Play Store, some of the most popular paid games are; Crashlands, Hearthstone: Heroes of Warcraft, Minecraft: Pocket Edition, Riptide GP Series, and Rollercoaster Tycoon.

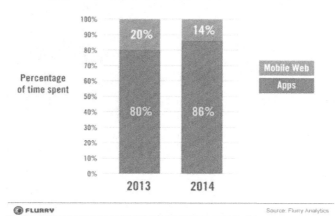

5. Social Networking Apps such asFacebook, WhatsApp, Messenger, WeChat, Instagram, Qzone, Weibo, Twitter, Pinterest, Snapchat and LinkedIn, have become top of the list of downloadable applications for smartphones.

6.   Productivity applications forsmartphones are highly praised for helping tech savvy users to keep their lives organized. With the advances made in mobile technology over the last few years and greater reliance on remote working, many businesses use mobile devices like smartphones and tablets to help them in managing their operations. Generally speaking, the days of relying on a PC to do everything are over - you can do it all from apps on your iPhone, iPad or Android. Examples include Boomerang, Doodle, FocusList, Genius Scan, etc.

7.   Search Tools have also been highlysuccessful mobile apps; particularly search tools that capitalize on the GPS capabilities of smart-phones. Avoid typing in your current location, and use apps such as Urban Spoon to search for nearbyrestaurants, Foursquare or Yelp for information on local shopping, nightlife, entertainment, and even maps.

8.   Financial tools – such as mobile bill payand mobile banking have become popular applications for professional's on-the-go. The capabilities of these apps are projected to increase in the future. Some of the best include Mint, You Need a Budget, Wally, and Acorns.

9.   Mailing/Postal Services - UPS Mobilefor iPhones and Androids allows users to print shipping labels, find UPS locations, estimate shipment costs, and delivery times, and track both incoming and outgoing shipping deliveries and packages.

Futuristic – Science Fiction fans willsurely be fans of some of the latest, futuristic apps such as holographic images and projectors, augmented reality applications, interactivity and crowd sourcing and real time collaboration apps.

CHAPTER FOUR

THE TOOLS OF THE MOBILE MILLIONAIRES

Mobile Marketing

Mobile marketing is marketing on or witha mobile device, such as a smartphone. Mobile marketing can provide customerswith timeand location-sensitive,

personalized information that promotes goods, services and ideas. Mobile (Digital) Marketing is a veritable tool both as a business and business-promoting tool. Personally, I make thousands of dollars each month doing mobile marketing (alone). It should be noted that mobile marketing can be both a business, and can also be a business-promoting tool.

This section seeks to explore some of the most common mobile marketing platformsexplored by the mobile millionaires (of which I am a player too).

Mobile Ads

This is a form of advertising viamobile phones or other mobile devices. It is a subset of mobile marketing. Mobile advertising is targeted at mobile phones, a cost value that came estimably to a global total of 4.6 billion as of 2009. The 50 emergence of this form of advertising is so real that there is now a dedicated global awards ceremony organized every year by Visiongain.

As mobile phones outnumberTV sets by over 3 to 1, and PC-based internet users by over 4 to 1, and the total laptop and desktop PC population by nearly 5 to 1, advertisers in many markets have recently rushed to this media. In Spain 75% of mobile phone owners receive ads, in France 62% and in Japan 54%. More remarkably as mobile advertising matures, like in the most advanced markets, the user involvement also matures. In Japan today, already 44% of mobile phone owners click on ads they receive on their phones. Mobile advertising was worth 900 million dollars in Japan alone. According to the research, theglobal mobile advertising market that is estimated to be $3 billion in 2014.

Furthermore, Berg Insight forecasts the global mobile advertising market to grow at a compound annual growth rate of 43 percent to €8.7 billion in 2014.

It is my earnest hope and desire that such data will be made available for Africa, especially Nigeria, the most populous black nation, so that we can maximize this invaluable asset.

Common Types of Mobile Ads

Mobile Web Banner (top of page) Mobile Web Poster (bottom of pagebanner),SMS advertising (which has been estimated at over 90%of mobile marketing revenue worldwide).

MMS advertising,

Advertising within mobile games Advertising within mobile videos, and during mobile

TV receipt,Full-screen interstitials, which appear while a requested item of mobile content or mobile web page is loading up andAudio advertisements that can take the form of a jingle before a voicemail recording, or an audio recording played while interacting with a telephone-based service such as movie ticketing or directory assistance.

How to Measure the Effectiveness of Mobile Ad Campaigns

The effectiveness of a mobile media ad campaign can be measured in a variety of ways. The main measurements are;

Views (Cost per Impression): thenumber of times target customers view the ad campaign.

Click-through (Cost per Click): thisinvolves the target clicking on the ad; he may or may not make a buying decision eventually.

Click-to-call rates: this involves thetarget clicking the ad, and eventually making a decision either to call formore information, or actually making a buying decision.

Cost per Install (CPI) where there thepricing model is based on the user installing an App on their mobile phone. CPI Mobile Advertising Networks work either as incent ornon-incent. In the incent model the user is given virtual points or rewards to install the game or App.

SMS Marketing: This is marketing that isdone through mobile phones' SMS (Short Message Service). It became increasingly popular in the early 2000s in Europe and other parts of the world when businesses started to collect mobile phone numbers and send off wanted (or unwanted) content.On average, SMS messages are read within four minutes, making them highly convertible.

Mobile Commerce: The phrasemobilecommercewas originally coined in 1997 tomean "the delivery of electronic commerce capabilities directly into the consumer's hand, anywhere, via wireless technology." Itis the use of wireless handheld devices such as cellular phones and laptops to conduct commercial transactions online. Mobilecommerce transactions continue to grow, and the term includes the purchase and sale of a wide range of goods and services, online banking, bill payment, information delivery and so on.

It is also known as e-commerce 62% of smartphone users havemade a purchase online using their mobile device in the last 6 months. One third of all ecommerce purchases during the 2015 holiday season were made on a smartphone. Ecommerce dollars now comprise 10% of ALL retail revenue. 80% of shoppers used a mobile phone inside of a physical store to either look up product reviews, compare prices or find alternative store locations. An estimated 10 Billion Mobile Connected Devices are currently in use.

Common Products and Services Available

The most common products and services available through the mobile commerce include (but not limited to) the following:

Mobile Money Transfer: This generallyrefers to payment services operated under financial regulations and performed from or via a mobile device. Instead of paying with cash, cheque, or credit cards, a consumer can use amobile phone to pay for a wide range of services and digital or hard goods.

Common mobile payment platforms in Nigeria are: Paypal, Flutterwave, Stripe, Alat, Paga, M-Teller, M-Naira, VTN, M - Wallet, Monitise, Access Mobile, Enterprise Mobile, Diamond Mobile, SwipeMax Wallet, Breeze Nigeria, Sterling Mobile, Wema Verve, EaZyMoney, QuickTeller, etc.

 Mobile ATM: The mobile ATM deviceeasily attaches to most Smartphones and dispenses money instantly and effortlessly – forever ending your search for the nearest bank or ATM. Just type in your personal pin code on your cell phone and access all your cash from the palm of your hand.

Mobile Ticketing:This is the processwhereby customers can order, pay for, obtain and validate tickets from any location and at any time using mobile phones or other mobile handsets. Mobile ticketing reduces the production and distribution costs connected with traditional paper-based ticketing channels and increase customer convenience by providing new and simple ways to purchase ticket.

Mobile Vouchers, Coupons and Loyalty Cards: Mobile ticketingtechnology can also be used for the distribution of vouchers, coupons, and loyalty cards. These items are represented by a virtual token that is sent to the mobile phone. A customer presenting a mobile phone with one of these tokens at the point of sale receives the same benefits as if they had the traditional token. Stores may send coupons to customers using location-based services to determine when the customer is nearby.

Content Purchase and Delivery: Currently, mobile content purchase and delivery mainly consists of the sale of ring-tones, wallpapers, and games for mobile phones. The convergence of mobile phones, portable audio players, and video players into a single device is increasing the purchase and delivery of full-length music tracks and video. The download speedsavailable with 4G networks make it possible to buy a movie on a mobile device in a couple of seconds.

Location-BasedServices:

Location-based services (LBS) are a general class of computer program-level services that use location data to control features. As such LBS is an information service and has a number of uses in social networking today as an entertainment service, which is accessible with mobile devices through the mobile network and which uses information on the geographical position of the mobile device. This has become more and more important with the expansion of the smartphone and tablet markets as well. The location of the mobile phone user is an important piece of information used during mobile commerce or m - commerce transactions. Knowing the location of the user allows for location-based services such as:

- Local Reporting

- Tracking People

Information Services: A widevariety of information services can be delivered to mobile phone users in much the same way as it is delivered to PCs. These services include:

- Stock quotes
- News
- Sports Score
- Financial Report
- Traffic Reporting

Customized traffic information, based on a user's actual travel patterns, can be sent to a mobile device. This customized data is more useful than a generic traffic-report broadcast, but was impractical before the invention of modern mobile devices due to the bandwidth requirements.

Mobile Banking: Banks and otherfinancial institutions use mobile commerce to allow their customers to access account information and make transactions, such as purchasing stocks, remitting money. This service is often referred to as Mobile Banking, or M-Banking.

Mobile Brokerage: Stock marketservices offered via mobile devices have also become more popular and are known as Mobile Brokerage. They allow the subscriber to react to market developments in a timely fashion and irrespective of their physical location.

Auctions: Over the past three yearsmobile reverse auction solutions have grown in popularity. Unlike traditional auctions, the reverse auction (or low-bid auction) bills the consumer's phone each time they place a bid. Many mobile SMS commerce solutions rely on a one-time purchase or one-time subscription; however, reverse auctions offer a high return for the mobile vendor as they require the consumer to make multiple transactions over a long period of time.

Mobile Browsing: Using a mobilebrowser — a World Wide Web browser on a mobile device — customercan shop online without having to be at their personal computer.

Mobile Purchase: Catalog merchantscan accept orders from customers electronically, via the customer's mobile device. In some cases, the merchant may even deliver the catalog electronically, rather than mailing a paper catalog to the customer. Some merchants provide mobile websites that are customized for the smaller screen and limited user interface of a mobile device.

In-Application Mobile Phone Payments: Payments can be madedirectly inside of an application running on a popular smartphone operating system, such as Google's Android OS. In-app purchases can be used to buy virtual goods, new and other mobile content and is ultimately billed by mobile carriers rather than the app stores themselves. Ericsson's IPX mobile commerce system is used by 120 mobile carriers to offer payment options such as try-before-you-buy, rentals and subscriptions

Mobile Marketing and Advertising:Email marketing is directly marketing a commercial message to a group of people using email. In its broadest sense, every email sent to a potential or current customer could be considered email marketing. It usually involves using email to send ads, request business, or solicit sales or donations, and is meant to build loyalty, trust, or brand awareness.

Types of Email Marketing

Transactional emails:These are emailssent to clients with whom you have some form of business transactions. The purpose of these emails is tofacilitate, complete, or confirm a transaction that the recipient has previously agreed to enter into with the sender, along with a few other narrow definitions of transactional messaging. Triggered transactional messages include dropped basket messages, password reset emails, purchase or order confirmation emails, order status emails, reorder emails and email receipts.

Direct emails:This involves sending anemail solely to communicate a promotional message (for example, an announcement of a special offer or a catalogue of products.

Uses of Email Marketing

There are three (3) basic uses of email marketing. They include;

- Sending email messages with the purpose of enhancing the relationship of a merchant with its current or previous customers, to encourage customer loyalty and repeat business.

- Sending email messages with the purpose of acquiring new customers or convincing current customers to purchase something immediately.

- Adding advertisements to email messages sent by other companies to their customers.

Opt-in emails: This is also known as *permission marketing*.

It is a method ofemail marketing where the recipient has already consented to receive it, either by direct or indirect subscriptions. Under this type of marketing, the recipient is always anticipating the email. This is mainly because the content of the email is somewhat relevant to her personal or business development.

How to Generate Lists of Email Clients

1. Keep a blog where people can have access to information that will help them become better in their life endeavors. You can then make them fill a form where they can subscribe for updates or newsletters.

2. You can give free materials that people will be interested in, but let them subscribe via email where you can send them a download link.

You can also rent (or buy)email addresses from service companies that offer such services.

Factors to Consider for Effective Email Marketing Campaigns

I. Pricing:People have a lot ofmessages and other activities competing for their attention. What will attract

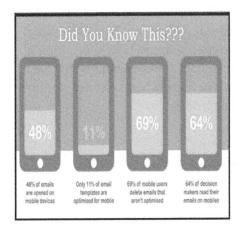

them to read and respond to your email will be your pricing offering. Make sure your price is competitive and reasonable enough for people to want to make a commitment to your services.

II. Duration:When you give abonus, specify when the offering opens and when it closes. Be keen on how long the discount opens for subscription. Make it short enough so as to generate more sales.

III. Flexibility:Be flexible in yourmethod of reply. It shouldn't necessarily be that your recipients must also reply you by email. Include your phone number, toll-free lines, social media handles and chat ID's like BlackBerryMessenger, WhatsApp, Twitter, etc.

The Principles of The Mobile Money

There are quite some principles that the *mobile millionaires* adopt. Knowing andpracticing these principles has made me a big player in the mobile world. These principles include:

The Principle of Simplicity: Thisprinciple states that whatever you do on the internet, especially with mobile technology, it must be easy enough for even the least educated person to use. Whenever I consider this principle, I think of www.google.com. The searchengine is so easy that every *John Doe* can use it.

The Principle of More: This principle isalso called *The Power of More*. It states that you must be willing to offer more than the users *deserve*. Do not hold back anything from your users. Whatever it is you are offering – a product, service (as discussed in previous chapters), or an app, give your intended users more.

The Principle of Niche: This principlestates that every offering must have a clearly marked out audience in view. Do not try to be everything to everybody. Do not try to be a *jack-of-all-trades*. If, for example, you are composing a message for email marketing, have a target

"IN MATTERS OF STYLE, SWIM WITH THE CURRENT; IN MATTERS OF PRINCIPLE, STAND LIKE A ROCK"

– Thomas Jefferson

in view. Not everyone will be interested in your offering –
no matter how appealing. But you can tailor your
message to get the attention of your intended audience. If
you don't, your message will be too watery to attract any
response.

The Principle of Customer-
Centeredness: This principle
states thatyou must work with
your target customer (or client)
in mind. It is not about what
you like; it is about what
yourcustomer needs. No matter
how bright your idea, no matter
how brilliant your offering, if it
does not meet the needs and aspirations of your clients, it
will be a waste. While writing this book, I had a challenge
with one of my web designers. He had this beautiful
concept about a particular website he developed for me,
the website was beautiful, the concept was great, he was
so enthusiastic about it, but all my clients complained that
they had difficulties navigating the website. The concept
was great but it did not meetmy needs. *Do not try this
with yourclients.*

The Principle of Cross -Platform: Thisprinciple states that
all your offerings, especially websites and apps, must be
designed to work on every available device. Take for
example a website; design your websites bearing in mind
that not everyone will view it from a PC (computer). You

must ensure that whateverthe device, visitors to your website will not have any issues viewing and navigating through the pages.

The Principle of Creativity: Thisprinciple states that you must be different to make a difference. People are used to the ordinary, general, *as usual* offerings. Give your clients some reasons to think you are *crazy*. Do something unique and a bit out of this world. *Wow* your clients – while not breaking the other principles. They will respect you for your creativity and be willing to pay for your services – even more than you ask.

The Principle of Visibility: Thisprinciple states that your positioning determines your profiting. You must know how to position yourself via marketing. No matter how great what you are offering, if people don't know about it, you are like a handsome guy winking at a lady in the dark: there will be no response. You are doing something but only you know about it.

General Guidelines for Joining the Mobile Millionaires

• Identify your strengths, and work on them. Mobile millionaires don't do things they are not good at.

They focus on their strengths and delegate their weaknesses.

- Have a plan. Don't just breeze in to the mobile (or internet) world aimlessly. If you don't have a roadmap, you will soon lose your way to others who know why they are here

- Fail forward. You will make mistakes and do things that will not work – that sounds normal. But it is insanity to make the same mistake twice. Fail. Learn. And move forward. Be better today than you wereyesterday.

- Be tenacious. Don't think people will just make way for you because you have a full proof idea. You can take my word for this – you will be kicked and tossed around till you can stand your ground. You must then make up your mind that it is not over till you win.

Winners are losers who refuse to quit.

- Be consistent. You must always be in the face of thepeople. Once you begin, hang in there till you win.

- Don't undulate. Don't be away today, back tomorrow.
- Be predictable (that you will always be there).

Be compassionate. Be genuinely interested in meeting the needs of your clients. Stay through with them till you solve their problems. Compassion is the only guarantee for an expansion. The more compassionate you are, themore attracted and connected you are to your clients

Be prompt. Be swift. Let your service delivery be unbeatable – in terms of speed and quality. The faster your delivery; the more jobs you can take on; the more money you make. Riches answer to volume of businesses done within the shortest space possible.

CHAPTER FIVE

THE FUTURE OF THE MOBILE DEVICE

Some trends to watch out for in the mobile business include the following:

Mixed Reality, VR, AR, and Bots(Forbes)

According to blogger, futurist, and life-streamer *Scoble*, Apple's still-in-development iPhone 8 will do almost science-fiction level mixed reality, showing a nuanced, tagged, and enhanced form of reality. Futurist and author Jesse Stay is convinced, adding that "Apple will also enter the VR race through mobile, and VR/mixed reality will become a mainstream tool."

"Right now we have been and are building the future of computing of computing, and what it means to be connected to the internet, for the vast majority of human beings."

– Dieter Bohn, The Verge

Artificial intelligence expert Sarah Austin says the 2017 will be about bots... specifically, chat bots.

Giant Leaps Forward forHardware (Idealog)

While there have been reports that the next iPhone might be designed as a retro-style flipper-phone and there is support for a movement towards other vintage-inspired tech, for most people the future of mobile technology is focused on wearables. Many suggest that devices for communication and other mobile functions might not be phones at all.

The latest generation of smart watches are all untethered, and perform more functions than before. Headsets have already gone wireless, and may soon be untethered too. Soft contact lenses rather than head-mounted gear are also not beyond the realm of imagination

Several concept phones such as the Motorola Piccolo and Kyocera's EOS folding phone have been developed by creative designers, stretching the boundaries of what a smartphone can physically be.

Features of concept phones include wrist-worn hologram projectors, fully functional wrist cuffsand phones that are flexible enough to be folded or crumpled.

The idea that a hologram or a malleable phone could be expanded or contracted to suit whatever an individual is doing is an elegant next step, and simpler hardware enhancements are already a reality. For example, Sony is has developed a lens that enables users to take advantage of the digital cameras on smartphones on a whole new level.

Maturationof M2M Communication:

Examples:

Qualcomm AllJoyn: This open-source software platform enables the "Internet of

There is an increase in the number of consumer-facing applications of machine -to-machine communication (objects wirelessly communicating with each other through embedded sensors and other devices). More companies are collaborating to make connectivity possible and easy across different device platforms. Worldwide M2M connections are forecast to grow at a compound annual rate of 36% between 2011 and 2021, reaching 2.1 billion.

There is an increasein the number of consumer-
facing applications of machine -to-machine
communication (objects wirelessly communicating
with each other through embedded sensors and
other devices). More companies are collaborating to
make connectivity possible and easy across different
device platforms. Worldwide M2M connections are
forecast to grow at a compound annual rate of 36%
between 2011 and 2021, reaching 2.1 billion.

— Analysys Mason, May 2012.

Everything," allowing any devices that use AllJoyn to communicate. For instance, a washing machine could send an alert about an unbalanced load to an Internet-enabled TV. Qualcomm demonstrated a system that allowed remote control of a coffee maker using a tablet; when the beverage was ready, the machine sent alerts to a tablet, smartphone and television, and could turn the TV on as well.

Fujitsu Next Generation Cane: Fujitsu demonstrated a prototype Wi-Fi-enabled cane that includes a GPS sensor to help elderly people find their way around; when needed, the cane can point users in the right direction via a vibrate function and built -in LED screen. A heart rate monitor in the handle automatically alerts authorities in case of a cardiac emergency.

In 2015, for the first time ever, there will be more U.S. consumers accessing the Internet through mobile devices than through PCs.

Mini tablets will account for as much as 60% of unit shipments

— a remarkable leap from just 33% in 2012

CHAPTER SIX

SUCCESS STORIES OF MOBILE MILLIONAIRES

Richard Branson

Sir Richard Charles Nicholas
Branson (born 18 July 1950) is an
English business magnate, investor
and philanthropist.[4] He founded
the Virgin Group, which controls
more than 400 companies.[5]

Branson expressed his desire to
become an entrepreneur at a young age. His first business
venture, at the age of 16, was a magazine
called *Student*.[6] In 1970, he set up a mail-order record
business. He opened a chain of record stores, Virgin
Records—later known as Virgin Megastores—in 1972.
Branson's Virgin brand grew rapidly during the 1980s, as
he set up Virgin Atlantic airline and expanded the Virgin
Records music label.

In March 2000, Branson was knighted at Buckingham
Palace for "services to entrepreneurship".[7] For his work
in retail, music and transport (with interests in land, air,
sea and space travel), his taste for adventure, and for his

humanitarian work, he became a prominent figure.[8][9] In 2002, he was named in the BBC's poll of the 100 Greatest Britons.[10] In 2004, he founded spaceflight corporation Virgin Galactic, noted for the SpaceShipOne project.

In November 2017, *Forbes* listed Branson's estimated net worth at $5.1 billion.[11]

Early life

Branson was born in Blackheath, London, the eldest of three children of Eve Branson (*née* Evette Huntley Flindt; born 1924), a former ballet dancer and air hostess, and Edward James Branson (1918–2011), a barrister.[12][13] He has two younger sisters.[14] His grandfather, the Right Honourable Sir George Arthur Harwin Branson, was a judge of the High Court of Justice and a Privy Councillor.[15] Branson was educated at Scaitcliffe School, a prep school in Surrey, before briefly attending Cliff View House School in Sussex.[16]His third great-grandfather, John Edward Branson, left England for India in 1793; John Edward's father, Harry Wilkins Branson, later joined him in Madras. On the show *Finding Your Roots*, Branson was shown to have 3.9% South Asian (Indian) DNA, likely through intermarriage.[13] He attended Stowe School, an independent school in Buckinghamshire until the age of sixteen.[16]

Branson has dyslexia and had poor academic performance; on his last day at school, his headmaster, Robert Drayson, told him he would either end up in prison or become a millionaire.[16] Branson's parents were supportive of his endeavours from an early age.[17] His mother was an entrepreneur; one of her most successful ventures was building and selling wooden tissue boxes and wastepaper bins.[18]

Career

Record business

Branson started his record business from the church where he ran *Student* magazine. He interviewed several prominent personalities of the late 1960s for the magazine including Mick Jagger and R. D. Laing.[19] Branson advertised popular records in *Student*, and it was an overnight success.[20] Trading under the name "Virgin", he sold records for considerably less than the "High Street" outlets, especiallythe chain W. H. Smith. Branson once said, "There is no point in starting your own business unless you do it out of a sense of frustration." The name "Virgin" was suggested by one of Branson's early employees because they were all new at business.[21] At the time, many products were sold under restrictive marketing agreements that limited discounting, despite efforts in the 1950s and 1960s to limit so-called resale price maintenance.[22]

Branson eventually started a record shop in Oxford Street in London. In 1971, he was questioned in connection with the selling of records in Virgin stores that had been declared export stock. The matter was never brought before a court because Branson agreed to repay any unpaid tax and a fine. His mother Eve re-mortgaged the family home in order to help pay the settlement.[21]

The Manor Studio, Richard Branson's recording studio in the manor house at the village of Shipton-on-Cherwell in Oxfordshire.

Earning enough money from his record store, Branson in 1972 launched the record label Virgin Records with Nik Powell, and bought a country estate north of Oxford in which he installed a residential recording studio, The Manor Studio.[23] He leased studio time to fledgling artists, including multi-instrumentalist Mike Oldfield, whose

74

debut album *Tubular Bells* (1973) was the first release for Virgin Records and became a chart-topping best-seller.[24]

Virgin signed such controversial bands as the Sex Pistols, which other companies were reluctant to sign. Virgin Records would go on to sign other artists including the Rolling Stones, Peter Gabriel, UB40, Steve Winwood and Paula Abdul, and to become the world's largest independent record label.[25] It also won praise for exposing the public to such obscure avant-garde music as Faust and Can. Virgin Records also introduced Culture Club to the music world. In 1982, Virgin purchased the gay nightclub Heaven. In 1991, in a consortium with David Frost, Branson made an unsuccessful bid for three ITV franchisees under the CPV-TV name. The early 1980s also saw his only attempt as a producer—on the novelty record "Baa, Baa, Black Sheep", by Singing Sheep in association with Doug McLean and Grace McDonald. The recording was a series of sheep baa-ing along to a drum-machine-produced track and reached number 42 in the UK charts in 1982.[26] In 1992, to keep his airline company afloat, Branson sold the Virgin label to EMI for £500 million.[27] Branson said that he wept when the sale was completed because the record business had been the very start of the Virgin empire. He created V2 Records in 1996 in order to re-enter the music business, owning 5% himself.[28]

Business ventures

Branson formed Virgin Atlantic Airways in 1984, launched Virgin Mobile in 1999, and Virgin Blue in Australia (now named Virgin Australia) in 2000. He was ninth in *The Sunday Times* Rich List 2006 of the wealthiest people or families in the UK, worth slightly more than £3 billion. Branson wrote in his autobiography of the decision to start an airline:

"My interest in life comes from setting myself huge, apparently unachievable challenges and trying to rise above them ... from the perspective of wanting to live life to the full, I felt that I had to attempt it."

Branson's first successful entry into the airline industry was during a trip to Puerto Rico. His flight was cancelled, so he decided to charter his own plane the rest of the way and offer a ride to the rest of the stranded passengers for a small fee in order to cover the cost.[29]

In 1993, Branson took what many saw as being one of his riskier business exploits by entering into the railway business. Virgin Trains won the franchises for the former Intercity West Coast and Cross-Country sectors of British Rail.

Virgin acquired European short-haul airline Euro Belgian Airlines in 1996 and renamed it Virgin Express. In 2006,

the airline was merged with SN Brussels
Airlines forming Brussels Airlines. It also started a national
airline based in Nigeria, called Virgin Nigeria. Another
airline, Virgin America, began flying out of San Francisco
International Airport in August 2007.

A series of disputes in the early 1990s caused tension
between Virgin Atlantic and British Airways, which
viewed Virgin as an emerging competitor. Virgin
subsequently accused British Airways of poaching its
passengers, hacking its computers, and leaking stories to
the press that portrayed Virgin negatively. After the so-
called campaign of "dirty tricks", British Airways settled
the case, giving £500,000 to Branson, a further £110,000 to
his airline, and had to pay legal fees of up to £3 million.
Branson distributed his compensation (the so-called "BA
bonus") among his staff.[30]

On 25 September 2004, Branson announced the signing
of a deal under which a new space
tourism company, Virgin Galactic, will license the
technology behind Spaceship One—funded
by Microsoft co-founder Paul Allen and designed by
legendary American aeronautical engineer and
visionary Burt Rutan—to take paying passengers
into suborbital space. Virgin Galactic (wholly owned by
Virgin Group) plans to make flights available to the
public with tickets priced at US$200,000 using Scaled
Composites White Knight Two.[31] At the time, Branson

said that he planned to take his two children, 31-year-old Holly and 28-year-old Sam, on a trip to outer space when they ride the SpaceShipTwo rocket plane on its first public flight then planned for 2014.[32] As part of his promotion of the firm, Branson has added a variation of the Virgin Galactic livery to his personal business jet, the Dassault Falcon 900EX "Galactic Girl" (G-GALX).[33][34]

Branson's next venture with the Virgin group was Virgin Fuels, which was set up to respond to global warming and exploit the recent spike in fuel costs by offering a revolutionary, cheaper fuel for automobiles and, in the near future, aircraft. Branson has stated that he was formerly a global warming sceptic and was influenced in his decision by a breakfast meeting with Al Gore.[35]

On 21 September 2006, Branson pledged to invest the profits of Virgin Atlantic and Virgin Trains in research for environmentally-friendly fuels. The investment is estimated to be worth $3 billion.[36][37]

On 4 July 2006, Branson sold his Virgin Mobile company to UK cable TV, broadband, and telephone company NTL/NTL:Telewest for almost £1 billion. A new company was launched with much fanfare and publicity on 8 February 2007, under the name Virgin Media. The decision to merge his Virgin Media Company with NTL was to integrate both of the companies' compatible parts of commerce. Branson used to own three-quarters of Virgin Mobile, whereas now he owns 15 percent of the new Virgin Media company.[38]

In 2006, Branson formed Virgin Comics and Virgin Animation, an entertainment company focused on creating new stories and characters for a global audience. The company was founded with author Deepak Chopra, filmmaker Shekhar Kapur, and entrepreneurs Sharad Devarajan and Gotham Chopra. Branson also launched the Virgin Health Bank on 1 February 2007, offering

parents-to-be the opportunity to store their baby's umbilical cord blood stem cells in private and public stem-cell banks.

Branson with Alberto Hazan in June 2007 helping launch Virgin Radio Italia

In June 2006, a tip-off from Virgin Atlantic led both UK and US competition authorities to investigate price-fixing attempts between Virgin Atlantic and British Airways. In August 2007, British Airways was fined £271 million over the allegations. Virgin Atlantic was given immunity for tipping off the authorities and received no fine—a controversial decision the Office of Fair Trading defended as being in the public interest.[39]

On 9 February 2007, Branson announced the setting up of a new global science and technology prize—The Virgin Earth Challenge—in the belief that history has shown that prizes of this nature encourage technological advancements for the good of mankind. The Virgin Earth Challenge was to award $25 million to the individual or group who are able to demonstrate a commercially viable design thatwill result in the net removal of anthropogenic, atmospheric greenhouse gases each year for at least ten years without countervailing harmful effects. This removal must have long-term effects and contribute materially to the stability of the Earth's climate. Branson also announced that he would be joined in the adjudication of the prize by a panel of five judges, all world authorities in

their respective fields: Al Gore, Sir Crispin Tickell, Tim Flannery, James E. Hansen, and James Lovelock.

In July 2007, Branson purchased his Australian home, Makepeace Island, in Noosa.[40] In August

2007, Branson announced that he bought a 20-percent stake in Malaysia's AirAsia X.[41]

Branson in April 2009 at the launch of Virgin America in Orange County, California.

On 13 October 2007, Branson's Virgin Group sought to add Northern Rock to its empire after submitting an offer that would result in Branson personally owning 30% of the company and changing the company's name from Northern Rock to Virgin Money.[42] The *Daily Mail* ran a campaign against his bid; Vince Cable, financial spokesperson for the Liberal Democrats, suggested in the House of Commons that Branson's criminal conviction for tax evasion might be felt by some as a good enough reason not to trust him with public money.[43]

On 10 January 2008, Branson's Virgin Healthcare announced that it would open a chain of health care clinics that would offer conventional medical care alongside homeopathic and complementary therapies, a development that was welcomed by Ben Bradshaw, the UK's health minister.[44]

Plans where GPs could be paid for referring National Health Service (NHS) patients to private Virgin services were abandoned in June 2008. The BMA warned the plan would "damage clinical objectivity", there would be a financial incentive for GPs to push patients toward the Virgin services at the centre.[45] Plans to take over an NHS Practice in Swindon were abandoned in late September 2008.[46]

In February 2009, Branson's Virgin organisation was reported as bidding to buy the former Honda Formula One team. Branson later stated an interest in Formula One, but claimed that, before the Virgin brand became involved with Honda or any other team, Formula One would have to develop a more economically efficient and environmentally responsible image. At the start of the 2009 Formula One season on 28 March, it was announced that Virgin would be sponsoring the new Brawn GP team,[47] with discussions also under way about introducing a less "dirty" fuel in the medium term.[48] After the end of the season and the subsequent purchase of Brawn GP by Mercedes Benz, Branson invested in an 80% buyout of Manor Grand Prix,[49][50] with the team being renamed Virgin Racing.

Branson and Tony Fernandes, owner of Air Asia and Lotus F1 Racing, had a bet for the 2010 F1 season where the team's boss should work on the winner's airline during a charity flight dressed as a stewardess. Fernandes escaped as the winner of the bet, as Lotus Racing ended tenth in the championship, while Virgin

Racing ended twelfth and last. Branson kept his word after losing the bet, as he served his duty as a stewardess on an Air Asia flight between Perth and Kuala Lumpur on 12 May 2013.[51]

Branson at the Time 100 Gala in May 2010. Known for his informal dress code, this was a rare occasion he didn't wear an open shirt.

In 2010, Branson became patron of the UK's Gordon Bennett 2010 gas balloon race, which has 16 hydrogen balloons flying across Europe.[52] In April 2010, Branson described the closure of large parts of European airspace owing to volcanic ash as "beyond a joke". Some scientists later concluded that serious structural damage to aircraft could have occurred if passenger planes had continued to fly.[53]

In April 2012, Virgin Care commenced a five-year contract for provision of a range of health services which had previously been under the aegis of NHS Surrey, the local primary care trust.[54] By March 2015 Virgin Care was in charge of over 230 services nationwide.[55]

In July 2012, Branson announced plans to build an orbital space launch system, designated LauncherOne.[56] Four commercial customers have already contracted for launches and two companies are developing standardised satellite buses optimised to the design of LauncherOne, in expectation of business opportunities created by the new *smallsat* launcher.[57]

In August 2012, the franchise for the West Coast Main Line, managed by Virgin Rail since 1997, came to an end. The contract was awarded to FirstGroup after a competitive tender process overseen by the Department for Transport. Branson had expressed his concerns about the tender process and questioned the validity of the business plan submitted by FirstGroup. When Virgin Rail lost the contract, Branson said he was convinced the civil servants had "got their maths wrong". In October, after an investigation into the bidding process, the deal was scrapped. The Transport Secretary Patrick McLoughlin announced there were "significant technical flaws" in the process and mistakes had been made by transport staff. Virgin Rail continues to operate the West Coast line.[58]

In September 2014, Branson announced his investment in drone company 3D Robotics stating, "It's amazing to see what a little flying object with a GoPro attached can do.

Before they came along the alternative was an expensive helicopter and crew. I'm really excited about the potential 3D Robotics sees in drones. They can do a lot of good in the world, and I hope this affordable technology will give many more people the chance to see our beautiful planet from such a powerful perspective."[59]

In November 2015, Branson announced the addition of Moskito Island to the Virgin Limited Edition portfolio. This resort, The Branson Estate on Moskito Island, offers 11 bedrooms for 22 guests.[60]

Branson has been involved in many failed business ventures, such as Virgin Cola, Virgin Cars, Virgin Publishing, Virgin Clothing and Virgin Brides.[61]

Tax

Branson's business empire is owned by a complicated series of offshore trusts and companies. *The Sunday*

Times stated that his wealth is calculated at £3 billion; if he were to retire to his Caribbean island and liquidate all of this, he would pay relatively little in tax.[62][*dead link*] Branson has been criticised for his business strategy, and has been accused of being a carpetbagger.[63][64][65][66] Branson responded that he is living on Necker for health rather than tax reasons.[67]

SeaWorld

Branson has been criticised by the Whale and Dolphin Conservation organisation for profiting from selling trips to SeaWorld and similar themed parks that hold dolphins, whales and other sea life in captivity for entertainment purposes.[68][69]

World Record Attempts

The capsule from the Virgin Atlantic Flyer balloon on display at the Imperial War Museum, Duxford, England

A 1998 attempt at an around-the-world balloon flight by Branson, Fossett, and Lindstrand ends in the Pacific

Ocean on 25 December 1998Branson made several world record-breaking attempts after 1985, when in the spirit of the Blue Riband he attempted the fastest Atlantic Ocean crossing. His first attempt in the "Virgin Atlantic Challenger" led to the boat capsizing in British waters and a rescue by RAF helicopter, which received wide media coverage. Some newspapers called for Branson to reimburse the government for the rescue cost. In 1986, in his "Virgin Atlantic

Challenger II", with sailing expert Daniel McCarthy, he beat the record by two hours.[6] A year later his hot air balloon "Virgin Atlantic Flyer" crossed the Atlantic.[70]

In January 1991, Branson crossed the Pacific from Japan to Arctic Canada, 6,700 miles (10,800 km), in a balloon of 2,600,000 cubic feet (74,000 m^3). This broke the record, with a speed of 245 miles per hour (394 km/h).

Between 1995 and 1998, Branson, Per Lindstrand, Vladimir Dzhanibekov, Larry Newman, and Steve Fossett made attempts to circumnavigate the globe by balloon. In late 1998 they made a record-breaking flight from Morocco to Hawaii but were unable to complete a global flight before Bertrand Piccard and Brian Jones in *Breitling Orbiter 3* in March 1999.

In March 2004, Branson set a record by travelling from Dover to Calais in a Gibbs Aquada in 1 hour, 40 minutes and 6 seconds, the fastest crossing of the English Channel in an amphibious vehicle. The previous record of six hours was set by two Frenchmen.[71] The cast of *Top Gear*, Jeremy Clarkson, James May and Richard Hammond, attempted to break this record in an amphibious vehicle which they had constructed and, while successfully crossing the channel, did not break Branson's record. After being intercepted by the Coast Guard and asked what their intentions were, Clarkson remarked "..Our intentions are to go across the Channel faster than 'Beardy' Branson!". The Coast Guard wished them good luck and left.[72]

In September 2008, Branson and his children made an unsuccessful attempt at an eastbound record crossing of the Atlantic Ocean under sail in the 99 feet (30 m) sloop *Virgin Money*.[73] The boat, also known as *Speedboat*, is owned by NYYC member Alex Jackson, who was a co-skipper on this passage, with Branson and Mike Sanderson. After two days, four hours, winds of force 7 to 9 (strong gale), and seas of 40 feet (12 m), a 'monster wave' destroyed the spinnaker, washed a ten-man life raft overboard and severely ripped the mainsail. She eventually continued to St. George's, Bermuda.[74]

Television, film and print[edit]

Branson at the 2008 Toronto International Film Festival.

Branson has guest starred, usually playing himself, on several television shows, including *Friends*, *Baywatch*, *Birds of a Feather*, *Only Fools and Horses*, *The Day Today*, a special episode of the comedy *Goodness Gracious Me* and *Tripping Over*. Branson made several appearances during the nineties on the BBC Saturday morning show *Live & Kicking*, where he was referred to as 'the pickle man' by comedy act Trev and Simon (in reference to Branston Pickle).[75]

Branson also appears in a cameo early in XTC's "Generals and Majors" video. He was also the star of a reality television show on Fox called *The Rebel Billionaire: Branson's Quest for the Best* (2004), in which sixteen contestants were tested for their entrepreneurship and sense of adventure. It did not succeed as a rival show to Donald Trump's *The Apprentice* and only lasted one season. According to Trump, Branson's "show was terrible. And I thought he was terribly miscast. He's a lot of hot air, like his balloons".[61]

His high public profile often leaves him open as a figure of satire—the 2000 AD series *Zenith* features a parody of Branson as a super villain, as the comic's publisher and favoured distributor and the Virgin group were in competition at the time. He is also caricatured in *The Simpsons* episode "Monty Can't Buy Me Love" as the tycoon Arthur Fortune, as the ballooning megalomaniac Richard Chutney (a pun on Branson, as in Branston Pickle) in *Believe Nothing*, and voiced himself in "The Princess Guide". The character Grandson Richard 39 in Terry Pratchett's Wings is modelled on Branson.

He has a cameo appearance in several films: *Around the World in 80 Days* (2004), where he played a hot-air balloon operator, and *Superman Returns* (2006), where he was credited as a 'Shuttle Engineer' and appeared alongside his son, Sam, with a Virgin Galactic-style commercial suborbital shuttle at the center of his storyline. He also has a cameo in the James Bond film *Casino Royale* (2006). Here, he is seen as a passenger going through Miami Airportsecurity check-in and being frisked – several Virgin Atlantic planes appear soon after. British Airways edited out Branson's cameo in their in-flight screening of the movie.[76] He makes a number of brief and disjointed appearances in the documentary *Derek and Clive Get the Horn* (1979), which follows the exploits of Peter Cook and Dudley Moore recording their final comedy album. Branson and his mother were also featured in the documentary film *Lemonade Stories*. On the TV series *Rove Live* in early 2006, Rove McManus and Sir Richard pushed each other into a swimming pool fully clothed live on TV during a "Live at your house" episode.

Branson is a *Star Trek* fan and named his new spaceship VSS *Enterprise* in honour of the *Star Trek* spaceships, and in 2006, reportedly offered actor William Shatner a ride on the inaugural space launch of Virgin Galactic. In an interview in *Time* magazine, published on 10 August 2009, Shatner claimed that Branson approached him asking how much he would pay for a ride on the spaceship. In response, Shatner asked "how much would you pay *me* to do it?"

In August 2007, Branson announced on *The Colbert Report* that he had named a new aircraft Air Colbert. He later doused political satirist and talk show host Stephen Colbert with water from his mug. Branson subsequently took a retaliatory splash from Colbert. The interview quickly ended, with both laughing[77] as shown on the episode aired on Comedy Central on 22 August 2007. The interview was promoted on *The Report* as the *Colbert-Branson Interview Trainwreck*. Branson then made a cameo appearance in *The Soup*, playing an intern working under Joel McHale who had been warned against getting into water fights with Stephen Colbert, and being subsequently fired.

In March 2008, he launched Virgin Mobile in India; during that period, he made a cameo appearance in Bollywood film *London Dreams*.[78] In July 2010, Branson narrated Australian sailor Jessica Watson's documentary about her solo sailing trip around the world.

In April 2011, Branson appeared on CNN's Mainsail with Kate Winslet.[79] Together they re-enacted a famous scene from the 1997 film *Titanic* for the cameras.[80] On 17 August 2011, he was featured in the premier episode of Hulu's first long-form original production entitled, *A Day in the Life*.[81]

At the 2012 Pride of Britain Awards on ITV on 30 October, Branson, along with Michael Caine, Elton John, Simon Cowell and Stephen Fry, recited Rudyard Kipling's poem "If—" in tribute to the 2012 British Olympic and Paralympics athletes.[82]

Humanitarian initiatives

In the late 1990s, Branson and musician Peter Gabriel discussed with Nelson Mandela their idea of a small group of leaders working to solve difficult global conflicts.[83] On 18 July 2007, in Johannesburg, South Africa, Mandela announced the formation of a new group, The Elders. Kofi Annan serves as Chair of The Elders and Gro Harlem Brundtland as Deputy Chair. The Elders is funded by a group of donors, including Branson and Gabriel.

Richard Branson with his mother Eve, and the Board of Directors of the International Centre for Missing & Exploited Children

In 1999, Branson became a founding sponsor of the International Centre for Missing & Exploited Children ("ICMEC"), the goal of which is to help find missing children, and to stop the exploitation of children, as his mother Eve became a founding member of ICMEC's Board of Directors.[84][85]

Through the Carbon War Room, founded in 2009, the entrepreneur sought solutions for global warming and the energy crisis. "We all have a part to play, but I believe entrepreneurs will have a really significant role to play in bringing investment and commercial skills to help develop the new technologies needed to grow a post-carbon economy", he said in his interview with *Vision*. Through Carbon War Room initiative he has focused efforts on finding sustainable alternatives for three industry sectors: shipping, energy efficiency and aviation and renewable jet fuels.[86]

He also launched Virgin Startup, an official delivery partner for the UK's Start Up Loans programme. Through this new organisation, he was to provide loans to entrepreneurs between the ages of 18 and 30 UK-wide. A pilot of the scheme, which ran over 11 months, injected £600,000 into 100 businesses.[86]

Branson's other work in South Africa includes the Branson School of Entrepreneurship, set up in 2005 as a partnership between Virgin Unite, the non-profit foundation of Virgin, and entrepreneur Taddy Blecher, the founder of CIDA City Campus, a university in Johannesburg. The school aims to improve economic growth in South Africa by supporting start-ups and micro-enterprises with skills, mentors, services, networks and finance arrangements.[87][88] Fundraising activity to support the school is achieved by *The Sunday Times* Fast Track 100, sponsored by Virgin Group, at its yearly event, where places to join Richard Branson on trips to South Africa to provide coaching and mentoring to students are auctioned to attendees. In 2009, Jason Luckhurst and Boyd Kershaw of Practicus, Martin Ainscough of the Ainscough Group and Matthew Riley of Daisy Communications helped raise £150,000 through the auction.[89]

In March 2008, Branson hosted an environmental gathering at his private island, Necker Island, in the Caribbean with several prominent entrepreneurs, celebrities, and world leaders. They discussed global warming-related problems facing the world, hoping that the meeting would be a precursor to future discussions regarding similar problems. Former British Prime Minister Tony Blair, Wikipedia co-founder Jimmy Wales, and Larry Page of Google were in attendance.[90]

On 8 May 2009, Branson took over Mia Farrow's hunger strike for three days in protest of the Sudanese government expulsion of aid groups from the Darfur region.[91] In 2010, he and the Nduna Foundation (founded by Amy Robbins), and Humanity United (an organization backed by Pam Omidyar, the wife of eBay founder Pierre Omidyar) founded Enterprise Zimbabwe.[92]

Branson at the United Nations Conference on Sustainable Development in 2012.

Branson is a signatory of Global Zero campaign, a non-profit international initiative for the elimination of all nuclear weapons worldwide.[93] Since its launch in Paris in December 2008,[94] Global Zero has grown to 300 leaders, including current and former heads of state, national security officials and military commanders, and 400,000 citizens worldwide; developed a practical step-by-step plan to eliminate nuclear weapons; launched an international student campaign with 75 campus chapters in eight countries; and produced a documentary film, *Countdown to Zero*, in partnership with Lawrence Bender and Participant Media.[95]

Since 2010, Branson has served as a Commissioner on the Broadband Commission for Digital Development, a UN initiative which promotes universal access to broadband services.[96] In 2011, Branson served on the Global Commission on Drug Policy with former political and cultural leaders of Latin America and elsewhere, "in a bid to boost the effort to achieve more humane and rational drug laws."[97]

In December 2013, Branson urged companies to boycott Uganda because of its "anti-homosexuality bill". Branson stated that it would be "against my conscience to support this country...governments must realize that people should be able to love whoever they want."[98]

In 2014, Branson joined forces with African Wildlife Foundation and partner WildAid for the "Say No" Campaign, an initiative to bring public awareness to the issues of wildlife poaching and trafficking.[99]

Branson is an opponent of the death penalty, stating: "the death penalty is always cruel, barbaric and inhumane. It has no place in the world."[100] The U.S. is one of the few countries that practiced the death penalty in 2015, and on 30 September 2015 Branson released a letter in support of American inmate Richard Glossip on the day he was due to be executed, buying an ad in *The Oklahoman* newspaper which had advocated the execution.[101] Branson stated the evidence against Glossip was flawed and that "every person is deserving of a fair trial", adding: "Your state is about to execute a man whose guilt has not been proven beyond a reasonable doubt."[101]

Climate change pledge

In 2006, Branson made a high-profile pledge to invest $3 billion toward addressing global warming over the course of the following decade.[102][103] However, author and activist Naomi Klein has criticised Branson for contributing "well under $300 million" as of 2014, far below the originally stated goal.[104] Additionally, Klein says Virgin airlines' greenhouse gas emissions increased considerably in the years following his pledge.[105]

Politics

In the 1980s, Branson was briefly given the post of "litter Tsar" by Margaret Thatcher—charged with "keeping Britain tidy".[106][107] In 2005 he declared that there were only negligible differences between the two main parties on economic matters.[108] He was suggested as a candidate for Mayor of London before the first 2000 election, with polls indicating he would be a viable candidate, but he did not express interest.[109][110][111]

Branson has supported continuing British membership of the European Union and was opposed to the 2016 referendum.[112] On 28 June 2016, interviewed for ITV's *Good Morning Britain*, he said that his company had lost a third of its value as a result of the referendum result and that a planned venture, employing over 3,000 people, which he had announced before the referendum, had been shelved. He gave his backing for a second referendum.[113]

Honours and awards

Branson at a conference in San Diego, California, on 8 July 2013

In 1993, Branson was awarded an honorary degree of Doctor of Technology from Loughborough University.[114]

In the New Years Honours list dated 30 December 1999, Elizabeth II signified her intention to confer the honour of Knight Bachelor on him for his "services to entrepreneurship".[115][116] He was knighted by Charles, Prince of Wales on 30 March 2000 at an investiture in Buckingham Palace.[117] Also in 2000, Branson received the Tony Jannus Award for his accomplishments in commercial air transportation.

Branson appears at No. 85 on the 2002 list of 100 Greatest Britons on the BBC and voted for by the public. Branson was also ranked in 2007's *Time* magazine "Top 100 Most Influential People in the World". On 7 December 2007, United Nations Secretary General Ban Ki-Moon presented Branson with the United Nations Correspondents Association Citizen of the World Award for his support for environmental and humanitarian causes.[118]

In 2009, Branson was voted the UK's "Celebrity Dream Boss" in an opinion poll by Cancer Research UK.[119] On 24 January 2011, Branson was awarded the German Media Prize (organised by "Media Control Charts"), previously handed to former US president Bill Clinton and the Dalai Lama. On 14 November 2011, Branson was awarded the ISTA Prize by the International Space Transport Association in The Hague for his pioneering achievements in the development of suborbital transport systems with "Virgin Galactic".[120] On 11 February 2012, Branson was honoured with the National Academy of Recording Arts and Sciences' President's Merit Award for his contributions to the music industry.[121]

On 2 June 2013, Branson received an honorary degree of Doctor Honoris Causa from Kaunas Technology University in Kaunas, Lithuania.[122] On 15 May 2014,

Branson received the 2014 Business for Peace Award, awarded annually by the Business for Peace Foundation in Oslo, Norway.[123]

On 21 September 2014, Branson was recognized by *The Sunday Times* as the most admired business person over the last five decades.[124] On 9 October 2014, Branson was named as the No. 1 LGBT ally by the OUTstanding organisation.[125] On 29 October 2015, Branson was listed by UK-based company Richtopia at number 1 in the list of 100 Most Influential British Entrepreneurs.[126][127] In October 2015, Branson received the International Crisis Group Chairman's Award at the United Nations Development Programme's In Pursuit of Peace Awards Dinner.[128]

Personal life

Branson kite surfing at Necker Island

Branson married Kristen Tomassi in 1972 and divorced her in 1979. He remarried in 1989, at Necker Island, a 74-acre (30 ha) island owned by Branson in the British Virgin Islands.[129] Branson owns a yacht that is named after his island - the Necker Belle.[130] He has a daughter Holly (born 1981) and a son Sam (born 1985) with his second wife, Joan Templeman (born 1945). He met her in 1976. He stated in an interview with Piers Morgan that he and Joan also had a daughter named Clare Sarah, who died when she was four days old in 1979.[131]

In 1998, Branson released his autobiography, titled *Losing My Virginity*, an international best-seller.[132] Branson was deeply saddened by the disappearance of fellow adventurer Steve Fossett in September 2007; the following month he wrote an article for *Time* magazine, titled "My Friend, Steve Fossett".[133]

In 2013 Branson became President of the Old Stoic Society of Stowe School.[134] In March 2015 Branson said that almost all drug use should be decriminalised in the UK, following the example of Portugal.[135]

Branson was ordained as a minister by the Universal Life Church Monastery.[136] Branson is also an experienced kitesurfer, holding some world records in the sport.[137][138] In August 2016 Branson was injured while riding his bicycle in the British Virgin Islands and suffered torn ligaments and a cracked cheek as a result. He was taken to hospital in Miami for X-rays and scans.[139]

In 2017, Branson's Necker Island home was left uninhabitable after Hurricane Irma hit. It is the second time the Necker Island home has been severely damaged after the building caught fire when it was struck by lightning caused by Hurricane Irene in 2011.[140]

On 27 November 2017 Richard Branson was accused of sexual assault to a singer Antonia Jenae. A spokesperson to Branson confirmed to *The Sun* that members of Joss Stone band were invited for a party in 2010.[141]

Informal dress code

Branson is known for his preference of casual clothing both at home and the workplace. On his dislike of ties, he says "I have been carrying out a lifelong campaign to say bye to the tie. I often carry a pair of scissors with me, ready to cut off the tie of any unsuspecting wearer. I even have a cushion on Necker Island made up of some of my victims! I remain convinced that ties only exist because managers, after spending years being forced to wear ties by their bosses, decide to force the next generation to do the same. They subtly encourage conformity. Most people in business dress the same and that contributes to them acting the same. Wearing a tie really can restrict new ideas and innovative thoughts – not to mention breath!"[142]

Influences

Branson has stated in a number of interviews that he has been much influenced by non-fiction books. He most commonly mentions Nelson Mandela's autobiography, *Long Walk to Freedom*, explaining that Mandela was "one of the most inspiring men I have ever met and had the honour to call my friend." Owing to his interest in humanitarian and ecological issues, Branson also lists Al Gore's best-selling book, *An Inconvenient Truth*, and *The Revenge of Gaia* by James Lovelock amongst his favourites. According to Branson's book, *Screw It, Let's Do It: Lessons in Life*, he is also a fan of Jung Chang's *Wild Swans* and Antony Beevor's *Stalingrad*.[143][144] In fiction, Branson has long admired the character Peter Pan,[145] and in 2006 he founded Virgin Comics LLC, stating that Virgin Comics will give "a whole generation of young, creative thinkers a voice".[146][147]

Bibliography

Steve Jobs

Steven Paul Jobs (/dʒɒbz/; February 24, 1955 –

October 5, 2011) was an
American entrepreneur, business magnate, inventor,
and industrial designer. He was the chairman, chief
executive officer (CEO), and co-founder of Apple Inc.;
CEO and majority shareholder of Pixar;[3] a member
of The Walt Disney Company's board of directors
following its acquisition of Pixar; and the founder,
chairman, and CEO of NeXT. Jobs and Apple co-
founder Steve Wozniak are widely recognized as
pioneers of the microcomputer revolution of the 1970s
and 1980s.

He was born in San Francisco to parents who had to put
him up for adoption at birth; he was raised in the San
Francisco Bay Areaduring the 1960s.[4] Jobs then
attended Reed College in 1972 before dropping
out,[5] and traveled through India in 1974 seeking
enlightenment and studying Zen Buddhism.[6] Jobs's
declassified FBI report stated that an acquaintance knew
that Jobs had used marijuana and LSD while he was in
college.[7] Jobs once told a reporter that taking LSD was
"one of the two or three most important things" he did in
his life.[8]

Jobs and Wozniak co-founded Apple in 1976 to sell
Wozniak's Apple I personal computer. The visionaries
gained fame and wealth a year later for the Apple II, one

of the first highly successful mass-produced personal computers. In 1979, after a tour of PARC, Jobs saw the commercial potential of the Xerox Alto, which was mouse-driven and had a graphical user interface (GUI). This led to development of the unsuccessful Apple Lisa in 1983, followed by the breakthrough Macintosh in 1984. In addition to being the first mass-produced computer with a GUI, the Macintosh introduced the sudden rise of the desktop publishing industry in 1985 with the addition of the Apple LaserWriter, the first laser printer to feature vector graphics. Following a long power struggle, Jobs was forced out of Apple in 1985.[9]

After leaving Apple, Jobs took a few of its members with him to found NeXT, a computer platform development company that specialized in state-of-the-art computers for higher-education and business markets. In addition, Jobs helped to initiate the development of the visual effects industry when he funded the spinout of the computer graphics division of George Lucas's Lucasfilm in 1986.[10] The new company, Pixar, would eventually produce the first fully computer-animated film, *Toy Story*—an event made possible in part because of Jobs's financial support.

In 1997, Apple merged with NeXT. Within a few months of the merger, Jobs became CEO of his former company; he revived Apple at the verge of bankruptcy. Beginning in 1997 with the "Think different" advertising campaign, Jobs worked closely with designer Jonathan Ive to develop a line of products that would have larger cultural ramifications: the iMac, iTunes and iTunes Store, Apple Store, iPod, iPhone, App Store, and the iPad. In 2001, the original Mac OS was replaced with a completely new Mac OS X, based on NeXT's NeXTSTEP platform, giving the OS a modern Unix-based foundation for the first time.

Jobs was diagnosed with a pancreatic neuroendocrine tumor in 2003 and died on October 5, 2011, of respiratory arrest related to the tumor.

Steve Jobs's biological parents were Abdulfattah Jandali and Joanne Schieble. His adoptive parents were Paul Jobs and Clara Hagopian.

His biological father, Abdulfattah "John" Jandali (Arabic: عبدالفتاح الجندلي) (b. March 15, 1931), grew up in Homs, Syria and was born into an Arab Muslim household.[11] Jandali is the son of a self-made millionaire who did not go to college and a mother who was a traditional housewife.[11] While an undergraduate at the American University of

Beirut, Lebanon, he was a student activist and spent time in jail for his political activities.[11] Although Jandali initially wanted to study law, he eventually decided to study economics and political science.[11] He pursued a PhD in the latter subject at the University of Wisconsin, where he met Joanne Carole Schieble (b. August 1, 1932), a Catholic of Swiss and German descent, who grew up on a farm in Wisconsin.[12][11][13] As a doctoral candidate, Jandali was a teaching assistant for a course Schieble was taking, although both were the same age.[14] Mona Simpson, Jobs's full biological sister, notes that her maternal grandparents were not happy that their daughter was dating Jandali: "it wasn't that he was Middle-Eastern so much as that he was a Muslim. But there are a lot of Arabs in Michigan and Wisconsin. So it's not that unusual."[14] Walter Isaacson, Steve Jobs's official biographer, additionally states that Schieble's father "threatened to cut Joanne off completely" if she continued the relationship.[12]

Jobs's adoptive father, Paul Reinhold Jobs (1922–1993), grew up in a Calvinist household,[15] the son of an "alcoholic and sometimes abusive" father.[12] The family lived on a farm in Germantown, Wisconsin.[12][15] Paul bore an ostensible resemblance to James Dean; he had tattoos, dropped out of high school, and traveled around the Midwest for several years during the 1930s looking for work.[12][15] He eventually joined the United States Coast Guard as an engine-room machinist.[15] After World War II, Paul Jobs decided to leave the Coast Guard when his ship docked in San Francisco.[15] He made a bet that he would find his wife in San Francisco and promptly went on a blind date with Clara Hagopian (1924–1986). They were engaged ten days later and married in 1946.[12] Clara, the daughter of Armenian immigrants, grew up in San Francisco and had been married before, but her husband had been killed in the war. After a series of moves, Paul and Clara settled in San Francisco's Sunset District in 1952.[12] As a hobby, Paul Jobs rebuilt cars, but his career was as a "repo man", which suited his "aggressive, tough personality."[15] Meanwhile, their attempts to start a family were halted after Clara had an ectopic pregnancy, leading them to consider adoption in 1955.[12]

Birth

"Of all the inventions of humans, the computer is going to rank near or at the top as history unfolds and we look back. It is the most awesome tool that we have ever invented. I feel incredibly lucky to be at exactly the right place in Silicon Valley, at exactly the right time, historically, where this invention has taken form."

Jobs's biological mother Schieble became pregnant with him in 1954 when she and Jandali spent the summer with his family in Homs, Syria. Jandali has stated that he "was very much in love with Joanne ... but sadly, her father was a tyrant, and forbade her to marry me, as I was from Syria. And so she told me she wanted to give the baby up for adoption."[17] Jobs told his official biographer that Schieble's father was dying at the time, Schieble did not want to aggravate him, and both felt that at 23 they were too young to marry.[12] In addition, as there was a strong stigma against bearing a child out of wedlock and raising it as a single mother, and as abortions were illegal and dangerous, adoption was the only option women had in the United States in 1954.[15] According to Jandali, Schieble deliberately did nothis child." A few weeks before she was due to give birth, Brennan was invited to deliver her baby at the All One Farm and she accepted the offer.[18] When Jobs was 23 (the same age as his biological parents when they had him)[12] Brennan gave birth to her baby, Lisa Brennan, on May 17, 1978.[18][55]"Dear Mike, This morning's papers carried suggestions that Apple is considering removing me as chairman. I don't know the source of these reports, but they are both misleading to the public and unfair to me. You will recall that at last Thursday's Board meeting I stated I had decided to start a new venture, and I tendered my resignation as chairman. The Board declined to accept my resignation and asked me to defer it for a week. I agreed to do so in light of the encouragement the Board offered with regard to the proposed new venture and the indications that Apple would invest in it. On Friday, after I told John Sculley who would be joining me, he confirmed Apple's willingness to discuss areas of possible collaboration between Apple and my new venture. Subsequently the Company appears to be adopting a hostile posture toward me and the new venture. Accordingly, I must insist upon the immediate acceptance of my resignation.

I would hope that in any statement it feels it must issue, the

Company will make it clear that the decision to resign as chairman was mine. I find myself both saddened and perplexed by the management's conduct in this matter which seems to me contrary to Apple's best interests. Those interests remain a matter of deep concern to me, both because of my past association with Apple and the substantial investment I retain in it. I continue to hope that calmer voices within the Company may yet be heard. Some Company representatives have said they fear I will use proprietary

Apple technology in my new venture. There is no basis for any such concern. If that concern is the real source of Apple's hostility to the venture, I can allay it. As you know, the company's recent re-organization left me with no work to do and no access even to regular management reports. I am but 30 and want still to contribute and achieve. After what we have accomplished together, I would wish our parting to be both amicable and dignified. Yours sincerely, Steven P. Jobs."

—*Steve Jobs, letter of resignation from Apple Computer, September 17th, 1985.*[15]

Jobs went there for the birth after he was contacted by Robert Friedland, their mutual friend and the farm owner. While distant, Jobs worked with her on a name for the baby, which they discussed while sitting in the fields on a blanket. Brennan suggested the name "Lisa" which Jobs also liked and notes that Jobs was very attached to the name "Lisa" while he "was also publicly denying paternity." She would discover later that during this time, Jobs was preparing to unveil a new kind of computer that he wanted to give a female name (his first choice was "Claire" after St. Clare). She also stated that she never gave him permission to use the baby's name for a computer and he hid the plans from her. Jobs also worked with his team to come up with the phrase, "Local Integrated Software Architecture" as an alternative explanation for the Apple Lisa[56] (decades later, however, Jobs admitted to his biographer Walter Isaacson that "obviously, it was named for my daughter"[57]). Brennan would come under intense criticism from Jobs, who claimed that "she doesn't want money, she just wants me." According to Brennan, Apple's Mike Scott wanted Jobs to give her money, while other Apple executives "advised him to ignore me or fight if I tried to go after a paternity settlement."[18]

When Jobs denied paternity, a DNA test established him as Lisa's father. It required him to give Brennan $385 a month in addition to returning the welfare money she had received. Jobs gave her $500 a month at the time when Apple went public, and Jobs became a millionaire. Brennan worked as a waitress in Palo Alto. Later, Brennan agreed to give an interview with Michael Moritz for *Time* magazine for its Time Person of the Year special, released on January 3, 1983, in which she discussed her relationship with Jobs. Rather than name Jobs the Person of the Year, the magazine named the computer the "Machine of the Year".[58] In the issue, Jobs questioned the reliability of the paternity test (which stated that the "probability of paternity for Jobs, Steven... is 94.1%").[59] Jobs responded by arguing that "28% of the male population of the United States could be the father."[18][59] *Time* also noted that "the baby girl and the machine on which Apple has placed so much hope for the future share the same name: Lisa."[59]

Jobs was worth a million dollars when he was 23 in 1978, 10 million when he was 24, and over 100 million when he was 25. He was also one of the youngest "people ever to make the Forbes list of the nation's richest people – and one of only a handful to have done it themselves, without inherited wealth."[15]

In 1978, Apple recruited Mike Scott from National Semiconductor to serve as CEO for what turned out to be several turbulent years. In 1983, Jobs lured John Sculley away from Pepsi-Cola to serve as Apple's CEO, asking, "Do you want to spend the rest of your life selling sugared water, or do you want a chance to change the world?"[60]In 1982, Jobs bought an apartment in the two top floors of The San Remo, a Manhattan building with a politically progressive reputation. Although he never lived there,[61] he spent years renovating it with the help of I. M. Pei. In 2003, he sold it to U2 singer Bono.

In 1984, Jobs bought the Jackling House and estate, and resided there for a decade. After that, he leased it out for several years until 2000 when he stopped maintaining the house, allowing exposure to the weather to degrade it. In 2004, Jobs received permission from the town of Woodside to demolish the house in order to build a smaller contemporary styled one. After a few years in court, the house was finally demolished in 2011, a few months before he died.[62]

In early 1984, Apple introduced the Macintosh, which was based on The Lisa (and Xerox PARC's mouse-driven graphical user interface).[63][64] The following year, Apple aired a Super Bowl television commercial titled "1984." At Apple's annual shareholders meeting on January 24, 1984, an emotional Jobs introduced the Macintosh to a wildly enthusiastic audience; Andy Hertzfeld described the scene as "pandemonium."[65]

Despite the fanfare, the expensive Macintosh was a hard sell.[66] Shortly after its release in 1985, Bill Gates's then-developing company, Microsoft, threatened to stop developing Mac applications unless it was granted "a license for the Mac operating system software. Microsoft was developing its graphical user interface ... for DOS, which it was calling Windows and didn't want Apple to sue over the similarities between the Windows GUI and the Mac interface."[67] Sculley granted Microsoft the license which later led to problems for Apple.[67] In addition, cheap IBM PC clones that ran on Microsoft software and had a graphical user interface began to appear. Although the Macintosh preceded the clones, it was far more expensive, so "through the late '80s, the Windows user interface was getting better and better and was thus taking increasingly more share from Apple."[68] Windows based IBM-PC clones also led to the development of additional GUIs such as IBM's TopView or Digital Research's GEM,[68] and thus "the graphical user interface was beginning to be taken for granted, undermining the most apparent advantage of the Mac...it seemed clear as the '80s wound down that Apple couldn't go it alone indefinitely against the whole IBM-clone market."[68]

Sculley's and Jobs's respective visions for the company greatly differed. The former favored open architecture computers like the Apple II, sold to education, small business, and home markets less vulnerable to IBM. Jobs wanted the company to focus on the closed architecture Macintosh as a business alternative to the IBM PC. President and CEO Sculley had little control over chairman of the board Jobs's Macintosh division; it and the Apple II division operated like separate companies, duplicating services.[70] Although its products provided 85% of Apple's sales in early 1985, the company's January

1985 annual meeting did not mention the Apple II
division or employees. Many left including Wozniak,
who stated that the company had "been going in the
wrong direction for the last five years" and sold most of
his stock.[71] The Macintosh's failure to defeat the PC
strengthened Sculley's position in the company.

In May 1985, Sculley—encouraged by Arthur Rock—
decided to reorganize Apple, and proposed a plan to the
board that would remove Jobs from the Macintosh
group and put him in charge of "New Product
Development." This move would effectively render Jobs
powerless within Apple.[15] In response, Jobs then
developed a plan to get rid of Sculley and take over
Apple. However, Jobs was confronted after the plan was
leaked, and he said that he would leave Apple. The
Board declined his resignation and asked him to
reconsider. Sculley also told Jobs that he had all of the
votes needed to go ahead with the reorganization. A few
months later, on September 17, 1985, Jobs submitted a

'My favorite things in life
don't cost any money.
It's really clear that the
most precious resource
we all have is time'

Steve Jobs

letter of
resignation to
the Apple
Board. Five
additional
senior Apple
employees also

resigned and joined Jobs in his new venture, NeXT.[15]

1985–1997

NeXT computer

Following his resignation from Apple in 1985, Jobs founded NeXT Inc.[72] with $7 million. A year later he was running out of money, and he sought venture capital with no product on the horizon. Eventually, Jobs attracted the attention of billionaire Ross Perot, who invested heavily in the company.[73] The NeXT computer was shown to the world in what was considered Jobs's comeback event,[74] a lavish invitation only gala launch event[75] that was described as a multimedia extravaganza.[76] The celebration was held at the Louise M. Davies Symphony Hall, San Francisco, California on Wednesday October 12, 1988. Steve Wozniak said in a 2013 interview that while Jobs was at NeXT he was "really getting his head together".[77]

NeXT workstations were first released in 1990 and priced at US$9,999. Like the Apple Lisa, the NeXT workstation was technologically advanced and designed for the education sector, but was largely dismissed as cost-prohibitive for educational institutions.[78] The NeXT workstation was known for its technical strengths, chief among them its object-orientedsoftware development system. Jobs marketed NeXT products to the financial, scientific, and academic community, highlighting its innovative, experimental new technologies, such as the Mach kernel, the digital signal processor chip, and the built-in Ethernet port. Making use of a NeXT computer, English computer scientist Tim Berners-Lee invented the World Wide Web in 1989 at CERN in Switzerland.[79]

The revised, second generation NeXTcube was released in 1990. Jobs touted it as the first "interpersonal" computer that would replace the personal computer. With its innovative NeXTMail multimedia email system, NeXTcube could share voice, image, graphics, and video in email for the first time. "Interpersonal computing is going to revolutionize human communications and groupwork", Jobs told reporters.[80] Jobs ran NeXT with an obsession for aesthetic perfection, as evidenced by the development of and attention to NeXTcube's magnesium case.[81] This put considerable strain on NeXT's hardware division, and in 1993, after having sold only 50,000 machines, NeXT transitioned fully to software development with the release of NeXTSTEP/Intel.[82] The company reported its first profit of $1.03 million in 1994.[73] In 1996, NeXT Software, Inc. released WebObjects, a framework for Web application development. After NeXT was acquired by Apple Inc. in

1997, WebObjects was used to build and run the Apple Store,[82] MobileMe services, and the iTunes Store.

Pixar and Disney

In 1986, Jobs funded the spinout of The Graphics Group (later renamed Pixar) from Lucasfilm's computer graphics division for the price of $10 million, $5 million of which was given to the company as capital and $5 million of which was paid to Lucasfilm for technology rights.[10]

The first film produced by Pixar with its Disney partnership, *Toy Story* (1995), with Jobs credited as executive producer,[83] brought fame and critical acclaim to the studio when it was released. Over the next 15 years, under Pixar's creative chief John Lasseter, the company produced box-office hits *A Bug's Life* (1998); *Toy Story 2* (1999); *Monsters, Inc.* (2001); *Finding Nemo* (2003); *The Incredibles* (2004); *Cars* (2006); *Ratatouille* (2007); *WALL-E* (2008); *Up* (2009); and *Toy Story 3* (2010). *Finding Nemo, The Incredibles, Ratatouille, WALL-E, Up* and *Toy Story 3* each received the Academy Award for Best Animated Feature, an award introduced in 2001.[84]

In 2003 and 2004, as Pixar's contract with Disney was running out, Jobs and Disney chief executive Michael

Eisner tried but failed to negotiate a new partnership,[85] and in early 2004, Jobs announced that Pixar would seek a new partner to distribute its films after its contract with Disney expired.

The Only way to do Great Work is to Love what you do.

Steve Jobs

In October 2005, Bob Iger replaced Eisner at Disney, and Iger quickly worked to mend relations with Jobs and Pixar. On January 24, 2006, Jobs and Iger announced that Disney had agreed to purchase Pixar in an all-stock transaction worth $7.4 billion. When the deal closed, Jobs became The Walt Disney Company's largest single shareholder with approximately seven percent of the company's stock.[86] Jobs's holdings in Disney far exceeded those of Eisner, who holds 1.7 percent, and of Disney family member Roy E. Disney, who until his 2009 death held about one percent of the company's stock and whose criticisms of Eisner – especially that he soured Disney's relationship with Pixar – accelerated Eisner's ousting. Upon completion of the merger, Jobs received 7% of Disney shares, and joined the board of directors as the largest individual shareholder.[86][87][88] Upon Jobs's death his shares in Disney were transferred to the Steven P. Jobs Trust led by Laurene Jobs.[89]

Floyd Norman, of Pixar, described Jobs as a "mature, mellow individual" who never interfered with the creative process of the filmmakers.[90] In early June 2014, Pixar cofounder and Walt Disney Animation Studios President Ed Catmull revealed that Jobs once advised him to "just explain it to them until they understand" in disagreements. Catmull released the book *Creativity Inc.* in 2014, in which he recounts numerous experiences of working with Jobs. Regarding his own manner of dealing with Jobs, Catmull writes:

In all the 26 years with Steve, Steve and I never had one of these loud verbal arguments and it's not my nature to do that. ... but we did disagree fairly frequently about things. ... I would say something to him and he would immediately shoot it down because he could think faster than I could. ... I would then wait a week ... I'd call him up and I give my counter argument to what he had said and he'd immediately shoot it down. So I had to wait another week, and sometimes this went on for months. But in the end one of three things happened. About a third of the time he said, 'Oh, I get it, you're right.' And that was the end of it. And it was another third of the time in which [I'd] say, 'Actually I think he is right.' The other third of the time, where we didn't reach consensus, he just let me do it my way, never said anything more about it.[91]

Family

Steve Jobs's house in Palo Alto

Steve Jobs's house, as viewed from an adjacent sidewalk. Abundant fruit trees are visible next to the house.

Chrisann Brennan notes that after Jobs was forced out of Apple, "he apologized many times over for his behavior" towards her and Lisa. She also states that Jobs "said that he never took responsibility when he should have, and that he was sorry."[18] By this time, Jobs had developed a strong relationship with Lisa and when she was nine, Jobs had her name on her birth certificate changed from "Lisa Brennan" to "Lisa Brennan-Jobs."[18] In addition, Jobs and Brennan developed a working relationship to co-parent Lisa, a change Brennan credits to the influence of his newly found biological sister, Mona Simpson (who worked to repair the relationship between Lisa and Jobs).[18] Jobs found Mona after first finding his birth mother, Joanne Schieble Simpson, shortly after he left Apple.[12]

Jobs did not contact his birth family during Clara's (his adoptive mother) lifetime, however. He would later tell his official biographer Walter Isaacson: "I never wanted [Paul and Clara] to feel like I didn't consider them my parents, because they were totally my parents [...] I loved them so much that I never wanted them to know of my search, and I even had reporters keep it quiet when any of them found out."[12] However, in 1986 when he was 31, Clara was diagnosed with lung cancer. He began to spend a great deal of time with her and learned more details about her background and his adoption, information that motivated him to find his biological mother. Jobs found on his birth certificate the name of the San Francisco doctor to whom Schieble had turned when she was pregnant. Although the doctor did not help Jobs while he was alive, he left a letter for Jobs to be opened upon his death. As he died soon afterwards, Jobs was given the letter which stated that "his mother had been an unmarried graduate student from Wisconsin named Joanne Schieble."[12]

Jobs only contacted Schieble after Clara died and after he received permission from his father, Paul. In addition, out of respect for Paul, he asked the media not to report on his search.[12] Jobs stated that he was motivated to find his birth mother out of both curiosity and a need "to see if she was okay and to thank her, because I'm glad I didn't end up as an abortion. She was twenty-three and she went through a lot to have me."[12] Schieble was emotional during their first meeting (though she wasn't familiar with the history of Apple or Jobs's role in it) and told him that she had been pressured into signing the adoption papers. She said that she regretted giving him up and repeatedly apologized to him for it. Jobs and Schieble would develop a friendly relationship throughout the rest of his life and would spend Christmas together.[12] When Jobs died in 2011, Schieble was suffering from dementia and living in a nursing home. She was not told about his death.[92]

During this first visit, Schieble told Jobs that he had a sister, Mona, who was not aware that she had a brother.[12] Schieble then arranged for them to meet in New York where Mona worked. Her first impression of Jobs was that "he was totally straightforward and lovely, just a normal and sweet guy."[12] Simpson and Jobs then went for a long walk to get to know each other.[12] Jobs later told his biographer that "Mona was not completely thrilled at first to have me in her life and have her mother so emotionally affectionate toward me . . . . As we got to know each other, we became really good friends, and she is my family. I don't know what I'd do without her. I can't imagine a better sister. My adopted sister, Patty, and I were never close."[12]

"I grew up as an only child, with a single mother. Because we were poor and because I knew my father had emigrated from Syria, I imagined he looked like Omar Sharif. I hoped he would be rich and kind and would come into our lives (and our not-yet-furnished apartment) and help us. Later, after I'd met my father, I tried to believe he'd changed his number and left no forwarding address because he was an idealistic revolutionary, plotting a new world for the Arab people. Even as a feminist, my whole life I'd been waiting for a man to love, who could love me. For decades, I'd thought that man would be my father. When I was 25, I met that man, and he was my brother."

—*Mona Simpson*[93]

Jobs then learned his family history. Six months after he was given up for adoption, Schieble's father died, she wed Jandali, and they had a daughter, Mona.[12][11] Jandali states that after finishing his PhD he returned to Syria to work and that it was during this period that Schieble left him[11] (they divorced in 1962).[12] He also states that after the divorce he lost contact with Mona for a period of time:

I also bear the responsibility for being away from my daughter when she was four years old, as her mother divorced me when I went to Syria, but we got back in touch after 10 years. We lost touch again when her mother moved and I didn't know where she was, but since 10 years ago we've been in constant contact, and I see her three times a year. I organized a trip for her last year to visit Syria and Lebanon and she went with a relative from Florida.[11]

A few years later, Schieble married an ice skating teacher, George Simpson. Mona Jandali took her stepfather's last name thus became Mona Simpson. In 1970, after they divorced, Schieble took Mona to Los Angeles and raised her on her own.[12]

Jobs told his official biographer that after meeting Simpson, he wanted to become involved in her ongoing search for their father. When he was found working in Sacramento, they decided that only Simpson would meet him. Jandali and Simpson spoke for several hours at which point he told her that he had left teaching for the restaurant business. He also said that he and Schieble had given another child away for adoption but that "we'll never see that baby again. That baby's gone." (Simpson did not mention that she had met Jobs).[12]Jandali further told Simpson that he once managed a Mediterranean restaurant near San Jose and that "all of the successful technology people used to come there. Even Steve Jobs ... oh yeah, he used to come in, and he was a sweet guy and a big tipper."[12] After hearing about the visit, Jobs recalled that "it was amazing .... I had been to that restaurant a few times, and I remember meeting the owner. He was Syrian. Balding. We shook hands."[12] However, Jobs did not want to meet Jandali because "I was a wealthy man by then, and I didn't trust him not to try to blackmail me or go to the press about it ... I asked Mona not to tell him about me."[12] Jandali later discovered his relationship to Jobs through an online blog. He then contacted Simpson and asked "what is this thing about Steve Jobs?" Simpson told him that it was true and later commented, "My father is thoughtful and a beautiful storyteller, but he is very, very passive ... He never contacted Steve."[12] Because Simpson, herself, researched her Syrian roots and began to meet members of the family, she assumed that Jobs would eventually want to meet their father, but he never did.[12] Jobs also never showed an interest in his Syrian heritage or the Middle East.[12] Simpson fictionalized the search for their father in the 1992 novel, *The Lost Father*.[12]

In 1989, Jobs first met his future wife, Laurene Powell, when he gave a lecture at the Stanford Graduate School of Business, where she was a student. Soon after the event, he stated that Laurene "was right there in the front row in the lecture hall, and I couldn't take my eyes off of her ... kept losing my train of thought, and started feeling a little giddy."[19]After the lecture, Jobs met up with her in the parking lot and invited her out to dinner. From that point forward, they were together, with a few minor exceptions, for the rest of his life.[19] Powell's father died when she was very young, and her mother raised her in a middle class New Jersey home similar to the one Jobs grew up in. After she received her B.A. from the University of Pennsylvania, she spent a short period in high finance but found it didn't interest her, so she decided to pursue her MBA at Stanford instead. In addition, unlike Jobs, she was athletic and followed professional sports. She also brought as much self-sufficiency to the relationship as he did and was more of a private than public person.[19]

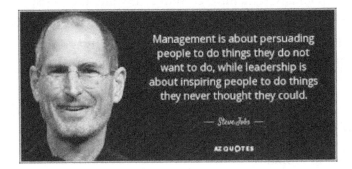

Jobs proposed on New Year's Day 1990 with "a fistful of freshly picked wildflowers."[19] They married on March 18, 1991, in a Buddhist ceremony at the Ahwahnee Hotel in Yosemite National Park.[19] Fifty people, including his father, Paul, and his sister, Mona, attended. The ceremony was conducted by Jobs's guru, Kobun Chino Otogawa. The vegan wedding cake was in the shape of Yosemite's Half Dome, and the wedding ended with a hike (during which Laurene's brothers had a snowball fight). Jobs is reported to have said to Mona: "You see, Mona [...], Laurene is descended from Joe Namath, and we're descended from John Muir."[12]

Jobs and Powell's first child, Reed, was born September 1991.[73] Jobs's father, Paul, died a year and a half later, on March 5, 1993. Jobs and Powell had two more children, Erin, born in August 1995, and Eve, born in 1998.[73] The family lived in Palo Alto, California.[94] A journalist who grew up locally remembered him as owning the house with "the scariest [Hallow'een] decorations in Palo Alto...I don't remember seeing him. I was busy being terrified."[95]

1997–2011

Return to Apple

Jobs on stage at Macworld Conference & Expo, San Francisco, January 11, 2005

In 1996, Apple announced that it would buy NeXT for $427 million. The deal was finalized in February 1997,[96] bringing Jobs back to the company he had cofounded. Jobs became *de facto* chief after then-CEO Gil Amelio was ousted in July 1997. He was formally named interim chief executive in September.[97] In March 1998, to concentrate Apple's efforts on returning to profitability, Jobs terminated a number of projects, such as Newton, Cyberdog, and OpenDoc. In the coming months, many employees developed a fear of encountering Jobs while riding in the elevator, "afraid that they might not have a job when the doors opened. The reality was that Jobs's summary executions were rare, but a handful of victims was enough to terrorize a whole company."[98] Jobs changed the licensing program for Macintosh clones, making it too costly for the manufacturers to continue making machines.

With the purchase of NeXT, much of the company's technology found its way into Apple products, most notably NeXTSTEP, which evolved into Mac OS X. Under Jobs's guidance, the company increased sales significantly with the introduction of the iMac and other new products; since then, appealing designs and powerful branding have worked well for Apple. At the 2000 Macworld Expo, Jobs officially dropped the "interim" modifier from his title at Apple and became permanent CEO.[99] Jobs quipped at the time that he would be using the title "iCEO".[100]

The company subsequently branched out, introducing and improving upon other digital appliances. With the introduction of the iPod portable music player, iTunes digital music software, and the iTunes Store, the company made forays into consumer electronics and music distribution. On June 29, 2007, Apple entered the cellular phone business with the introduction of the iPhone, a multi-touch display cell phone, which also included the features of an iPod and, with its own mobile browser, revolutionized the mobile browsing scene. While nurturing innovation, Jobs also reminded his employees that "real artists ship [deliver product]."[101]

Jobs had a public war of words with Dell Computer CEO Michael Dell, starting in 1987, when Jobs first criticized Dell for making "un-innovative beige boxes".[102] On October 6, 1997, at a Gartner Symposium, when Dell was asked what he would do if he ran the then-troubled Apple Computer company, he said: "I'd shut it down and give the money back to the shareholders."[103] Then, in 2006, Jobs sent an email to all employees when Apple's market capitalization rose above Dell's:

Team, it turned out that Michael Dell wasn't perfect at predicting the future. Based on today's stock market close, Apple is worth more than Dell. Stocks go up and down, and things may be different tomorrow, but I thought it was worth a moment of reflection today. Steve.[104]

Jobs was both admired and criticized for his consummate skill at persuasion and salesmanship, which has been dubbed the "reality distortion field" and was particularly evident during his keynote speeches (colloquially known as "Stevenotes") at Macworld Expos and at Apple Worldwide Developers Conferences.[105]

Jobs was a board member at Gap Inc. from 1999 to 2002.[106]

Steve Jobs and Bill Gates at the fifth *D: All Things Digital* conference (*D5*) in May 2007

In 2001, Jobs was granted stock options in the amount of 7.5 million shares of Apple with an exercise price of $18.30. It was alleged that the options had been backdated, and that the exercise price should have been $21.10. It was further alleged that Jobs had thereby incurred taxable income of $20,000,000 that he did not report, and that Apple overstated its earnings by that same amount. As a result,

Jobs potentially faced a number of criminal charges and civil penalties. The case was the subject of active criminal and civil government investigations,[107] though an independent internal Apple investigation completed on December 29, 2006 found that Jobs was unaware of these issues and that the options granted to him were returned without being exercised in 2003.[108]

In 2005, Jobs responded to criticism of Apple's poor recycling programs for e-waste in the US by lashing out at environmental and other advocates at Apple's annual meeting in Cupertino in April. A few weeks later, Apple announced it would take back iPods for free at its retail stores. The Computer TakeBack Campaign responded by flying a banner from a plane over the Stanford University graduation at which Jobs was the commencement speaker. The banner read "Steve, don't be a mini-player— recycle all e-waste."

In 2006, he further expanded Apple's recycling programs to any US customer who buys a new Mac. This program includes shipping and "environmentally friendly disposal" of their old systems.[109] The success of Apple's unique products and services provided several years of stable financial returns, propelling Apple to become the world's most valuable publicly traded company in 2011.[110]

Jobs was perceived as a demanding perfectionist [111][112] who always aspired to position his businesses and their products at the forefront of the information technology industry by foreseeing and setting innovation and style trends. He summed up this self-concept at the end of his keynote speech at the Macworld Conference and Expo in January 2007, by quoting ice hockey player Wayne Gretzky:

There's an old Wayne Gretzky quote that I love. "I skate to where the puck is going to be, not where it has been." And we've always tried to do that at Apple. Since the very, very beginning. And we always will.[113]

On July 1, 2008, a US$7 billion class action suit was filed against several members of the Apple board of directors for revenue lost because of alleged securities fraud.[114][115]

In a 2011 interview with biographer Walter Isaacson, Jobs revealed that he had met with U.S. President Barack Obama, complained about the nation's shortage of software engineers, and told Obama that he was "headed for a one-term presidency".[116] Jobs proposed that any foreign student who got an engineering degree at a U.S. university should automatically be offered a green card. After the meeting, Jobs commented, "The president is very smart, but he kept explaining to us reasons why things can't get done . . . . It infuriates me."[116]

Health issues

In October 2003, Jobs was diagnosed with cancer.[117] In mid-2004, he announced to his employees that he had a cancerous tumor in his pancreas.[118] The prognosis for pancreatic cancer is usually very poor;[119] Jobs stated that he had a rare, much less aggressive type, known as islet cell neuroendocrine tumor.[118]

Despite his diagnosis, Jobs resisted his doctors' recommendations for medical intervention for nine months,[120] instead relying on a pseudo-medicine diet to try natural healing to thwart the disease. According to Harvard researcher Ramzi Amri, his choice of alternative treatment "led to an unnecessarily early death".[117] other doctors agree that Jobs's diet was insufficient to address his disease. Cancer researcher and alternative medicine critic David Gorski, for instance, said, "My best guess was that Jobs probably only modestly decreased his chances of survival, if that."[121] Barrie R. Cassileth, the chief of Memorial Sloan Kettering Cancer Center's integrative medicine department,[122] said, "Jobs's faith in alternative medicine likely cost him his life.... He had the only kind of pancreatic cancer that is treatable and curable.... He essentially committed suicide."[123] According to Jobs's biographer, Walter Isaacson, "for nine months he refused to undergo surgery for his pancreatic cancer – a decision he later regretted as his health declined".[124] "Instead, he tried a vegan diet, acupuncture, herbal remedies, and other treatments he found online, and even consulted a psychic. He was also influenced by a doctor who ran a clinic that advised juice fasts, bowel cleansings and other unproven approaches, before finally having surgery in July 2004."[125] He eventually underwent a pancreaticoduodenectomy (or "Whipple procedure") in July 2004, that appeared to remove the tumor successfully.[126][127] Jobs did not receive chemotherapy or radiation therapy.[118][128] During Jobs's absence, Tim Cook, head of worldwide sales and operations at Apple, ran the company.[118]

In early August 2006, Jobs delivered the keynote for Apple's annual Worldwide Developers Conference. His "thin, almost gaunt" appearance and unusually "listless" delivery,[129][130] together with his choice to delegate significant portions of his keynote to other presenters, inspired a flurry of media and Internet speculation about the state of his health.[131] In contrast, according to an *Ars Technica* journal report, Worldwide Developers Conference (WWDC) attendees who saw Jobs in person said he "looked fine".[132] Following the keynote, an Apple spokesperson said that "Steve's health is robust."[133]

Two years later, similar concerns followed Jobs's 2008 WWDC keynote address.[134] Apple officials stated that Jobs was victim to a "common bug" and was taking antibiotics,[135]while others surmised his cachectic appearance was due to the Whipple procedure.[128] During a July conference call discussing Apple earnings, participants responded to repeated questions about Jobs's health by insisting that it was a "private matter". Others said that shareholders had a right to know more, given Jobs's hands-on approach to running his company.[136][137] Based on an off-the-record phone conversation with Jobs, *The New York Times* reported, "While his health problems amounted to a good deal more than 'a common bug', they weren't life-threatening and he doesn't have a recurrence of cancer."[138]

On August 28, 2008, Bloomberg mistakenly published a 2,500-word obituary of Jobs in its corporate news service, containing blank spaces for his age and cause of death. (News carriers customarily stockpile up-to-date obituaries to facilitate news delivery in the event of a well-known figure's death.) Although the error was promptly rectified, many news carriers and blogs reported on it,[139] intensifying rumors concerning Jobs's health.[140] Jobs responded at Apple's September 2008 *Let's Rock* keynote by paraphrasing Mark Twain: "Reports of my death are greatly exaggerated."[141][142] At a subsequent media event, Jobs concluded his presentation with a slide reading "110/70", referring to his blood pressure, stating he would not address further questions about his health.[143]

On December 16, 2008, Apple announced that marketing vice-president Phil Schiller would deliver the company's final keynote address at the Macworld Conference and Expo 2009, again reviving questions about Jobs's health.[144][145] In a statement given on January 5, 2009, on Apple.com, Jobs said that he had been suffering from a "hormone imbalance" for several months.[146][147]

On January 14, 2009, Jobs wrote in an internal Apple memo that in the previous week he had "learned that my health-related issues are more complex than I originally thought".[148]He announced a six-month leave of absence until the end of June 2009, to allow him to better focus on his health. Tim Cook, who previously acted as CEO in Jobs's 2004 absence, became acting CEO of Apple, with Jobs still involved with "major strategic decisions".[148]

In 2009, Tim Cook offered a portion of his liver to Jobs, since both share a rare blood type. (The donor liver can regenerate tissue after such an operation.) Jobs yelled, "I'll never let you do that. I'll never do that."[149]

In April 2009, Jobs underwent a liver transplant at Methodist University Hospital Transplant Institute in Memphis, Tennessee.[150][151][152] Jobs's prognosis was described as "excellent".[150]

Resignation

On January 17, 2011, a year and a half after Jobs returned to work following the liver transplant, Apple announced that he had been granted a medical leave of absence. Jobs announced his leave in a letter to employees, stating his decision was made "so he could focus on his health." As it did at the time of his 2009 medical leave, Apple announced that Tim Cook would run day-to-day operations and that Jobs would continue to be involved in major strategic decisions at the company.[153][154] Despite the leave, Jobs appeared at the iPad 2 launch event (March 2), the WWDC keynote introducing iCloud (June 6), and before the Cupertino City Council (June 7).[155]

On August 24, 2011, Jobs announced his resignation as Apple's CEO, writing to the board, "I have always said if there ever came a day when I could no longer meet my duties and expectations as Apple's CEO, I would be the first to let you know. Unfortunately, that day has come."[156] Jobs became chairman of the board and named Tim Cook as his successor as CEO.[157][158] Jobs continued to work for Apple until the day before his death six weeks later.[159][160][161]

Death

Flags flying at half-staff outside
Apple HQ in Cupertino, on the
evening of Steve Jobs's death

Memorial candles and iPads
pay tribute to Steve Jobs
outside the Apple Store in
Palo Alto, California, shortly
after his death.

Jobs died at his Palo Alto,
California home around
3 p.m. (PDT) on October 5,
2011, due to complications from a relapse of his
previously treated islet-cell neuroendocrine pancreatic
cancer,[45][162][163] which resulted in respiratory
arrest.[164] He had lost consciousness the day before and
died with his wife, children, and sisters at his side.[93] His
sister, Mona Simpson, described his death thus: "Steve's
final words, hours earlier, were monosyllables, repeated

three times. Before embarking, he'd looked at his sister Patty, then for a long time at his children, then at his life's partner, Laurene, and then over their shoulders past them. Steve's final words were: 'Oh wow. Oh wow. Oh wow.'" He then lost consciousness and died several hours later.[93] A small private funeral was held on October 7, 2011, the details of which were not revealed out of respect for Jobs's family.[165] At the time of his death, his biological mother, Joanne Schieble Simpson, was living in a nursing home and suffering from dementia. She was not told that he died.[92]

Apple[166] and Pixar each issued announcements of his death.[167] Apple announced on the same day that they had no plans for a public service, but were encouraging "well-wishers" to send their remembrance messages to an email address created to receive such messages.[168] Apple and Microsoft both flew their flags at half-staff throughout their respective headquarters and campuses.[169][170] Bob Iger ordered all Disney properties, including Walt Disney World and Disneyland, to fly their flags at half-staff from October 6 to 12, 2011.[171] For two weeks following his death, Apple displayed on its corporate Web site a simple page that showed Jobs's name and lifespan next to his grayscale portrait.[172][173][174] On October 19, 2011, Apple employees held a private memorial service for Jobs on the Apple campus in Cupertino. Jobs's widow, Laurene, was in attendance, as well as Cook, Bill Campbell, Norah Jones, Al Gore, and Coldplay.[175] Some of Apple's retail stores closed briefly so employees could attend the memorial. A video of the service was uploaded to Apple's website.[175]

Governor Jerry Brown of California declared Sunday, October 16, 2011, to be "Steve Jobs Day."[176] On that day, an invitation-only memorial was held at Stanford University. Those in attendance included Apple and other tech company executives, members of the media, celebrities, close friends of Jobs, and politicians, along with Jobs's family. Bono, Yo Yo Ma, and Joan Baez performed at the service, which lasted longer than an hour. The service was highly secured, with guards at all of the university's gates, and a helicopter flying overhead from an area news station.[177][178] Each attendee was given a small brown box as a "farewell gift" from Jobs. The box contained a copy of the *Autobiography of a Yogi* by Paramahansa Yogananda.[179]

Apple co-founder Steve Wozniak,[180] former owner of what would become Pixar, George Lucas,[181] former rival, Microsoft co-founder Bill Gates,[182] and

President Barack Obama[183] all offered statements in response to his death.

Jobs is buried in an unmarked grave at Alta Mesa Memorial Park, the only nonsectarian cemetery in Palo Alto.[184][185]

Portrayals and coverage in books, film, and theater

Steve Jobs is the subject of a number of books and films.

Innovations and designsJobs's design aesthetic was influenced by the modernist architectural style of Joseph Eichler, by the industrial designs of Braun's Dieter Rams, and by Buddhism. In India, he experienced Buddhism while on his seven-month spiritual journey,[186] and his sense of intuition was influenced by the spiritual people with whom he studied.[186]

According to Apple cofounder Steve Wozniak "Steve didn't ever code. He wasn't an engineer and he didn't do any original design..."[187][188] Daniel Kottke, one of Apple's earliest employees and a college friend of Jobs's, stated that "Between Woz and Jobs, Woz was the innovator, the inventor. Steve Jobs was the marketing person."[189]

He is listed as either primary inventor or co-inventor in 346 United States patents or patent applications related to a range of technologies from actual computer and portable devices to user interfaces (including touch-based), speakers, keyboards, power adapters, staircases, clasps, sleeves, lanyards and packages. Jobs's contributions to most of his patents were to "the look and feel of the product". His industrial design chief Jonathan Ive had his name along with him for 200 of the patents.[190] Most of these are design patents (specific product designs; for example, Jobs listed as primary inventor in patents for both original and lamp-style iMacs, as well as PowerBook G4 Titanium) as opposed to utility patents (inventions).[191][192] He has 43 issued US patents on inventions.[191] The patent on the Mac OS X Dock user interface with "magnification" feature was issued the day before he died.[193] Although Jobs had little involvement in the engineering and technical side of the original Apple computers,[188] Jobs later used his CEO position to directly involve himself with product design.[194]

Involved in many projects throughout his career was his long-time marketing executive and confidant Joanna Hoffman, known as one of the few employees at Apple and NeXT who could successfully stand up to Jobs while also engaging with him.[195]

Even while terminally ill in the hospital, Jobs sketched new devices that would hold the iPad in a hospital bed.[196] He also despised the oxygen monitor on his finger and suggested ways to revise the design for simplicity.[197]

Since his death, the former Apple CEO has won 141 patents, more than most inventors win during their lifetimes. Currently, Jobs holds over 450 patents.[198]

Apple II

The Apple II is an 8-bit home computer, one of the first highly successful mass-produced microcomputer products,[50] designed primarily by Steve Wozniak (Jobs oversaw the development of the Apple II's unusual case[12] and Rod Holt developed the unique power supply[51]). It was introduced in 1977 at the West Coast Computer Faire by Jobs and was the first consumer product sold by Apple Computer.

Apple Lisa

The Lisa is a personal computer designed by Apple Computer, Inc. during the early 1980s. It was the first personal computer to offer a graphical user interface in a machine aimed at individual business users. Development of the Lisa began in 1978.[199] The Lisa sold poorly, with only 100,000 units sold.[200]

In 1982, after Jobs was forced out of the Lisa project,[201] he joined the Macintosh project. The Macintosh is not a direct descendant of Lisa, although there are obvious similarities between the systems. The final revision, the Lisa 2/10, was modified and sold as the Macintosh XL.[202]

Macintosh

Once he joined the original Macintosh team, Jobs took over the project after Wozniak had experienced a traumatic airplane accident and temporarily left the company.[77] Jobs introduced the Macintosh computer on January 24, 1984. This was the first mass-market personal computer featuring an integral graphical user interface and mouse.[203] This first model was later renamed to "Macintosh 128k" for uniqueness amongst a populous family of subsequently updated models which are also based on Apple's same proprietary architecture. Since 1998, Apple has largely phased out the Macintosh name in favor of "Mac", though the product family has been nicknamed "Mac" or "the Mac" since the development of the first model. The Macintosh was introduced by a US$1.5 million Ridley Scott television commercial, "1984".[204] It most notably aired during the third quarter of Super Bowl XVIII on January 22, 1984, and some people consider the ad a "watershed event"[205] and a "masterpiece."[206]

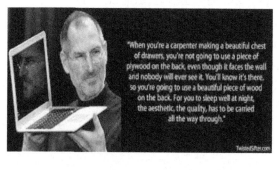

Regis McKenna called the ad "more successful than the Mac itself."[207] "1984" used an unnamed heroine to represent the coming of the Macintosh (indicated by a Picasso-style picture of the computer on her white tank top) as a means of saving humanity from the "conformity" of IBM's attempts to dominate the computer industry. The ad alludes to George Orwell's novel, *Nineteen Eighty-Four*, which described a dystopian future ruled by a televised "Big Brother."[208][209]

The Macintosh, however, was expensive, which hindered its ability to be competitive in a market already dominated by the Commodore 64 for consumers, as well as the IBM Personal Computer and its accompanying clone market for businesses.[210] Macintosh systems still found success in education and desktop publishing and kept Apple as the second-largest PC manufacturer for the next decade.

NeXT Computer

After Jobs was forced out of Apple in 1985, he started a company that built workstation computers. The NeXT Computer was introduced in 1988 at a lavish launch event. Tim Berners-Lee created the world's first web browser (WorldWideWeb) using the NeXT Computer. The NeXT Computer was the basis for today's macOS (formerly OS X) and iOS(formerly iPhone OS).[211][212]

iMac

Apple iMac was introduced in 1998 and its innovative design was directly the result of Jobs's return to Apple. Apple boasted "the back of our computer looks better than the front of anyone else's."[213] Described as "cartoonlike", the first iMac, clad in Bondi Blue plastic, was unlike any personal computer that came before. In

1999, Apple introduced the Graphite gray Apple iMac and since has varied the shape, colour and size considerably while maintaining the all-in-one design. Design ideas were intended to create a connection with the user such as the handle and a breathing light effect when the computer went to sleep.[214] The Apple iMac sold for $1,299 at that time. The iMac also featured some technical innovations, such as having USB ports as the only device inputs. This latter change resulted, through the iMac's success, in the interface being popularised among third party peripheral makers – as evidenced by the fact that many early USB peripherals were made of translucent plastic (to match the iMac design).[215]

iTunes

iTunes is a media player, media library, online radio broadcaster, and mobile device management application developed by Apple Inc. It is used to play, download, and organize digital audio and video (as well as other types of media available on the iTunes Store) on personal computers running the macOS and Microsoft Windows operating systems. The iTunes Store is also available on the iPod Touch, iPhone, and iPad.

Through the iTunes Store, users can purchase and download music, music videos, television shows, audiobooks, podcasts, movies, and movie rentals in some countries, and ringtones, available on the iPhone and iPod Touch (fourth generation onward). Application software for the iPhone, iPad and iPod Touch can be downloaded from the App Store.

iPod

The first generation of iPod was released October 23, 2001. The major innovation of the iPod was its small size achieved by using a 1.8" hard drive compared to the 2.5" drives common to players at that time. The capacity of the first generation iPod ranged from 5 GB to 10 GB.[216] The iPod sold for US$399 and more than 100,000 iPods were sold before the end of 2001. The introduction of the iPod resulted in Apple becoming a major player in the music industry.[217] Also, the iPod's success prepared the way for the iTunes music store and the iPhone.[218] After the 1st generation of iPod, Apple released the hard drive-based iPod Classic, the touchscreen iPod Touch, the video-capable iPod Nano, and the screenless iPod Shuffle in the following years.[217]

iPhone

Apple began work on the first iPhone in 2005 and the first iPhone was released on June 29, 2007. The iPhone created such a sensation that a survey indicated six out of ten Americans were aware of its release. *Time Magazine* declared it "Invention of the Year" for 2007.[219] The Apple iPhone is a small device with multimedia capabilities and functions as a quad-band touch screen smartphone.[220] A year later, the iPhone 3G was released in July 2008 with three key features: support for GPS, 3G data and tri-band UMTS/HSDPA. In June 2009, the iPhone 3GS, whose improvements included voice control, a better camera, and a faster processor, was introduced by Phil Schiller.[221] The iPhone 4 is thinner than previous models, has a five megapixel camera capable of recording video in 720p HD, and adds a secondary front-facing camera for video calls.[222] A major feature of the iPhone 4S, introduced in October 2011, was Siri, a virtual assistant capable of voice recognition.[219]

iPad

Jobs introducing the iPad, San Francisco, January 27, 2010

iPad is an iOS-based line of tablet computers designed and marketed by Apple Inc. The first iPad was released on April 3, 2010; the most recent iPad models, the iPad (2017), iPad Pro, and iPad Mini 4, were released on September 9, 2015 and March 24, 2017. The user interface is built around the device's multi-touch screen, including a virtual keyboard. The iPad includes built-in Wi-Fi and cellular connectivity on select models. As of April 2015, there have been over 250 million iPads sold.[223]

Mark Zuckerberg

Mark Elliot Zuckerberg (/ˈzʌkərbɜːrg/; born May 14, 1984) is an American computer programmer and Internet entrepreneur. He is a co-founder of Facebook, and currently operates as its chairman and chief executive officer.[4][5] His net worth is estimated to be US

$74.2 billion as of November 2017, and in 2016 was ranked by *Forbes* as the fifth richest person in the world.[3][6]

Zuckerberg launched Facebook from his Harvard University dormitory room on February 4, 2004. He was assisted by his college roommates and fellow Harvard students Eduardo Saverin, Andrew McCollum, Dustin Moskovitz, and Chris Hughes.[7] The group then introduced Facebook to other college campuses. Facebook expanded rapidly, reaching one billion users by 2012. Meanwhile, Zuckerberg was involved in various legal disputes brought by others in the group, who claimed a share of the company based upon their involvement during the development phase of Facebook.[8]

In December 2012, Zuckerberg and his wife Priscilla Chan announced that over the course of their lives they would give the majority of their wealth to "advancing human potential and promoting equality" in the spirit of The Giving Pledge.[9] On December 1, 2015, they announced they would eventually give 99 percent of their Facebook shares (worth about US$45 billion at the time) to the Chan Zuckerberg Initiative.[10][11]

Since 2010, *Time* magazine has named Zuckerberg among the 100 wealthiest and most influential people in the world as a part of its Person of the Year award.[3][12][13] In December 2016, Zuckerberg was ranked 10th on *Forbes* list of The World's Most Powerful People.[14]

 Zuckerberg was born in 1984 in White Plains, New York.[16] He is the son of Karen (née Kempner), a psychiatrist, and Edward Zuckerberg, a dentist.[17] His ancestors came from Germany, Austria and Poland.[18] He and his three sisters, Randi, Donna, and Arielle, were brought up in Dobbs Ferry, New York, a small Westchester County village about 21 miles north of Midtown Manhattan.[19] Zuckerberg was raised Jewish and became a Bar Mitzvah when he turned 13.[20]

At Ardsley High School, Zuckerberg excelled in classes. He transferred to the exclusive private school Phillips Exeter Academy, in New Hampshire, in his junior year, where he won prizes in science (math, astronomy, and physics) and classical studies. In his youth, he also attended the Johns Hopkins Center for Talented Youth summer camp. On his college application, Zuckerberg stated that he could read and write French, Hebrew, Latin, and ancient Greek. He was captain of the fencing team.[21][22][23]

Software developer

Early years

Zuckerberg began using computers and writing software in middle school. His father taught him Atari BASIC Programming in the 1990s, and later hired software developer David Newman to tutor him privately. Zuckerberg took a graduate course in the subject at Mercy College near his home while still in high school. In one program, since his father's dental practice was operated from their home, he built a software program he called "ZuckNet" that allowed all the computers between the house and dental office to communicate with each other. It is considered a "primitive" version of AOL's Instant Messenger, which came out the following year.[24][25]

According to writer Jose Antonio Vargas, "some kids played computer games. Mark created them." Zuckerberg himself recalls this period: "I had a bunch of friends who were artists. They'd come over, draw stuff, and I'd build a game out of it." However, notes Vargas, Zuckerberg was not a typical "geek-klutz", as he later became captain of his prep school fencingteam and earned a classics diploma. Napster co-founder Sean Parker, a close friend, notes that Zuckerberg was "really into Greek odysseys and all that stuff", recalling how he once quoted lines from the Roman epic poem *Aeneid*, by Virgil, during a Facebook product conference.[19]

During Zuckerberg's high school years, he worked under the company name Intelligent Media Group to build a music player called the Synapse Media Player. The device used machine learning to learn the user's listening habits, which was posted to *Slashdot*[26] and received a rating of 3 out of 5 from *PC Magazine*.[27]

College years

Vargas noted that by the time Zuckerberg began classes at Harvard, he had already achieved a "reputation as a programming prodigy". He studied psychology and computer scienceand belonged to Alpha Epsilon Pi and Kirkland House.[12][19][28] In his sophomore year, he wrote a program that he called CourseMatch, which allowed users to make class selection decisions based on the choices of other students and also to help them form study groups. A short time later, he created a different program he initially called Facemash that let students select the best looking person from a choice of photos. According to Arie Hasit, Zuckerberg's roommate at the time, "he built the site for fun". Hasit explains:

We had books called Face Books, which included the names and pictures of everyone who lived in the student dorms. At first, he built a site and placed two pictures, or pictures of two males and two females. Visitors to the site had to choose who was "hotter" and according to the votes there would be a ranking.[29]

The site went up over a weekend, but by Monday morning, the college shut it down, because its popularity had overwhelmed one of Harvard's network switches and prevented students from accessing the Internet. In addition, many students complained that their photos were being used without permission. Zuckerberg apologized publicly, and the student paper ran articles stating that his site was "completely improper."[29]

The following semester, in January 2004, Zuckerberg began writing code for a new Web site.[30] On February 4,

2004, Zuckerberg launched "Thefacebook", originally located at thefacebook.com.[31]

Six days after the site launched, three Harvard seniors, Cameron Winklevoss, Tyler Winklevoss, and Divya Narendra, accused Zuckerberg of intentionally misleading them into believing he would help them build a social network called HarvardConnection.com, while he was instead using their ideas to build a competing product.[32] The three complained to *The Harvard Crimson*, and the newspaper began an investigation in response.

Following the official launch of the Facebook social media platform, the three filed a lawsuit against Zuckerberg that resulted in a settlement.[33] The agreed settlement was for 1.2 million Facebook shares that were worth US$300 million at Facebook's IPO.[34]

Zuckerberg dropped out of Harvard in his sophomore year in order to complete his project.[35] In January 2014, he recalled:

I remember really vividly, you know, having pizza with my friends a day or two after—I opened up the first version of Facebook at the time I thought, "You know, someone needs to build a service like this for the world." But I just never thought that we'd be the ones to help do it. And I think a lot of what it comes down to is we just cared more.[36]

On May 28, 2017, Zuckerberg received an honorary degree from Harvard.[37][38]

Career

Zuckerberg listening to President Barack Obama before a private meeting where Obama dined with technology business leaders in Woodside, California, February 17, 2011.

Facebook

On February 4, 2004, Zuckerberg launched Facebook from his Harvard dormitory room.[39][40] An earlier inspiration for Facebook may have come from Phillips Exeter Academy, the prep school from which Zuckerberg graduated in 2002. It published its own student directory, "The Photo Address Book", which students referred to as "The Facebook". Such photo directories were an important part of the student social experience at many private schools. With them, students were able to list attributes such as their class years, their friends, and their telephone numbers.[39]

Once at college, Zuckerberg's Facebook started off as just a "Harvard thing" until Zuckerberg decided to spread it to other schools, enlisting the help of roommate Dustin Moskovitz. They began with Columbia University, New York University, Stanford, Dartmouth, Cornell, University of Pennsylvania, Brown, and Yale.[41] Samyr Laine, a triple jumper representing Haiti at the 2012 Summer Olympics, shared a room with Zuckerberg during Facebook's founding. "Mark was clearly on to great things," said Laine, who was Facebook's fourteenth user.[42]

Zuckerberg, Moskovitz and some friends moved to Palo Alto, California in Silicon Valley where they leased a small house that served as an office. Over the summer, Zuckerberg met Peter Thiel, who invested in the company. They got their first office in mid-2004. According to Zuckerberg, the group planned to return to Harvard, but eventually decided to remain in California.[43][44] They had already turned down offers by major corporations to buy the company. In an interview in 2007, Zuckerberg explained his reasoning: "It's not because of the amount of money. For me and my colleagues, the most important thing is that we create an open information flow for people. Having media corporations owned by conglomerates is just not an attractive idea to me."[40]

He restated these goals to *Wired* magazine in 2010: "The thing I really care about is the mission, making the world open."[45] Earlier, in April 2009, Zuckerberg sought the advice of former Netscape CFO Peter Currie about financing strategies for Facebook.[46] On July 21, 2010, Zuckerberg reported that the company reached the 500 million-user mark.[47] When asked whether Facebook could earn more income from advertising as a result of its phenomenal growth, he explained:

I guess we could ... If you look at how much of our page is taken up with ads compared to the average search query. The average for us is a little less than 10 percent of the pages and the average for search is about 20 percent taken up with ads ... That's the simplest thing we could do. But we aren't like that. We make enough money. Right, I mean, we are keeping things running; we are growing at the rate we want to.[45]

In 2010, Steven Levy, who wrote the 1984 book *Hackers: Heroes of the Computer Revolution*, wrote that

Zuckerberg "clearly thinks of himself as a hacker". Zuckerberg said that "it's OK to break things" "to make them better".[48][49] Facebook instituted "hackathons" held every six to eight weeks where participants would have one night to conceive of and complete a project.[48] The company provided music, food, and beer at the hackathons, and many Facebook staff members, including Zuckerberg, regularly attended.[49] "The idea is that you can build something really good in a night", Zuckerberg told Levy. "And that's part of the personality of Facebook now ... It's definitely very core to my personality."[48]

Vanity Fair magazine named Zuckerberg number 1 on its 2010 list of the Top 100 "most influential people of the Information Age".[50] Zuckerberg ranked number 23 on the *Vanity Fair* 100 list in 2009.[51] In 2010, Zuckerberg was chosen as number 16 in *New Statesman*'s annual survey of the world's 50 most influential figures.[52] In a 2011 interview with PBS shortly after the death of Steve Jobs, Zuckerberg said that Jobs had advised him on how to create a management team at Facebook that was "focused on building as high quality and good things as you are".[53]

On October 1, 2012, Zuckerberg visited Russian Prime Minister Dmitry Medvedev in Moscow to stimulate social media innovation in Russia and to boost Facebook's position in the Russian market.[54] Russia's communications minister tweeted that Prime Minister Dmitry Medvedev urged the social media giant's founder to abandon plans to lure away Russian programmers and instead consider opening a research center in Moscow. In 2012, Facebook had roughly 9 million users in Russia, while domestic clone VK had around 34 million.[55] Rebecca Van Dyck, Facebook's head of consumer marketing, claimed that 85 million American Facebook users were exposed to the first day of the Home promotional campaign on April 6, 2013.[56]

On August 19, 2013, *The Washington Post* reported that Zuckerberg's Facebook profile was hacked by an unemployed web developer.[57]

At the 2013 TechCrunch Disrupt conference, held in September, Zuckerberg stated that he is working towards registering the 5 billion humans who were not connected to the Internet as of the conference on Facebook. Zuckerberg then explained that this is intertwined with the aim of the Internet.org project, whereby Facebook, with the support of other technology companies, seeks to increase the number of people connected to the internet.[58][59]

Zuckerberg was the keynote speaker at the 2014 Mobile World Congress (MWC), held in Barcelona, Spain, in

March 2014, which was attended by 75,000 delegates. Various media sources highlighted the connection between Facebook's focus on mobile technology and Zuckerberg's speech, claiming that mobile represents the future of the company.[60]Zuckerberg's speech expands upon the goal that he raised at the TechCrunch conference in September 2013, whereby he is working towards expanding Internet coverage into developing countries.[61]

Alongside other American technology figures like Jeff Bezos and Tim Cook, Zuckerberg hosted visiting Chinese politician Lu Wei, known as the "Internet czar" for his influence in the enforcement of China's online policy, at Facebook's headquarters on December 8, 2014. The meeting occurred after Zuckerberg participated in a Q&A session at Tsinghua University in Beijing, China, on October 23, 2014, where he attempted to converse in Mandarin Chinese; although Facebook is banned in China, Zuckerberg is highly regarded among the people and was at the university to help fuel the nation's burgeoning entrepreneur sector.[62]

Zuckerberg fielded questions during a live Q&A session at the company's headquarters in Menlo Park on December 11, 2014. The founder and CEO explained that he does not believe Facebook is a waste of time, because it facilitates social engagement, and participating in a public session was so that he could "learn how to better serve the community".[63][64]

Zuckerberg receives a one-dollar salary as CEO of Facebook.[2] In June 2016, Business Insider named Zuckerberg one of the "Top 10 Business Visionaries Creating Value for the World" along with Elon Musk and Sal Khan, due to the fact that he and his wife "pledged to give away 99% of their wealth — which is estimated at over $52.1 billion."[65]

Wirehog

A month after Zuckerberg launched Facebook in February 2004, i2hub, another campus-only service, created by Wayne Chang, was launched. i2hub focused on peer-to-peer file sharing. At the time, both i2hub and Facebook were gaining the attention of the press and growing rapidly in users and publicity. In August 2004, Zuckerberg, Andrew McCollum, Adam D'Angelo, and Sean Parker launched a competing peer-to-peer file sharing service called Wirehog, a precursor to Facebook Platform applications.[66][67]

Platform, Beacon, and Connect

 Zuckerberg at the World Economic Forum in Davos, Switzerland (January 2009).

On May 24, 2007, Zuckerberg announced Facebook Platform, a development platform for programmers to create social applications within Facebook. Within weeks, many applications had been built and some already had millions of users. It grew to more than 800,000 developers around the world building applications for Facebook Platform.[68]

On November 6, 2007, Zuckerberg announced Beacon, a social advertising system that enabled people to share information with their Facebook friends based on their browsing activities on other sites. For example, eBay sellers could let friends know automatically what they have for sale via the Facebook news feed as they listed items for sale. The program came under scrutiny because of privacy concerns from groups and individual users. Zuckerberg and Facebook failed to respond to the concerns quickly, and on December 5, 2007, Zuckerberg wrote a blog post on Facebook,[69] taking responsibility for the concerns about

Beacon and offering an easier way for users to opt out of the service.

In 2007, Zuckerberg was added to MIT Technology Review's TR35 list as one of the top 35 innovators in the world under the age of 35.[70]On July 23, 2008, Zuckerberg announced Facebook Connect, a version of Facebook Platform for users.

Internet.org

In a public Facebook post, Zuckerberg launched the Internet.org project in late August 2013. Zuckerberg explained that the primary aim of the initiative is to provide Internet access to the 5 billion people who are not connected as of the launch date. Using a three-tier strategy, Internet.org will also create new jobs and open up new markets, according to Zuckerberg. He stated in his post:

The world economy is going through a massive transition right now. The knowledge economy is the future. By bringing everyone online, we'll not only improve billions of lives, but we'll also improve our own as we benefit from the ideas and productivity they contribute to the world. Giving everyone the opportunity to connect is the foundation for enabling the knowledge economy. It is not the only thing we need to do, but it's a fundamental and necessary step.[59]

To stay proven on the efforts of bringing in the concept of net neutrality, Mark Zuckerberg met Narendra Modi, Satya Nadella and Sundar Pichai at the Silicon Valley, to discuss on how to effectively establish affordable internet access to the less developed countries.[71] As a token of initiation, Mark Zuckerberg changed his Facebook profile picture to extend his support to the Digital India to help the rural communities to stay connected to the internet.[72]

Legal controversies

ConnectU lawsuits

Harvard students Cameron Winklevoss, Tyler Winklevoss, and Divya Narendra accused Zuckerberg of intentionally making them believe he would help them build a social network called HarvardConnection.com (later called ConnectU).[73] They filed a lawsuit in 2004, but it was dismissed on a technicality on March 28, 2007. It was refiled soon thereafter in federal court in Boston. Facebook countersued in regards to Social Butterfly, a project put out by The Winklevoss Chang Group, an alleged partnership between ConnectU and i2hub. On

June 25, 2008, the case settled and Facebook agreed to transfer over 1.2 million common shares and pay $20 million in cash.[74]

In November 2007, confidential court documents were posted on the website of *02138*, a magazine that catered to Harvard alumni. They included Zuckerberg's Social Security number, his parents' home address, and his girlfriend's address. Facebook filed to have the documents removed, but the judge ruled in favor of *02138*.[75]

Saverin lawsuit

A lawsuit filed by Eduardo Saverin against Facebook and Zuckerberg was settled out of court. Though terms of the settlement were sealed, the company affirmed Saverin's title as co-founder of Facebook. Saverin signed a non-disclosure contract after the settlement.[76]

Pakistan criminal investigation

In June 2010, Pakistani Deputy Attorney General Muhammad Azhar Sidiqque launched a criminal investigation into Zuckerberg and Facebook co-founders Dustin Moskovitz and Chris Hughes after a "Draw Muhammad" contest was hosted on Facebook. The investigation named the anonymous German woman who created the contest. Sidiqque asked the country's police to contact Interpol to have Zuckerberg and the three others arrested for blasphemy. On May 19, 2010, Facebook's website was temporarily blocked in Pakistan until Facebook removed the contest from its website at the end of May. Sidiqque also asked its UN representative to raise the issue with the United Nations General Assembly.[77][78]

Paul Ceglia

In June 2010, Paul Ceglia, the owner of a wood pellet fuel company in Allegany County, upstate New York, filed suit against Zuckerberg, claiming 84 percent ownership of Facebook and seeking monetary damages. According to Ceglia, he and Zuckerberg signed a contract on April 28, 2003, that an initial fee of $1,000 entitled Ceglia to 50% of the website's revenue, as well as an additional 1% interest in the business per day after January 1, 2004, until website completion. Zuckerberg was developing other projects at the time, among which was *Facemash*, the predecessor of Facebook, but did not register the domain name *thefacebook.com* until January 1, 2004. Facebook management dismissed the lawsuit as "completely frivolous". Facebook spokesman Barry Schnitt told a reporter that Ceglia's counsel had unsuccessfully sought an out-of-court settlement.[79][80]

On October 26, 2012, federal authorities arrested Ceglia, charging him with mail and wire fraud and of "tampering with, destroying and fabricating evidence in a scheme to defraud the Facebook founder of billions of dollars." Ceglia is accused of fabricating emails to make it appear that he and Zuckerberg discussed details about an early version of Facebook, although after examining their emails, investigators found there was no mention of Facebook in them.[81] Some law firms withdrew from the case before it was initiated and others after Ceglia's arrest.[82][83]

Palestinian terror attacks

On July 2, 2016, Israeli cabinet minister Gilad Erdan accused Zuckerberg of having some responsibility for deadly attacks by Palestinians against Israelis.[84] According to him, the social network was not doing enough to ban posts to its platform that incite violence against Israelis.[85] "Some of the victims' blood is on Zuckerberg's hands", Erdan said.[86]

Hawaiian land ownership

In January 2017, Zuckerberg filed eight "quiet title and partition" lawsuits against hundreds of native Hawaiians to get them to sell their land to him. This land is contained within the 700 acres of land in the Hawaiian island of Kauai that Zuckerberg had purchased in 2014. When he learned that Hawaiian land ownership law differs from that of the other 49 states, he dropped the lawsuits.[87][88]

Depictions in media

The Social Network

A movie based on Zuckerberg and the founding years of Facebook, *The Social Network* was released on October 1, 2010, and stars Jesse Eisenberg as Zuckerberg. After Zuckerberg was told about the film, he responded, "I just wished that nobody made a movie of me while I was still alive."[89] Also, after the film's script was leaked on the Internet and it was apparent that the film would not portray Zuckerberg in a wholly positive light, he stated that he wanted to establish himself as a "good guy".[90] The film is based on the book *The Accidental Billionaires* by Ben Mezrich, which the book's publicist once described as "big juicy fun" rather than "reportage".[91] The film's screenwriter Aaron Sorkin told *New York* magazine, "I don't want my fidelity to be the truth; I want it to be storytelling", adding, "What is the big deal about accuracy purely for accuracy's sake, and can we not have the true be the enemy of the good?"[92]

Upon winning the Golden Globe Award for Best Picture on January 16, 2011, producer Scott Rudin thanked Facebook and Zuckerberg "for his willingness to allow us to use his life and work as a metaphor through which to tell a story about communication and the way we relate to each other."[93] Sorkin, who won for Best Screenplay, retracted some of the impressions given in his script:[94]

"I wanted to say to Mark Zuckerberg tonight, if you're watching, Rooney Mara's character makes a prediction at the beginning of the movie. She was wrong. You turned out to be a great entrepreneur, a visionary, and an incredible altruist."

On January 29, 2011, Zuckerberg made a surprise guest appearance on *Saturday Night Live*, which was being hosted by Jesse Eisenberg. They both said it was the first time they ever met.[95] Eisenberg asked Zuckerberg, who had been critical of his portrayal by the film, what he thought of the movie. Zuckerberg replied, "It was interesting."[96] In a subsequent interview about their meeting, Eisenberg explains that he was "nervous to meet him, because I had spent now, a year and a half thinking about him ..." He adds, "Mark has been so gracious about something that's really so uncomfortable ... The fact that he would do *SNL* and make fun of the situation is so sweet and so generous. It's the best possible way to handle something that, I think, could otherwise be very uncomfortable."[97][98]

Disputed accuracy

Jeff Jarvis, author of the book *Public Parts*, interviewed Zuckerberg and believes Sorkin made up too much of the story. He states, "That's what the internet is accused of doing, making stuff up, not caring about the facts."[99]

According to David Kirkpatrick, former technology editor at *Fortune* magazine and author of *The Facebook Effect: The Inside Story of the Company That Is Connecting the World,*(2011),[100] "the film is only "40% true ... he is not snide and sarcastic in a cruel way, the way Zuckerberg is played in the movie." He says that "a lot of the factual incidents are accurate, but many are distorted and the overall impression is false", and concludes that primarily "his motivations were to try and come up with a new way to share information on the Internet".[99]

Although the film portrays Zuckerberg's creation of Facebook in order to elevate his stature after not getting into any of the elite final clubs at Harvard, Zuckerberg said he had no interest in joining the clubs.[19] Kirkpatrick agrees that the impression implied by the film is "false". Karel Baloun, a former senior engineer at Facebook, notes that the "image of Zuckerberg as a socially inept nerd is overstated ... It is fiction ..." He likewise dismisses the film's assertion that he "would deliberately betray a friend".[99]

Other depictions

Zuckerberg voiced himself on an episode of *The Simpsons* titled "Loan-a Lisa", which first aired on October 3, 2010. In the episode, Lisa Simpson and her friend Nelson encounter Zuckerberg at an entrepreneurs' convention. Zuckerberg tells Lisa that she does not need to graduate from college to be wildly successful, referencing Bill Gates and Richard Branson as examples.[101]

On October 9, 2010, *Saturday Night Live* lampooned Zuckerberg and Facebook.[102] Andy Samberg played Zuckerberg. The real Zuckerberg was reported to have been amused: "I thought this was funny."[103]

Stephen Colbert awarded a "Medal of Fear" to Zuckerberg at the Rally to Restore Sanity and/or Fear on October 30, 2010, "because he values his privacy much more than he values yours".[104]

Zuckerberg appears in the climax of the documentary film *Terms and Conditions May Apply*.[105][106][107]

Philanthropy

Chan and Zuckerberg in Prague (2013

Zuckerberg donated an undisclosed amount to Diaspora, an open-source personal Web server that implements a distributed social networking service. He called it a "cool idea".[45]

Zuckerberg founded the Start-up: Education foundation.[108][109] On September 22, 2010, it was reported that Zuckerberg had donated $100 million to Newark Public Schools, the public school system of Newark, New Jersey.[110][111] Critics noted the timing of the donation as being close to the release of *The Social*

Network, which painted a somewhat negative portrait of Zuckerberg.[112] Zuckerberg responded to the criticism, saying, "The thing that I was most sensitive about with the movie timing was, I didn't want the press about *The Social Network*movie to get conflated with the Newark project. I was thinking about doing this anonymously just so that the two things could be kept separate."[113] Newark Mayor Cory Booker stated that he and New Jersey Governor Chris Christie had to convince Zuckerberg's team not to make the donation anonymously.[113] The money was largely wasted, according to journalist Dale Russakoff.[114][115]

On December 9, 2010, Zuckerberg, Bill Gates, and investor Warren Buffett signed "The Giving Pledge", in which they promised to donate to charity at least half of their wealth over the course of time, and invited others among the wealthy to donate 50 percent or more of their wealth to charity.[116]

On December 19, 2013, Zuckerberg announced a donation of 18 million Facebook shares to the Silicon Valley Community Foundation, to be executed by the end of the month—based on Facebook's valuation as of then, the shares totaled $990 million in value. On December 31, 2013, the donation was recognized as the largest charitable gift on public record for 2013.[117] *The*

Chronicle of Philanthropy placed Zuckerberg and his wife at the top of the magazine's annual list of 50 most generous Americans for 2013, having donated roughly $1 billion to charity.[118]

In October 2014, Zuckerberg and his wife Priscilla Chan donated US$25 million to combat the Ebola virus disease, specifically the West African Ebola virus epidemic.[119][120] in 2016, the Chan Zuckerberg Initiative announced that it would give $600 million to Biohub, a location in San Francisco's Mission Bay District near the University of California, San Francisco, to allow for easy interaction and collaboration between scientists at UCSF; University of California, Berkeley; Stanford University.

On December 1, 2015, Zuckerberg and Chan announced the birth of their first daughter Max, and in an open letter to Max, they pledged to donate 99 percent of their Facebook shares, then valued at US$45 billion, to the Chan Zuckerberg Initiative, their new organization that will focus on health and education. The donation will not be given immediately, but over the course of their lives.[121][122] However, instead of forming a charitable corporation to donate the value of the stock to, as Bill Gates, Warren Buffett, Larry Page, Sergey Brinand other tech billionaires have done, Zuckerberg and Chan chose to use the structure of a limited liability company. This has drawn criticism from a number of journalists.[123][124][125][126] Chan and Zuckerberg also signed The Giving Pledge.[127]

On August 28, 2017, Zuckerberg and Chan announced the birth of their second daughter August.[128]

Politics

In 2002, Zuckerberg registered to vote in Westchester County, New York, where he grew up, but did not cast a ballot until November 2008. Santa Clara County Registrar of Voters Spokeswoman, Elma Rosas, told Bloomberg that Zuckerberg is listed as "no preference" on voter rolls, and he voted in at least two of the past three general elections, in 2008 and 2012.[129][130]

Zuckerberg has never revealed his own political views: some consider him a conservative,[131][132] while others consider him liberal.[133]

On February 13, 2013, Zuckerberg hosted his first ever fundraising event for New Jersey Governor Chris Christie. Zuckerberg's particular interest on this occasion was education reform, and Christie's education reform work focused on teachers unions and the expansion of charter schools.[134][135] Later that year, Zuckerberg hosted a campaign fundraiser for Newark mayor Cory Booker, who was running in the 2013 New Jersey special Senate election.[136] In September 2010, with the support of Governor Chris Christie, Booker obtained a US$100 million pledge from Zuckerberg to Newark Public Schools.[137] In December 2012, Zuckerberg donated 18 million shares to the Silicon Valley Community Foundation, a community organization that includes education in its list of grant-making areas.[138][139]

On April 11, 2013, Zuckerberg led the launch of a 501(c)(4) lobbying group called FWD.us. The founders and contributors to the group were primarily Silicon Valley entrepreneurs and investors, and its president was Joe Green, a close friend of Zuckerberg.[140][141][142][143] The goals of the group include immigration reform, improving the state of education in the United States, and enabling more technological breakthroughs that benefit the public,[144][145] yet it has also been criticized for financing ads advocating a variety of oil and gas development initiatives, including drilling in the Arctic National Wildlife Refuge and the Keystone XL pipeline.[146] In 2013, numerous liberal and progressive groups, such as The League of Conservation Voters, MoveOn.org, the Sierra Club, Democracy for America, CREDO, Daily Kos, 350.org, and Presente and Progressives United agreed to either pull their Facebook ad buys or not buy Facebook ads for at least two weeks, in protest of Zuckerberg ads funded by FWD.us that were in support of oil drilling and the Keystone XL pipeline, and in opposition to Obamacare among Republican United States senators who back immigration reform.[

A media report on June 20, 2013 revealed that Zuckerberg actively engaged with Facebook users on his own profile page after the online publication of a FWD.us video. In response to a claim that the FWD.us organization is "just about tech wanting to hire more people", the Internet entrepreneur replied: "The bigger problem we're trying to address is ensuring the 11 million undocumented folks living in this country now and similar folks in the future are treated fairly."[148]

In June 2013, Zuckerberg joined Facebook employees in a company float as part of the annual San Francisco Lesbian, Gay, Bisexual, and Transgender Pride Celebration. The company first participated in the event in

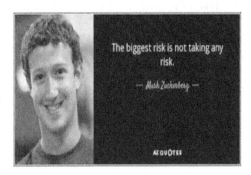

2011, with 70 employees, and this number increased to 700 for the 2013 march. The 2013 pride celebration was especially significant, as it followed a U.S. Supreme Court ruling that deemed the Defense of Marriage Act (DOMA) unconstitutional.[149][150]

When questioned about the mid-2013 PRISM scandal at the TechCrunch Disrupt conference in September 2013, Zuckerberg stated that the U.S. government "blew it." He further explained that the government performed poorly in regard to the protection of the freedoms of its citizens, the economy, and companies.[58]Zuckerberg placed a statement on his Facebook wall on December 9, 2015 which said that he wants "to add my voice in support of Muslims in our community and around the world" in response to the aftermath of the November 2015 Paris attacks and the 2015 San Bernardino attack.[151][152][153][154] The statement also said that Muslims are "always welcome" on Facebook, and that his position was a result of the fact that "as a Jew, my parents taught me that we must stand up against attacks on all communities."[155][156]

On February 24, 2016, Zuckerberg sent out a company-wide internal memo to employees formally rebuking employees who had crossed out handwritten "Black Lives

Matter" phrases on the company walls and had written "All Lives Matter" in their place. Facebook allows employees to free-write thoughts and phrases on company walls. The memo was then leaked by several employees. As Zuckerberg had previously condemned this practice at previous company meetings, and other similar requests had been issued by other leaders at Facebook, Zuckerberg wrote in the memo that he would now consider this overwriting practice not only disrespectful, but "malicious as well." According to Zuckerberg's memo, "*Black Lives Matter* doesn't mean other lives don't – it's simply asking that the black community also achieves the justice they deserve." The memo also noted that the act of crossing something out in itself, "means silencing speech, or that one person's speech is more important than another's." Zuckerberg also said in the memo that he would be launching investigations into the incidents.[157][158][159] The *New York Daily News* interviewed Facebook employees who commented anonymously that, "Zuckerberg was genuinely angry about the incident and it really encouraged staff that Zuckerberg showed a clear understanding of why the phrase 'Black Lives Matter' must exist, as well as why writing through it is a form of harassment and erasure." [157]

In January 2017, Zuckerberg criticized Donald Trump's executive order to severely limit immigrants and refugees from some countries.[160]

Personal life

Zuckerberg met his future wife, fellow student Priscilla Chan, at a fraternity party during his sophomore year at Harvard. They began dating in 2003.[161][162]

In September 2010, Zuckerberg invited Chan, by then a medical student at the University of California, San Francisco,[163] to move into his rented Palo Alto house. Zuckerberg studied Mandarin in preparation for the couple's visit to China in December 2010.[164][165] On May 19, 2012, Zuckerberg and Chan married in Zuckerberg's backyard in an event that also celebrated her graduation from medical school.[166][167][168] On July 31, 2015, Zuckerberg announced that he and Chan were expecting a baby girl. He said he felt confident that the risk of miscarrying was low so far into the pregnancy, after Chan had already suffered three miscarriages.[169] On December 1, Zuckerberg announced the birth of their daughter, Maxima Chan Zuckerberg ("Max").[170][171] The couple announced on their Chinese New Year video, published on February 6, 2016, that Maxima's official Chinese name is Chen Mingyu

(Chinese: 陈明宇).[172] They welcomed their second daughter, August, in August 2017.[173]

Some people dream of success...while others wake up and work hard at it.

Mark Zuckerberg

Zuckerberg has also been very active in China, and he has been a member of Tsinghua University business school's advisory board since 2014.[174]

While raised Jewish, Zuckerberg later identified as an atheist,[21][175][176] a position he has since renounced.[177] He has shown an appreciation for Buddhism.[178][179] With regard to Christianity, both Zuckerberg and his wife told Pope Francis in August 2016 "how much we admire his message of mercy and tenderness, and how he's found new ways to communicate with people of every faith around the world."[180][181][182] In December 2016, when asked "Aren't you an atheist?" in response to a Christmas Day post on Facebook, Zuckerberg responded, "No. I was raised Jewish and then I went through a period where I questioned things, but now I believe religion is very important."[177] As he closed his commencement address at Harvard University in May 2017, Zuckerberg shared the Jewish prayer *Mi Shebeirach*, which he stated he says when he faces challenges in life.[183][184]

Jan Koum

Jan Koum (Ukrainian: ЯнКум; born February 24, 1976) is a Ukrainian-American internet inventor[2] and computer programmer. He is the CEO and co-founder of WhatsApp, a mobile messaging application which was acquired by Facebook Inc. in February 2014 for US$19.3 billion. In 2014, he entered the Forbes list of the 400 richest Americans at position 62, with an estimated worth of more than $7.5 billion dollars. He was the highest-ranked newcomer to the list that year.[3]

Life and Career

Koum was born in Kiev, Ukraine (then part of the Soviet Union). He is of Jewish origin.[4] He grew up in Fastiv, outside Kiev, and moved with his mother and grandmother to Mountain View, California in 1992,[5] where a social support program helped the family to get a small two-bedroom apartment,[6] at the age of 16. His father had intended to join the family later, but finally remained in Ukraine.[7] At first Koum's mother worked as a babysitter, while he himself worked as a cleaner at a grocery store. By the age of 18 he became interested in programming. He enrolled at San Jose State University and simultaneously worked at Ernst & Young as a security tester.[6]

In February 1996, a restraining order was granted against Koum in state court in San Jose, California. An ex-girlfriend detailed incidents in which she said Koum verbally and physically threatened her. In October 2014, Koum said about the restraining order, "I am ashamed of the way I acted, and ashamed that my behavior forced her to take legal action".[8]

In 1997, Jan Koum was hired by Yahoo as an infrastructure engineer, shortly after he met Brian Acton while working at Ernst & Young as a security tester.[6] Over the next nine years, they worked at Yahoo. In September 2007 Koum and Acton left Yahoo and took a year off, traveling around South America and playing ultimate frisbee. Both applied, and failed, to work at Facebook. In January 2009, he bought an iPhone and realized that the then-seven-month-old App Store was about to spawn a whole new industry of apps. He visited his friend Alex Fishman and the two talked for hours about Koum's idea for an app over tea at Fishman's kitchen counter.[6] Koum almost immediately chose the name WhatsApp because it sounded like "what's up", and a week later on his birthday, February 24, 2009, he incorporated WhatsApp Inc. in California.[6]

WhatsApp became popular in just a short amount of time, and this caught Facebook's attention. Facebook's founder Mark Zuckerberg first contacted Koum in the spring 2012. The two began meeting at a coffee shop in Los Altos, California, then began a series of dinners and walks in the hills above Silicon Valley.[9]

On February 9, 2014 Zuckerberg asked Koum to have dinner at his home, and formally proposed Koum a deal to join the Facebook board - 10 days later Facebook announced it was acquiring WhatsApp for US$19 Billion USD.[10][11][12][13][14]

Over the first half of 2016, Koum sold more than $2.4 billion worth of Facebook stock, which was about a half of his total holdings. He is estimated to still own another $2.4 billion in Facebook stock.[15]

Trivia—

Jan Koum was part of a group of hackers called w00w00, where he met[6][16] the future founders of Napster, Shawn Fanning and Jordan Ritter.

In November 2014, Koum donated one million dollars to The FreeBSD Foundation, and close to $556 million to the Silicon Valley Community Foundation (SVCF) the same year.[17]

Bill Gates

William Henry Gates III (born October 28, 1955) is an American business magnate, investor, author, philanthropist, and co-founder of the Microsoft Corporation along with Paul Allen.[2][3]

In 1975, Gates and Allen launched Microsoft, which became the world's largest PC software company. During his career at Microsoft, Gates held the positions of chairman, CEO and chief software architect, while also being the largest individual shareholder until May 2014.[4][a] Gates stepped down as chief executive officer of Microsoft in January 2000, but he remained as chairman and created the position of chief software architect for himself.[7] In June 2006, Gates announced that he would be transitioning from full-time work at Microsoft to part-time work and full-time work at the Bill & Melinda Gates Foundation.[8] He gradually transferred his duties to Ray Ozzieand Craig Mundie.[9] He stepped down as chairman of Microsoft in February 2014 and assumed a new post as technology adviser to support the newly appointed CEO Satya Nadella.[10]

Gates is one of the best-known entrepreneurs of the personal computer revolution. He has been criticized for his business tactics, which have been considered anti-competitive. This opinion has been upheld by numerous court rulings.[11] Later in his career, Gates pursued a number of philanthropic endeavors. He donated large amounts of money to various charitable organizations and scientific research programs through the Bill & Melinda Gates Foundation, which was established in 2000.

Since 1987, Gates has been included in the *Forbes* list of the world's wealthiest people, an index of the wealthiest documented individuals, excluding and ranking against those with wealth that is not able to be completely ascertained.[12][13] From 1995 to 2017, he held the *Forbes* title of the richest person in the world all but four of those years, and held it consistently from March 2014–July 2017, with an estimated net worth of US$89.9 billion as of October 2017.[1] However, on July 27, 2017, and since October 27, 2017, he has been surpassed by Amazon.com founder Jeff Bezos, who had an estimated net worth of US$90.6 billion at the time.[14] In 2009, Gates and Warren Buffett founded The Giving Pledge, whereby they and other billionaires pledge to give at least half of their wealth to philanthropy.[15] The foundation works to save lives and improve global health, and is working with Rotary International to eliminate polio.[16]

Early life

Gates was born in Seattle, Washington on October 28, 1955. He is the son of William H. Gates Sr.[b] (b. 1925) and Mary Maxwell Gates (1929–1994). His ancestry includes English, German, Irish, and Scots-Irish.[17][18] His father was a prominent lawyer, and his mother served on the board of directors for First Interstate BancSystem and the United Way. Gates's maternal grandfather was JW Maxwell, a national bank president. Gates has one elder sister, Kristi (Kristianne), and one younger sister, Libby. He is the fourth of his name in his family, but is known as William Gates III or "Trey" because his father had the "II" suffix.[19] Early on in his life, Gates's parents had a law career in mind for him.[20] When Gates was young, his family regularly attended a church of the Congregational Christian Churches, a Protestant Reformed denomination.[21][22][23] The family encouraged competition; one visitor reported that "it didn't matter whether it was hearts or pickleball or swimming to the dock ... there was always a reward for winning and there was always a penalty for losing".[24]

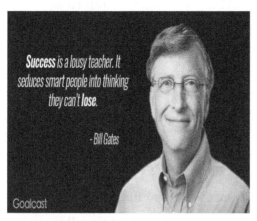

Success is a lousy teacher. It seduces smart people into thinking they can't lose.

- Bill Gates

Goalcast

At 13, he enrolled in the Lakeside School, a private preparatory school.[25] When he was in the eighth grade, the Mothers' Club at the school used proceeds from Lakeside School's rummage sale to buy a Teletype Model 33 ASR terminal and a block of computer time on a General Electric (GE) computer for the school's students.[26] Gates took an interest in programming the GE system in BASIC, and was excused from math classes to pursue his interest. He wrote his first computer program on this machine: an implementation of tic-tac-toe that allowed users to play games against the computer. Gates was fascinated by the machine and how it would always execute software code perfectly. When he reflected back on that moment, he said, "There was just something neat about the machine."[27] After the Mothers Club donation was exhausted, he and other students sought time on systems including DEC PDP minicomputers. One of these systems was a PDP-10 belonging to Computer Center Corporation (CCC), which banned four Lakeside

students – Gates, Paul Allen, Ric Weiland, and Kent
Evans – for the summer after it caught them exploiting
bugs in the operating system to obtain free computer
time.[28][29]

At the end of the ban, the four students offered to find
bugs in CCC's software in exchange for extra computer
time. Rather than use the system via Teletype.
Subsequently, Gates went to CCC's offices and
studied source code for various programs that ran on the
system, including programs in Fortran, Lisp, and machine
language. The arrangement with CCC continued until
1970, when the company went out of business. The
following year, Information Sciences, Inc. hired the four
Lakeside students to write a payroll program in COBOL,
providing them computer time and royalties. After his
administrators became aware of his programming
abilities, Gates wrote the school's computer program to
schedule students in classes. He modified the code so that
he was placed in classes with "a disproportionate number
of interesting girls."[30] He later stated that "it was hard to
tear myself away from a machine at which I could so
unambiguously demonstrate success."[27] At age 17, Gates
formed a venture with Allen, called Traf-O-Data, to
make traffic counters based on the Intel
8008 processor.[31] In early 1973, Bill Gates served as a

congressional page in the U.S. House of Representatives.[32]

Gates was a National Merit Scholar when he graduated from Lakeside School in 1973.[33] He scored 1590 out of 1600 on the Scholastic Aptitude Tests (SAT) and enrolled at Harvard College in the autumn of 1973.[34][35] He chose a pre-law major but took mathematics and graduate level computer science courses.[36] While at Harvard, he met fellow student Steve Ballmer. Gates left Harvard after two years while Ballmer would stay and graduate *magna cum laude*. Years later, Ballmer succeeded Gates as Microsoft's CEO. He maintained that position from 2000 until his resignation from the company in 2014.[37]

In his second year, Gates devised an algorithm for pancake sorting as a solution to one of a series of unsolved problems[38] presented in a combinatorics class by Harry Lewis, one of his professors. Gates's solution held the record as the fastest version for over thirty years;[38][39] its successor is faster by only one percent.[38] His solution was later formalized in a published paper in collaboration with Harvard computer scientist Christos Papadimitriou.[40]

While Gates was a student at Harvard,[41] he did not have a definite study plan, and he spent a lot of time using the school's computers. Gates remained in contact with Paul Allen, and he joined him at Honeywell during the summer of 1974.[42] The MITS Altair 8800 was released the following year. The new computer was based on the Intel 8080 CPU, and Gates and Allen saw this as the opportunity to start their own computer software company.[43] Gates dropped out of Harvard at this time. He had talked over this decision with his parents, who were supportive of him after seeing how much their son wanted to start his own company.[41] Gates explained his decision to leave Harvard, saying "...if things [Microsoft] hadn't worked out, I could always go back to school. I was officially on [a] leave [of absence]."[44]

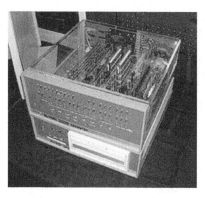

Microsoft

BASIC

MITS Altair 8800 Computer with 8-inch (200 mm) floppy disk system

After Gates read the January 1975 issue of *Popular Electronics*, which demonstrated the Altair 8800, he contacted Micro Instrumentation and Telemetry Systems (MITS), the creators of the new microcomputer, to inform them that he and others were working on a BASIC interpreter for the platform.[45] In reality, Gates and Allen did not have an Altair and had not written code for it; they merely wanted to gauge MITS's interest. MITS president Ed Roberts agreed to meet them for a demo, and over the course of a few weeks they developed an Altair emulatorthat ran on a minicomputer, and then the BASIC interpreter. The demonstration, held at MITS's offices in Albuquerque, was a success and resulted in a deal with MITS to distribute the interpreter as Altair BASIC. Paul Allen was hired into MITS,[46] and Gates took a leave of absence from Harvard to work with Allen at MITS in Albuquerque in November 1975. They named their partnership "Micro-Soft" and had their first office located in Albuquerque.[46] Within a year, the hyphen was dropped, and on November 26, 1976, the trade name "Microsoft" was registered with the Office of the Secretary of the State of New Mexico.[46] Gates never returned to Harvard to complete his studies.

Microsoft's Altair BASIC was popular with computer hobbyists, but Gates discovered that a pre-market copy had leaked into the community and was being widely copied and distributed. In February 1976, Gates wrote an Open Letter to Hobbyists in the MITS newsletter in which he asserted that more than 90 percent of the users of Microsoft Altair BASIC had not paid Microsoft for it and by doing so the Altair "hobby market" was in danger of eliminating the incentive for any professional developers to produce, distribute, and maintain high-quality software.[47] This letter was unpopular with many computer hobbyists, but Gates persisted in his belief that software developers should be able to demand payment. Microsoft became independent of MITS in late 1976, and it continued to develop programming language software for various systems.[46] The company moved from Albuquerque to its new home in Bellevue, Washington, on January 1, 1979.[45]

During Microsoft's early years, all employees had broad responsibility for the company's business. Gates oversaw the business details, but continued to write code as well. In the first five years, Gates personally reviewed every line of code the company shipped, and often rewrote parts of it as he saw fit.[48][

IBM partnership

IBM approached Microsoft in July 1980 in reference to an operating system for its upcoming personal computer, the IBM PC.[49] Big Blue first proposed that Microsoft write the BASIC interpreter. When IBM's representatives mentioned that they needed an operating system, Gates referred them to Digital Research (DRI), makers of the widely used CP/Moperating system.[50] IBM's discussions with Digital Research went poorly, and they did not reach a licensing agreement. IBM representative Jack Sams mentioned the licensing difficulties during a subsequent meeting with Gates and told him to get an acceptable operating system. A few weeks later, Gates proposed using 86-DOS (QDOS), an operating system similar to CP/M that Tim Paterson of Seattle Computer Products (SCP) had made for hardware similar to the PC. Microsoft made a deal with SCP to become the exclusive licensing agent, and later the full owner, of 86-DOS. After adapting the operating system for the PC, Microsoft delivered it to IBM as PC DOS in exchange for a one-time fee of $50,000.[51]

Gates did not offer to transfer the copyright on the operating system, ecause he believed that other hardware vendors would clone IBM's system.[51] They did, and the sales of MS-DOS made Microsoft a major player in the industry.[52] Despite IBM's name on the operating system, the press quickly identified Microsoft as being very influential on the new computer. *PC*

Magazine asked if Gates were "the man behind the machine?",[49] and *InfoWorld* quoted an expert as stating "it's Gates' computer".[53] Gates oversaw Microsoft's company restructuring on June 25, 1981, which re-incorporated the company in Washington State and made Gates the president of Microsoft and its board chairman.[45]

Windows

Microsoft launched its first retail version of Microsoft Windows on November 20, 1985. In August of the following year, the company struck a deal with IBM to develop a separate operating system called OS/2. Although the two companies successfully developed the first version of the new system, the partnership deteriorated due to mounting creative differences.[54]

Management style

Bill Gates in January 2008

From Microsoft's founding in 1975 until 2006, Gates had primary responsibility for the company's product strategy. He gained a reputation for being distant from others; as early as 1981 an industry executive complained in public that "Gates is notorious for not being reachable by phone and for not returning phone calls."[55] Another executive recalled that he showed Gates a game and defeated him 35 of 37 times. When they met again a month later, Gates "won or tied every game. He had studied the game until he solved it. That is a competitor."[56]

Gates was an executive who met regularly with Microsoft's senior managers and program managers. In firsthand accounts of these meetings, the managers described him being verbally combative. He also berated managers for perceived holes in their business strategies or proposals that placed the company's long-term interests at risk.[57][58] He interrupted presentations with such comments as "That's the stupidest thing I've ever heard!"[59] and "Why don't you just give up your options and join the Peace Corps?"[60] The target of his outburst then had to defend the proposal in detail until, hopefully, Gates was fully convinced.[59] When subordinates appeared to be procrastinating, he was known to remark sarcastically, "I'll do it over the weekend."[61][62][63]

During Microsoft's early history, Gates was an active software developer, particularly in the company's programming language products, but his basic role in most of the company's history was primarily as a manager and executive. Gates has not officially been on a development team since working on the TRS-80 Model 100,[64] but as late as 1989 he wrote code that shipped with the company's products.[62] He remained interested in technical details; in 1985, Jerry Pournelle wrote that when he watched Gates announce Microsoft Excel, "Something else impressed me. Bill Gates likes the program, not because it's going to make him a lot of money (although I'm sure it will do that), but because it's a neat hack."[65]

On June 15, 2006, Gates announced that over the next two years he would transition out of his day-to-day role to dedicate more time to philanthropy. He divided his responsibilities between two successors when he placed Ray Ozzie in charge of day-to-day management and Craig Mundie in charge of long-term product strategy.[66]

Antitrust litigation

Gates giving his deposition at Microsoft on August 27, 1998

Many decisions that led to antitrust litigation over Microsoft's business practices have had Gates's approval. In the 1998 *United States v. Microsoft* case, Gates gave deposition testimony that several journalists characterized as evasive. He argued with examiner David Boiesover the contextual meaning of words such as, "compete", "concerned", and "we". The judge and other observers in the court room were seen laughing at various points during the deposition.[67] *BusinessWeek* reported:

Early rounds of his deposition show him offering obfuscatory answers and saying 'I don't recall,' so many times that even the presiding judge had to chuckle. Worse, many of the technology chief's denials and pleas of ignorance were directly refuted by prosecutors with snippets of e-mail that Gates both sent and received.[68]

Gates later said he had simply resisted attempts by Boies to mischaracterize his words and actions. As to his demeanor during the deposition, he said, "Did I fence with Boies? ... I plead guilty. Whatever that penalty is should be levied against me: rudeness to Boies in the first degree."[69] Despite Gates's denials, the judge ruled that Microsoft had committed monopolization and tying, and blocking competition, both in violation of the Sherman Antitrust Act.[69]

Appearance in Ads

Mugshots of 22-year-old Gates following his 1977 arrest for a traffic violation
in Albuquerque, New Mexico

In 2008, Gates appeared in a series of ads to promote Microsoft. The first commercial, co-starring Jerry Seinfeld, is a 90-second talk between strangers as Seinfeld walks up on a discount shoe store (Shoe Circus) in a mall and notices Gates buying shoes inside. The salesman is trying to sell Mr. Gates shoes that are a size too big. As Gates is buying the shoes, he holds up his discount card, which uses a slightly altered version of his own mugshot of his arrest in New Mexico in 1977, for a traffic violation.[70] As they are walking out of the mall, Seinfeld asks Gates if he has melded his mind to other developers, after getting a "Yes", he then asks if they are working on a way to make computers edible, again getting a "Yes". Some say that this is an homage to Seinfeld's own show about "nothing"

(*Seinfeld*).[71] In a second commercial in the series, Gates and Seinfeld are at the home of an average family trying to fit in with normal people.[72]

Post-Microsoft

Gates meets with U.S. Secretary of Defense James Mattis, February 2017

Since leaving day-to-day operations at Microsoft, Gates has continued his philanthropy and works on other projects.

According to the Bloomberg Billionaires Index, Gates was the world's highest-earning billionaire in 2013, as his net worth increased by US$15.8 billion to US$78.5 billion. As of January 2014, most of Gates's assets are held in Cascade Investment LLC, an entity through which he owns stakes in numerous businesses, including Four Seasons Hotels and Resorts, and Corbis Corp.[73] On February 4, 2014, Gates stepped down as chairman of Microsoft to become Technology Advisor alongside new CEO Satya Nadella.[10][74]

Gates provided his perspective on a range of issues in a substantial interview that was published in the March 27, 2014 issue of *Rolling Stone* magazine. In the interview, Gates provided his perspective on climate change, his charitable activities, various tech companies and people involved in them, and the state of America. In response to a question about his greatest fear when he looks 50 years into the future, Gates stated: "... there'll be some really bad things that'll happen in the next 50 or 100 years, but hopefully none of them on the scale of, say, a million people that you didn't expect to die from a pandemic, or nuclear or bioterrorism." Gates also identified innovation as the "real driver of progress" and pronounced that "America's way better today than it's ever been."[75]

Gates has recently expressed concern about the existential threats of superintelligence; in a Reddit "ask me anything", he stated that

First the machines will do a lot of jobs for us and not be super intelligent. That should be positive if we manage it well. A few decades after that though the intelligence is strong enough to be a concern. I agree with Elon Musk and some others on this and don't understand why some people are not concerned.[76][77][78][79]

In a March 2015 interview, with Baidu's CEO, Robin Li, Gates claimed he would "highly recommend" Nick

Bostrom's recent work, *Superintelligence: Paths, Dangers, Strategies.*[80]

Gates's days are planned for him, similar to the US President's schedule, on a minute-by-minute basis.[81]

Personal life

Bill and Melinda Gates in June 2009

Gates married Melinda French on a golf course on the Hawaiian island of Lanai on January 1, 1994; he was 38 and she was 29. They have three children: Jennifer Katharine (b. 1996), Rory John (b. 1999), and Phoebe Adele (b. 2002). The family resides in a modern design mansion, which is an earth-sheltered house in the side of a hill overlooking Lake Washington in Medina near Seattle in Washington state, United States. According to 2007 King County public records, the total assessed value of the property (land and house) is $125 million, and the annual property taxes are $991,000. The

66,000 sq ft (6,100 m^2) estate has a 60-foot (18 m) swimming pool with an underwater music system, as well as a 2,500 sq ft (230 m^2) gym and a 1,000 sq ft (93 m^2) dining room.[82]

In an interview with *Rolling Stone*, Gates stated in regard to his faith:

The moral systems of religion, I think, are super important. We've raised our kids in a religious way; they've gone to the Catholic church that Melinda goes to and I participate in. I've been very lucky, and therefore I owe it to try and reduce the inequity in the world. And that's kind of a religious belief. I mean, it's at least a moral belief.[83]

In the same interview, Gates said: "I agree with people like Richard Dawkins that mankind felt the need for creation myths. Before we really began to understand disease and the weather and things like that, we sought false explanations for them. Now science has filled in some of the realm – not all – that religion used to fill. But the mystery and the beauty of the world is overwhelmingly amazing, and there's no scientific explanation of how it came about. To say that it was generated by random numbers, that does seem, you know, sort of an uncharitable view [laughs]. I think it makes sense to believe in God, but exactly what decision in your life you make differently because of it, I don't know."[83]

The Codex Leicester is one of Gates's private acquisitions. He purchased the collection of famous scientific writings by Leonardo da Vinci for $30.8 million at an auction in 1994.[84]Gates is also known for being an avid reader, and the ceiling of his large home library is engraved with a quotation from *The Great Gatsby*.[85] He also enjoys playing bridge, tennis, and golf.[86][87]

In 1999, his wealth briefly surpassed $101 billion.[88] Despite his wealth and extensive business travel, Gates usually flew coach in commercial aircraft until 1997, when he bought a private jet.[89] Since 2000, the nominal value of his Microsoft holdings has declined due to a fall in Microsoft's stock price after the dot-com bubble burst and the multibillion-dollar donations he has made to his charitable foundations. In a May 2006 interview, Gates commented that he wished that he were not the richest man in the world because he disliked the attention it brought.[90] In March 2010, Gates was the second wealthiest person behind Carlos Slim, but regained the top position in 2013, according to the Bloomberg Billionaires List.[91][92] Carlos Slim retook the position again in June 2014[93][94] (but then lost the top position back to Gates). Between 2009 and 2014, his wealth doubled from US$40 billion to more than US$82 billion.[95] Since October 2017, Gates was surpassed by Amazon.com founder Jeff Bezos as the richest person in the world.[14]

Bill Gates has held the top spot on the list of The World's Billionaires for 18 out of the past 23 years.[96]

Gates has several investments outside Microsoft, which in 2006 paid him a salary of $616,667 and $350,000 bonus totaling $966,667.[97] In 1989, he founded Corbis, a digital imaging company. In 2004, he became a director of Berkshire Hathaway, the investment company headed by long-time friend Warren Buffett.[98] In 2016, he was discussing his gaming habits when he revealed that he was color-blind.[99]

In a BBC interview, Gates claimed "I've paid more tax than any individual ever, and gladly so... I've paid over $6 billion in taxes."[100] He is a proponent of higher taxes, particularly for the rich.[101]

Philanthropy

Gates
with Bono, Queen

Rania of Jordan, former British Prime Minister Gordon Brown, President Umaru Yar'Adua of Nigeria and others during the Annual Meeting 2008 of the World Economic Forum in Switzerland

In 2009, Gates and Warren Buffett founded The Giving Pledge, whereby they and other billionaires pledge to give at least half of their wealth to philanthropy.[15]

Bill and Melinda Gates Foundation

Gates studied the work of Andrew Carnegie and John D. Rockefeller, and donated some of his Microsoft stock in 1994 to create the "William H. Gates Foundation." In 2000, Gates and his wife combined three family foundations and Gates donated stock valued at $5 billion to create the charitable Bill & Melinda Gates Foundation, which was identified by the Funds for NGOs company in 2013, as the world's wealthiest charitable foundation, with assets reportedly valued at more than $34.6 billion.[102][103] The Foundation allows benefactors to access information that shows how its money is being spent, unlike other major charitable organizations such as the Wellcome Trust.[104][105]

Gates has credited the generosity and extensive philanthropy of David Rockefeller as a major influence. Gates and his father met with Rockefeller several times,

and their charity work is partly modeled on
the Rockefeller family's philanthropic focus, whereby they
are interested in tackling the global problems that are
ignored by governments and other organizations.[106] As
of 2007, Bill and Melinda Gates were the second-most
generous philanthropists in America, having given over
$28 billion to charity;[107] the couple plan to eventually
donate 95 percent of their wealth to charity.[108]

The foundation is organized into four program areas:
Global Development Division, Global Health Division,
United States Division, and Global Policy & Advocacy
Division.[109] The foundation supports the use
of genetically modified organisms in agricultural
development. Specifically, the foundation is supporting
the International Rice Research Institute in
developing Golden Rice, a genetically modified rice
variant used to combat Vitamin A deficiency.[110]

Personal donations

Melinda Gates suggested that people should emulate the
philanthropic efforts of the Salwen family, which had sold
its home and given away half of its value, as detailed
in *The Power of Half*.[111] Gates and his wife invited Joan
Salwen to Seattle to speak about what the family had

done, and on December 9, 2010, Gates, investor Warren Buffett, and Facebook founder and CEO Mark Zuckerberg signed a commitment they called the "Gates-Buffet Giving Pledge." The pledge is a commitment by all three to donate at least half of their wealth over the course of time to charity.[112][113][114]

Gates has also provided personal donations to educational institutions. In 1999, Gates donated $20 million to the Massachusetts Institute of Technology (MIT) for the construction of a computer laboratory named the "William H. Gates Building" that was designed by architect Frank Gehry. While Microsoft had previously given financial support to the institution, this was the first personal donation received from Gates.[115]

The Maxwell Dworkin Laboratory of the Harvard John A. Paulson School of Engineering and Applied Sciences is named after the mothers of both Gates and Microsoft President Steven A. Ballmer, both of whom were students (Ballmer was a member of the School's graduating class of 1977, while Gates left his studies for Microsoft), and donated funds for the laboratory's construction.[116] Gates also donated $6 million to the construction of the Gates Computer Science Building, completed in January 1996, on the campus of Stanford University. The building contains the Computer Science Department (CSD) and the Computer Systems Laboratory (CSL) of Stanford's Engineering department.[117]

On August 15, 2014, Bill Gates posted a video of himself on Facebook in which he is seen dumping a bucket of ice water on his head. Gates posted the video after Facebook founder Mark Zuckerberg challenged him to do so in order to raise awareness for the disease ALS (amyotrophic lateral sclerosis).[118]

Since about 2005, Bill Gates and his foundation have taken an interest in solving global sanitation problems. For example, they announced the "Reinvent the Toilet Challenge", which has received considerable media interest.[119] To raise awareness for the topic of sanitation and possible solutions, Gates drank water that was "produced from human feces" in 2014 – in fact it was produced from a sewage sludge treatment process called the Omni-processor.[120][121] In early 2015, he also appeared with Jimmy Fallon on *The Tonight Show* and challenged him to see if he could taste the difference between this reclaimed water or bottled water.[122]

In November 2017, Gates said he would give $50 million to the Dementia Discovery Fund, a venture capital that seeks treatment for Alzheimer's disease. He also pledged an additional $50 million to start-up ventures working in Alzheimer's research.[123]

Bill and Melinda Gates have said that they intend to leave their three children $10 million each as their inheritance. With only $30 million kept in the family, they appear to be on a course to give away about 99.96 percent of their wealth.[124]

Criticism

In 2007, the *Los Angeles Times* criticized the foundation for investing its assets in companies that have been accused of worsening poverty, polluting heavily, and pharmaceutical companies that do not sell to the developing world.[125] In response to press criticism, the foundation announced a review of its investments to assess social responsibility.[126] It subsequently canceled the review and stood by its policy of investing for maximum return, while using voting rights to influence company practices.[127] The Gates Millennium Scholars program has been criticized by Ernest W. Lefever for its exclusion of Caucasian students.[128] The scholarship program is administered by the United Negro College Fund.[129] In 2014, Bill Gates sparked a protest in Vancouver when he decided to donate $50 million to UNAIDS through the Bill & Melinda Gates Foundation for the purpose of mass circumcision in Zambia and Swaziland.[130][131]

Charity sports events

On April 29, 2017, Bill Gates partnered with Swiss tennis legend Roger Federer in playing a noncompetitive tennis match to a packed house at Key Arena in Seattle. The event was in support of Roger Federer Foundation's charity efforts in Africa.[132] Federer and Gates played against John Isner and Pearl Jam lead guitarist Mike McReady. Gates and Federer won the game 6–4.

Recognition

Gates and Steve Jobs at the fifth *D: All Things Digital* conference (*D5*) in 2007

In 1987, Gates was listed as a billionaire in *Forbes* magazine's 400 Richest People in America issue. He was worth $1.25 billion and was the world's youngest self-made billionaire.[13] Since 1987, Gates has been included in the *Forbes* The World's Billionaires list and was the wealthiest from 1995 to 1996,[133] 1998 to 2007, 2009, and has been since 2014.[1] Gates was number one on *Forbes'* 400 Richest Americans list from 1993 through to 2007, 2009, and 2014 through 2017.[134][135]

Time magazine named Gates one of the 100 people who most influenced the 20th century, as well as one of the 100 most influential people of 2004, 2005, and 2006. *Time* also collectively named Gates, his wife Melinda and U2's lead singer Bono as the 2005 Persons of the Year for their humanitarian efforts.[136] In 2006, he was voted eighth in the list of "Heroes of our time".[137] Gates was listed in the *Sunday Times* power list in 1999, named CEO of the year by *Chief Executive Officers magazine* in 1994, ranked number one in the "Top 50 Cyber Elite" by *Time* in 1998, ranked number two in the *Upside* Elite 100 in 1999, and was included in *The Guardian* as one of the "Top 100 influential people in media" in 2001.[138]

According to *Forbes*, Gates was ranked as the fourth most powerful person in the world in 2012,[139] up from fifth in 2011.[140]

In 1994, he was honored as the twentieth Distinguished Fellow of the British Computer Society. In 1999, Gates received New York Institute of Technology's President's Medal.[141] Gates has received honorary doctorates from Nyenrode Business Universiteit, Breukelen, The

Netherlands, in 2000;[142] the Royal Institute of Technology, Stockholm, Sweden, in 2002;[143] Waseda University, Tokyo, Japan, in 2005; Tsinghua University, Beijing, China, in April 2007;[144] Harvard University in June 2007;[145] the Karolinska Institute, Stockholm, in 2007,[146] and Cambridge University in June 2009.[147] He was also made an honorary trustee of Peking University in 2007.[148]

Gates was made an Honorary Knight Commander of the Order of the British Empire (KBE) by Queen Elizabeth II in 2005.[149] In November 2006, he was awarded the Placard of the Order of the Aztec Eagle, together with his wife Melinda who was awarded the Insignia of the same order, both for their philanthropic work around the world in the areas of health and education, particularly in Mexico, and specifically in the program "*Un país de lectores*".[150] Gates received the 2010 Bower Award for Business Leadership from The Franklin Institutefor his achievements at Microsoft and his philanthropic work.[151] Also in 2010, he was honored with the Silver Buffalo Award by the Boy Scouts of America, its highest award for adults, for his service to youth.[152]

David Packard

David Packard (/ˈpækərd/ *PACK-erd*; September 7, 1912 – March 26, 1996) was an electrical engineer and co-founder, with William Hewlett, of Hewlett-Packard (1939), serving as president (1947–64), CEO (1964–68), and Chairman of the Board (1964–68, 1972–93). He served as U.S. Deputy Secretary of Defense from 1969 to 1971 during the Nixon administration. Packard served as President of the Uniformed Services University of the Health Sciences (USU) from 1976 to 1981. He was also chairman of the Board of Regents from 1973 to 1982. Packard was the recipient of the Presidential Medal of Freedom in 1988 and is noted for many technological innovations and philanthropic

Personal life

David Packard was born in Pueblo, Colorado, and attended Centenn

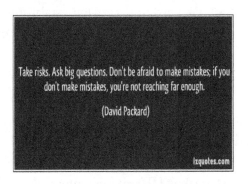

ial High School, where early on he showed an interest in science, engineering, sports, and leadership.[1] His father was an attorney. He earned his B.A. from Stanford University in 1934, where he earned letters in football and basketball and attained membership in the Phi Beta

Kappa Society and was a Brother of the Alpha Delta Phi Literary Fraternity.[2] Stanford is where he met two people who were important to his life, Lucile Salter and Bill Hewlett.[3] Packard then briefly attended the University of Colorado before he left to work for the General Electric Company in Schenectady, New York. In 1938, he returned to Stanford from New York, where he earned a master's degree in Electrical Engineering in 1938.[3] In the same year, he married Lucile Salter, with whom he had four children: David, Nancy, Susan, and Julie. Lucile Packard died in 1987.

Hewlett-Packard

In 1940, Packard and Hewlett established Hewlett-Packard (HP) in Packard's garage with an initial capital investment of $538 (equivalent to US$9,465 in 2017).[1][3] Packard mentions in his book *The HP Way* that the name Hewlett-Packard was determined by the flip of a coin: HP, rather than PH.[3][4] Their first product was an audio frequency oscillator sold to Walt Disney Studios for use on the soundtrack of *Fantasia*.[3] The *HP Way* describes HP's management philosophy, which encourages creativity and shuns traditional business hierarchy and formality.[5] During World War II HP produced radio, sonar, radar, nautical, and aviation devices.[5]

The company, where Packard proved to be an expert administrator and Hewlett provided many technical innovations,[3] gr

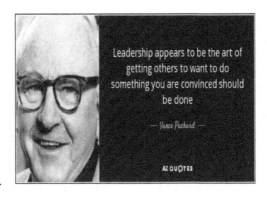

Leadership appears to be the art of getting others to want to do something you are convinced should be done

— *Vance Packard* —

AZ QUOTES

ew into the world's largest producer of electronic testing and measurement devices. It also became a major producer of calculators, computers, and laser and ink jet printers.

HP incorporated in 1947, with Packard becoming its first president, serving in that role until 1964; he was then elected Chief Executive Officer and Chairman of the Board, holding these positions through 1968.[6] He left HP in 1969 to serve in the Nixon administration until 1971, at which time he returned to HP and was re-elected Chairman of the Board, serving from 1972 to 1993. In 1991, Packard oversaw a major reorganization at HP.[5] He retired from HP in 1993. At the time of his death in 1996, Packard's stake in the company was worth more than $1 billion.

At Packard's instruction,[7] the domain name "HP.com" was registered on March 3, 1986, and as such was one of the earliest to be registered.[8]

Department of Defense

Upon entering office in 1969, President Richard M. Nixon appointed Packard U.S. Deputy Secretary of Defense under Secretary of Defense Melvin Laird.[3] Packard resigned in December 1971[9][10] and returned to Hewlett-Packard in 1972 as Chairman of the Board.

While serving in the Department of Defense (DoD), he brought concepts of resource management used in business to the military, as well as establishing the Defense Systems Management College.[11] In 1970, Packard issued a memorandum that contained a number of major reforms designed to address "the real mess we have on our hands."[12] A key reform was elimination of Robert MacNamara's Total Package Procurement except in rare situations.[12]

Near the end of his time at DoD, Packard wrote the "Packard Memo" or "Employment of Military Resources in the Event of Civil Disturbances".[13] Enacted in February 1972, the Act[14] describes exceptions to the 1878 Posse Comitatus Act, which limited the powers of the federal government to use the U.S. military for law enforcement, except where expressly authorized by the Constitution or Act of Congress — noting that the Constitution provides an exception when needed "to prevent loss of life or wanton destruction of property and to restore governmental functioning and public order when sudden and unexpected civil disturbances, disasters, or calamities seriously endanger life and property and disrupt normal governmental functions to such an extent that duly constituted local authorities are unable to control the situations" and "to protect Federal property and Federal governmental functions when the need for protection exists and duly constituted local authorities are unable or decline to provide adequate protection".[15] § 214.5 states that "employment of DoD military resources for assistance to civil authorities in controlling civil disturbances will normally be predicated upon the issuance of a Presidential Executive order or Presidential directive authorizing", with exceptions "limited to:

1. Cases of sudden and unexpected emergencies as described in §215.4(c)(1)(i), which require that immediate military action be taken.
2. Providing military resources to civil authorities as prescribed in §215.9 of this part."[16]

According to Lindorff, these exceptions essentially reinstate the possibility of martial law in the U.S., prohibited since 1878.[17]

In the 1970s and 1980s Packard was a prominent advisor to the White House on defense procurement and management. He served as Chairman of The Business

Council in 1973 and 1974.[18] In 1985-86, he served as chairman of The Packard Commission.

Philanthropy

From the early 1980s until his death in 1996, Packard dedicated much of his time and money to philanthropic projects.[19] Prompted by his daughters Nancy Packard Burnett and Julie Packard, in 1978 Dave and Lucile Packard created the Monterey Bay Aquarium Foundation. The couple eventually donated $55 million to build the new aquarium, which opened in 1984 with Julie Packard as executive director.[1] In 1987, Packard gave $13 million to create the Monterey Bay Aquarium Research Institute,[1] and the David and Lucile Packard Foundation has since provided about 90% of the Institute's operating budget.

In 1964, the couple founded the David and Lucile Packard Foundation. In 1986, they donated $40 million toward building what became the Lucile Packard Children's Hospital at Stanford University; the new hospital opened in June 1991. Packard and Hewlett made a combined donation of $77 million to Stanford in 1994,[20] for which the university named the David Packard Electrical Engineering Building in his honor.[21] The building is located adjacent to the William Hewlett Teaching Center.

Packard was a member of the American Enterprise Institute's board of trustees. He died on March 26, 1996 at age 83 in Stanford, California, leaving approximately $4 billion (the bulk of his estate) to the David and Lucile Packard Foundation,[5] including large amounts of valuable real property in Los Altos Hills. All three Packard daughters sit on the Foundation's board of trustees. David Woodley Packard, his son, currently serves as president of the Packard Humanities Institute.[22]

Ma Huateng

Ma Huateng (Chinese: 马化腾; pinyin: *Mǎ Huàténg*, born on October 29, 1971), also known as Pony 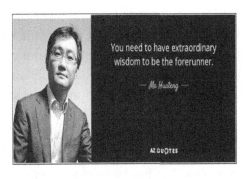 Ma, is a Chinese business magnate, investor, philanthropist, engineer, internet and technology entrepreneur. He is the founder, chairman and chief executive officer of Tencent, Asia's most valuable company, one of the largest Internet and technology companies, and the biggest investment, gaming and entertainment conglomerate in the world.[2][3][4] The company controls China's biggest mobile instant messaging service and its subsidiaries provide media, entertainment, payment systems, smartphones, internet-related services, value-added services and online advertising services, both in China and globally.

In 2007 and 2014[5] *Time* magazine called him one of the world's most influential people[6], while in 2015, Forbes credited him as one of the world's most powerful people. In 2017, Fortune ranked him as among the top businessmen of the year.[7][8] Ma is a deputy to the Shenzhen Municipal People's Congress and served in the 12th National People's Congress.[4]

Ma Huateng has been lauded as one of the world's smartest and greatest leaders, one of the most successful investors, as well as one of the premier leaders in the AI, Internet and technology industry. He is also known to be one of the greatest philanthropists in the world, setting up charity foundations as well as donating Tencent's shares, and in 2016, was named China's most generous philanthropist. Known for his low profile entrepreneur style as compared to Jack Ma's outgoing personality, Ma has been closely compared to Warren Buffett for their similarity in investments, and often described as an "aggressive acquisitor".[9][10][11][12][13][14][15]

As of January 2018, he is China's richest man, as well as the wealthiest person in Asia, with a net worth of US$49.2 billion. On 21 November 2017, he surpassed both Larry Pageand Sergey Brin to become the ninth richest man in the world, and the first Asian to enter Forbes' top 10 richest men list.[16][17][18][19]

Early life and education

Ma was born in Chaoyang District, Shantou, Guangdong. When his father, Ma Chenshu, got a job as a port manager in Shenzhen, near Hong Kong, the young Ma accompanied him.[20] He was enrolled in Shenzhen University in 1989 and then graduated in 1993 with a Bachelor of Science in computer science.[21]

Career

Founding of Tencent and early Career

Ma's first job was with China Motion Telecom Development, a supplier of telecommunications services and products, where he was in charge of developing software for pagers. He reportedly earned $176 per month.[22] He also worked for Shenzhen Runxun Communications Co. Ltd. in the research and development department for Internet calling services.[23]

Alongside four other classmates, Ma Huateng went on to co-found Tencent in 1998. The company's first product came after Ma participated in a presentation for ICQ, the world's first Internet instant messaging service, founded in 1996 by an Israeli company.[23] Inspired by the idea,

Ma and his team launched in February 1999 a similar software, with a Chinese interface and a slightly different name – OICQ (or, Open ICQ).[24] The product quickly became popular and garnered more than a million registered users by the end of 1999, making it one of the largest such services in China.[25]

Talking about the founding of Tencent, he told *China Daily* in a 2009 interview that "If I have seen further, it is by standing on the shoulders of giants," paraphrasing a quote attributed to Isaac Newton and referencing the similarities between ICQ and OICQ. "We knew our product had a future, but at that time we just couldn't afford it," Ma remembered.[23] In order to solve the problem, Ma asked for bank loans and even talked about selling the company.[26]

Since Tencent's prized service OICQ was offered free of charge, the company looked to venture capitalists to finance its growing operational costs. In 2000, Ma turned to US investment firm IDC and Hong Kong's telecom carrier Pacific Century CyberWorks (PCCW) who bought 40% of Tencent's shares for $2.2 million.[27] With the pager market declining, Ma improved the messaging platform by allowing QQ users to send messages to mobile handsets. Afterwards, 80% of the company's revenue came from deals struck with telecom operators who agreed to share message fees.[26]

AOL lawsuit and business expansion

The leader of the market today may not necessarily be the leader tomorrow.

Ma Huateng

After AOL (America Online) bought ICQ in 1998, the company filed a lawsuit against Tencent with the National Arbitration Forum in the United States, claiming that QICQ's domain names QICQ.com and QICQ.net were in violation of ICQ's intellectual property rights. Tencent lost and had to shut down the websites.[23] In December 2000, in order to stave off other costly lawsuit, Ma changed the name of the software to QQ (with "Q" and "QQ" used to stand for the word "cute")[28]

After the AOL lawsuit, Ma Huateng decided to expand the business portfolio of Tencent. In 2003, Tencent released its own portal (QQ.com) and made forays into the online games market. By 2004, Tencent became the largest Chinese instant messaging service (holding 74% of the market),[26] prompting Ma to list the company on the Hong Kong Stock Exchange.[23] After the company raised $200 million in June's IPO, Ma quickly became one of the richest people in China's telecom industry.

In 2004, Tencent launched an online gaming platform and started selling virtual goods to support the games published on that platform (weapons, gaming power), as well as emoticons and ringtones.[25]

At Ma's behest, Tencent launched in 2005 the C2C platform Paipai.com, a direct competitor to e-ecommerce giant Alibaba.[29]

Mimicking Bill Gates' Microsoft, Ma Huateng created two competing teams of engineers in 2010 and charged them with creating a new product. After two months, one team presented an app for text messaging and group chat – Weixin – which launched in January 2011. In 2015, Weixin (or WeChat in English), is the largest instant messaging platform in the world, used by 48% of all Internet users.[25][30]

Other diverse services provided by Tencent include web portals, e-commerce, and multiplayer online games.[8] Online games such as Legend of Yulong and Legend of Xuanyuan boosted revenue by more than half, up to US$ 5.1 billion, with a US$ 1.5 billion profit margin.[7]

In December 2015, Ma Huateng announced that Tencent will build an "internet hospital" set up in Wuzhen that will provide long-distance diagnoses and medicine delivery.[31]

Politics

According to the official Tencent website, Ma is a deputy to the 5th Shenzhen Municipal People's Congress and serves in the 12th National People's Congress.[4]

Because of Tencent's dominance of the social network and instant messaging markets in China, Ma Huateng' relationship with the Chinese Communist Party has repeatedly come under scrutiny.

Speaking of censorship at a tech conference in Singapore, Ma was quoted as saying "Lots of people think they can speak out and that they can be irresponsible. I think that's wrong [...] We are a great supporter of the government in terms of the information security. We try to have a better management and control of the Internet".[32]

Personal life

Ma uses the nickname Pony, derived from the English translation of his family name, which means "horse."[26] Ma Huateng seldom appears in the media and is known for his secretive lifestyle.[33] He believes in the maxim: "Ideas are not important in China – execution is."[30]

Ma Huateng's wealth comes from the 9.7% stake in Tencent Holdings. He reportedly owns property in Hong Kong and art pieces worth $150 million.[34] He owns a redeveloped palatial residence of 19,600 sq ft in Hong Kong.[34]

In 2016, Ma transferred $2 billion worth of Tencent shares, to his charitable foundation. However Forbes has not decreased his net worth as the shares are still listed under his name.[35]

Michael Dell

Michael Saul Dell (born February 23, 1965) is an American businessman, investor, philanthropist, and author. He is the founder and CEO of Dell Technologies, one of the world's largest technology infrastructure companies.  He is ranked as the 37th richest person in the world by *Forbes*, with a net worth of US$20.8 billion as of February 2017.[2]

In 2011, his 243.35 million shares of Dell Inc. stock were worth $3.5 billion, giving him 12% ownership of the company.[3] His remaining wealth of roughly $10 billion is invested in other companies and is managed by a firm whose name, MSD Capital, incorporates Dell's initials.[4] On January 5, 2013 it was announced that Michael Dell had bid to take Dell Inc. private for $24.4

billion in the biggest management buyout since the Great Recession. Dell Inc. officially went private on October 29, 2013.[5]

On October 12, 2015, Dell Inc. announced its intent to acquire the enterprise software and storage company EMC Corporation. At $67 billion, it has been labeled the "highest-valued tech acquisition in history".[6][7] The acquisition was finalized September 7, 2016.[8]

Early life

Michael Dell was born in 1965 in Houston, to a Jewish family whose surname reflects the translation into English of the original German/Yiddish *Thal* ("valley" or "dale [*q.v.*]"; modern common-noun spelling *Tal*) upon the family's immigration to the United States.[9] The son of Lorraine Charlotte (née Langfan), a stockbroker,[10] and Alexander Dell, an orthodontist, Michael Dell attended Herod Elementary School in Houston.[11] In a bid to enter business early, he applied to take a high school equivalency exam at age eight. In his early teens, he invested his earnings from part-time jobs in stocks and precious metals.[12]

Dell purchased his first calculator at age seven and encountered an early teletype terminal in junior high. At age 15, after playing with computers at Radio Shack, he got his first computer, an Apple II, which he promptly disassembled to see how it worked.[13] He got a job as a dishwasher at age 12 and was quickly promoted to maitre d'.[14] Dell attended Memorial High School in Houston, selling subscriptions to the *Houston Post* in the summer. While making cold calls, he noted that the people most likely to purchase subscriptions were those in the process of establishing permanent geographic and social presence. He then hired some friends who scoured local court records so he could target this demographic group by collecting names from marriage and mortgage applications. He then segmented those leads by the size of mortgage, calling on those with the highest mortgages first. Dell earned $18,000 that year, exceeding the annual income of his history and economics teacher.[15]

Business career

A PC's Limited Turbo PC signed by Dell

Michael Dell lecturing at the Oracle OpenWorld, San Francisco 2010

While a freshman pre-med student at the University of Texas, Dell started an informal business putting together and selling upgrade kits for personal computers[16] in Room 2713 of the Dobie Center residential building. He then applied for a vendor license to bid on contracts for the State of Texas, winning bids by not having the overhead of a computer store.[17][18][19]

In January 1984, Dell banked on his conviction that the potential cost savings of a manufacturer selling PCs directly had enormous advantages over the conventional indirect retail channel. In January 1984, Dell registered his company as "PC's Limited". Operating out of a condominium, the business sold between $50,000 and $80,000 in upgraded PCs, kits, and add-on components. In May, Dell incorporated the company as "Dell Computer Corporation" and relocated it to a business center in North Austin. The company employed a few order takers, a few more people to fulfill them, and, as Dell recalled, a manufacturing staff "consisting of three guys with screwdrivers sitting at six-foot tables". The venture's capitalization cost was $1,000.[20][21]

In 1992, aged 27, he became the youngest CEO of a company ranked in *Fortune* magazine's list of the top 500 corporations.[22] In 1996, Dell started selling computers over the Web, the same year his company launched its

first servers. Dell Inc. soon reported about $1 million in sales per day from dell.com.[23] In the first quarter of 2001, Dell Inc. reached a world market share of 12.8 percent, passing Compaq to become the world's largest PC maker. The metric marked the first time the rankings had shifted over the previous seven years. The company's combined shipments of desktops, notebooks and servers grew 34.3 percent worldwide and 30.7 percent in the United States at a time when competitor's sales were shrinking.[24]

In 1998, Dell founded MSD Capital L.P. to manage his family's investments. Investment activities include publicly traded securities, private equity activities, and real estate. The firm employs 80 people and has offices in New York, Santa Monica and London. Dell himself is not involved in day-to-day operations.[25] On March 4, 2004, Dell stepped down as CEO, but stayed as chairman of Dell Inc.'s board, while Kevin Rollins, then president and COO, became president and CEO. On January 31, 2007, Dell returned as CEO at the request of the board, succeeding Rollins.[26]

In 2013, Michael Dell with the help of Silver Lake Partners, Microsoft, and a consortium of lenders, took Dell, Inc. private. The deal was reportedly worth $25 billion and faced difficulties during its execution. Notable resistance came from Carl Icahn, but after several months he stepped aside. Michael Dell received a 75% stake in the private company.[27]

On October 12, 2015, Dell Inc. announced its intent to acquire the enterprise software and storage company EMC Corporation. At $67 billion, it has been labeled the "highest-valued tech acquisition in history".[6][7] The acquisition was finalized September 7, 2016.[8]

Penalty

In July 2010 Dell Inc. agreed to pay a $100 million penalty to settle SEC charges[28] of disclosure and accounting fraud in relation to undisclosed payments from Intel Corporation. Michael Dell and former CEO Kevin Rollins agreed to pay $4 million each, former CFO James Schneider to pay $3 million to settle the charges.[28]

Accolades

Accolades for Dell include "Entrepreneur of the Year" (at age 24) from *Inc.* magazine;[29] "Top CEO in American Business" from *Worth* magazine; "CEO of the Year" from *Financial World*, *Industry Week* and *Chief Executive* magazines. Dell also received the 2013 Franklin Institute's Bower Award for Business Leadership.[30]

Affiliations

Dell serves on the Foundation Board of the World Economic Forum, the executive committee of the International Business Council, the U.S. Business Council, and the governing board of the Indian School of Business in Hyderabad, India. He previously served as a member of the U.S. President's Council of Advisors on Science and Technology.[31]

Writings

Dell's 1999 book, *Direct from Dell: Strategies That Revolutionized an Industry* (by HarperBusiness), is an account of his early life, his company's founding, growth and missteps, as well as lessons learned. The book was written in collaboration with Catherine Fredman.[32]

Wealth and personal life

Forbes estimates Dell's net worth as of February 2017 at $20.8 billion.[33] Dell married Susan Lieberman on October 28, 1989, in Austin, Texas; the couple reside there with their four children.[34][35][36]

Philanthropy

In 1999, Michael and Susan Dell established the Michael and Susan Dell Foundation, which focuses on, among other causes, grants, urban education, childhood health and family economic stability. In 2006, the foundation provided $50 million in grants to three health-related organizations associated with the University of Texas: the Michael & Susan Dell Center for Advancement of Healthy Living, the Dell Pediatric Research Institute to compliment the Dell Children's Medical Center, as well as funding for a new computer science building at the University of Texas at Austin campus.[37] In 2013, the foundation provided an additional $50 million commitment to establish the Dell Medical School at the University of Texas at Austin. [38] Since 1999, the MSDF has committed $1.23 billion to non-profits and social enterprises in the United States, India and South Africa.[39] Dell is also behind the founding of the Dell Jewish Community Campus in the Northwest Hills neighborhood of Austin.[40]

By 2010, the foundation had committed more than $650 million to children's issues and community initiatives in the United States, India and South Africa.[41] Today the foundation has over $466 million assets under management.[42]

In 2002, Dell received an honorary doctorate in Economic Science from the University of Limerick in honor of his investment in Ireland and the local community and for his support for educational initiatives.[43]

In 2012, the Michael and Susan Dell Foundation committed $50 million for medical education. The Dell Medical School began enrolling students in 2016.[44]

In 2014, he donated $1.8 million to the Friends of the Israel Defense Forces.[45]

In 2017, in the wake of Hurricane Harvey, Dell, a Houston native, pledged $36 million to relief efforts. [46]

Steve Ballmer

Steven Anthony Ballmer (/ˈbɔːlmər/; born March 24, 1956[3]) is an American businessman, investor and philanthropist who was the chief executive officer of Microsoft from January 2000 to February 2014,[4] and is the current owner of the Los Angeles Clippers of the National Basketball  Association (NBA). As of December 11, 2017, his personal wealth is estimated at US$37.1 billion,[5] ranking him the 21st richest person in the world.[6]

Ballmer was hired by Bill Gates at Microsoft in 1980 after dropping out of Stanford University. He eventually

240

became President in 1998, and replaced Gates as CEO in 2000. It was announced on August 23, 2013, that he would step down as Microsoft's CEO within 12 months. On February 4, 2014, Ballmer retired as CEO and was succeeded by Satya Nadella; Ballmer resigned from the Board of Directors on August 19, 2014 to prepare for teaching a new class and for the start of the NBA season.[7][8] On May 29, 2014, Ballmer placed a bid of $2 billion to purchase the NBA's Los Angeles Clippers after NBA commissioner Adam Silver forced Donald Sterling to sell the team.[9] He officially became the Clippers owner on August 12, 2014; Microsoft co-founder Paul Allen is a fellow owner in the NBA, himself having owned the Portland Trail Blazers since 1988.

His time as Microsoft CEO has been seen as mixed, with critics noting the company's tripling of sales and doubling of profits, but losing its market dominance and missing out on 21st century technology trends.[10][11][12]

Early life

Ballmer was born in Detroit; he was the son of Beatrice Dworkin and Frederic Henry Ballmer (Fritz Hans Ballmer),[13] a manager at the Ford Motor Company.[14] His father was a Swiss immigrant, and his mother was Jewish (her family was from Belarus).[15] Through his mother, Ballmer is a second cousin of actress and comedian Gilda Radner.[16] Ballmer grew up in the affluent community of Farmington

Hills, Michigan. Ballmer also lived in Brussels from for three years in 1964, where he attended the International School of Brussels.[17] In 1973, he attended college prep and engineering classes at Lawrence Technological University. He graduated valedictorian from Detroit Country Day School, a private college preparatory school in Beverly Hills, Michigan, with a score of 800 on the mathematical section of the SAT[18][19] and was a National Merit Scholar.[20] He now sits on the school's board of directors. In 1977, he graduated *magna cum laude* from Harvard University with a B.A. in applied mathematics and economics.[21][22]

At college, Ballmer was a manager for the Harvard Crimson football team, worked on *The Harvard Crimson* newspaper as well as the *Harvard Advocate*, and lived down the hall from fellow sophomore Bill Gates. He scored highly in the William Lowell Putnam Mathematical Competition, an exam sponsored by the Mathematical Association of America, scoring higher than Bill Gates.[23] He then worked as an assistant product manager at Procter & Gamble for two years, where he shared an office with Jeffrey R. Immelt, who later became CEO of General Electric.[24] In 1980, he dropped out of the Stanford Graduate School of Business to join Microsoft.[25]

History with Microsoft

Steve Ballmer joined Microsoft on June 11, 1980, and became Microsoft's 30th employee, the first business manager hired by Gates.[26]

Ballmer was initially offered a salary of $50,000 as well as a percentage of ownership of the company. When Microsoft was incorporated in 1981, Ballmer owned 8% of the company. In 2003, Ballmer sold 39.3 million Microsoft shares equating to approximately $955 million, thereby reducing his ownership to 4%.[27] The same year, he replaced Microsoft's employee stock options program.[28]

In the 20 years following his hire, Ballmer headed several Microsoft divisions, including operations, operating systems development, and sales and support. From February 1992 onwards, he was Executive Vice President, Sales and Support. Ballmer led Microsoft's development of the .NET Framework. Ballmer was then promoted to President of Microsoft, a title that he held from July 1998 to February 2001, making him the de facto number two in the company to the chairman and CEO, Bill Gates.[29]

Chief Executive Officer (2000–2014)

Steve Ballmer at Mobile World Congress 2010.

On January 13, 2000 Ballmer was officially named chief executive officer.[4][30] As CEO, Ballmer handled company finances and daily operations, but Gates remained chairman of the board and still retained control of the "technological vision" as chief software architect.[31]Gates relinquished day-to-day activities when he stepped down as chief software architect in 2006, while staying on as chairman, and that gave Ballmer the autonomy needed to make major management changes at Microsoft.[32]

When Ballmer took over as CEO, the company was fighting an antitrust lawsuit brought on by the U.S. government and 20 states, plus class-action lawsuits and complaints from rival companies. While it was said that Gates would have continued fighting the suit, Ballmer made it his priority to settle these saying: "Being the object of a lawsuit, effectively, or a complaint from your government is a very awkward, uncomfortable position to be in. It just has all downside. People assume if the government brought a complaint that there's really a problem, and your ability to say we're a good, proper, moral place is tough. It's actually tough, even though you feel that way about yourselves."[33]

Upon becoming CEO, Ballmer required detailed business justification in order to approve of new products, rather than allowing hundreds of products that sounded potentially interesting or trendy. In 2005, he recruited B. Kevin Turner from Wal-Mart, who was the

President and CEO of Sam's Club, to become Microsoft's Chief Operating Officer.[34] Turner was hired at Microsoft to lead the company's sales, marketing and services group and to instill more process and discipline in the company's operations and salesforce.[35]

Since Bill Gates' retirement, Ballmer oversaw a "dramatic shift away from the company's PC-first heritage", replacing most major division heads in order to break down the "talent-hoarding fiefdoms", and *Businessweek* said that the company "arguably now has the best product lineup in its history". Ballmer was instrumental in driving Microsoft's connected computing strategy, with acquisitions such as Skype.[32]

Under Ballmer's tenure as CEO, Microsoft's annual revenue surged from $25 billion to $70 billion, while its net income increased 215 percent to $23 billion, and its gross profit of 75 cents on every dollar in sales is double that of Google or IBM[36] In terms of leading the company's total annual profit growth, Ballmer's tenure at Microsoft (16.4%) surpassed the performances of other well-known CEOs such as General Electric's Jack Welch (11.2%) and IBM's Louis V. Gerstner Jr. (2%).[32] These gains came from the existing Windows and Office franchises, with Ballmer maintaining their profitability, fending off threats from cheaper competitors such as GNU/Linux and other open-source operating systems and Google Docs.[37] Ballmer also built half-a-dozen new businesses[38] such as the data centers division and the Xbox entertainment and devices division

($8.9 billion)[39] (which has prevented the
Sony PlayStation and other gaming consoles from
undermining Windows),[40] and oversaw the acquisition
of Skype. Ballmer also constructed the company's
$20 billion Enterprise Business, consisting of new
products and services such as Exchange, Windows
Server, SQL Server, SharePoint, System Center, and
Dynamics CRM, each of which initially faced an uphill
battle for acceptance but have emerged as leading or
dominant in each category.[40] This diversified product
mix helped to offset the company's reliance on PCs and
mobile computing devices as the company entered
the Post-PC era; in reporting quarterly results during
April 2013, while Windows Phone 8 and Windows 8 had
not managed to increase their market share above single
digits, the company increased its profit 19% over the
previous quarter in 2012, as the Microsoft Business
Division (including Office 365) and Server and Tools
division (cloud services) are each larger than the
Windows division.[41][42]

Ballmer attracted criticism for failing to capitalize on
several new consumer technologies, forcing Microsoft to
play catch-up in the areas of tablet computing,
smartphones and music players with mixed
results.[32][42] Under Ballmer's watch, "In many cases,
Microsoft latched onto technologies like smartphones,
touchscreens, 'smart' cars and wristwatches that read
sports scores aloud long before Apple or Google did.
But it repeatedly killed promising projects if they

threatened its cash cows [Windows and Office]."[43] Microsoft's share price stagnated during Ballmer's tenure. As a result, in May 2012, hedge fund manager David Einhorn called on Ballmer to step down as CEO of Microsoft. "His continued presence is the biggest overhang on Microsoft's stock," Einhorn said in reference to Ballmer.[44] In a May 2012 column in *Forbes* magazine, Adam Hartung described Ballmer as "the worst CEO of a large publicly traded American company", saying he had "steered Microsoft out of some of the fastest growing and most lucrative tech markets (mobile music, headsets and tablets)".[45]

In 2009, and for the first time since Bill Gates resigned from day-to-day management at Microsoft, Ballmer delivered the opening keynote at CES.[46]

Ballmer at MIX 08 in 2008

As part of his plans to expand on hardware, on June 19, 2012, Ballmer revealed Microsoft's first ever computer device, a tablet called Microsoft Surface at an event held in Hollywood, Los Angeles.[47] He followed this

by announcing the company's purchase of Nokia's mobile phone division in September 2013,[48] his last major acquisition for Microsoft as CEO.

On August 23, 2013, Microsoft announced that Ballmer would retire within the next 12 months. A special committee that included Bill Gates would decide on the next CEO.[49]

There was a list of potential successors to Ballmer as Microsoft CEO, but all had departed the company: Jim Allchin, Brad Silverberg, Paul Maritz, Nathan Myhrvold, Greg Maffei, Pete Higgins, Jeff Raikes, J. Allard, Robbie Bach, Bill Veghte, Ray Ozzie, Bob Muglia and Steven Sinofsky.[50][51] B. Kevin Turner, Microsoft's Chief Operating Officer (COO), was considered by some to be a *de facto* number two to Ballmer, with Turner having a strong grasp of business and operations but lacking technological vision.[52] On February 4, 2014, Satya Nadella succeeded Ballmer as CEO.[8]

Personality

Ballmer is known for his energetic and exuberant personality, which is meant to motivate employees and partners.[53] His flamboyant stage appearances at Microsoft events are widely circulated on the Internet as viral videos.[54][55][56]

One of his earliest known viral videos was his promotion of Windows 1.0 for a Crazy Eddie commercial in 1985, where he energetically shouts "How much do YOU think this advanced operating environment is worth? WAIT just one minute before you answer".[57][58] Ballmer and Brian Valentine repeated this in a spoof promotion of Windows XP later on.

A widely circulated video was his entrance on stage at Microsoft's 25th anniversary event in September 2000,[59] where he shouted and jumped across the stage, and saying "I love this company". It has been nicknamed 'monkey boy dance'.[60][61] Another well known viral video was one captured at a Windows 2000 developers' conference, featuring a perspiring Ballmer chanting the word "developers".[62][63]

Relationship with Bill Gates

The *Wall Street Journal* has reported that there was tension surrounding the 2000 transition of authority from Bill Gates to Ballmer. Things became so bitter that, on one occasion, Gates stormed out of a meeting in a huff after a shouting match in which Ballmer jumped to the defense of several colleagues, according to an individual present at the time. After the exchange, Ballmer seemed "remorseful", the person said. Once Gates leaves, "I'm not going to need him for anything. That's the principle," Ballmer said. "Use him, yes, need him, no."[64]

In October 2014, a few months after Ballmer left his post at Microsoft, a *Vanity Fair* profile stated that Ballmer and

Gates no longer talk to each other due to animosity over Ballmer's resignation.[65] In a November 2016 interview, Ballmer said he and Gates have "drifted apart" ever since, saying that they always had a "brotherly relationship" beforehand.[66] He said that his push into the hardware business, specifically smartphones, which Gates did not support, contributed to their relationship breakdown.[67]

Retirement

After saying in 2008 that he intended to remain CEO for another decade, Ballmer announced his retirement in 2013, after losing billions of dollars in acquisitions and on the Surface tablet. Microsoft's stock price rebounded on the news.[68]

Ballmer says that he regretted the lack of focus on Windows Mobile in the early 2000s, leaving Microsoft a distant third in the current smartphone market.[69] Moreover, he attributed the success of the expensively-priced iPhones to carrier subsidies.[70] He went on to say,

People like to point to this quote where I said iPhones will never sell, because the price at $600 or $700 was too high. And there was business model innovation by Apple to get it essentially built into the monthly cellphone bill.

He called the acquisition of the mobile phone division of Nokia as his "toughest decision" during his tenure, as it was overseeing the changing profile of Microsoft as it was expanding on hardware.[71]

Ballmer hosted his last company meeting in September 2013,[72] and stepped down from the company's board of directors, in August 2014.[73]

On December 24, 2014, the Seattle Times reported that the IRS sued Ballmer, Craig Mundie, Jeff Raikes, Jim Allchin, Orlando Ayala and David Guenther in an effort to compel them to testify in Microsoft's corporate tax audit. The IRS has been looking into how Microsoft and other companies deal with transfer pricing.[74]

Other positions

Ballmer served as director of Accenture Ltd. and a general partner of Accenture SCA from 2001 to 2006.[75]

On competing companies and software

Apple

In 2007, Ballmer said "There's no chance that the [Apple] iPhone is going to get any significant market share. No chance."[76]

Speaking at a conference in NYC in 2009, Ballmer criticized Apple's pricing, saying, "Now I think the tide has turned back the other direction (against Apple). The economy is helpful. Paying an extra $500 for a computer in this environment—same piece of hardware—paying $500 more to get a logo on it? I think that's a more challenging proposition for the average person than it used to be."[77]

In 2015, Ballmer called Microsoft's decision to invest in Apple to save it from bankruptcy in 1997 as the "craziest thing we ever did". By 2015 Apple was the world's most valuable company.[78]

Free and open source software

In July 2000, Ballmer called the free software Linux kernel "communism"[79] as it infringed with Microsoft's intellectual property.[80] In June 2001 he called Linux a "cancer that attaches itself in an intellectual property sense to everything it touches".[81] Ballmer used the notion of "viral" licensing terms to express his concern over the fact that the GNU General Public License (GPL) employed by such software requires that all derivative software be under the GPL or a compatible license. In April 2003 he even interrupted his skiing holiday in Switzerland to personally plea the mayor of Munich not to switch to GNU/Linux.[82] But he did not succeed with this and Munich uses LiMux now, despite his offering a 35% discount at his lobbying visit.[83]

In March 2016, Ballmer changed his stance on Linux, saying that he supports his successor Satya Nadella's open source commitments. He maintained that his comments in 2001 were right at the time but that times have changed.[84][85]

Google

In 2005, Microsoft sued Google for hiring one of its previous vice presidents, Kai-Fu Lee, claiming it was in violation of his one-year non-compete clause in his contract. Mark Lucovsky, who left for Google in 2004, alleged in a sworn statement to a Washington state court that Ballmer became enraged upon hearing that Lucovsky was about to leave Microsoft for Google, picked up his chair, and threw it across his office, and that, referring to former Google CEO Eric Schmidt (who previously worked for competitors Sun and Novell), Ballmer vowed to "kill Google."[86] Lucovsky reports:[87]

At some point in the conversation Mr. Ballmer said: "Just tell me it's not Google." I told him it was Google. At that point, Mr. Ballmer picked up a chair and threw it across the room hitting a table in his office. Mr. Ballmer then said: "Fucking Eric Schmidt is a fucking pussy. I'm going to fucking bury that guy, I have done it before, and I will do it again. I'm going to fucking kill Google."[88]

Ballmer then resumed attempting to persuade Lucovsky to stay at Microsoft. Ballmer has described Lucovsky's account of the incident as a "gross exaggeration of what actually took place".[86]

During the 2011 Web 2.0 Summit in San Francisco, he said: "You don't need to be a computer scientist to use a Windows Phone and you do to use an Android phone ... It is hard for me to be excited about the Android phones."[89][90]

There's no chance that the iPhone is going to get any significant market share. No chance.

Steve Ballmer, 2007

In 2013, Ballmer said that Google was a "monopoly" that should be pressured from market competition authorities.[91]

Sports

On March 6, 2008, Seattle mayor Greg Nickels announced that a local ownership group involving Ballmer made a "game changing" commitment to invest $150 million in cash toward a proposed $300 million renovation of KeyArena and were ready to purchase the Seattle SuperSonics from the Professional Basketball Club LLC in order to keep the team in Seattle. However, this initiative failed, and the

SuperSonics relocated to Oklahoma City, Oklahoma, where they now play as the Oklahoma City Thunder.[92]

In June 2012, Ballmer was an investor in Chris R. Hansen's proposal to build a new arena in the SoDo neighborhood of Seattle and bring the SuperSonics back to Seattle.[93] On January 9, 2013, Ballmer and Hansen led a group of investors in an attempt to purchase the Sacramento Kings from the Maloof family and relocate them to Seattle for an estimated $650 million. However, this attempt also fell through.[94]

Following the Donald Sterling scandal in May 2014, Ballmer was the highest bidder in an attempt to purchase the Los Angeles Clippers for a reported price of $2 billion, which is the second highest bid for a sports franchise in North American sports history (after the $2.15 billion sale of the Los Angeles Dodgers in 2012). After a California court confirmed the authority of Shelly Sterling to sell the team, it was officially announced on August 12, 2014 that Ballmer would become the Los Angeles Clippers owner.[95]

On September 25, 2014, Ballmer said he would bar the team from using Apple products such as iPads, and replace them with Microsoft products.[96] It has been reported that he had previously also barred his household family from using iPhones.[97]

Wealth

Ballmer was the second person after Roberto Goizueta to become a billionaire in U.S. dollars based on stock options received as an employee of a corporation in which he was neither a founder nor a relative of a founder. As of December 11, 2017, his personal wealth is estimated at US$37.1 billion.[5] While CEO of Microsoft in 2009, Ballmer earned a total compensation of $1,276,627, which included a base salary of $665,833, a cash bonus of $600,000, no stock or options, and other compensation of $10,794.[98]

Philanthropy

On November 12, 2014, it was announced that Ballmer and his wife Connie donated $50 million to the University of Oregon. Connie Ballmer is a University of Oregon alumna, and serves on the institution's board of trustees. The funds will go towards the university's $2 billion fundraising effort, and will focus towards scholarships, public health research and advocacy, and external branding/communications.[99]

On November 13, 2014, it was announced that Ballmer would provide a gift, estimated at $60 million, to Harvard University's computer science department. The gift would allow the department to hire new faculty, and hopefully increase the national stature of the program. Ballmer previously donated $10 million to the same department in 1994, in a joint-gift with Bill Gates.[100]

Ballmer serves on the World Chairman's Council of the Jewish National Fund, which means he has donated US$1 million or more to the JNF.[101]

USAFacts

Ballmer launched USAFacts.org in 2017, a non-profit organization whose goal is to allow people to understand US government revenue, spending and societal impact. He is reported to have contributed $10 million to fund teams of researchers who populated the website's database with official data.[102][103][104]

Personal life

In 1990, he married Connie Snyder;[105] they have three sons.[106]

The Ballmers live in Hunts Point, Washington.[107]

CHAPTER SEVEN

LESSONS IN LIFE AND BUSINESS MENTORS

Pursue a Lateral Path

One of my mentors pointed out that the general public tends to think in verticals: "I'm climbing up the career ladder," or "I  had a setback that knocked me down a notch," but truly successful people think laterally. As one moves along from point A to point B, what else can also be accomplished along the same path? Think of your path as speeding trains, running along side by side. You can hop on and hop off as needed. Instead of starting one company, start two that can share many of the same staff and skill sets. Look around at who you know and leverage your goals based on that. Do you have a sibling or business partner who is pursuing endeavors you have an interest in? Who best to learn from and grow than someone who you already have an in with? Grow congruently and when you encounter an obstacle, consider visualizing the issue as a "decision tree."

Even When You're Tired, Don't Cut Corners

We sometimes wear "busy" as a badge and run the risk of sloppy or incomplete performance. One of my mentors owns an internationally successful jewelry company. The labor of hand-pouring precious metal is a lost art in this day and age of machines and factories. She has a collection that is all hand-poured and the attention to detail is exquisite. As you pour the heated metal layer by layer, if any air gets in, the metal must be re-poured; otherwise the final, finished product could end up defective. Perhaps a defect could be so small that no one would notice, but attention to detail is precise and accurate. As a result, running the risk of a defect isn't an option and the metal is simply re-poured until each layer is perfect.

This story was so poignant for me because it speaks directly to our lives as busy Americans. The lesson here is simple: just do it the right way. Even when you're tired, even when you're mad, and even if no one else is doing it the right way and it's unfair.

Instill Confidence in Others

One of my mentors told me that we all have unlimited currency–and that currency is to do good. The best mark of leadership is leading by example. It's your job to instill confidence in others. Besides those around you (family, friends, business partners, employees etc.), consider broadening your reach. Get engaged and involved in your local community. Volunteer to read to a class during elementary school reading week. Serve dinner to the homeless. Visit a children's hospital or nursing home. The return on your time is immeasurable and you will be able to truly ingratiate philanthropy as part of your lifestyle.

What You Have in the Bank is Not What You're Worth

One of my mentors shared a story with me about how his company wanted to acquire this other company. They made offers that became more grandiose over the course of nearly two years. Regardless of how much money they threw at this company, their CEO kept rejecting it, not even countering. My mentor's CFO threw a tantrum, clearly at wit's end, and made some absurd statement about how if they don't sell, they'll get buried in court because "money is no object." That's when my mentor had an epiphany: This other company isn't choosing not to sell because they don't want to sell. It's just that they want to sell to a buyer who has compassion and understands their company. The other company had some of the same employees for 20-plus years. The CEO wanted to protect his employees from being terminated the moment the company was sold and he knew that in selling to my mentor's company, it was inevitable. They restructured the agreement, and the hiring and retention clause was modified to keep all existing employees. The price was less than the inflated offers that came during the desperate bargaining.

Be a person of principle and reach a level of empathy with the person on the other side of the table. It will result in a win-win every time.

Be Proud to Know Yourself

One of my mentors comes from a long lineage of successful businessmen. He has reminded me over the years to pay attention to how you can help others. One night, he was watching late night TV and a story came on about how a retired NHL player was trying to obtain a very special hockey puck that his daughter inadvertently gave away decades ago. Understanding the nostalgia, my mentor located the puck on eBay, won the bid and gave the puck back to its rightful owner.

Sometimes you don't do things for personal gain or attention, you just do it because it's the right and kind thing to do. On your path to success, there will be people out there who will support you and others who won't, but the most important person to know and rely on is yourself.

Success takes time.

Many entrepreneurs go into business thinking that they have raised enough

money to launch the business. But, the foundation of a business doesn't happen overnight. It typically takes two or three years to build a solid foundation and ensure the business is on steady ground.

I use a phrase that I call "TGFO" (Thank God For Oprah), because when she started the *Oprah Winfrey Network*, it took her just about three years to get her foundation settled. Now, I have that to point to as a benchmark.

If it takes Oprah, who had every business resource in the world at her disposal – capital, fans, a great brand and more – around three years to have a solid business foundation, that means it will likely take you the same. Make sure you have planned not just for the launch of the business, but to support it – and yourself – financially or otherwise for up to three years before you know if the business will work.

Promote yourself.

Self-promoters often get a bad rap. As someone who often gets accused of this myself, I retort, "Well, if I don't promote myself, who will?"

Oprah is a noted champion of this strategy. She has built her brand around being her, even making herself the cover model to every edition of her magazine.

This keeps her brand very consistent, and clearly, her promoting works, because just about everyone on the planet knows who she is. Take the lead from Oprah here and be willing to promote yourself, your business and your products and services consistently.

Work with great talent.

While Oprah has mastered the art of self-promotion, she's also surrounded herself with great people. She not only hires the best-of-the-best internally, like Adam Glassman, her creative director for *The Oprah Magazine,* but she has also launched the careers of designer Nate Berkus, self-help guru Dr. Phil, personal finance whiz Suze Orman and many more.

By working with this great pool of talent, she has been able to broaden what she gives her customer in terms of content and products. Make sure you look for the best talent – either to hire or to collaborate with – to take your business to the next level.

Craft a great deal.

Oprah has always been a master of the deal. When she became a top TV personality, instead of renegotiating her salary, she renegotiated ownership of the program, as well as the studio where it was produced and a stake in its distributor. That's what helped her become a billionaire.

When she decided to become a spokeswoman for Weight Watchers, she also bought a stake in the company, and the stock has recently risen as her weight has fallen.

Creating a good deal has been a hallmark from Oprah that you can learn from. See where you can improve your deal-making to amp up the long-term value of your business and your overall wealth.

Give to get.

You can't think of Oprah without thinking of her giveaways. "You get a car!" endures as a favorite internet meme years after it happened on her show. Her giveaway strategy created a ton of excitement, not just with the people who benefitted, but with everyone who heard about it after the fact.

While you are probably not going to be giving away free cars or even a full slew of your "favorite things," perhaps you can give away some free samples of new products and services to existing clients. Or, start with a free consultation to entice new customers.

Whatever you might give away, just make sure you're creating excitement – for your clients, for your company and for your brand.

1. Build something that actually solves a problem.

If you want to build a valuable and sustainable business, approach your venture with a problem-solution framework. The most successful companies in the world emerge from genuine needs and consequently create real opportunities and value. "Innovation" is just the process of solving a problem with a creative solution that's *never* been thought of or executed before.

2. Fail fast.

Your first attempt to develop something that has the right product-to-market fit probably won't work. The sooner you understand what's not working, the sooner you'll arrive at a working solution. Therefore, the key is to iterate quickly and ship frequently. Building something that provides value to its respective market will require multiple attempts and failures. This was the case with every company I've built.

3. Build a great team and you'll typically end up with a great product or service.

Most entrepreneurs think startups are all about the idea. They're not. Initially, most ideas are way off base and don't have product-to-market fit.

Investors such as Cuban and Branson look at the team as much as the product. If you have a team that knows how to problem-solve and persevere, you can brainstorm, iterate and prototype until you arrive at the *right* idea. The right team has the right blend of attitude, intelligence, perseverance, passion and domain expertise. Investors know it when they see it.

4. Build culture from the start.

Culture is the foundation of your company, and culture comes from people, not theory. Today, I follow the SWAN formula: Smart, Works Hard, Ambitious and Nice. If you hire SWANs from the start, the company culture will be organic and build itself. Ultimately, culture will give your company the momentum it needs to barrel through the roughest parts of entrepreneurship.

5. Don't be afraid to push the boundaries.

Both Cuban and Branson have said that the most successful companies in the world create a legacy by breaking the rules and *not* following common beliefs or thinking. When you think unconventionally, true innovation and disruption can occur. Call it a "paradigm shift," "transformation" or whatever term gets you motivated. Take the "road less travelled" if you really want to upend an existing business model or traditional industry.

Now, do your own thing. If you based your entire startup strategy around something I wrote here, you're contradicting tip number five about pushing boundaries. Mentors and commentators should push you to form your own strategy rather than provide fill-in-the-blank answers that apply to each and every scenario. No two startups follow the same path.

So use these tips, but if you want to create something the world can't ignore, go do your own thing. Make something we can't read about in a blog post today. If you really want to emulate Cuban or Branson's model, go build a company they wish they could invest in. Maybe they will.

CHAPTER EIGHT

DISRUPTIVE INNOVATION

Disruptive innovation is a term in the field of business administration which refers to an innovation that creates a new market and value network and eventually disrupts an existing market and value network, displacing established market leading firms, products, and alliances. [2] The term was defined and first analyzed by the American scholar Clayton M. Christensen and his collaborators beginning in 1995,[3] and has been called the most influential business idea of the early 21st century.[4]

Not all innovations are disruptive, even if they are revolutionary. For example, the first automobiles in the late 19th century were not a disruptive innovation, because early automobiles were expensive luxury items that did not disrupt the market

ELEMENTS OF DISRUPTIVE INNOVATION

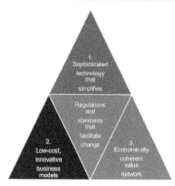

for horse-drawn vehicles. The market for transportation essentially remained intact until the debut of the lower-priced Ford Model T in 1908.[5] The *mass-produced*automobile was a disruptive innovation, because it changed the transportation market, whereas the first thirty years of automobiles did not.

Disruptive innovations tend to be produced by outsiders and entrepreneurs, rather than existing market-leading companies. The business environment of market leaders does not allow them to pursue disruptive innovations when they first arise, because they are not profitable enough at first and because their development can take scarce resources away from sustaining innovations (which are needed to compete against current competition).[6] A disruptive process can take longer to develop than by the conventional approach and the risk associated to it is higher than the other more incremental or evolutionary forms of innovations, but once it is deployed in the market, it achieves a much faster penetration and higher degree of impact on the established markets.[7]

Beyond business and economics disruptive innovations can also be considered to disrupt complex systems, including economic and business-related aspects.[8]

History and usage of the term

The term disruptive technologies was coined by Clayton M. Christensen and introduced in his 1995 article *Disruptive Technologies: Catching the Wave*,[9] which he cowrote with Joseph Bower. The article is aimed at management executives who make the funding or purchasing decisions in companies, rather than the research community. He describes the term further in his book *The Innovator's Dilemma*.[10] *Innovator's Dilemma* explored the cases of the disk drive industry (which, with its rapid generational change, is to the study of business what fruit flies are to the study of genetics, as Christensen was advised in the 1990s[11]) and the excavating equipment industry (where hydraulic actuation slowly displaced cable-actuated movement). In his sequel with Michael E. Raynor, *The Innovator's Solution*,[12]

Christensen replaced the term *disruptive technology* with *disruptive innovation* because he recognized that few technologies are intrinsically disruptive or sustaining in character; rather, it is the *business model* that the technology enables that creates the disruptive impact. However, Christensen's evolution from a technological focus to a business-modelling focus is central to understanding the evolution of business at the market or industry level. Christensen and Mark W. Johnson, who cofounded the management consulting firm Innosight, described the dynamics of "business model innovation" in the 2008 *Harvard Business Review* article "Reinventing Your Business Model".[13] The concept of disruptive technology continues a long tradition of identifying radical technical change in the study of innovation by economists, and the development of tools for its management at a firm or policy level.

The term "disruptive innovation" is misleading when it is used to refer to a product or service at one fixed point, rather than to the evolution of that product or service over time.

In the late 1990s, the automotive sector began to embrace a perspective of "constructive disruptive technology" by working with the consultant David E. O'Ryan, whereby the use of current off-the-shelf technology was integrated with newer innovation to create what he called "an unfair advantage". The process or technology change as a whole had to be "constructive" in improving the current method of manufacturing, yet disruptively impact the whole of the business case model, resulting in a significant reduction of waste, energy, materials, labor, or legacy costs to the user.

In keeping with the insight that what matters economically is the business model, not the technological sophistication itself, Christensen's theory explains why many disruptive innovations are *not* "advanced technologies", which the technology mudslide hypothesis would lead one to expect. Rather, they are often novel combinations of existing off-the-shelf components, applied cleverly to a small, fledgling value network.

Theory

The current theoretical understanding of disruptive innovation is different from what might be expected by default, an idea that Clayton M. Christensen called the "technology mudslide hypothesis". This is the simplistic idea that an established firm fails because it doesn't "keep up technologically" with other firms. In this hypothesis, firms are like climbers scrambling upward on crumbling footing, where it takes constant upward-climbing effort just to stay still, and any break from the effort (such as complacency born of profitability) causes a rapid downhill slide. Christensen and colleagues have shown that this simplistic hypothesis is wrong; it doesn't model reality. What they have shown is that good firms are usually aware of the innovations, but their business environment does not allow them to pursue them when they first arise, because they are not profitable enough at first and because their development can take scarce resources away from that of sustaining innovations (which are needed to compete against current competition). In Christensen's terms, a firm's existing *value networks* place insufficient value on the disruptive innovation to allow its pursuit by that firm. Meanwhile, start-up firms inhabit different value networks, at least until the day that their disruptive innovation is able to invade the older value network. At that time, the established firm in that network can at best only fend off the market shareattack with a me-too entry, for which survival (not thriving) is the only reward.[6]

Christensen defines a disruptive innovation as a product or service designed for a new set of customers.

"Generally, disruptive innovations were technologically straightforward, consisting of off-the-shelf components put together in a product architecture that was often simpler than prior approaches. They offered less of what customers in established markets wanted and so could rarely be initially employed there. They offered a different package of attributes valued only in emerging markets remote from, and unimportant to, the mainstream."[14]

Christensen argues that disruptive innovations can hurt successful, well-managed companies that are responsive to

273

their customers and have excellent research and development. These companies tend to ignore the markets most susceptible to disruptive innovations, because the markets have very tight profit margins and are too small to provide a good growth rate to an established (sizable) firm.[15] Thus, disruptive technology provides an example of an instance when the common business-world advice to "focus on the customer" (or "stay close to the customer", or "listen to the customer") can be strategically counterproductive.

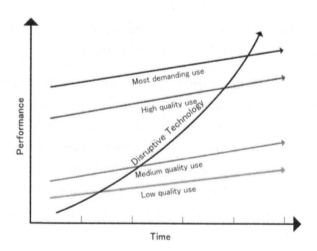

While Christensen argued that disruptive innovations can hurt successful, well-managed companies, O'Ryan countered that "constructive" integration of existing, new, and forward-thinking innovation could improve the economic benefits of these same well-managed companies, once decision-making management understood the systemic benefits as a whole.

How low-end disruption occurs over time.Christensen distinguishes between "low-end disruption", which targets customers who do not need the full performance valued by customers at the high end of the market, and "new-market disruption", which targets customers who have needs that were previously unserved by existing incumbents.[16]

"Low-end disruption" occurs when the rate at which products improve exceeds the rate at which customers can adopt the new performance. Therefore, at some point the performance of the product overshoots the needs of certain customer segments. At this point, a disruptive technology may enter the market and provide a product that has lower performance than the incumbent but that exceeds the requirements of certain segments, thereby gaining a foothold in the market.

In low-end disruption, the disruptor is focused initially on serving the least profitable customer, who is happy with a good enough product. This type of customer is not willing to pay premium for enhancements in product functionality. Once the disruptor has gained a foothold in this customer segment, it seeks to improve its profit margin. To get higher profit margins, the disruptor needs to enter the segment where the customer is willing to pay a little more for higher quality. To ensure this quality in its product, the disruptor needs to innovate. The incumbent will not do much to retain its share in a not-so-profitable segment, and will move up-market and focus on its more attractive customers. After a number of such encounters, the incumbent is squeezed into smaller markets than it was previously serving. And then, finally, the disruptive technology meets the demands of the most profitable segment and drives the established company out of the market.

"New market disruption" occurs when a product fits a new or emerging market segment that is not being served by existing incumbents in the industry.

The extrapolation of the theory to all aspects of life has been challenged,[17][18] as has the methodology of relying on selected case studies as the principal form of evidence.[17] Jill Lepore points out that some companies identified by the theory as victims of disruption a decade or more ago, rather than being defunct, remain dominant in their industries today (including Seagate Technology, U.S. Steel, and Bucyrus).[17] Lepore questions whether the theory has been oversold and misapplied, as if it were able to explain everything in every sphere of life, including not just business but education and public institutions.[17]

Disruptive technology

In 2009, Milan Zeleny described high technology as disruptive technology and raised the question of what is being disrupted. The answer, according to Zeleny, is the *support network* of high technology.[19] For example, introducing electric cars disrupts the support network for gasoline cars (network of gas and service stations). Such disruption is fully expected and therefore effectively resisted by support net owners. In the long run, high

(disruptive) technology bypasses, upgrades, or replaces the outdated support network. Questioning the concept of a disruptive technology, Haxell (2012) questions how such technologies get named and framed, pointing out that this is a positioned and retrospective act.[20][21]

Technology, being a form of social relationshipalways evolves. No technology remains fixed. Technology starts, develops, persists, mutates, stagnates, and declines, just like living organisms.[22] The evolutionary life cycle occurs in the use and development of any technology. A new high-technology core emerges and challenges existing technology support nets (TSNs), which are thus forced to coevolve with it. New versions of the core are designed and fitted into an increasingly appropriate TSN, with smaller and smaller high-technology effects. High technology becomes regular technology, with more efficient versions fitting the same support net. Finally, even the efficiency gains diminish, emphasis shifts to product tertiary attributes (appearance, style), and technology becomes TSN-preserving appropriate technology. This technological equilibrium state becomes established and fixated, resisting being interrupted by a technological mutation; then new high technology appears and the cycle is repeated.

Regarding this evolving process of technology, Christensen said:

"The technological changes that damage established companies are usually not radically new or difficult from a technological point of view. They do, however, have two important characteristics: First, they typically present a different package of performance attributes—ones that, at least at the outset, are not valued by existing customers. Second, the performance attributes that existing customers do value improve at such a rapid rate that the new technology can later invade those established markets."[23]

Joseph Bower[24] explained the process of how disruptive technology, through its requisite support net, dramatically transforms a certain industry.

"When the technology that has the potential for revolutionizing an industry emerges, established companies typically see it as unattractive: it's not something their mainstream customers want, and its projected profit margins aren't sufficient to cover big-company cost structure. As a result, the new technology tends to get ignored in favor of what's currently popular with the best customers. But then another company steps in to bring the innovation to a new market. Once the disruptive technology becomes established there, smaller-scale innovation rapidly raise the technology's performance on attributes that mainstream customers' value."[25]

The automobile was high technology with respect to the horse carriage; however, it evolved into technology and finally into appropriate technology with a stable, unchanging TSN. The main high-technology advance in the offing is some form of electric car—whether the energy source is the sun, hydrogen, water, air pressure, or traditional charging outlet. Electric cars preceded the gasoline automobile by many decades and are now returning to replace the traditional gasoline automobile. The printing press was a development that changed the way that information was stored, transmitted, and replicated. This allowed empowered authors but it also promoted censorship and information overload in writing technology.

Milan Zeleny described the above phenomenon.[26] He also wrote that:

"Implementing high technology is often resisted. This resistance is well understood on the part of active participants in the requisite TSN. The electric car will be resisted by gas-station operators in the same way automated teller machines (ATMs) were resisted by bank tellers and automobiles by horsewhip makers. Technology does not qualitatively restructure the TSN and therefore will not be resisted and never has been resisted. Middle management resists business process reengineering because BPR represents a direct assault on the support net (coordinative hierarchy) they thrive on. Teamwork and multi-functionality is resisted by those whose TSN provides the comfort of narrow specialization and command-driven work."[27]

Social media could be considered a disruptive innovation within sports. More specifically, the way that news in sports circulates nowadays versus the pre-internet era where sports news was mainly on T.V., radio, and newspapers. Social media has created a new market for sports that was not around before in the sense that players and fans have instant access to information related to sports.

High-technology effects

High technology is a technology core that changes the very architecture (structure and organization) of the components of the technology support net. High technology therefore transforms the qualitative nature of the TSN's tasks and their relations, as well as their requisite physical, energy, and information flows. It also affects the skills required, the roles played, and the styles of management and coordination—the organizational culture itself.

This kind of technology core is different from regular technology core, which preserves the qualitative nature of flows and the structure of the support and only allows users to perform the same tasks in the same way, but faster, more reliably, in larger quantities, or more efficiently. It is also different from appropriate technology core, which preserves the TSN itself with the purpose of technology implementation and allows users to do the same thing in the same way at comparable levels of efficiency, instead of improving the efficiency of performance.[28]

As for the difference between high technology and low technology, Milan Zeleny once said:

" The effects of high technology always breaks the direct comparability by changing the system itself, therefore requiring new measures and new assessments of its productivity. High technology cannot be compared and evaluated with the existing technology purely on the basis of cost, net present value or return on investment. Only within an unchanging and relatively stable TSN would such direct financial comparability be meaningful. For example, you can directly compare a manual typewriter with an electric typewriter, but not a typewriter with a word processor. Therein lies the management challenge of high technology. "[29]

However, not all modern technologies are high technologies. They have to be used as such, function as such, and be embedded in their requisite TSNs. They have to empower the individual because only through the individual can they empower knowledge. Not all information technologies have integrative effects. Some information systems are still designed to improve the traditional hierarchy of command and thus preserve and entrench the existing TSN. The administrative model of management, for instance, further aggravates the division of task and labor, further specializes knowledge, separates management from workers, and concentrates information and knowledge in centers.

As knowledge surpasses capital, labor, and raw materials as the dominant economic resource, technologies are also starting to reflect this shift. Technologies are rapidly shifting from centralized hierarchies to distributed networks. Nowadays knowledge does not reside in a super-mind, super-book, or super-database, but in a complex relational pattern of networks brought forth to coordinate human action.

Practical example of disruption

In the practical world, the popularization of personal computers illustrates how knowledge contributes to the ongoing technology innovation. The original centralized concept (one computer, many persons) is a knowledge-defying idea of the prehistory of computing, and its inadequacies and failures have become clearly apparent. The era of personal computing brought powerful computers "on every desk" (one person, one computer). This short transitional period was necessary for getting used to the new computing environment, but was inadequate from the vantage point of producing knowledge. Adequate knowledge creation and management come mainly from networking and distributed computing (one person, many computers). Each person's computer must form an access point to the entire computing landscape or ecology through the Internet of other computers, databases, and mainframes, as well as production, distribution, and retailing facilities, and the like. For the first time, technology empowers individuals rather than external hierarchies. It transfers influence and power where it optimally belongs: at the loci of the useful knowledge. Even though hierarchies and bureaucracies do not innovate, free and empowered individuals do; knowledge, innovation, spontaneity, and self-reliance are becoming increasingly valued and promoted.[30]

Innovation

Innovation is often also viewed as the application of better solutions that meet new requirements, unarticulated needs, or existing market needs.[1] This is accomplished through more-
effective products, processes, services, technologies, or business models that are readily available
to markets, governments and society. The term "innovation" can be defined as something original and more effective and, as a consequence, new, that "breaks into" the market or society.[2] It is related to, but not the same as, invention,[3] as innovation is more apt to involve the practical implementation of an invention (i.e. new/improved ability) to make a meaningful impact in the market or society,[4] and not all innovations require an invention. Innovation is often manifested via the engineering process, when the problem being solved is of a technical or scientific nature. The opposite of innovation is exnovation.

While a novel device is often described as an innovation, in economics, management science, and other fields of practice and analysis, innovation is generally considered to be the result of a process that brings together various novel ideas in a way that they affect society. In industrial economics, innovations are created and found empirically

from services to meet the
growing consumer demand.[5][6][7]

Definition

A 2013 survey of literature on innovation found over 40 definitions. In an industrial survey of how the software industry defined innovation, the following definition given by Crossan and Apaydin was considered to be the most complete, which builds on the Organisation for Economic Co-operation and Development (OECD) manual's definition:[8]

Innovation is: production or adoption, assimilation, and exploitation of a value-added novelty in economic and social spheres; renewal and enlargement of products, services, and markets; development of new methods of production; and establishment of new management systems. It is both a process and an outcome.

Two main dimensions of innovation were degree of novelty (patent) (i.e. whether an innovation is new to the firm, new to the market, new to the industry, or new to the world) and type of innovation (i.e. whether it is process or product-service system innovation).[8]

Inter-disciplinary views

Business and economics

In business and in economics, innovation can become a catalyst for growth. With rapid advancements in transportation and communications over the past few decades, the old-world concepts of factor endowments and comparative advantage which focused on an area's unique inputs are outmoded for today's global economy. Economist Joseph Schumpeter(1883-1950), who contributed greatly to the study of innovation economics, argued that industries must incessantly revolutionize the economic structure from within, that is innovate with better or more effective processes and products, as well as market distribution, such as the connection from the craft shop to factory. He famously asserted that "creative destruction is the essential fact about capitalism".[9] Entrepreneurs continuously look for better ways to satisfy their consumer base with improved quality, durability, service, and price which come to fruition in innovation with advanced technologies and organizational strategies.[10][*need quotation to verify*]

A prime example of innovation involved the explosive boom of Silicon Valley startups out of the Stanford Industrial Park. In 1957, dissatisfied employees of Shockley Semiconductor, the company of Nobel laureate and co-inventor of the transistor William Shockley, left to form an independent firm, Fairchild Semiconductor. After several years, Fairchild developed into a formidable presence in the sector. Eventually, these founders left to start their own companies based on their own, unique, latest ideas, and then leading employees started their own firms. Over the next 20 years, this snowball process launched the momentous startup-company explosion of information-technology firms. Essentially, Silicon Valley began as 65 new enterprises born out of Shockley's eight former employees.[11] Since then, hubs of innovation have sprung up globally with similar metonyms, including Silicon Alleyencompassing New York City.

Another example involves business incubators - a phenomenon nurtured by governments around the world, close to knowledge clusters (mostly research-based) like universities or other Government Excellence Centres - which aim primarily to channel generated knowledge to applied innovation outcomes in order to stimulate regional or national economic growth.[12]

Organizations

In the organizational context, innovation may be linked to positive changes
in efficiency, productivity, quality, competitiveness, and market share. However, recent research findings highlight the complementary role of organizational culture in enabling organizations to translate innovative activity into tangible performance improvements.[13] Organizations can also improve profits and performance by providing work groups opportunities and resources to innovate, in addition to employee's core job tasks.[14] Peter Drucker wrote:

Innovation is the specific function of entrepreneurship, whether in an existing business, a public service institution, or a new venture started by a lone individual in the family kitchen. It is the means by which the entrepreneur either creates new wealth-producing resources or endows existing resources with enhanced potential for creating wealth. –Drucker[15]

According to Clayton Christensen, disruptive innovation is the key to future success in business.[16] The organisation requires a proper structure in order to retain competitive advantage. It is necessary to create and nurture an environment of innovation. Executives and managers need to break away from traditional ways of thinking and use change to their advantage. It is a time of risk but even greater opportunity.[17] The world of work is changing with the increase in the use of technology and both companies and businesses are becoming increasingly competitive. Companies will have to downsize and re-engineer their operations to remain competitive. This will affect employment as businesses will be forced to reduce the number of people employed while accomplishing the same amount of work if not more.[18]

While disruptive innovation will typically "attack a traditional business model with a lower-cost solution and overtake incumbent firms quickly,"[19] foundational innovation is slower, and typically has the potential to create new foundations for global technology systems over the longer term. Foundational innovation tends to transform business operating modelsas entirely new business models emerge over many years, with gradual and steady adoption of the innovation leading to waves of technological and institutional change that gain momentum more slowly.[19] The advent of the packet-switched communication protocol TCP/IP—originally introduced in 1972 to support a single use case for United

States Department of Defense electronic communication (email), and which gained widespread adoption only in the mid-1990s with the advent of the World Wide Web—is a foundational technology.[19]

All organizations can innovate, including for example hospitals, universities, and local governments.[20] For instance, former Mayor Martin O'Malley pushed the City of Baltimore to use CitiStat, a performance-measurement data and management system that allows city officials to maintain statistics on crime trends to condition of potholes. This system aids in better evaluation of policies and procedures with accountability and efficiency in terms of time and money. In its first year, CitiStat saved the city $13.2 million.[21] Even mass transitsystems have innovated with hybrid bus fleets to real-time tracking at bus stands. In addition, the growing use of mobile data terminals in vehicles, that serves as communication hubs between vehicles and a control center, automatically send data on location, passenger counts, engine performance, mileage and other information. This tool helps to deliver and manage transportation systems.[22]

Still other innovative strategies include hospitals digitizing medical information in electronic medical records. For example, the U.S. Department of Housing and Urban

Development's HOPE VI initiatives turned severely distressed public housing in urban areas into revitalized, mixed-income environments; the Harlem Children's Zone used a community-based approach to educate local area children; and the Environmental Protection Agency's brownfield grants facilitates turning over brownfields for environmental protection, green spaces, community and commercial development.

Sources

There are several sources of innovation. It can occur as a result of a focus effort by a range of different agents, by chance, or as a result of a major system failure.

According to Peter F. Drucker, the general sources of innovations are different changes in industry structure, in market structure, in local and global demographics, in human perception, mood and meaning, in the amount of already available scientific knowledge, etc.[15]

Original model of three phases of the process of Technological Change

In the simplest linear model of innovation the traditionally recognized source is *manufacturer innovation*. This is where an agent (person or business) innovates in order to sell the innovation. Specifically, R&D measurement is the commonly used input for innovation, in particular in the business sector, named Business Expenditure on R&D (BERD) that grew over the years on the expenses of the declining R&D invested by the public sector.[23]

Another source of innovation, only now becoming widely recognized, is *end-user innovation*. This is where an agent (person or company) develops an innovation for their own (personal or in-house) use because existing products do not meet their needs. MIT economist Eric von Hippel has identified end-user innovation as, by far, the most important and critical in his classic book on the subject, *The Sources of Innovation*.[24]

The robotics engineer Joseph F. Engelberger asserts that innovations require only three things:

1. A recognized need,
2. Competent people with relevant technology, and
3. Financial support.[25]

However, innovation processes usually involve: identifying customer needs, macro and mess trends, developing competences, and finding financial support.

The Kline chain-linked model of innovation [26] places emphasis on potential market needs as drivers of the innovation process, and describes the complex and often iterative feedback loops between marketing, design, manufacturing, and R&D.

Innovation by businesses is achieved in many ways, with much attention now given to formal research and development (R&D) for "breakthrough innovations". R&D help spur on patents and other scientific innovations that leads to productive growth in such areas as industry, medicine, engineering, and government.[27] Yet, innovations can be developed by less formal on-the-job modifications of practice, through exchange and combination of professional experience and by many other routes. Investigation of relationship between the concepts of innovation and technology transfer revealed overlap.[28] The more radical and revolutionary innovations tend to emerge from R&D, while more incremental innovations may emerge from practice – but there are many exceptions to each of these trends.

Information technology and changing business processes and management style can produce a work climate favorable to innovation.[29] For example, the software tool company Atlassian conducts quarterly "ShipIt Days" in which employees may work on anything related to the company's products.[30] Google employees work on self-directed projects for 20% of their time (known as Innovation Time Off). Both companies cite these bottom-up processes as major sources for new products and features.

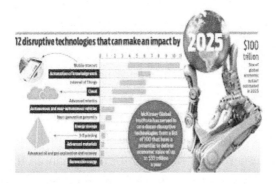

An important innovation factor includes customers buying products or using services. As a result, firms may incorporate users in focus groups (user centred approach), work closely with so called lead users (lead user approach) or users might adapt their products themselves. The lead user method focuses on idea generation based on leading users to develop breakthrough innovations. U-STIR, a project to innovate Europe's surface transportation system, employs such workshops.[31] Regarding this user innovation, a great deal of innovation is done by those actually implementing and using technologies and products as part of their normal activities. Sometimes user-innovators may become entrepreneurs, selling their product, they may choose to trade their innovation in exchange for other innovations, or they may be adopted by their suppliers. Nowadays, they may also choose to freely reveal their innovations, using methods like open source. In such networks of innovation the users or communities of users can further develop technologies and reinvent their social meaning.[32][33]

One technique for innovating a solution to an identified problem is to actually attempt an experiment with many possible solutions.[34] This technique was famously used by Thomas Edison's laboratory to find a version of the incandescent light bulb economically viable for home use, which involved searching through thousands of possible filament designs before settling on carbonized bamboo.

This technique is sometimes used in pharmaceutical drug discovery. Thousands of chemical compounds are subjected to high-throughput screening to see if they have any activity against a target molecule which has been identified as biologically significant to a disease. Promising compounds can then be studied; modified to improve efficacy, reduce side effects, and reduce cost of manufacture; and if successful turned into treatments.

The related technique of A/B testing is often used to help optimize the design of web sites and mobile apps. This is used by major sites such as amazon.com, Facebook, Google, and Netflix.[35] Procter & Gamble uses computer-simulated products and onlinen user panels to conduct larger numbers of experiments to guide the design, packaging, and shelf placement of consumer products.[36] Capital One uses this technique to drive credit card marketing offers.[35]

Goals and failures

Programs of organizational innovation are typically tightly linked to organizational goals and objectives, to the business plan, and to market competitive positioning. One driver for innovation programs in corporations is to achieve growth objectives. As Davila et al. (2006) notes, "Companies cannot grow through cost reduction and reengineering alone... Innovation is the key element in providing aggressive top-line growth, and for increasing bottom-line results".[37]

One survey across a large number of manufacturing and services organizations found, ranked in decreasing order of popularity, that systematic programs of organizational

innovation are most frequently driven by:
improved quality, creation of new markets, extension of
the product range, reduced labor costs,
improved production processes, reduced materials,
reduced environmental damage, replacement
of products/services, reduced energy consumption,
conformance to regulations.[37]

These goals vary between improvements to products,
processes and services and dispel a popular myth that
innovation deals mainly with new product development.
Most of the goals could apply to any organization be it a
manufacturing facility, marketing firm, hospital or local
government. Whether innovation goals are successfully
achieved or otherwise depends greatly on the
environment prevailing in the firm.[38]

Conversely, failure can develop in programs of
innovations. The causes of failure have been widely
researched and can vary considerably. Some causes will
be external to the organization and outside its influence of
control. Others will be internal and ultimately within the
control of the organization. Internal causes of failure can
be divided into causes associated with the cultural
infrastructure and causes associated with the innovation
process itself. Common causes of failure within the
innovation process in most organizations can be distilled
into five types: poor goal definition, poor alignment of
actions to goals, poor participation in teams, poor

monitoring of results, poor communication and access to information.[39]

Diffusion

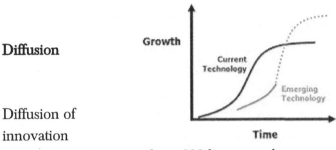

Diffusion of innovation research was first started in 1903 by seminal researcher Gabriel Tarde, who first plotted the S-shaped diffusion curve. Tarde defined the innovation-decision process as a series of steps that includes:[40]

1. First knowledge
2. Forming an attitude
3. A decision to adopt or reject
4. Implementation and use
5. Confirmation of the decision

Once innovation occurs, innovations may be spread from the innovator to other individuals and groups. This process has been proposed that the life cycle of innovations can be described using the 's-curve' or diffusion curve. The s-curve maps growth of revenue or productivity against time. In the early stage of a particular innovation, growth is relatively slow as the new product establishes itself. At some point customers begin to demand and the product growth increases more rapidly. New incremental innovations or changes to the product

299

allow growth to continue. Towards the end of its lifecycle, growth slows and may even begin to decline. In the later stages, no amount of new investment in that product will yield a normal rate of return

The s-curve derives from an assumption that new products are likely to have "product life" – i.e., a start-up phase, a rapid increase in revenue and eventual decline. In fact the great majority of innovations never get off the bottom of the curve, and never produce normal returns.

Innovative companies will typically be working on new innovations that will eventually replace older ones. Successive s-curves will come along to replace older ones and continue to drive growth upwards. In the figure above the first curve shows a current technology. The second shows an emerging technology that currently yields lower growth but will eventually overtake current technology and lead to even greater levels of growth. The length of life will depend on many factors.[41]

Measures

Measuring innovation is inherently difficult as it implies commensurability so that comparisons can be made in quantitative terms. Innovation, however, is by definition novelty. Comparisons are thus often meaningless across products or service.[42] Nevertheless, Edison et al.[8] in their review of literature on innovation management found 232 innovation metrics. They categorized these measures along five dimensions i.e. inputs to the innovation process, output from the innovation process, effect of the innovation output, measures to access the activities in an innovation process and availability of factors that facilitate such a process.[8]

There are two different types of measures for innovation: the organizational level and the political level.

Organizational level

The measure of innovation at the organizational level relates to individuals, team-level assessments, and private companies from the smallest to the largest company. Measure of innovation for organizations can be conducted by surveys, workshops, consultants, or internal benchmarking. There is today no established general way to measure organizational innovation. Corporate measurements are generally structured around balanced scorecards which cover several aspects of innovation such as business measures related to finances, innovation process efficiency, employees' contribution and motivation, as well benefits for customers. Measured values will vary widely between businesses, covering for example new product revenue, spending in R&D, time to market, customer and employee perception & satisfaction, number of patents, additional sales resulting from past innovations.[43]

Political level

For the political level, measures of innovation are more focused on a country or region competitive advantage through innovation. In this context, organizational capabilities can be evaluated through various evaluation frameworks, such as those of the European Foundation for Quality Management. The OECD Oslo Manual (1995) suggests standard guidelines on measuring technological product and process innovation. Some people consider the Oslo Manual complementary to the Frascati Manual from 1963. The new Oslo manual from 2005 takes a wider perspective to innovation, and includes marketing and organizational innovation. These standards are used for example in the European Community Innovation Surveys.[44]

Other ways of measuring innovation have traditionally been expenditure, for example, investment in R&D (Research and Development) as percentage of GNP (Gross National Product). Whether this is a good measurement of innovation has been widely discussed and the Oslo Manual has incorporated some of the critique against earlier methods of measuring. The traditional methods of measuring still inform many policy decisions. The EU Lisbon Strategy has set as a goal that their average expenditure on R&D should be 3% of GDP.[45]

Indicators

Many scholars claim that there is a great bias towards the "science and technology mode" (S&T-mode or STI-mode), while the "learning by doing, using and interacting mode" (DUI-mode) is ignored and measurements and research about it rarely done. For example, an institution may be high tech with the latest equipment, but lacks crucial doing, using and interacting tasks important for innovation.

A common industry view (unsupported by empirical evidence) is that comparative cost-effectiveness research is a form of price control which reduces returns to industry, and thus limits R&D expenditure, stifles future innovation and compromises new products access to markets.[46] Some academics claim cost-effectiveness

303

research is a valuable value-based measure of innovation which accords "truly significant" therapeutic advances (i.e. providing "health gain") higher prices than free market mechanisms.[47] Such pricing has been viewed as a means of indicating to industry the type of innovation that should be rewarded from the public purse.[48]

An Australian academic developed the case that national comparative cost-effectiveness analysis systems should be viewed as measuring "health innovation" as an evidence-based policy concept for valuing innovation distinct from valuing through competitive markets, a method which requires strong anti-trust laws to be effective, on the basis that both methods of assessing pharmaceutical innovations are mentioned in annex 2C.1 of the Australia-United States Free Trade Agreement.[49][year needed][50][51]

Indices

Several indices attempt to measure innovation and rank entities based on these measures, such as:

- The Bloomberg Innovation Index
- The "Bogota Manual"[52] similar to the Oslo Manual, is focused on Latin America and the Caribbean countries.
- The "Creative Class" developed by Richard Florida
- The EIU Innovation Ranking

- The Global Competitiveness Report
- The Global Innovation Index (GII), by INSEAD[53]
- The Information Technology and Innovation Foundation (ITIF) Index
- Innovation 360 - From the World Bank. Aggregates innovation indicators (and more) from a number of different public sources
- The Innovation Capacity Index (ICI) published by a large number of international professors working in a collaborative fashion. The top scorers of ICI 2009–2010 were: 1. Sweden 82.2; 2. Finland 77.8; and 3. United States 77.5.[54]
- The Innovation Index, developed by the Indiana Business Research Center, to measure innovation capacity at the county or regional level in the United States.[55]
- The Innovation Union Scoreboard
- The innovationsindikator for Germany, developed by the Federation of German Industries (Bundesverband der Deutschen Industrie) in 2005[56]
- The INSEAD Innovation Efficacy Index[57]
- The International Innovation Index, produced jointly by The Boston Consulting Group, the National Association of Manufacturers and its nonpartisan research affiliate The Manufacturing Institute, is a worldwide index measuring the level of innovation in a country. NAM describes

it as the "largest and most comprehensive global index of its kind".[citation needed]

- The Management Innovation Index - Model for Managing Intangibility of Organizational Creativity: Management Innovation Index[58]
- The NYCEDC Innovation Index, by the New York City Economic Development Corporation, tracks New York City's "transformation into a center for high-tech innovation. It measures innovation in the City's growing science and technology industries and is designed to capture the effect of innovation on the City's economy."[59]
- The Oslo Manual is focused on North America, Europe, and other rich economies.
- The State Technology and Science Index, developed by the Milken Institute, is a U.S.-wide benchmark to measure the science and technology capabilities that furnish high paying jobs based around key components.[60]
- The World Competitiveness Scoreboard[61]

Rankings

Many research studies try to rank countries based on measures of innovation. Common areas of focus include: high-
tech companies, manufacturing, patents, post-secondary education, research and development, and research

personnel. The left ranking of the top 10 countries below is based on the 2016 Bloomberg Innovation Index.[62] However, studies may vary widely; for example the Global Innovation Index 2016 ranks Switzerland as number one wherein countries like South Korea and Japan do not even make the top ten.[63]

Future

In 2005 Jonathan Huebner, a physicist working at the Pentagon's Naval Air Warfare Center, argued on the basis of both U.S. patents and world technological breakthroughs, per capita, that the rate of human technological innovation peaked in 1873 and has been slowing ever since.[64][65] In his article, he asked "Will the level of technology reach a maximum and then decline as in the Dark Ages?"[64] In later comments to *New Scientist* magazine, Huebner clarified that while he believed that we will reach a rate of innovation in 2024 equivalent to that of the Dark Ages, he was not predicting the reoccurrence of the Dark Ages themselves.[66]

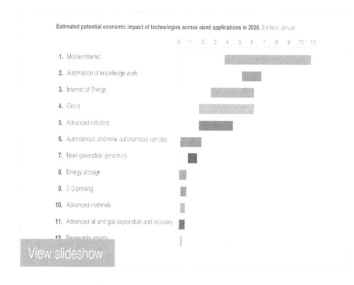

Estimated potential economic impact of technologies across sized applications in 2025, $ trillion, annual

1. Mobile Internet
2. Automation of knowledge work
3. Internet of Things
4. Cloud
5. Advanced robotics
6. Autonomous and near-autonomous vehicles
7. Next-generation genomics
8. Energy storage
9. 3-D printing
10. Advanced materials
11. Advanced oil and gas exploration and recovery
12. Renewable energy

View slideshow

John Smart criticized the claim and asserted that technological singularity researcher Ray Kurzweil and others showed a "clear trend of acceleration, not deceleration" when it came to innovations.[67] The foundation replied to Huebner the journal his article was published in, citing Second Life and eHarmony as proof of accelerating innovation; to which Huebner replied.[68] However, Huebner's findings were confirmed in 2010 with U.S. Patent Office data.[69] and in a 2012 paper.[70]

Innovation and international development

308

The theme of innovation as a tool to disrupting patterns of poverty has gained momentum since the mid-2000s among major international development actors such as DFID,[71]Gates Foundation's use of the Grand Challenge funding model,[72] and USAID's Global Development Lab.[73] Networks have been established to support innovation in development, such as D-Lab at MIT.[74] Investment funds have been established to identify and catalyze innovations in developing countries, such as DFID's Global Innovation Fund,[75] Human Development Innovation Fund,[76] and (in partnership with USAID) the Global Development Innovation Ventures.[77]

Government policies

Given the noticeable effects on efficiency, quality of life, and productive growth, innovation is a key factor in society and economy. Consequently, policymakers have long worked to develop environments that will foster innovation and its resulting positive benefits, from funding Research and Development to supporting regulatory change, funding the development of innovation clusters, and using public purchasing and standardisation to 'pull' innovation through.

For instance, experts are advocating that the U.S. federal government launch a National Infrastructure Foundation, a nimble, collaborative strategic intervention organization that will house innovations programs from fragmented silos under one entity, inform federal officials on innovation performance metrics, strengthen industry-university partnerships, and support innovation economic development initiatives, especially to strengthen regional clusters. Because clusters are the geographic incubators of innovative products and processes, a cluster development grant program would also be targeted for implementation. By focusing on innovating in such areas as precision manufacturing, information technology, and clean energy, other areas of national concern would be tackled including government debt, carbon footprint, and oil dependence.[27] The U.S. Economic Development Administration understand this reality in their continued Regional Innovation Clusters initiative.[78] In addition, federal grants in R&D, a crucial driver of innovation and productive growth, should be expanded to levels similar to Japan, Finland, South Korea, and Switzerland in order to stay globally competitive. Also, such grants should be better procured to metropolitan areas, the essential engines of the American economy.[27]

Many countries recognize the importance of research and development as well as innovation including

Japan's Ministry of Education, Culture, Sports, Science and Technology(MEXT);[79] Germany's Federal Ministry of Education and Research;[80] and the Ministry of Science and Technology in the People's Republic of China. Furthermore, Russia's innovation programme is the Medvedev modernisation programme which aims at creating a diversified economy based on high technology and innovation. Also, the Government of Western Australia has established a number of innovation incentives for government departments. Landgate was the first Western Australian government agency to establish its Innovation Program.[81]

CHAPTER NINE

INTERNET

Internet users per 100
population members
and GDP per capita for
selected countries.

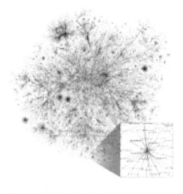

The Internet is the global
system of
interconnected computer
networks that use
the Internet protocol suite (TCP/IP) to link devices
worldwide. It is a *network of networks* that consists of
private, public, academic, business, and government
networks of local to global scope, linked by a broad
array of electronic, wireless, and optical networking
technologies. The Internet carries a vast range of
information resources and services, such as the inter-
linked hypertext documents and applications of
the World Wide Web (WWW), electronic
mail, telephony, and file sharing.

The origins of the Internet date back to research
commissioned by the United States Federal

Government in the 1960s to build robust, fault-tolerant communication via computer networks.[1] The linking of commercial networks and enterprises in the early 1990s marked the beginning of the transition to the modern Internet,[2] and generated rapid growth as institutional, personal, and mobile computers were connected to the network. By the late 2000s, its services and technologies had been incorporated into virtually every aspect of everyday life.

Most traditional communications media, including telephony, radio, television, paper mail and newspapers are being reshaped, redefined, or even bypassed by the Internet, giving birth to new services such as email, Internet telephony, Internet television, online music, digital newspapers, and video streaming websites.

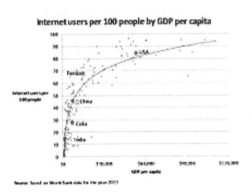

Internet users per 100 people by GDP per capita

Newspaper, book, and other print publishing are adapting to websitetechn ology, or are reshaped into blogging, w eb feeds and online news aggregators. The Internet has enabled and accelerated new forms of personal interactions through instant messaging, Internet forums, and social networking. Online shopping has grown exponentially both for major retailers and small businesses and entrepreneurs, as it enables firms to extend their "brick and mortar" presence to serve a larger market or even sell goods and services entirely online. Business-to-business and financial services on the Internet affect supply chains across entire industries.

The Internet has no centralized governance in either technological implementation or policies for access and usage; each constituent network sets its own policies.[3] Only the overreaching definitions of the two principal name spaces in the Internet, the Internet Protocol address (IP address) space and the Domain Name System (DNS), are directed by a maintainer organization, the Internet Corporation for Assigned Names and Numbers (ICANN). The technical underpinning and standardization of the core protocols is an activity of the Internet Engineering Task Force (IETF), a non-profit organization of loosely affiliated international participants that anyone may associate with by contributing technical expertise.[4]

Terminology

The Internet Messenger by Buky Schwartz, located in Holon, Israel

When the term *Internet* is used to refer to the specific global system of interconnected Internet Protocol (IP) networks, the word is a proper noun[5] that should be written with an initial capital letter. In common use and the media, it is often erroneously not capitalized, viz. *the internet.* Some guides specify that the word should be capitalized when used as a noun, but not capitalized when used as an adjective.[6] The Internet is also often referred to as *the Net,* as a short form of *network.* Historically, as early as 1849, the word *internetted* was used uncapitalized as an adjective, meaning *interconnected* or *interwoven.*[7] The designers of early computer networks used *internet* both as a noun and as a verb in shorthand form of internetwork or internetworking, meaning interconnecting computer networks.[8]

The terms *Internet* and *World Wide Web* are often used interchangeably in everyday speech; it is common to speak of "*going on the Internet*" when using a web browser to view web pages. However, the World Wide Web or *the Web* is only one of a large number of Internet services. The Web is a collection of interconnected documents (web pages) and other web resources, linked by hyperlinks and URLs.[9] As another point of comparison, Hypertext Transfer Protocol, or HTTP, is the language used on the Web for information transfer, yet it is just one of many languages or protocols that can be used for communication on the Internet.[10] The term *Interweb* is a portmanteau of *Internet* and *World Wide Web* typically used sarcastically to parody a technically unsavvy user.

History

Research into packet switching by Paul Baran and Donald Davies emerged in the early to mid-1960s,[11] and packet switched networks such as the NPL network,[12] ARPANET, Tymnet, the Merit Network,[13] Telenet, and CYCLADES,[14][15] were developed in the late 1960s and 1970s using a variety of protocols.[16] The ARPANET project led to the development of protocols for internetworking, by which multiple separate networks could be joined into a single network of networks.[17] ARPANET development began with two network nodes which were interconnected between the Network Measurement Center at

the University of California, Los Angeles (UCLA) Henry
Samueli School of Engineering and Applied
Science directed by Leonard Kleinrock, and the NLS
system at SRI International (SRI) by Douglas
Engelbart in Menlo Park, California, on 29 October
1969.[18] The third site was the Culler-Fried Interactive
Mathematics Center at the University of California, Santa
Barbara, followed by the University of Utah Graphics
Department. In an early sign of future growth, fifteen
sites were connected to the young ARPANET by the
end of 1971.[19][20] These early years were documented in
the 1972 film *Computer Networks: The Heralds of
Resource Sharing.*

Early international collaborations on the ARPANET
were rare. European developers were concerned with
developing the X.25 networks.[21] Notable exceptions
were the Norwegian Seismic Array (NORSAR) in June
1973, followed in 1973 by Sweden with satellite links to
the Tanum Earth Station and Peter T. Kirstein's research

NSFNET T3 Network 1992

group in the United
Kingdom, initially
at the Institute of
Computer
Science, University
of London and
later at University
College

317

London.[22][23][24] In December 1974, RFC
675 (*Specification of Internet Transmission Control Program*), by Vinton Cerf, Yogen Dalal, and Carl Sunshine, used the term *internet* as a shorthand for *internetworking* and later RFCs repeated this use.[25] Access to the ARPANET was expanded in 1981 when the National Science Foundation (NSF) funded the Computer Science Network (CSNET). In 1982, the Internet Protocol Suite (TCP/IP) was standardized, which permitted worldwide proliferation of interconnected networks.

T3 NSFNET Backbone, c. 1992.

TCP/IP network access expanded again in 1986 when the National Science Foundation Network (NSFNet) provided access to supercomputer sites in the United States for researchers, first at speeds of 56 kbit/s and later at 1.5 Mbit/s and 45 Mbit/s.[26] Commercial Internet service providers (ISPs) emerged in the late 1980s and early 1990s. The ARPANET was decommissioned in 1990. By 1995, the Internet was fully commercialized in the U.S. when the NSFNet was decommissioned, removing the last restrictions on use of the Internet to carry commercial traffic.[27] The Internet rapidly expanded in Europe and Australia in the mid to late 1980s [28][29] and to Asia in the late 1980s and early

1990s.[30] The beginning of
dedicated transatlantic communication between the
NSFNET and networks in Europe was established with a
low-speed satellite relay between Princeton
University and Stockholm, Sweden in December
1988.[31] Although other network protocols such
as UUCP had global reach well before this time, this
marked the beginning of the Internet as an
intercontinental network.

Public commercial use of the Internet began in mid-1989
with the connection of MCI Mail and Compuserve's
email capabilities to the 500,000 users of the
Internet.[32] Just months later on 1 January
1990, PSInet launched an alternate Internet backbone for
commercial use; one of the networks that would grow
into the commercial Internet we know today. In March
1990, the first high-speed T1 (1.5 Mbit/s) link between
the NSFNET and Europe was installed between Cornell
University and CERN, allowing much more robust
communications than were capable with satellites.[33] Six
months later Tim Berners-Lee would begin
writing WorldWideWeb, the first web browser after two
years of lobbying CERN management. By Christmas
1990, Berners-Lee had built all the tools necessary for a
working Web: the HyperText Transfer Protocol (HTTP)
0.9,[34] the HyperText Markup Language (HTML), the

first Web browser (which was also a HTML editor and could access Usenet newsgroups and FTP files), the first HTTP server software(later known as CERN httpd), the first web server,[35] and the first Web pages that described the project itself. In 1991 the Commercial Internet eXchange was founded, allowing PSInet to communicate with the other commercial networks CERFnet and Alternet. Since 1995 the Internet has tremendously impacted culture and commerce, including the rise of near instant communication by email, instant messaging, telephony (Voice over Internet Protocol or VoIP), two-way interactive video calls, and the World Wide Web[36] with its discussion forums, blogs, social networking, and online shopping sites. Increasing amounts of data are transmitted at higher and higher speeds over fiber optic networks operating at 1-Gbit/s, 10-Gbit/s, or more.

The Internet continues to grow, driven by ever greater amounts of online information and knowledge, commerce, entertainment and social networking.[39] During the late 1990s, it was estimated that traffic on the public Internet grew by 100 percent per year, while the mean annual growth in the number of Internet users was thought to be between 20% and 50%.[40] This growth is often attributed to the lack of central administration, which allows organic growth of the network, as well as the non-proprietary nature of the Internet protocols, which encourages vendor interoperability and prevents any one company from exerting too much control over the network.[41] As of 31 March 2011, the estimated total number of Internet users was 2.095 billion (30.2% of world population).[42] It is estimated that in 1993 the Internet carried only 1% of the information flowing through two-way telecommunication, by 2000 this figure had grown to 51%, and by 2007 more than 97% of all telecommunicated information was carried over the Internet.[43]

Governance

ICANN headquarters in the Playa Vista neighborhood of Los Angeles, California, United States.

The Internet is a global network that comprises many voluntarily interconnected autonomous networks. It operates without a central governing body. The technical underpinning and standardization of the core protocols (IPv4 and IPv6) is an activity of the Internet Engineering Task Force (IETF), a non-profit organization of loosely affiliated international participants that anyone may associate with by contributing technical expertise. To maintain interoperability, the principal name spaces of the Internet are administered by the Internet Corporation for Assigned Names and Numbers (ICANN). ICANN is governed by an international board of directors drawn from across the Internet technical, business, academic, and other non-commercial communities. ICANN coordinates the assignment of unique identifiers for use on the Internet, including domain names, Internet Protocol (IP) addresses, application port numbers in the transport protocols, and many other parameters. Globally unified name spaces are essential for maintaining the global reach of the Internet. This role of ICANN distinguishes it as perhaps the only central coordinating body for the global Internet.[44]

Regional Internet Registries (RIRs) allocate IP addresses:

- African Network Information Center (AfriNIC) for Africa
- American Registry for Internet Numbers (ARIN) for North America
- Asia-Pacific Network Information Centre (APNIC) for Asia and the Pacific region

- Latin American and Caribbean Internet Addresses Registry (LACNIC) for Latin America and the Caribbean region
- Réseaux IP Européens – Network Coordination Centre (RIPE NCC) for Europe, the Middle East, and Central Asia

The National Telecommunications and Information Administration, an agency of the United States Department of Commerce, had final approval over changes to the DNS root zoneuntil the IANA stewardship transition on 1 October 2016.[45][46][47][48] The Internet Society (ISOC) was founded in 1992 with a mission to *"assure the open development, evolution and use of the Internet for the benefit of all people throughout the world"*.[49] Its members include individuals (anyone may join) as well as corporations, organizations, governments, and universities. Among other activities ISOC provides an administrative home for a number of less formally organized groups that are involved in developing and managing the Internet, including: the Internet Engineering Task Force (IETF), Internet Architecture Board (IAB), Internet Engineering Steering Group (IESG), Internet Research Task Force (IRTF), and Internet Research Steering Group (IRSG). On 16 November 2005, the United Nations-sponsored World Summit on the Information Society in Tunis established the Internet Governance Forum (IGF) to discuss Internet-related issues.

Infrastructure

2007 map showing submarine fiberoptic telecommunication cables around the world.

The communications infrastructure of the Internet consists of its hardware components and a system of software layers that control various aspects of the architecture.

Routing and service tiers

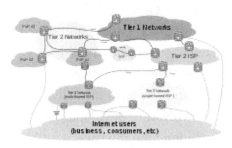

Packet routing across the Internet involves several tiers of Internet service providers.

Internet service providers establish the worldwide connectivity between individual networks at various levels of scope. End-users who only access the Internet when needed to perform a function or obtain information, represent the bottom of the routing hierarchy. At the top of the routing hierarchy are the tier 1 networks, large telecommunication companies that exchange traffic directly with each other via peeringagreements. Tier 2 and lower level networks buy Internet transit from other providers to reach at least some parties on the global Internet, though they may also engage in peering. An ISP may use a single upstream provider for connectivity, or implement multihoming to achieve redundancy and load balancing. Internet exchange points are major traffic exchanges with physical connections to multiple ISPs. Large organizations, such as academic institutions, large enterprises, and governments, may perform the same function as ISPs, engaging in peering and purchasing transit on behalf of their internal networks. Research networks tend to interconnect with large subnetworks such as GEANT, GLORIAD, Internet2, and the UK's national research and education network, JANET. Both the Internet IP routing structure and hypertext links of the World Wide Web are examples of scale-free networks.[50] Computers and routers use routing tables in their operating system to direct IP packets to the next-hop router or destination. Routing tables are maintained by manual configuration or automatically by routing protocols. End-nodes typically use a default route that points toward an ISP providing transit, while ISP routers use the Border Gateway Protocol to establish the most efficient routing across the complex connections of the global Internet.

Access

Common methods of Internet access by users include dial-up with a computer modem via telephone circuits, broadband over coaxial cable, fiber optics or copper wires, Wi-Fi, satellite and cellular telephone technology (3G, 4G). The Internet may often be accessed from computers in libraries and Internet cafes. Internet access points exist in many public places such as airport halls and coffee shops. Various terms are used, such as *public Internet kiosk, public access terminal*, and *Web payphone*. Many hotels also have public terminals, though these are usually fee-based. These terminals are widely accessed for various usages, such as ticket booking, bank deposit, or online payment. Wi-Fi provides wireless access to the Internet via local computer networks. Hotspots providing such access include Wi-Fi cafes, where users need to bring their own wireless devices such as a laptop or PDA. These services may be free to all, free to customers only, or fee-based.

Grassroots efforts have led to wireless community networks. Commercial Wi-Fi services covering large city areas are in place in New York, London, Vienna, Toronto, SanFrancisco, Philadelphia, Chicago and Pittsburgh. The Internet can then be accessed from such places as a park bench.[51]

Apart from Wi-Fi, there have been experiments with proprietary mobile wireless networks like Ricochet, various high-speed data services over cellular phone networks, and fixed wireless services. High-end mobile phones such as smartphones in general come with Internet access through the phone network. Web browsers such as Opera are available on these advanced handsets, which can also run a wide variety of other Internet software. More mobile phones have Internet access than PCs, though this is not as widely used.[52] An Internet access provider and protocol matrix differentiates the methods used to get online.

Protocols

While the hardware components in the Internet infrastructure can often be used to support other software systems, it is the design and the standardization process of the software that characterizes the Internet and provides the foundation for its scalability and success. The responsibility for the architectural design of the Internet software systems has been assumed by the Internet Engineering Task Force (IETF).[53] The IETF conducts standard-setting work groups, open to any individual, about the various aspects of Internet architecture. Resulting contributions and standards are published as *Request for Comments* (RFC) documents on the IETF web site. The principal methods of networking that enable the Internet are contained in specially designated RFCs that constitute the Internet Standards. Other less rigorous documents are simply informative, experimental, or historical, or document the best current practices (BCP) when implementing Internet technologies.

The Internet standards describe a framework known as the Internet protocol suite. This is a model architecture that divides methods into a layered system of protocols, originally documented in RFC 1122 and RFC 1123. The layers correspond to the environment or scope in which their services operate. At the top is the application layer, space for the application-specific networking methods used in software applications.

For example, a web browser program uses the client-server application model and a specific protocol of interaction between servers and clients, while many file-sharing systems use a peer-to-peer paradigm. Below this top layer, the transport layer connects applications on different hosts with a logical channel through the network with appropriate data exchange methods.

Underlying these layers are the networking technologies that interconnect networks at their borders and exchange traffic across them. The Internet layer enables computers to identify and locate each other via Internet Protocol (IP) addresses, and routes their traffic via intermediate (transit) networks. Last, at the bottom of the architecture is the link layer, which provides logical connectivity between hosts on the same network link, such as a local area network (LAN) or a dial-up connection. The model, also known as TCP/IP, is designed to be independent of the underlying hardware used for the physical connections, which the model does not concern itself with in any detail. Other models have been developed, such as the OSI model, that attempt to be comprehensive in every aspect of communications. While many similarities exist between the models, they are not compatible in the details of description or implementation. Yet, TCP/IP protocols are usually included in the discussion of OSI networking.

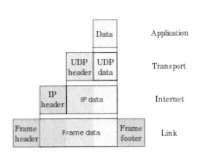

As user data is processed through the protocol stack, each abstraction layer adds encapsulation information at the sending host. Data is transmitted *over the wire* at the link level between hosts and routers. Encapsulation is removed by the receiving host. Intermediate relays update link encapsulation at each hop, and inspect the IP layer for routing purposes.

The most prominent component of the Internet model is the Internet Protocol (IP), which provides addressing systems, including IP addresses, for computers on the network. IP enables internetworking and, in essence, establishes the Internet itself. Internet Protocol Version 4 (IPv4) is the initial version used on the first generation of the Internet and is still in dominant use. It was designed to address up to ~4.3 billion (10^9) hosts. However, the explosive growth of the Internet has led to IPv4 address exhaustion, which entered its final stage in 2011,[54] when the global address allocation pool was exhausted. A new protocol version, IPv6, was developed in the mid-1990s, which provides vastly larger addressing capabilities and more efficient routing of Internet traffic. IPv6 is currently in growing deployment around the world, since Internet address registries (RIRs) began to urge all resource managers to plan rapid adoption and conversion.[55]

IPv6 is not directly interoperable by design with IPv4. In essence, it establishes a parallel version of the Internet not directly accessible with IPv4 software. Thus, translation facilities must exist for internetworking or nodes must have duplicate networking software for both networks. Essentially all modern computer operating systems support both versions of the Internet Protocol. Network infrastructure, however, has been lagging in this development. Aside from the complex array of physical connections that make up its infrastructure, the Internet is facilitated by bi- or multi-lateral commercial contracts, e.g., peering agreements, and by technical specifications or protocols that describe the exchange of data over the network. Indeed, the Internet is defined by its interconnections and routing policies.

Services

The Internet carries many network services, most prominently mobile apps such as social media apps, the World Wide Web, electronic mail, multiplayer online games, Internet telephony, and file sharing services.

World Wide Web

This NeXT Computer was used by Tim Berners-Lee at CERN and became the world's first Web server.

Many people use the terms *Internet* and *World Wide Web*, or just the *Web*, interchangeably, but the two terms are not synonymous. The World Wide Web is the primary application program that billions of people use on the Internet, and it has changed their lives immeasurably.[56][57] However, the Internet provides many other services. The Web is a global set of documents, images and other resources, logically interrelated by hyperlinks and referenced with Uniform Resource Identifiers (URIs). URIs symbolically identify services, servers, and other databases, and the documents and resources that they can provide. Hypertext Transfer Protocol (HTTP) is the main access protocol of the World Wide Web. Web services also use HTTP to allow software systems to communicate in order to share and exchange business logic and data.

World Wide Web browser software, such as Microsoft's Internet Explorer/Edge, Mozilla Firefox, Opera, Apple's Safari, and Google Chrome, lets users navigate from one web page to another via hyperlinks embedded in the documents. These documents may also contain any combination of computer data, including graphics, sounds, text, video, multimedia and interactive content that runs while the user is interacting with the page. Client-side software can include

animations, games, office applications and scientific demonstrations. Through keyword-driven Internet research using search
engines like Yahoo!, Bing and Google, users worldwide have easy, instant access to a vast and diverse amount of online information. Compared to printed media, books, encyclopedias and traditional libraries, the World Wide Web has enabled the decentralization of information on a large scale.

The Web has also enabled individuals and organizations to publish ideas and information to a potentially large audience online at greatly reduced expense and time delay. Publishing a web page, a blog, or building a website involves little initial cost and many cost-free services are available. However, publishing and maintaining large, professional web sites with attractive, diverse and up-to-date information is still a difficult and expensive proposition. Many individuals and some companies and groups use *web logs* or blogs, which are largely used as easily updatable online diaries. Some commercial organizations encourage staff to communicate advice in their areas of specialization in the hope that visitors will be impressed by the expert knowledge and free information, and be attracted to the corporation as a result.

Advertising on popular web pages can be lucrative, and e-commerce, which is the sale of products and services directly via the Web, continues to grow. Online advertising is a form of marketing and advertising which uses the Internet to deliver promotional marketing messages to consumers. It includes email marketing, search engine marketing (SEM), social media marketing, many types of display advertising (including web banner advertising), and mobile advertising. In 2011, Internet advertising revenues in the United States surpassed those of cable television and nearly exceeded those of broadcast television.[58]:19 Many common online advertising practices are controversial and increasingly subject to regulation.

When the Web developed in the 1990s, a typical web page was stored in completed form on a web server, formatted in HTML, complete for transmission to a web browser in response to a request. Over time, the process of creating and serving web pages has become dynamic, creating a flexible design, layout, and content. Websites are often created using content management software with, initially, very little content. Contributors to these systems, who may be paid staff, members of an organization or the public, fill underlying databases with content using editing pages designed for that purpose while casual visitors view and read this content in HTML form. There may or may not be editorial, approval and security systems built into the process of taking newly entered content and making it available to the target visitors.

Communication

Email is an important communications service available on the Internet. The concept of sending electronic text messages between parties in a way analogous to mailing letters or memos predates the creation of the Internet. Pictures, documents, and other files are sent as email attachments. Emails can be cc-ed to multiple email addresses.

Internet telephony is another common communications service made possible by the creation of the Internet. VoIP stands for Voice-over-Internet Protocol, referring to the protocol that underlies all Internet communication. The idea began in the early 1990s with walkie-talkie-like voice applications for personal computers. In recent years many VoIP systems have become as easy to use and as convenient as a normal telephone. The benefit is that, as the Internet carries the voice traffic, VoIP can be free or cost much less than a traditional telephone call, especially over long distances and especially for those with always-on Internet connections such as cable or ADSL. VoIP is maturing into a competitive alternative to traditional telephone service. Interoperability between different providers has improved and the ability to call or receive a call from a traditional telephone is available. Simple, inexpensive VoIP network adapters are available that eliminate the need for a personal computer.

Voice quality can still vary from call to call, but is often equal to and can even exceed that of traditional calls. Remaining problems for VoIP include emergency telephone numberdialing and reliability. Currently, a few VoIP providers provide an emergency service, but it is not universally available. Older traditional phones with no "extra features" may be line-powered only and operate during a power failure; VoIP can never do so without a backup power source for the phone equipment and the Internet access devices. VoIP has also become increasingly popular for gaming applications, as a form of communication between players. Popular VoIP clients for gaming include Ventrilo and Teamspeak. Modern video game consoles also offer VoIP chat features.

Data Transfer

File sharing is an example of transferring large amounts of data across the Internet. A computer file can be emailed to customers, colleagues and friends as an attachment. It can be uploaded to a website or File Transfer Protocol (FTP) server for easy download by others. It can be put into a "shared location" or onto a file server for instant use by colleagues. The load of bulk downloads to many users can be eased by the use of "mirror" servers or peer-to-peer networks. In any of these cases, access to the file may be controlled by user authentication, the transit of the file over the Internet may be obscured by encryption, and money may change hands for access to the file. The price can be paid by the remote charging of funds from, for example, a credit card whose details are also passed – usually fully encrypted – across the Internet. The origin and authenticity of the file received may be checked by digital signatures or by MD5 or other message digests. These simple features of the Internet, over a worldwide basis, are changing the production, sale, and distribution of anything that can be reduced to a computer file for transmission. This includes all manner of print publications, software products, news, music, film, video, photography, graphics and the other arts. This in turn has caused seismic shifts in each of the existing industries that previously controlled the production and distribution of these products.

Streaming media is the real-time delivery of digital media for the immediate consumption or enjoyment by end users. Many radio and television broadcasters provide Internet feeds of their live audio and video productions. They may also allow time-shift viewing or listening such as Preview, Classic Clips and Listen Again features. These providers have been joined by a range of pure Internet "broadcasters" who never had on-air licenses. This means that an Internet-connected device, such as a computer or something more specific, can be used to access on-line media in much the same way as was previously possible only with a television or radio receiver. The range of available types of content is much wider, from specialized technical webcasts to on-demand popular multimedia services. Podcasting is a variation on this theme, where – usually audio – material is downloaded and played back on a computer or shifted to a portable media player to be listened to on the move. These techniques using simple equipment allow anybody, with little censorship or licensing control, to broadcast audio-visual material worldwide.

Digital media streaming increases the demand for network bandwidth. For example, standard image quality needs 1 Mbit/s link speed for SD 480p, HD 720p quality requires 2.5 Mbit/s, and the top-of-the-line HDX quality needs 4.5 Mbit/s for 1080p.[59]

Webcams are a low-cost extension of this phenomenon. While some webcams can give full-frame-rate video, the picture either is usually small or updates slowly. Internet users can watch animals around an African waterhole, ships in the Panama Canal, traffic at a local roundabout or monitor their own premises, live and in real time. Video chat rooms and video conferencing are also popular with many uses being found for personal webcams, with and without two-way sound. YouTube was founded on 15 February 2005 and is now the leading website for free streaming video with a vast number of users. It uses a flash-based web player to stream and show video files. Registered users may upload an unlimited amount of video and build their own personal profile. YouTube claims that its users watch hundreds of millions, and upload hundreds of thousands of videos daily. Currently, YouTube also uses an HTML5 player.[60]

Social impact

The Internet has enabled new forms of social interaction, activities, and social associations. This phenomenon has given rise to the scholarly study of the sociology of the Internet.

Users

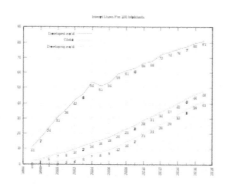

Internet users per 100 inhabitants

Source: International Telecommunications Union.[61][62]

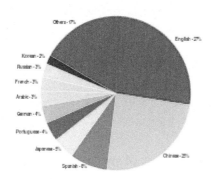

Internet users by language[63]

340

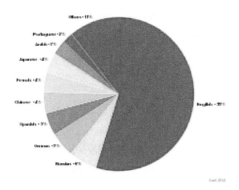

Website content languages[64]

Internet usage has seen tremendous growth. From 2000 to 2009, the number of Internet users globally rose from 394 million to 1.858 billion.[65] By 2010, 22 percent of the world's population had access to computers with 1 billion Google searches every day, 300 million Internet users reading blogs, and 2 billion videos viewed daily on YouTube.[66] In 2014 the world's Internet users surpassed 3 billion or 43.6 percent of world population, but two-thirds of the users came from richest countries, with 78.0 percent of Europe countries population using the Internet, followed by 57.4 percent of the Americas.[67]

The prevalent language for communication on the Internet has been English. This may be a result of the origin of the Internet, as well as the language's role as a lingua franca. Early computer systems were limited to the characters in the American Standard Code for Information Interchange (ASCII), a subset of the Latin alphabet.

After English (27%), the most requested languages on the World Wide Web are Chinese (25%), Spanish (8%), Japanese (5%), Portuguese and German (4% each), Arabic, French and Russian (3% each), and Korean (2%).[63] By region, 42% of the world's Internet users are based in Asia, 24% in Europe, 14% in North America, 10% in Latin America and the Caribbean taken together, 6% in Africa, 3% in the Middle East and 1% in Australia/Oceania.[68] The Internet's technologies have developed enough in recent years, especially in the use of Unicode, that good facilities are available for development and communication in the world's widely used languages. However, some glitches such as *mojibake* (incorrect display of some languages' characters) still remain.

In an American study in 2005, the percentage of men using the Internet was very slightly ahead of the percentage of women, although this difference reversed in those under 30. Men logged on more often, spent more time online, and were more likely to be broadband users, whereas women tended to make more use of opportunities to communicate (such as email). Men were more likely to use the Internet to pay bills, participate in auctions, and for recreation such as downloading music and videos. Men and women were equally likely to use the Internet for shopping and banking.[69] More recent studies indicate that in 2008, women significantly outnumbered men on most social networking sites, such as Facebook and Myspace, although the ratios varied with age.[70] In addition, women watched more streaming content, whereas men downloaded more.[71] In terms of blogs, men were more likely to blog in the first place; among those who blog, men were more likely to have a professional blog, whereas women were more likely to have a personal blog.[72]

According to forecasts by Euromonitor International, 44% of the world's population will be users of the Internet by 2020.[73] Splitting by country, in 2012 Iceland, Norway, Sweden, the Netherlands, and Denmark had the highest Internet penetration by the number of users, with 93% or more of the population with access.[74]

Several neologisms exist that refer to Internet users: Netizen (as in as in "citizen of the net")[75] refers to those actively involved in improving online communities, the Internet in general or surrounding political affairs and rights such as free speech,[76][77] Internaut refers to operators or technically highly capable users of the Internet,[78][79] digital citizen refers to a person using the Internet in order to engage in society, politics, and government participation.[80]

Usage

The Internet allows greater flexibility in working hours and location, especially with the spread of unmetered high-speed connections. The Internet can be accessed almost anywhere by numerous means, including through mobile Internet devices. Mobile phones, datacards, handheld game consoles and cellular routersallow users to connect to the Internet wirelessly. Within the limitations imposed by small screens and other limited facilities of such pocket-sized devices, the services of the Internet, including email and the web, may be available. Service providers may restrict the services offered and mobile data charges may be significantly higher than other access methods.

Educational material at all levels from pre-school to post-doctoral is available from websites. Examples range from CBeebies, through school and high-school revision guides and virtual universities, to access to top-end scholarly literature through the likes of Google Scholar.

For distance education, help with homework and other assignments, self-guided learning, whiling away spare time, or just looking up more detail on an interesting fact, it has never been easier for people to access educational information at any level from anywhere. The Internet in general and the World Wide Web in particular are important enablers of both formal and informal education. Further, the Internet allows universities, in particular, researchers from the social and behavioral sciences, to conduct research remotely via virtual laboratories, with profound changes in reach and generalizability of findings as well as in communication between scientists and in the publication of results.[81]

The low cost and nearly instantaneous sharing of ideas, knowledge, and skills have made collaborative work dramatically easier, with the help of collaborative software. Not only can a group cheaply communicate and share ideas but the wide reach of the Internet allows such groups more easily to form. An example of this is the free software movement, which has produced, among other things, Linux, Mozilla Firefox, and OpenOffice.org (later forked into LibreOffice). Internet chat, whether using an IRC chat room, an instant messagingsystem, or a social networking website, allows colleagues to stay in touch in a very convenient way while working at their computers during the day. Messages can be exchanged even more quickly and conveniently than via email. These systems may allow files to be exchanged, drawings and images to be shared, or voice and video contact between team members.

Content management systems allow collaborating teams to work on shared sets of documents simultaneously without accidentally destroying each other's work. Business and project teams can share calendars as well as documents and other information. Such collaboration occurs in a wide variety of areas including scientific research, software development, conference planning, political activism and creative writing. Social and political collaboration is also becoming more widespread as both Internet access and computer literacy spread.

The Internet allows computer users to remotely access other computers and information stores easily from any access point. Access may be with computer security, i.e. authentication and encryption technologies, depending on the requirements. This is encouraging new ways of working from home, collaboration and information sharing in many industries. An accountant sitting at home can audit the books of a company based in another country, on a server situated in a third country that is remotely maintained by IT specialists in a fourth. These accounts could have been created by home-working bookkeepers, in other remote locations, based on information emailed to them from offices all over the world. Some of these things were possible before the widespread use of the Internet, but the cost of private leased lines would have made many of them infeasible in practice. An office worker away from their desk, perhaps on the other side of the world on a business trip or a holiday, can access their emails, access their data using cloud computing, or open a remote desktop session into their office PC using a secure virtual private network (VPN) connection on the Internet. This can give the worker complete access to all of their normal files and data, including email and other applications, while away from the office. It has been referred to among system administrators as the Virtual Private Nightmare,[82] because it extends the secure perimeter of a corporate network into remote locations and its employees' homes.

Social networking and entertainment

Many people use the World Wide Web to access news, weather and sports reports, to plan and book vacations and to pursue their personal interests. People use chat, messaging and email to make and stay in touch with friends worldwide, sometimes in the same way as some previously had pen pals. Social networking websites such as Facebook, Twitter, and Myspace have created new ways to socialize and interact. Users of these sites are able to add a wide variety of information to pages, to pursue common interests, and to connect with others. It is also possible to find existing acquaintances, to allow communication among existing groups of people. Sites like LinkedIn foster commercial and business connections. YouTube and Flickr specialize in users' videos and photographs. While social networking sites were initially for individuals only, today they are widely used by businesses and other organizations to promote their brands, to market to their customers and to encourage posts to "go viral". "Black hat" social media techniques are also employed by some organizations, such as spam accounts and astroturfing.

A risk for both individuals and organizations writing posts (especially public posts) on social networking websites, is that especially foolish or controversial posts occasionally lead to an unexpected and possibly large-scale backlash on social media from other Internet users. This is also a risk in relation to controversial *offline* behavior, if it is widely made known. The nature of this backlash can range widely from counter-arguments and public mockery, through insults and hate speech, to, in extreme cases, rape and death threats. The online disinhibition effect describes the tendency of many individuals to behave more stridently or offensively online than they would in person. A significant number of feminist women have been the target of various forms of harassment in response to posts they have made on social media, and Twitter in particular has been criticised in the past for not doing enough to aid victims of online abuse.[83]

For organizations, such a backlash can cause overall brand damage, especially if reported by the media. However, this is not always the case, as any brand damage in the eyes of people with an opposing opinion to that presented by the organization could sometimes be outweighed by strengthening the brand in the eyes of others. Furthermore, if an organization or individual gives in to demands that others perceive as wrong-headed, that can then provoke a counter-backlash.

Some websites, such as Reddit, have rules forbidding the

posting of personal information of individuals (also known as doxxing), due to concerns about such postings leading to mobs of large numbers of Internet users directing harassment at the specific individuals thereby identified. In particular, the Reddit rule forbidding the posting of personal information is widely understood to imply that all identifying photos and names must be censored in Facebook screenshots posted to Reddit. However, the interpretation of this rule in relation to public Twitter posts is less clear, and in any case, like-minded people online have many other ways they can use to direct each other's attention to public social media posts they disagree with.

Children also face dangers online such as cyberbullying and approaches by sexual predators, who sometimes pose as children themselves. Children may also encounter material which they may find upsetting, or material which their parents consider to be not age-appropriate. Due to naivety, they may also post personal information about themselves online, which could put them or their families at risk unless warned not to do so. Many parents choose to enable Internet filtering, and/or supervise their children's online activities, in an attempt to protect their children from inappropriate material on the Internet. The most popular social networking websites, such as Facebook and

Twitter, commonly forbid users under the age of 13. However, these policies are typically trivial to circumvent by registering an account with a false birth date, and a significant number of children aged under 13 join such sites anyway. Social networking sites for younger children, which claim to provide better levels of protection for children, also exist.[84]

The Internet has been a major outlet for leisure activity since its inception, with entertaining social experiments such as MUDs and MOOs being conducted on university servers, and humor-related Usenet groups receiving much traffic.[citation needed] Many Internet forums have sections devoted to games and funny videos.[citation needed] The Internet pornographyand online gambling industries have taken advantage of the World Wide Web, and often provide a significant source of advertising revenue for other websites.[85] Although many governments have attempted to restrict both industries' use of the Internet, in general, this has failed to stop their widespread popularity.[86]

Another area of leisure activity on the Internet is multiplayer gaming.[87] This form of recreation creates communities, where people of all ages and origins enjoy the fast-paced world of multiplayer games. These range from MMORPG to first-person shooters, from role-playing video games to online gambling. While online gaming has been around since the 1970s, modern modes of online gaming began with subscription services such as GameSpy and MPlayer.[88] Non-subscribers were limited to certain types of game play or certain games. Many people use the Internet to access and download music, movies and other works for their enjoyment and relaxation. Free and fee-based services exist for all of these activities, using centralized servers and distributed peer-to-peer technologies. Some of these sources exercise more care with respect to the original artists' copyrights than others.

Internet usage has been correlated to users' loneliness.[89] Lonely people tend to use the Internet as an outlet for their feelings and to share their stories with others, such as in the "I am lonely will anyone speak to me" thread.

Cybersectarianism is a new organizational form which involves: "highly dispersed small groups of practitioners that may remain largely anonymous within the larger social context and operate in relative secrecy, while still linked remotely to a larger network of believers who share a set of practices and texts, and often a common devotion to a particular leader. Overseas supporters provide funding and support; domestic practitioners distribute tracts, participate in acts of resistance, and share information on the internal situation with outsiders. Collectively, members and practitioners of such sects construct viable virtual communities of faith, exchanging personal testimonies and engaging in the collective study via email, on-line chat rooms, and web-based message boards."[90] In particular, the British government has raised concerns about the prospect of young British Muslims being indoctrinated into Islamic extremism by material on the Internet, being persuaded to join terrorist groups such as the so-called "Islamic State", and then potentially committing acts of terrorism on returning to Britain after fighting in Syria or Iraq.

Cyberslacking can become a drain on corporate resources; the average UK employee spent 57 minutes a day surfing the Web while at work, according to a 2003 study by Peninsula Business Services.[91] Internet addiction disorder is excessive computer use that interferes with daily life. Nicholas G. Carr believes that Internet use has other effects on individuals, for instance improving skills of scan-reading and interfering with the deep thinking that leads to true creativity.[92]

Electronic business

Electronic business (*e-business*) encompasses business processes spanning the entire value chain: purchasing, supply chain management, marketing, sales, customer service, and business relationship. E-commerce seeks to add revenue streams using the Internet to build and enhance relationships with clients and partners. According to International Data Corporation, the size of worldwide e-commerce, when global business-to-business and - consumer transactions are combined, equate to $16 trillion for 2013. A report by Oxford Economics adds those two together to estimate the total size of the digital economy at $20.4 trillion, equivalent to roughly 13.8% of global sales.[93]

While much has been written of the economic advantages of Internet-enabled commerce, there is also evidence that some aspects of the Internet such as maps and location-aware services may serve to reinforce economic inequality and the digital divide.[94] Electronic commerce may be responsible for consolidation and the decline of mom-and-pop, brick and mortar businesses resulting in increases in income inequality.[95][96][97]

Author Andrew Keen, a long-time critic of the social transformations caused by the Internet, has recently focused on the economic effects of consolidation from Internet businesses. Keen cites a 2013 Institute for Local Self-Reliance report saying brick-and-mortar retailers employ 47 people for every $10 million in sales while Amazon employs only 14. Similarly, the 700-employee room rental start-up Airbnb was valued at $10 billion in 2014, about half as much as Hilton Hotels, which employs 152,000 people. And car-sharing Internet startup Uber employs 1,000 full-time employees and is valued at $18.2 billion, about the same valuation as Avis and Hertz combined, which together employ almost 60,000 people.[98]

Telecommuting

Telecommuting is the performance within a traditional worker and employer relationship when it is facilitated by tools such as groupware, virtual private networks, conference calling, videoconferencing, and voice over IP (VOIP) so that work may be performed from any location, most conveniently the worker's home. It can be efficient and useful for companies as it allows workers to communicate over long distances, saving significant amounts of travel time and cost. As broadband Internet connections become commonplace, more workers have adequate bandwidth at home to use these tools to link their home to their corporate intranet and internal communication networks.

Collaborative publishing

Wikis have also been used in the academic community for sharing and dissemination of information across institutional and international boundaries.[99] In those settings, they have been found useful for collaboration on grant writing, strategic planning, departmental documentation, and committee work.[100] The United States Patent and Trademark Office uses a wiki to allow the public to collaborate on finding prior art relevant to examination of pending patent applications. Queens, New York has used a wiki to allow citizens to collaborate on the design and planning of a local park.[101] The English Wikipedia has the largest user base

among wikis on the World Wide Web[102] and ranks in the top 10 among all Web sites in terms of traffic.[103]

Politics and political revolutions

356

Banner in Bangkok during the 2014 Thai coup d'état, informing the Thaipublic that 'like' or 'share' activities on social media could result in imprisonment (observed June 30, 2014).

The Internet has achieved new relevance as a political tool. The presidential campaign of Howard Dean in 2004 in the United States was notable for its success in soliciting donation via the Internet. Many political groups use the Internet to achieve a new method of organizing for carrying out their mission, having given rise to Internet activism, most notably practiced by rebels in the Arab Spring.[104][105] *The New York Times* suggested that social media websites, such as Facebook and Twitter, helped people organize the political revolutions in Egypt, by helping activists organize protests, communicate grievances, and disseminate information.[106]

The potential of the Internet as a civic tool of communicative power was explored by Simon R. B. Berdal in his 2004 thesis:

As the globally evolving Internet provides ever new access points to virtual discourse forums, it also promotes new civic relations and associations within which communicative power may flow and accumulate. Thus, traditionally ... national-embedded peripheries get entangled into greater, international peripheries, with stronger combined powers... The Internet, as a consequence, changes the topology of the "centre-periphery" model, by stimulating conventional peripheries to interlink into "super-periphery" structures, which enclose and "besiege" several centres at once.[107]

Berdal, therefore, extends the Habermasian notion of the *public sphere* to the Internet, and underlines the inherent global and civic nature that interwoven Internet technologies provide. To limit the growing civic potential of the Internet, Berdal also notes how "self-protective measures" are put in place by those threatened by it:

If we consider China's attempts to filter "unsuitable material" from the Internet, most of us would agree that this resembles a self-protective measure by the system against the growing civic potentials of the Internet. Nevertheless, both types represent limitations to "peripheral capacities". Thus, the Chinese government tries to prevent communicative power to build up and unleash (as the 1989 Tiananmen Square uprising suggests, the government may find it wise to install "upstream measures"). Even though limited, the Internet is proving to be an empowering tool also to the

Chinese periphery: Analysts believe that Internet petitions have influenced policy implementation in favour of the public's online-articulated will ...[107]

Incidents of politically motivated Internet censorship have now been recorded in many countries, including western democracies.

Philanthropy

The spread of low-cost Internet access in developing countries has opened up new possibilities for peer-to-peer charities, which allow individuals to contribute small amounts to charitable projects for other individuals. Websites, such as DonorsChoose and GlobalGiving, allow small-scale donors to direct funds to individual projects of their choice. A popular twist on Internet-based philanthropy is the use of peer-to-peer lending for charitable purposes. Kiva pioneered this concept in 2005, offering the first web-based service to publish individual loan profiles for funding. Kiva raises funds for local intermediary microfinance organizations which post stories and updates on behalf of the borrowers. Lenders can contribute as little as $25 to loans of their choice, and receive their money back as borrowers repay. Kiva falls short of being a pure peer-to-peer charity, in that loans are disbursed before being funded by lenders and borrowers do not communicate with lenders themselves.[108][109]

However, the recent spread of low-cost Internet access in developing countries has made genuine international person-to-person philanthropy increasingly feasible. In 2009, the US-based nonprofit Zidisha tapped into this trend to offer the first person-to-person microfinance platform to link lenders and borrowers across international borders without intermediaries. Members can fund loans for as little as a dollar, which the borrowers then use to develop business activities that improve their families' incomes while repaying loans to the members with interest.

Borrowers access the Internet via public cybercafes, donated laptops in village schools, and even smart phones, then create their own profile pages through which they share photos and information about themselves and their businesses. As they repay their loans, borrowers continue to share updates and dialogue with lenders via their profile pages. This direct web-based connection allows members themselves to take on many of the communication and recording tasks traditionally performed by local organizations, bypassing geographic barriers and dramatically reducing the cost of microfinance services to the entrepreneurs.[110]

Security

Internet resources, hardware, and software components are the target of criminal or malicious attempts to gain unauthorized control to cause interruptions, commit fraud, engage in blackmail or access private information.

Malware

Malicious software used and spread on the Internet includes computer viruses which copy with the help of humans, computer worms which copy themselves automatically, software for denial of service attacks, ransomware, botnets, and spyware that reports on the activity and typing of users. Usually, these activities constitute cybercrime. Defense theorists have also speculated about the possibilities of cyber warfare using similar methods on a large scale.

Surveillance

The vast majority of computer surveillance involves the monitoring of data and traffic on the Internet.[111] In the United States for example, under the Communications Assistance For Law Enforcement Act, all phone calls and broadband Internet traffic (emails, web traffic, instant messaging, etc.) are required to be available for unimpeded real-time monitoring by Federal law enforcement agencies.[112][113][114] Packet capture is the monitoring of data traffic on a computer network. Computers communicate over the Internet by breaking up messages (emails, images, videos, web pages, files, etc.) into small chunks called "packets", which are routed through a network of computers, until they reach their destination, where they are assembled back into a complete "message" again. Packet Capture Appliance intercepts these packets as they are traveling through the network, in order to examine their contents using other programs. A packet capture is an information *gathering* tool, but not an *analysis* tool. That is it gathers "messages" but it does not analyze them and figure out what they mean. Other programs are needed to perform traffic analysis and sift through intercepted data looking for important/useful information. Under the Communications Assistance For Law Enforcement Act all U.S. telecommunications providers are required to install packet sniffing technology to allow Federal law enforcement and intelligence agencies to intercept all of their customers' broadband Internet and voice over Internet protocol (VoIP) traffic.[115]

The large amount of data gathered from packet capturing requires surveillance software that filters and reports relevant information, such as the use of certain words or phrases, the access of certain types of web sites, or communicating via email or chat with certain parties.[116] Agencies, such as the Information Awareness Office, NSA, GCHQ and the FBI, spend billions of dollars per year to develop, purchase, implement, and operate systems for interception and analysis of data.[117] Similar systems are operated by Iranian secret police to identify and suppress dissidents. The required hardware and software was allegedly installed by German Siemens AG and Finnish Nokia.[118]

Censorship

Internet censorship and surveillance by country[119][120][121][122]

Pervasive

Substantial

Selective

Changing situation

Little or none

Not classified or no data

Some governments, such as those of Burma, Iran, North Korea, the Mainland China, Saudi Arabia and the United Arab Emirates restrict access to content on the Internet within their territories, especially to political and religious content, with domain name and keyword filters.[123]

In Norway, Denmark, Finland, and Sweden, major Internet service providers have voluntarily agreed to restrict access to sites listed by authorities. While this list of forbidden resources is supposed to contain only known child pornography sites, the content of the list is secret.[124] Many countries, including the United States, have enacted laws against the possession or distribution of certain material, such as child pornography, via the Internet, but do not mandate filter software. Many free or commercially available software programs, called content-control software are available to users to block offensive websites on individual computers or networks, in order to limit access by children to pornographic material or depiction of violence.

Performance

As the Internet is a heterogeneous network, the physical characteristics, including for example the data transfer rates of connections, vary widely. It exhibits emergent phenomena that depend on its large-scale organization.

Outages

An Internet blackout or outage can be caused by local signaling interruptions. Disruptions of submarine communications cables may cause blackouts or slowdowns to large areas, such as in the 2008 submarine cable disruption. Less-developed countries are more vulnerable due to a small number of high-capacity links. Land cables are also vulnerable, as in 2011 when a woman digging for scrap metal severed most connectivity for the nation of Armenia.[125] Internet blackouts affecting almost entire countries can be achieved by governments as a form of Internet censorship, as in the blockage of the Internet in Egypt, whereby approximately 93%[126] of networks were without access in 2011 in an attempt to stop mobilization for anti-government protests.[127]

Energy use

In 2011, researchers estimated the energy used by the Internet to be between 170 and 307 GW, less than two percent of the energy used by humanity. This estimate included the energy needed to build, operate, and periodically replace the estimated 750 million laptops, a billion smart phones and 100 million servers worldwide as well as the energy that routers, cell towers, optical

365

switches, Wi-Fi transmitters and cloud storage devices use when transmitting Internet traffic.[128][129]

4G

4G is the fourth generation of broadband cellular network technology, succeeding 3G. A 4G system must provide capabilities defined by ITU in IMT Advanced. Potential and current applications include amended mobile web access, IP telephony, gaming services, high-definition mobile TV, video conferencing, and 3D television.

The first-release Long Term Evolution (LTE) standard (a 4G candidate system) has been commercially deployed in Oslo, Norway, and Stockholm, Sweden since 2009. It has, however, been debated whether first-release versions should be considered 4G, as discussed in the technical understanding section below.

Technical understandings

In March 2008, the International Telecommunications Union-Radio communications sector (ITU-R) specified a set of requirements for 4G standards, named the International Mobile Telecommunications Advanced (IMT-Advanced) specification, setting peak speed requirements for 4G service at 100 megabits per second (Mbit/s) for high mobility communication (such as from trains and cars) and 1 gigabit per second (Gbit/s) for low mobility communication (such as pedestrians and stationary users).[1]

Since the first-release versions of Mobile WiMAX and LTE support much less than 1 Gbit/s peak bit rate, they are not fully IMT-Advanced compliant, but are often branded 4G by service providers. According to operators, a generation of the network refers to the deployment of a new non-backward-compatible technology. On December 6, 2010, ITU-R recognized that these two technologies, as well as other beyond-3G technologies that do not fulfill the IMT-Advanced requirements, could nevertheless be considered "4G", provided they represent forerunners to IMT-Advanced compliant versions and "a substantial level of improvement in performance and capabilities with respect to the initial third generation systems now deployed".[2]

Mobile WiMAX Release 2 (also known as *WirelessMAN-Advanced* or *IEEE 802.16m*) and LTE Advanced (LTE-A) are IMT-Advanced compliant backwards compatible versions of the above two systems, standardized during the spring 2011,and promising speeds in the order of 1 Gbit/s. Services were expected in 2013.

As opposed to earlier generations, a 4G system does not support traditional circuit-switched telephony service, but all-Internet Protocol (IP) based communication such as IP telephony. As seen below, the spread spectrum radio technology used in 3G systems, is abandoned in all 4G candidate systems and replaced by OFDMA multi-carrier transmission and other frequency-domain equalization (FDE) schemes, making it possible to transfer very high bit rates despite extensive multi-path radio propagation (echoes). The peak bit rate is further improved by smart antenna arrays for multiple-input multiple-output (MIMO) communications.

Background

In the field of mobile communications, a "generation" generally refers to a change in the fundamental nature of the service, non-backwards-compatible transmission technology, higher peak bit rates, new frequency bands, wider channel frequency bandwidth in Hertz, and higher capacity for many simultaneous data transfers (higher system spectral efficiencyin bit/second/Hertz/site).

New mobile generations have appeared about every ten years since the first move from 1981 analog (1G) to digital (2G) transmission in 1992. This was followed, in 2001, by 3G multi-media support, spread spectrum transmission and, at least, 200 kbit/s peak bit rate, in 2011/2012 to be followed by "real" 4G, which refers to all-Internet Protocol (IP) packet-switched networks giving mobile ultra-broadband (gigabit speed) access.

While the ITU has adopted recommendations for technologies that would be used for future global communications, they do not actually perform the standardization or development work themselves, instead relying on the work of other standard bodies such as IEEE, The Wi MAX Forum, and 3GPP.

In the mid-1990s, the ITU-R standardization organization released the IMT-2000 requirements as a framework for what standards should be considered 3G syst ems, requiring 200 kbit/s peak bit rate. In 2008, ITU -R specified the IMT – Advanced (Intern

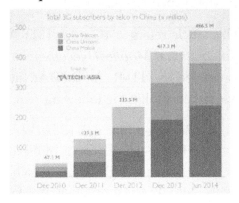

ational Mobile Telecommunications Advanced) requirements for 4G systems.

The fastest 3G-based standard in the UMTS family is the HSPA+ standard, which is commercially available since 2009 and offers 28 Mbit/s downstream (22 Mbit/s upstream) without MIMO, i.e. only with one antenna, and in 2011 accelerated up to 42 Mbit/s peak bit rate downstream using either DC-HSPA+ (simultaneous use of two 5 MHz UMTS carriers)[3] or 2x2 MIMO. In theory speeds up to 672 Mbit/s are possible, but have not been deployed yet. The fastest 3G-based standard in the CDMA2000 family is the EV-DO Rev. B, which is available since 2010 and offers 15.67 Mbit/s downstream.

IMT-Advanced requirements

This article refers to 4G using IMT-Advanced (*International Mobile Telecommunications Advanced*), as defined by ITU-R. An IMT-Advanced cellular system must fulfill the following requirements:[4]

- Be based on an all-IP packet switched network.
- Have peak data rates of up to approximately 100 Mbit/s for high mobility such as mobile access and up to approximately 1 Gbit/s for low mobility such as nomadic/local wireless access.[1]

- Be able to dynamically share and use the network resources to support more simultaneous users per cell.
- Use scalable channel bandwidths of 5–20 MHz, optionally up to 40 MHz.[1] *Rumney, Moray (September 2008). "IMT-Advanced: 4G Wireless Takes Shape in an Olympic Year"(PDF). Agilent Measurement Journal. Archived from the original (PDF) on January 17, 2016.*
- Have peak link spectral efficiency of 15-bit/s/Hz in the downlink, and 6.75-bit/s/Hz in the up link (meaning that 1 Gbit/s in the downlink should be possible over less than 67 MHz bandwidth).
- System spectral efficiency is, in indoor cases, 3-bit/s/Hz/cell for downlink and 2.25-bit/s/Hz/cell for uplink.[1]
- Smooth handovers across heterogeneous networks.

In September 2009, the technology proposals were submitted to the International Telecommunication Union (ITU) as 4G candidates.[5] Basically all proposals are based on two technologies.

- LTE Advanced standardized by the 3GPP
- 802.16m standardized by the IEEE

Implementations of Mobile WiMAX and first-release LTE are largely considered a stopgap solution that will offer a considerable boost until WiMAX 2 (based on the 802.16m spec) and LTE Advanced are deployed. The latter's standard versions were ratified in spring 2011, but are still far from being implemented.[4]

The first set of 3GPP requirements on LTE Advanced was approved in June 2008.[6] LTE Advanced was to be standardized in 2010 as part of Release 10 of the 3GPP specification. LTE Advanced will be based on the existing LTE specification Release 10 and will not be defined as a new specification series. A summary of the technologies that have been studied as the basis for LTE Advanced is included in a technical report.[7]

Some sources consider first-release LTE and Mobile WiMAX implementations as pre-4G or near-4G, as they do not fully comply with the planned requirements of 1 Gbit/s for stationary reception and 100 Mbit/s for mobile.

Confusion has been caused by some mobile carriers who have launched products advertised as 4G but which according to some sources are pre-4G versions, commonly referred to as '3.9G', which do not follow the ITU-R defined principles for 4G standards, but today can be called 4G according to ITU-R. Vodafone NL for example, advertised LTE as '4G', while advertising now

LTE Advanced as their '4G+' service which actually is (True) 4G. A common argument for branding 3.9G systems as new-generation is that they use different frequency bands from 3G technologies ; that they are based on a new radio-interface paradigm ; and that the standards are not backwards compatible with 3G, whilst some of the standards are forwards compatible with IMT-2000 compliant versions of the same standards.

System standards

IMT-2000 compliant 4G standards

As of October 2010, ITU-R Working Party 5D approved two industry-developed technologies (LTE Advanced and WirelessMAN-Advanced)[8] for inclusion in the ITU's International Mobile Telecommunications Advanced program (IMT-Advanced program), which is focused on global communication systems that will be available several years from now.

LTE Advanced

LTE Advanced (Long Term Evolution Advanced) is a candidate for IMT-Advanced standard, formally submitted by the 3GPP organization to ITU-T in the fall

2009, and expected to be released in 2013. The target of 3GPP LTE Advanced is to reach and surpass the ITU requirements.[9] LTE Advanced is essentially an enhancement to LTE. It is not a new technology, but rather an improvement on the existing LTE network. This upgrade path makes it more cost effective for vendors to offer LTE and then upgrade to LTE Advanced which is similar to the upgrade from WCDMA to HSPA. LTE and LTE Advanced will also make use of additional spectrums and multiplexing to allow it to achieve higher data speeds. Coordinated Multi-point Transmission will also allow more system capacity to help handle the enhanced data speeds. Release 10 of LTE is expected to achieve the IMT Advanced speeds. Release 8 currently supports up to 300 Mbit/s of download speeds which is still short of the IMT-Advanced standards.[10]

IEEE 802.16m or WirelessMAN-Advanced

The IEEE 802.16m or WirelessMAN-Advanced evolution of 802.16e is under development, with the objective to fulfill the IMT-Advanced criteria of 1 Gbit/s for stationary reception and 100 Mbit/s for mobile reception.[11]

Forerunner versions

3GPP Long Term Evolution (LTE)

Telia-branded Samsung LTE modem

The pre-4G 3GPP Long Term Evolution (LTE) technology is often branded "4G – LTE", but the first LTE release does not fully comply with the IMT-Advanced requirements. LTE has a theoretical net bit rate capacity of up to 100 Mbit/s in the downlink and 50 Mbit/s in the uplink if a 20 MHz channel is used – and more if multiple-input multiple-output (MIMO), i.e. antenna arrays, are used.

The physical radio interface was at an early stage named *High Speed OFDM Packet Access* (HSOPA), now named Evolved UMTS Terrestrial Radio Access (E-UTRA). The first LTE USB dongles do not support any other radio interface.

The world's first publicly available LTE service was opened in the two Scandinavian capitals, Stockholm (Ericsson and Nokia Siemens Networks systems) and Oslo (a Huawei system) on December 14, 2009, and branded 4G. The user terminals were manufactured by Samsung.[12] As of November 2012, the five publicly available LTE services in the United States are provided by MetroPCS,[13] Verizon Wireless,[14] AT&T Mobility, U.S. Cellular,[15] Sprint,[16] and T-Mobile US.[17]

T-Mobile Hungary launched a public beta test (called *friendly user test*) on 7 October 2011, and has offered commercial 4G LTE services since 1 January 2012.[*citation needed*]

In South Korea, SK Telecom and LG U+ have enabled access to LTE service since 1 July 2011 for data devices, slated to go nationwide by 2012.[18] KT Telecom closed its 2G service by March 2012, and complete the nationwide LTE service in the same frequency around 1.8 GHz by June 2012.

In the United Kingdom, LTE services were launched by EE in October 2012,[19] and by O2 and Vodafone in August 2013.[20]

Mobile WiMAX (IEEE 802.16e)

The Mobile WiMAX (IEEE 802.16e-2005) mobile wireless broadband access (MWBA) standard (also known as WiBro in South Korea) is sometimes branded 4G, and offers peak data rates of 128 Mbit/s downlink and 56 Mbit/s uplink over 20 MHz wide channels.[*citation needed*]

In June 2006, the world's first commercial mobile WiMAX service was opened by KT in Seoul, South Korea.[21]

Sprint has begun using Mobile WiMAX, as of 29 September 2008, branding it as a "4G" network even though the current version does not fulfill the IMT Advanced requirements on 4G systems.[22]

In Russia, Belarus and Nicaragua WiMax broadband internet access was offered by a Russian company Scartel, and was also branded 4G, Yota.[23]

In the latest version of the standard, WiMax 2.1, the standard have been updated to be not compatible with earlier WiMax standard, and is instead interchangeable with LTE-TDD system, effectively merging WiMax standard with LTE.

TD-LTE for China market

Just as Long-Term Evolution (LTE) and WiMAX are being vigorously promoted in the global telecommunications industry, the former (LTE) is also the most powerful 4G mobile communications leading technology and has quickly occupied the Chinese market. TD-LTE, one of the two variants of the LTE air interface technologies, is not yet mature, but many domestic and international wireless carriers are, one after the other turning to TD-LTE.

IBM's data shows that 67% of the operators are considering LTE because this is the main source of their future market. The above news also confirms IBM's statement that while only 8% of the operators are considering the use of WiMAX, WiMAX can provide the fastest network transmission to its customers on the market and could challenge LTE.

TD-LTE is not the first 4G wireless mobile broadband network data standard, but it is China's 4G standard that was amended and published by China's largest telecom operator – China Mobile. After a series of field trials, is expected to be released into the commercial phase in the next two years. Ulf Ewaldsson, Ericsson's vice president said: "the Chinese Ministry of Industry and China Mobile in the fourth quarter of this year will hold a large-scale field test, by then, Ericsson will help the hand." But viewing from the current development trend, whether this standard advocated by China Mobile will be widely recognized by the international market is still debatable.

Discontinued candidate systems

UMB (formerly EV-DO Rev. C)

UMB (Ultra Mobile Broadband) was the brand name for a discontinued 4G project within the 3GPP2 standardization group to improve the CDMA2000 mobile phone standard for next generation applications and requirements. In November 2008, Qualcomm, UMB's lead sponsor, announced it was ending development of the technology, favouring LTE instead.[24] The objective was to achieve data speeds over 275 Mbit/s downstream and over 75 Mbit/s upstream.

Flash-OFDM

At an early stage the Flash-OFDM system was expected to be further developed into a 4G standard.

iBurst and MBWA (IEEE 802.20) systems

The iBurst system (or HC-SDMA, High Capacity Spatial Division Multiple Access) was at an early stage considered to be a 4G predecessor. It was later further developed into the Mobile Broadband Wireless Access (MBWA) system, also known as IEEE 802.20.

Principal technologies in all candidate systems

Key features

The following key features can be observed in all suggested 4G technologies:

- Physical layer transmission techniques are as follows:[25]
- MIMO: To attain ultra-high spectral efficiency by means of spatial processing including multi-antenna and multi-user MIMO
- Frequency-domain-equalization, for example *multi-carrier modulation* (OFDM) in the downlink or *single-carrier frequency-domain-equalization* (SC-FDE) in the uplink: To exploit the frequency selective channel property without complex equalization
- Frequency-domain statistical multiplexing, for example (OFDMA) or (single-carrier FDMA) (SC-FDMA, a.k.a. linearly precoded OFDMA, LP-OFDMA) in the uplink: Variable bit rate by assigning different sub-channels to different users based on the channel conditions
- Turbo principle error-correcting codes: To minimize the required SNR at the reception side

- Channel-dependent scheduling: To use the time-varying channel
- Link adaptation: Adaptive modulation and error-correcting codes
- Mobile IP utilized for mobility
- IP-based femtocells (home nodes connected to fixed Internet broadband infrastructure)

As opposed to earlier generations, 4G systems do not support circuit switched telephony. IEEE 802.20, UMB and OFDM standards[26] lack soft-handover support, also known as cooperative relaying.

Multiplexing and access schemes

Recently, new access schemes like Orthogonal FDMA (OFDMA), Single Carrier FDMA (SC-FDMA), Interleaved FDMA, and Multi-carrier CDMA (MC-CDMA) are gaining more importance for the next generation systems. These are based on efficient FFT algorithms and frequency domain equalization, resulting in a lower number of multiplications per second. They also make it possible to control the bandwidth and form the spectrum in a flexible way. However, they require advanced dynamic channel allocation and adaptive traffic scheduling.

WiMax is using OFDMA in the downlink and in the uplink. For the LTE (telecommunication), OFDMA is used for the downlink; by contrast, Single-carrier FDMA is used for the uplink since OFDMA contributes more to the PAPR related issues and results in nonlinear operation of amplifiers. IFDMA provides less power fluctuation and thus requires energy-inefficient linear amplifiers. Similarly, MC-CDMA is in the proposal for the IEEE 802.20 standard. These access schemes offer the

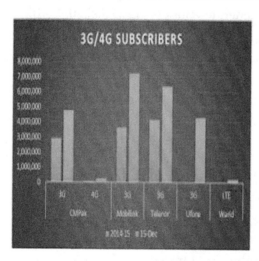

same efficiencies as older technologies like CDMA. Apart from this, scalability and higher data rates can be achieved.

The other important advantage of the above-mentioned access techniques is that they require less complexity for equalization at the receiver. This is an added advantage especially in the MIMO environments since the spatial multiplexing transmission of MIMO systems inherently require high complexity equalization at the receiver.

In addition to improvements in these multiplexing systems, improved modulation techniques are being used. Whereas earlier standards largely used Phase-shift keying, more efficient systems such as 64QAM are being proposed for use with the 3GPP Long Term Evolution standards.

IPv6 support

Unlike 3G, which is based on two parallel infrastructures consisting of circuit switched and packet switched network nodes, 4G is based on packet switching *only*. This requires low-latency data transmission.

As IPv4 addresses are (nearly) exhausted,[Note 1][27] IPv6 is essential to support the large number of wireless-enabled devices that communicate using IP. By increasing the number of IP addresses available, IPv6 removes the need for network address translation (NAT), a method of sharing a limited number of addresses among a larger group of devices, which has a number of problems and limitations. When using IPv6, some kind of NAT is still required for communication with legacy IPv4 devices that are not also IPv6-connected.

As of June 2009, Verizon has posted specifications that require any 4G devices on its network to support IPv6.[28]

Advanced Antenna Systems

The performance of radio communications depends on an antenna system, termed smart or intelligent antenna. Recently, multiple antenna technologies are emerging to achieve the goal of 4G systems such as high rate, high reliability, and long range communications. In the early 1990s, to cater for the growing data rate needs of data communication, many transmission schemes were proposed. One technology, spatial multiplexing, gained importance for its bandwidth conservation and power efficiency. Spatial multiplexing involves deploying multiple antennas at the transmitter and at the receiver. Independent streams can then be transmitted simultaneously from all the antennas. This technology, called MIMO(as a branch of intelligent antenna), multiplies the base data rate by (the smaller of) the number of transmit antennas or the number of receive antennas. Apart from this, the reliability in transmitting high speed data in the fading channel can be improved by using more antennas at the transmitter or at the receiver. This is called *transmit* or *rec eive diversity*. Both

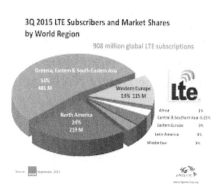

384

transmit/receive diversity and transmit spatial multiplexing are categorized into the space-time coding techniques, which does not necessarily require the channel knowledge at the transmitter. The other category is closed-loop multiple antenna technologies, which require channel knowledge at the transmitter.

Open-wireless Architecture and Software-defined radio (SDR)

One of the key technologies for 4G and beyond is called Open Wireless Architecture (OWA), supporting multiple wireless air interfaces in an open architecture platform.

SDR is one form of open wireless architecture (OWA). Since 4G is a collection of wireless standards, the final form of a 4G device will constitute various standards. This can be efficiently realized using SDR technology, which is categorized to the area of the radio convergence.

History of 4G and pre-4G technologies

The 4G system was originally envisioned by the Defense Advanced Research Projects Agency (DARPA).The DARPA selected the distributed architecture and end-to-end Internet protocol (IP), and believed at an early stage in peer-to-peer networking in which every mobile device would be both a transceiver and a router for other devices in the network, eliminating the spoke-and-hub weakness of 2G and 3G cellular systems.[29][*page needed*] Since the 2.5G GPRS system, cellular systems have provided dual infrastructures: packet switched nodes for data services, and circuit switched nodes for voice calls. In 4G systems, the circuit-switched infrastructure is abandoned and only a packet-switched network is provided, while 2.5G and 3G systems require both packet-switched and circuit-switched network nodes, i.e. two infrastructures in parallel. This means that in 4G, traditional voice calls are replaced by IP telephony.

- In 2002, the strategic vision for 4G — which ITU designated as IMT Advanced— was laid out.
- In 2004, LTE was first proposed by NTT DoCoMo of Japan.[30]
- In 2005, OFDMA transmission technology is chosen as candidate for the HSOPA downlink, later renamed 3GPP Long Term Evolution (LTE) air interface E-UTRA.
- In November 2005, KT demonstrated mobile WiMAX service in Busan, South Korea.[31]
- In April 2006, KT started the world's first commercial mobile WiMAX service in Seoul, South Korea.[32]

- In mid-2006, Sprint announced that it would invest about US$5 billion in a WiMAX technology buildout over the next few years[33] ($6.07 billion in real terms[34]). Since that time Sprint has faced many setbacks that have resulted in steep quarterly losses. On 7 May 2008, Sprint, Imagine, Google, Intel, Comcast, Bright House, and Time Warner announced a pooling of an average of 120 MHz of spectrum; Sprint merged its Xohm WiMAX division with Clearwire to form a company which will take the name "Clear".
- In February 2007, the Japanese company NTT DoCoMo tested a 4G communication system prototype with 4×4 MIMO called VSF-OFCDM at 100 Mbit/s while moving, and 1 Gbit/s while stationary. NTT DoCoMo completed a trial in which they reached a maximum packet transmission rate of approximately 5 Gbit/s in the downlink with 12×12 MIMO using a 100 MHz frequency bandwidth while moving at 10 km/h,[35] and is planning on releasing the first commercial network in 2010.
- In September 2007, NTT Docomo demonstrated e-UTRA data rates of 200 Mbit/s with power consumption below 100 mW during the test.[36]
- In January 2008, a U.S. Federal Communications Commission (FCC) spectrum auction for the 700 MHz former analog TV frequencies began. As a result, the biggest share of the spectrum

went to Verizon Wireless and the next biggest to AT&T.[37] Both of these companies have stated their intention of supporting LTE.

- In January 2008, EU commissioner Viviane Reding suggested re-allocation of 500–800 MHz spectrum for wireless communication, including WiMAX.[38]
- On 15 February 2008, Skyworks Solutions released a front-end module for e-UTRAN.[39][40][41]
- In November 2008, ITU-R established the detailed performance requirements of IMT-Advanced, by issuing a Circular Letter calling for candidate Radio Access Technologies (RATs) for IMT-Advanced.[42]
- In April 2008, just after receiving the circular letter, the 3GPP organized a workshop on IMT-Advanced where it was decided that LTE Advanced, an evolution of current LTE standard, will meet or even exceed IMT-Advanced requirements following the ITU-R agenda.
- In April 2008, LG and Nortel demonstrated e-UTRA data rates of 50 Mbit/s while travelling at 110 km/h.[43]
- On 12 November 2008, HTC announced the first WiMAX-enabled mobile phone, the Max 4G[44]
- On 15 December 2008, San Miguel Corporation, the largest food and beverage conglomerate in southeast Asia, has signed a memorandum of understanding with Qatar Telecom QSC (Qtel)

to build wireless broadband and mobile communications projects in the Philippines. The joint-venture formed wi-tribe Philippines, which offers 4G in the country.[45]Around the same time Globe Telecom rolled out the first WiMAX service in the Philippines.

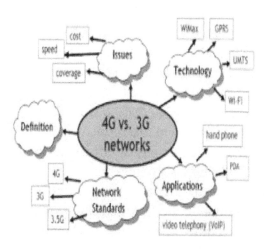

- On 3 March 2009, Lithuania's LRTC announcing the first operational "4G" mobile WiMAX network in Baltic states.[46]
- In December 2009, Sprint began advertising "4G" service in selected cities in the United States, despite average download speeds of only 3–6 Mbit/s with peak speeds of 10 Mbit/s (not available in all markets).[47]
- On 14 December 2009, the first commercial LTE deployment was in the Scandinavian

capitals Stockholm and Oslo by the Swedish-Finnish network operator TeliaSonera and its Norwegian brandname NetCom (Norway). TeliaSonera branded the network "4G". The modem devices on offer were manufactured by Samsung (dongle GT-B3710), and the network infrastructure created by Huawei (in Oslo) and Ericsson (in Stockholm). TeliaSonera plans to roll out nationwide LTE across Sweden, Norway and Finland.[48][49]TeliaSonera used spectral bandwidth of 10 MHz, and single-in-single-out, which should provide physical layer net bitrates of up to 50 Mbit/s downlink and 25 Mbit/s in the uplink. Introductory tests showed a TCP throughput of 42.8 Mbit/s downlink and 5.3 Mbit/s uplink in Stockholm.[50]

- On 4 June 2010, Sprint released the first WiMAX smartphone in the US, the HTC Evo 4G.[51]
- On November 4, 2010, the Samsung Craft offered by MetroPCS is the first commercially available LTE smartphone[52]
- On 6 December 2010, at the ITU World Radiocommunication Seminar 2010, the ITU stated that LTE, WiMax and similar "evolved 3G technologies" could be considered "4G".[2]
- In 2011, Argentina's Claro launched a pre-4G HSPA+ network in the country.
- In 2011, Thailand's Truemove-H launched a pre-4G HSPA+ network with nationwide availability.

- On March 17, 2011, the HTC Thunderbolt offered by Verizon in the U.S. was the second LTE smartphone to be sold commercially.[53][54]
- In February 2012, Ericsson demonstrated mobile-TV over LTE, utilizing the new eMBMS service (enhanced Multimedia Broadcast Multicast Service).[55]

Since 2009 the LTE-Standard has strongly evolved over the years, resulting in many deployments by various operators across the globe. For an overview of commercial LTE networks and their respective historic development see: List of LTE networks. Among the vast range of deployments many operators are considering

the deployment and operation of LTE networks. A compilation of planned LTE deployments can be found at: List of planned LTE networks.

Beyond 4G research

A major issue in 4G systems is to make the high bit rates available in a larger portion of the cell, especially to users in an exposed position in between several base stations. In current research, this issue is addressed by macro-diversity techniques, also known as group cooperative relay, and also by Beam-Division Multiple Access (BDMA).[56]

Pervasive networks are an amorphous and at present entirely hypothetical concept where the user can be simultaneously connected to several wireless access technologies and can seamlessly move between them (See vertical handoff, IEEE 802.21). These access technologies can be Wi-Fi, UMTS, EDGE, or any other future access technology. Included in this concept is also smart-radio (also known as cognitive radio) technology to efficiently manage spectrum use and transmission power as well as the use of mesh routing protocols to create a pervasive network.

CHAPTER TEN

TECHNOLOGY

A steam turbine with the case opened. Such turbines produce most of the electricity used today. Electricity consumption and living standards are highly correlated.[1] Electrification is believed to be the most important engineering achievement of the 20th century.

Technology ("science of craft", from Greek τέχνη, *techne*, "art, skill, cunning of hand"; and -λογία, *-logia*[2]) is the collection of techniques, skills, methods, and processes used in the production of goods or services or in the accomplishment of objectives, such as scientific investigation. Technology can be the knowledge of techniques, processes, and the like, or it can be embedded in machines to allow for operation without detailed knowledge of their workings.

The simplest form of technology is the development and use of basic tools. The prehistoric discovery of how to control fire and the later Neolithic Revolution increased the available sources of food, and the invention of the wheel helped humans to travel in and control their environment. Developments in historic times, including the printing press, the telephone, and the Internet, have lessened physical barriers to communication and allowed humans to interact freely on a global scale. The steady progress of military technology has brought weapons of ever-increasing destructive power, from clubs to nuclear weapons.

Technology has many effects. It has helped develop more advanced economies (including today's global economy) and has allowed the rise of a leisure class. Many technological processes produce unwanted by-products known as pollution and deplete natural resources to the detriment of Earth's environment. Innovations have always influenced the values of a society and raised new questions of the ethics of technology. Examples include the rise of the notion of efficiency in terms of human productivity, and the challenges of bioethics.

Philosophical debates have arisen over the use of technology, with disagreements over whether technology improves  the human condition or worsens it. Neo-Luddism, anarcho-primitivism, and similar reactionary movements criticize the pervasiveness of technology, arguing that it harms the environment and alienates people; proponents of ideologies such as transhumanism and techno-progressivism view continued technological progress as beneficial to society and the human condition.

Definition and usage

The spread of paper and printing to the West, as in this printing press, helped scientists and politicianscommunicate their ideas easily, leading to the Age of Enlightenment; an example of technology as cultural force.

The use of the term "technology" has changed significantly over the last 200 years. Before the 20th century, the term was uncommon in English, and it was used either to refer to the description or study of the useful arts[3] or to allude to technical education, as in the Massachusetts Institute of Technology (chartered in 1861).[4]

The term "technology" rose to prominence in the 20th century in connection with the Second Industrial Revolution. The term's meanings changed in the early 20th century when American social scientists, beginning with Thorstein Veblen, translated ideas from the German concept of *Technik* into "technology." In German and other European languages, a distinction exists between *technik* and *technologie* that is absent in English, which usually translates both terms as "technology." By the 1930s, "technology" referred not only to the study of the industrial arts but to the industrial arts themselves.[5]

In 1937, the American sociologist Read Bain wrote that "technology includes all tools, machines, utensils, weapons, instruments, housing, clothing, communicating and transporting devices and the skills by which we produce and use them."[6] Bain's definition remains common among scholars today, especially social scientists. Scientists and engineers usually prefer to define technology as applied science, rather than as the things that people make and use.[7] More recently, scholars have borrowed from European philosophers of "technique" to extend the meaning of technology to various forms of instrumental reason, as in Foucault's work on technologies of the self (*techniques de soi*).

Dictionaries and scholars have offered a variety of definitions. The *Merriam-Webster Learner's Dictionary* offers a definition of the term: "the use of science in industry, engineering, etc., to invent useful things or to solve problems" and "a machine, piece of equipment, method, etc., that is created by technology."[8] Ursula Franklin, in her 1989 "Real World of Technology" lecture, gave another definition of the concept; it is "practice, the way we do things around here."[9] The term is often used to imply a specific field of technology, or to refer to high technology or just consumer electronics, rather than technology as a whole.[10] Bernard Stiegler, in *Technics and Time, 1*, defines technology in two ways: as "the pursuit of life by means other than life," and as "organized inorganic matter."[11]

Technology can be most broadly defined as the entities, both material and immaterial, created by the application of mental and physical effort in order to achieve some value. In this usage, technology refers to tools and machines that may be used to solve real-world problems.

It is a far-reaching term that may include simple tools, such as a crowbar or wooden spoon, or more complex machines, such as a space station or particle accelerator. Tools and machines need not be material; virtual technology, such as computer software and business methods, fall under this definition of technology.[12] W. Brian Arthur defines technology in a similarly broad way as "a means to fulfill a human purpose."[13]

The word "technology" can also be used to refer to a collection of techniques. In this context, it is the current state of humanity's knowledge of how to combine resources to produce desired products, to solve problems, fulfill needs, or satisfy wants; it includes technical methods, skills, processes, techniques, tools and raw materials. When combined with another term, such as "medical technology" or "space technology," it refers to the state of the respective field's knowledge and tools. "State-of-the-art technology" refers to the high technology available to humanity in any field.

The invention of integrated circuits and the microprocessor (here, an Intel 4004 chip from

1971) led to the modern computer revolution.

Technology can be viewed as an activity that forms or changes culture.[14] Additionally, technology is the application of math, science, and the arts for the benefit of life as it is known. A modern example is the rise of communication technology, which has lessened barriers to human interaction and as a result has helped spawn new subcultures; the rise of cyberculture has at its basis the development of the Internetand the computer.[15] Not all technology enhances culture in a creative way; technology can also help facilitate political oppression and war via tools such as guns. As a cultural activity, technology predates both science and engineering, each of which formalize some aspects of technological endeavor.

Science, engineering and technology

Antoine Lavoisier conducting an experiment with combustion generated by amplified sun light

The distinction between science, engineering, and

technology is not always clear. Science is systematic knowledge of the physical or material world gained through observation and experimentation.[16] Technologies are not usually exclusively products of science, because they have to satisfy requirements such as utility, usability, and safety.

Engineering is the goal-oriented process of designing and making tools and systems to exploit natural phenomena for practical human means, often (but not always) using results and techniques from science. The development of technology may draw upon many fields of knowledge, including scientific, engineering, mathematical, linguistic, and historical knowledge, to achieve some practical result.

Technology is often a consequence of science and engineering, although technology as a human activity precedes the two fields. For example, science might study the flow of electrons in electrical conductors by using already-existing tools and knowledge. This new-found knowledge may then be used by engineers to create new tools and machines such as semiconductors, computers, and other forms of advanced technology. In this sense, scientists and engineers may both be considered technologists; the three fields are often considered as one for the purposes of research and reference.[17]

The exact relations between science and technology in particular have been debated by scientists, historians, and policymakers in the late 20th century, in part because the debate can inform the funding of basic and applied science. In the immediate wake of World War II, for example, it was widely considered in the United States that technology was simply "applied science" and that to fund basic science was to reap technological results in due time. An articulation of this philosophy could be found explicitly in Vannevar Bush's treatise on postwar science policy, *Science – The Endless Frontier*: "New products, new industries, and more jobs require continuous additions to knowledge of the laws of nature ...

This essential new knowledge can be obtained only through basic scientific research."[18] In the late-1960s, however, this view came under direct attack, leading towards initiatives to fund science for specific tasks (initiatives resisted by the scientific community). The issue remains contentious, though most analysts resist the model that technology simply is a result of scientific research.[19][20]

History

Main articles: History of technology, Timeline of historic inventions, and Timeline of electrical and electronic engineering

Paleolithic (2.5 Ma – 10 ka)

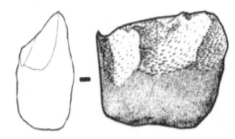

A primitive chopper

Further information: Outline of prehistoric technology

The use of tools by early humans was partly a process of discovery and of evolution. Early humans evolved from a species of foraginghominids which were already bipedal,[21] with a brain mass approximately one third of modern humans.[22] Tool use remained relatively unchanged for most of early human history. Approximately 50,000 years ago, the use of tools and complex set of behaviors emerged, believed by many archaeologists to be connected to the emergence of fully modern language.[23]

Stone tools

Hand axes from the Acheulian period

A Clovis point, made via pressure flaking

Hominids started using primitive stone tools millions of years ago. The earliest stone tools were little more than a fractured rock, but approximately 75,000 years ago,[24] pressure flaking provided a way to make much finer work.

Fire

Main article: Control of fire by early humans

The discovery and utilization of fire, a simple energy source with many profound uses, was a turning point in the technological evolution of humankind.[25] The exact date of its discovery is not known; evidence of burnt animal bones at the Cradle of Humankind suggests that the domestication of fire occurred before 1 Ma;[26] scholarly consensus indicates that *Homo erectus* had controlled fire by between 500 and 400 ka.[27][28] Fire, fueled with wood and charcoal, allowed early humans to cook their food to increase its digestibility, improving its nutrient value and broadening the number of foods that could be eaten.[29]

Clothing and shelter

Other technological advances made during the Paleolithic era were clothing and shelter; the adoption of both technologies cannot be dated exactly, but they were a key to humanity's progress. As the Paleolithic era progressed, dwellings became more sophisticated and more elaborate; as early as 380 ka, humans were constructing temporary wood huts.[30][31] Clothing, adapted from the fur and hides of hunted animals, helped humanity expand into colder regions; humans began to migrate out of Africa by 200 ka and into other continents such as Eurasia.[32]

Neolithic through classical antiquity (10 ka – 300 CE)

An array of Neolithic artifacts, including bracelets, axe heads, chisels, and polishing tools

Human's technological ascent began in earnest in what is known as the Neolithic Period ("New Stone Age"). The invention of polished stone axeswas a major advance that allowed forest clearance on a large scale to create farms. This use of polished stone axes increased greatly in the Neolithic, but were originally used in the preceding Mesolithic in some areas such as Ireland.[33] Agriculture fed larger populations, and the transition to sedentism allowed simultaneously raising more children, as infants no longer needed to be carried, as nomadic ones must. Additionally, children could contribute labor to the raising of crops more readily than they could to the hunter-gatherer economy.[34][35]

With this increase in population and availability of labor came an increase in labor specialization.[36] What triggered the progression from early Neolithic villages to the first cities, such as Uruk, and the first civilizations, such as Sumer, is not specifically known; however, the emergence of increasingly hierarchical social structures and specialized labor, of trade and war amongst adjacent cultures, and the need for collective action to overcome environmental challenges such as irrigation, are all thought to have played a role.[37]

Metal tools

Continuing improvements led to the furnace and bellows and provided, for the first time, the ability to smelt and forge of gold, copper, silver, and lead – native metals found in relatively pure form in nature.[38] The advantages of copper tools over stone, bone, and wooden tools were quickly apparent to early humans, and native copper was probably used from near the beginning of Neolithic times (about 10 ka).[39] Native copper does not naturally occur in large amounts, but copper ores are quite common and some of them produce metal easily when burned in wood or charcoal fires. Eventually, the working of metals led to the discovery of alloys such as bronze and brass (about 4000 BCE). The first uses of iron alloys such as steel dates to around 1800 BCE.[40][41]

Energy and transport

The wheel was invented circa 4000 BCE.

Main article: History of transport

Meanwhile, humans were learning to harness other forms of energy. The earliest known use of wind power is the sailing ship; the earliest record of a ship under sail is that of a Nile boat dating to the 8th millennium BCE.[42] From prehistoric times, Egyptians probably used the power of the annual flooding of the Nile to irrigate their lands, gradually learning to regulate much of it through purposely built irrigation channels and "catch" basins. The ancient Sumerians in Mesopotamia used a complex system of canals and levees to divert water from the Tigris and Euphrates rivers for irrigation.[43]

According to archaeologists, the wheel was invented around 4000 BCE probably independently and nearly simultaneously in Mesopotamia (in present-day Iraq), the Northern Caucasus (Maykop culture) and Central Europe.[44] Estimates on when this may have occurred range from 5500 to 3000 BCE with most experts putting it closer to 4000 BCE.[45] The oldest artifacts with drawings depicting wheeled carts date from about 3500 BCE;[46] however, the wheel may have been in use for millennia before these drawings were made. More recently, the oldest-known wooden wheel in the world was found in the Ljubljana marshes of Slovenia.[47]

The invention of the wheel revolutionized trade and war. It did not take long to discover that wheeled wagons could be used to carry heavy loads. The ancient Sumerians used the potter's wheel and may have invented it.[48] A stone pottery wheel found in the city-state of Ur dates to around 3429 BCE,[49] and even older fragments of wheel-thrown pottery have been found in the same area.[49] Fast (rotary) potters' wheels enabled early mass production of pottery, but it was the use of the wheel as a transformer of energy (through water wheels, windmills, and even treadmills) that revolutionized the application of nonhuman power sources. The first two-wheeled carts were derived from travois[50] and were first used in Mesopotamia and Iran in around 3000 BCE.[50]

The oldest known constructed roadways are the stone-paved streets of the city-state of Ur, dating to circa 4000 BCE[51] and timber roads leading through the swamps of Glastonbury, England, dating to around the same time period.[51] The first long-distance road, which came into use around 3500 BCE,[51] spanned 1,500 miles from the Persian Gulf to the Mediterranean Sea,[51] but was not paved and was only partially maintained.[51] In around 2000 BCE, the Minoans on the Greek island of Crete built a fifty-kilometer (thirty-mile) road leading from the palace of Gortyn on the south side of the island, through the mountains, to the palace of Knossos on the north side of the island.[51] Unlike the earlier road, the Minoan road was completely paved.[51]

Plumbing

Photograph of the Pont du Gard in France, one of the most famous ancient Roman aqueducts[52]

Ancient Minoan private homes had running water.[53] A bathtub virtually identical to modern ones was unearthed at the Palace of Knossos.[53][54] Several Minoan private homes also had toilets, which could be flushed by pouring water down the drain.[53] The ancient Romans had many public flush toilets,[54] which emptied into an extensive sewage system.[54] The primary sewer in Rome was the Cloaca Maxima;[54] construction began on it in the sixth century BCE and it is still in use today.[54]

The ancient Romans also had a complex system of aqueducts,[52] which were used to transport water across long distances.[52]The first Roman aqueduct was built in 312 BCE.[52] The eleventh and final ancient Roman aqueduct was built in 226 CE.[52] Put together, the Roman aqueducts extended over 450 kilometers,[52] but less than seventy kilometers of this was above ground and supported by arches.[52]

Medieval and modern history (300 CE – present)

Main articles: Medieval technology, Renaissance technology, Industrial Revolution, Second Industrial Revolution, Information Technology, and Productivity improving technologies (economic history)

Innovations continued through the Middle Ages with innovations such as silk, the horse collar and horseshoes in the first few hundred years after the fall of the Roman Empire. Medieval technology saw

the use of simple machines (such as the lever, the screw, and the pulley) being combined to form more complicated tools, such as
the wheelbarrow, windmills and clocks.
The Renaissance brought forth many of these innovations, including the printing press (which facilitated the greater communication of knowledge), and technology became increasingly associated with science, beginning a cycle of mutual advancement. The advancements in technology in this era allowed a more steady supply of food, followed by the wider availability of consumer goods.

The automobilerevolutio nized personal transportation.

Starting in the United Kingdom in the 18th century, the Industrial Revolution was a period of great technological discovery, particularly in the areas of agriculture, manufacturing, mining, metallurgy, and transport, driven by the discovery of steam power. Technology took another step in a second industrial revolution with the harnessing of electricity to create such innovations as the electric motor, light bulb, and countless others. Scientific advancement and the discovery of new concepts later allowed for powered flight and advancements in medicine, chemistry, physics, and engineering. The rise in technology has led to skyscrapers and broad urban areas whose inhabitants rely on motors to transport them and their food supply. Communication was also greatly improved with the invention of the telegraph, telephone, radio and television. The late 19th and early 20th centuries saw a revolution in transportation with the invention of the airplane and automobile.

F-15 and F-16 flying over Kuwaiti oil fires during the Gulf War in 1991.

The 20th century brought a host of innovations. In physics, the discovery of nuclear fission has led to both nuclear weapons and nuclear power. Computers were also invented and later miniaturized utilizing transistors and integrated circuits. Information technology subsequently led to the creation of the Internet, which ushered in the current Information Age. Humans have also been able to explore space with satellites(later used for telecommunication) and in manned missions going all the way to the moon. In medicine, this era brought innovations such as open-heart surgery and later stem cell therapy along with new medications and treatments.

Complex manufacturing and construction techniques and organizations are needed to make and maintain these new technologies, and entire industries have arisen to support and develop succeeding generations of increasingly more complex tools. Modern technology increasingly relies on training and education – their designers, builders, maintainers, and users often require sophisticated general and specific training. Moreover, these technologies have become so complex that entire fields have been created to support them, including engineering, medicine, and computer science, and other fields have been made more complex, such as construction, transportation and architecture.

Philosophy

Technicism

Generally, technicism is the belief in the utility of technology for improving human societies.[55] Taken to an extreme, technicism "reflects a fundamental attitude which seeks to control reality, to resolve all problems with the use of scientific-technological methods and

413

tools."[56] In other words, human beings will someday be able to master all problems and possibly even control the future using technology. Some, such as Stephen V. Monsma,[57] connect these ideas to the abdication of religion as a higher moral authority.

Optimism

Optimistic assumptions are made by proponents of ideologies suchas transhumanism and singularitarianism, which view technological development as generally having beneficial effects for the society and the human condition. In these ideologies, technological development is morally good.

Trans humanists generally believe that the point of technology is to overcome barriers, and that what we commonly refer to as the human condition is just another barrier to be surpassed. Singularitarians believe in some sort of "accelerating change"; that the rate of technological progress accelerates as we obtain more technology, and that this will culminate in a "Singularity" after artificial general intelligence is invented in which progress is nearly infinite; hence the term. Estimates for the date of this Singularity vary,[58] but prominent futurist Ray Kurzweil estimates the Singularity will occur in 2045.

Kurzweil is also known for his history of the universe in six epochs: (1) the physical/chemical epoch, (2) the life epoch, (3) the human/brain epoch, (4) the technology epoch, (5) the artificial intelligence epoch, and (6) the universal colonization epoch. Going from one epoch to the next is a Singularity in its own right, and a period of speeding up precedes it. Each epoch takes a shorter time, which means the whole history of the universe is one giant Singularity event.[59]

Some critics see these ideologies as examples of scientism and techno-utopianism and fear the notion of human enhancement and technological singularity which they support. Some have described Karl Marx as a techno-optimist.[60]

Skepticism and critics

Luddites smashing a power loom in 1812

On the somewhat skeptical side are certain philosophers like Herbert Marcuse and John Zerzan, who believe that technological societies are inherently flawed. They suggest that the inevitable result of such a society is to become evermore technological at the cost of freedom and psychological health.

Many, such as the Luddites and prominent philosopher Martin Heidegger, hold serious, although not entirely, deterministic reservations about technology (see "The Question Concerning Technology"[61]). According to Heidegger scholars Hubert Dreyfus and Charles Spinosa, "Heidegger does not oppose technology. He hopes to reveal the essence of technology in a way that 'in no way confines us to a stultified compulsion to push on blindly with technology or, what comes to the same thing, to rebel helplessly against it.' Indeed, he promises that 'when we once open ourselves expressly to the essence of technology, we find ourselves unexpectedly taken into a freeing claim.'[62] What this entails is a more complex relationship to technology than either techno-optimists or techno-pessimists tend to allow."[63]

Some of the most poignant criticisms of technology are found in what are now considered to be dystopian literary classics such as Aldous Huxley's *Brave New World*, Anthony Burgess's *A Clockwork Orange*, and George Orwell's *Nineteen Eighty-Four*. In Goethe's *Faust*, Faust selling his soul to the devil in return for power over the physical world is also often interpreted as a metaphor for the adoption of industrial technology. More recently, modern works of science fiction such as those by Philip K. Dick and William Gibson and films such as *Blade Runner* and *Ghost in the Shell* project highly ambivalent or cautionary attitudes toward technology's impact on human society and identity.

The late cultural critic Neil Postman distinguished tool-using societies from technological societies and from what he called "technopolies," societies that are dominated by the ideology of technological and scientific progress to the exclusion or harm of other cultural practices, values and world-views.[64]

Darin Barney has written about technology's impact on practices of citizenship and democratic culture, suggesting that technology can be construed as (1) an object of political debate, (2) a means or medium of discussion, and (3) a setting for democratic deliberation and citizenship. As a setting for democratic culture, Barney suggests that technology tends to make ethical questions, including the question of what a good life consists in, nearly impossible, because they already give an answer to the question: a good life is one that includes the use of more and more technology.[65]

Nikolas Kompridis has also written about the dangers of new technology, such as genetic engineering, nanotechnology, synthetic biology, and robotics. He warns that these technologies introduce unprecedented new challenges to human beings, including the possibility of the permanent alteration of our biological nature. These concerns are shared by other philosophers, scientists and public intellectuals who have written about similar issues (e.g. Francis Fukuyama, Jürgen Habermas, William Joy, and Michael Sandel).[66]

Another prominent critic of technology is Hubert Dreyfus, who has published books such as *On the Internet* and *What Computers Still Can't Do.*

A more infamous anti-technological treatise is *Industrial Society and Its Future*, written by the Unabomber Ted Kaczynski and printed in several major newspapers (and later books) as part of an effort to end his bombing campaign of the techno-industrial infrastructure.

Appropriate Technology

The notion of appropriate technology was developed in the 20th century by thinkers such as E. F. Schumacher and Jacques Ellul to describe situations where it was not desirable to use very new technologies or those that required access to some centralized infrastructure or parts or skills imported from elsewhere. The ecovillage movement emerged in part due to this concern.

Optimism and skepticism in the 21st century

This section mainly focuses on American concerns even if it can reasonably be generalized to other Western countries.

The inadequate quantity and quality of American jobs is one of the most fundamental economic challenges we face. [...] What's the linkage between technology and this fundamental problem?

— Bernstein, Jared, "It's Not a Skills Gap That's Holding Wages Down: It's the Weak Economy, Among Other Things," in The American Prospect, October 2014

In his article, Jared Bernstein, a Senior Fellow at the Center on Budget and Policy Priorities,[67] questions the widespread idea that automation, and more broadly, technological advances, have mainly contributed to this growing labor market problem. His thesis appears to be a third way between optimism and skepticism. Essentially,

he stands for a neutral approach of the linkage between technology and American issues
concerning unemployment and declining wages.

He uses two main arguments to defend his point. First, because of recent technological advances, an increasing number of workers are losing their jobs. Yet, scientific evidence fails to clearly demonstrate that technology has displaced so many workers that it has created more problems than it has solved.
Indeed, automation threatens repetitive jobs but higher-end jobs are still necessary because they complement technology and manual jobs that "requires flexibility judgment and common sense"[68] remain hard to replace with machines. Second, studies have not shown clear links between recent technology advances and the wage trends of the last decades.

Therefore, according to Bernstein, instead of focusing on technology and its hypothetical influences on current American increasing unemployment and declining wages, one needs to worry more about "bad policy that fails to offset the imbalances in demand, trade, income and opportunity."[68]

For people who use both the Internet and mobile devices in excessive quantities it is likely for them to experience fatigue and over exhaustion as a result of disruptions in their sleeping patterns. Continuous studies have shown that increased BMI and weight gain are associated with people who spend long hours online and not exercising frequently [69]. Heavy Internet use is also displayed in the school lower grades of those who use it in excessive amounts [70]. It has also been noted that the use of mobile phones whilst driving has increased the occurrence of road accidents – particularly amongst teen drivers. Statistically, teens reportedly have fourfold the amount of road traffic incidents as those who are 20 years or older, and a very high percentage of adolescents write (81%) and read (92%) texts while driving.[71] In this context, mass media and technology have a negative impact on people, on both their mental and physical health.

Complex technological systems

Thomas P. Hughes stated that because technology has been considered as a key way to solve problems, we need to be aware of its complex and varied characters to use it more efficiently.[72] What is the difference between a wheel or a compass and cooking machines such as an oven or a gas stove? Can we consider all of them, only a part of them, or none of them as technologies?

Technology is often considered too narrowly; according to Hughes, "Technology is a creative process involving human ingenuity".[73] This definition's emphasis on creativity avoids unbounded definitions that may mistakenly include cooking "technologies," but it also highlights the prominent role of humans and therefore their responsibilities for the use of complex technological systems.

Yet, because technology is everywhere and has dramatically changed landscapes and societies, Hughes argues that engineers, scientists, and managers have often believed that they can use technology to shape the world as they want. They have often supposed that technology is easily controllable and this assumption has to be thoroughly questioned.[72]For instance, Evgeny Morozov particularly challenges two concepts: "Internet-centrism" and "solutionism."[74] Internet-centrism refers to the idea that our society is convinced that the Internet is one of the most stable and coherent forces. Solutionism is the ideology that every social issue can be solved thanks to technology and especially thanks to the internet. In fact, technology intrinsically contains uncertainties and limitations. According to Alexis Madrigal's review of Morozov's theory, to ignore it will lead to "unexpected consequences that could eventually cause more damage than the problems they seek to address."[75] Benjamin R. Cohen and Gwen Ottinger also discussed the multivalent effects of technology.[76]

Therefore, recognition of the limitations of technology, and more broadly, scientific knowledge, is needed – especially in cases dealing with environmental justice and health issues. Ottinger continues this reasoning and argues that the ongoing recognition of the limitations of scientific knowledge goes hand in hand with scientists and engineers' new comprehension of their role. Such an approach of technology and science "[require] technical professionals to conceive of their roles in the process differently. [They have to consider themselves as] collaborators in research and problem solving rather than simply providers of information and technical solutions."[77]

Competitiveness

Technology is properly defined as any application of science to accomplish a function. The science can be leading edge or well established and the function can have high visibility or be significantly more mundane, but it is all technology, and its exploitation is the foundation of all competitive advantage.

Technology-based planning is what was used to build the US industrial giants before WWII (e.g., Dow, DuPont, GM) and it is what was used to transform the US into a superpower. It was not economic-based planning.

Other animal species

This adult gorilla uses a branch as a walking stick to gauge the water's depth, an example of technology usage by non-human primates.

The use of basic technology is also a feature of other animal species apart from humans. These include primates such as chimpanzees,[78] some dolphin communities,[79] and crows.[80][81] Considering a more generic perspective of technology as ethology of active environmental conditioning and control, we can also refer to animal examples such as beavers and their dams, or bees and their honeycombs.

The ability to make and use tools was once considered a defining characteristic of the genus Homo.[82] However, the discovery of tool construction among chimpanzees and related primates has discarded the notion of the use of technology as unique to humans. For example, researchers have observed wild chimpanzees utilising tools for foraging: some of the tools used include leaf sponges, termite fishing probes, pestles and levers.[83] West African chimpanzees also use stone hammers and anvils for cracking nuts,[84] as do capuchin monkeys of Boa Vista, Brazil.[85]

Future technology

Theories of technology often attempt to predict the future of technology based on the high technology and science of the time. As with all predictions of the future, however, technology's is uncertain.

In 2005, futurist Ray Kurzweil predicted that the future of technology would mainly consist of an overlapping "GNR Revolution" of genetics, nanotechnology and robotics, with robotics being the most important of the three.[86]

Mobile phone

Evolution of mobile phones, to an early smartphone.

A mobile phone, known as a cell phone in North America, is a portable telephone that can make and receive calls over a radio frequency link while the user is moving within a telephone service area. The radio frequency link establishes a connection to the switching systems of a mobile phone operator, which provides access to the public switched telephone network (PSTN). Modern mobile telephone services use a cellular networkarchitecture, and, therefore, mobile telephones are called *cellular telephones* or *cell phones*, in North America. In addition to telephony, 2000s-era mobile phones support a variety of other services, such as text messaging, MMS, email, Internet access, short-range wireless communications (infrared, Bluetooth), business applications, video games, and digital photography. Mobile phones offering only those capabilities are known as feature phones; mobile phones which offer greatly advanced computing capabilities are referred to as smartphones.

The first handheld mobile phone was demonstrated by John F. Mitchell[1][2] and Martin Cooper of Motorola in 1973, using a handset weighing c. 2 kilograms (4.4 lbs).[3] In 1979, Nippon Telegraph and Telephone (NTT) launched the world's first cellular network in Japan.[4] In 1983, the DynaTAC 8000x was the first commercially available handheld mobile phone. From 1983 to 2014, worldwide mobile phone subscriptions grew to over seven billion, penetrating virtually 100% of the global population and reaching even the bottom of the economic pyramid.[5] In first quarter of 2016, the top smartphone developers worldwide were Samsung, Apple, and Huawei (and "[s]martphone sales represented 78 percent of total mobile phone sales").[6] For feature phones (or "dumbphones") as of 2016, the largest were Samsung, Nokia, and Alcatel.[7]

Mobile Phones In Retrospect

Martin Cooper of Motorola made the first publicized handheld mobile phone call on a prototype DynaTAC model on April 4, 1973. This is a reenactment in 2007.

A handheld mobile radio telephone service was envisioned in the early stages of radio engineering. In 1917, Finnish inventor Eric Tigerstedt filed a patent for a "pocket-size folding telephone with a very thin carbon microphone". Early predecessors of cellular phones included analog radio communications from ships and trains. The race to create truly portable telephone devices began after World War II, with developments taking place in many countries. The advances in mobile telephony have been traced in successive "generations", starting with the early zeroth-generation (0G) services, such as Bell System's Mobile Telephone Service and its successor, the Improved Mobile Telephone Service. These 0G systems were not cellular, supported few simultaneous calls, and were very expensive.

The Motorola DynaTAC 8000X. First commercially available handheld cellular mobile phone, 1984.

The first handheld cellular mobile phone was demonstrated by John F. Mitchell[1][2] and Martin Cooper of Motorola in 1973, using a handset weighing c. 4.4 lbs (2 kg).[3] The first commercial automated cellular network was launched in Japan by Nippon Telegraph and Telephone in 1979. This was followed in 1981 by the simultaneous launch of the Nordic Mobile Telephone (NMT) system in Denmark, Finland, Norway, and Sweden.[8] Several other countries then followed in the early to mid-1980s. These first-generation (1G) systems could support far more simultaneous calls but still used analog cellular technology. In 1983, the DynaTAC 8000x was the first commercially available handheld mobile phone.

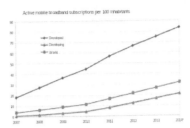

In 1991, the second-generation (2G) digital cellular technology was launched in Finland by Radiolinja on the GSM standard. This sparked competition in the sector as the new operators challenged the incumbent 1G network operators.

Ten years later, in 2001, the third generation (3G) was launched in Japan by NTT DoCoMo on the WCDMA standard.[9] This was followed by 3.5G, 3G+ or turbo 3G enhancements based on the high-speed packet access (HSPA) family, allowing UMTS networks to have higher data transfer speeds and capacity.

By 2009, it had become clear that, at some point, 3G networks would be overwhelmed by the growth of bandwidth-intensive applications, such as streaming media.[10] Consequently, the industry began looking to data-optimized fourth-generation technologies, with the promise of speed improvements up to ten-fold over existing 3G technologies. The first two commercially available technologies billed as 4G were the WiMAX standard, offered in North America by Sprint, and the LTE standard, first offered in Scandinavia by TeliaSonera.

Types

Smartphone

Active mobile broadband subscriptions per 100 inhabitants.[11]

Smartphones have a number of distinguishing features. The International Telecommunication Union measures those with Internet connection, which it calls *Active Mobile-Broadband subscriptions* (which includes tablets, etc.). In the developed world, smartphones have now overtaken the usage of earlier mobile systems. However, in the developing world, they account for around 50% of mobile telephony.

Feature phone

Feature phone is a term typically used as a retronym to describe mobile phones which are limited in capabilities in contrast to a modern smartphone. Feature phones typically provide voice calling and text messaging functionality, in addition to basic multimedia and Internet capabilities, and other services offered by the user's wireless service provider. A feature phone has additional functions over and above a basic mobile phone which is only capable of voice calling and text messaging.[12][13] Feature phones and basic mobile phones tend to use a proprietary, custom-designed software and user interface. By contrast, smartphones generally use a mobile operating system that often shares common traits across devices.

Kosher phone

There are Orthodox Jewish religious restrictions which, by some interpretations, standard mobile telephones overstep. To deal with this problem, some rabbinical organizations have recommended that phones with text-messaging capability not be used by children.[14] Phones with restricted features are known as kosher phones and have rabbinical approval for use in Israel and elsewhere by observant Orthodox Jews. Although these phones are intended to prevent immodesty, some vendors report good sales to adults who prefer the simplicity of the devices. Some phones are approved for use by essential workers (such as health, security, and public service workers) on the sabbath, even though the use of any electrical device is generally prohibited during this time.[15]

Hardware

The common components found on all phones are:

- A battery, providing the power source for the phone functions.
- An input mechanism to allow the user to interact with the phone. These are a keypad for feature phones and touch screens for most smartphones.
- A screen which echoes the user's typing displays text messages, contacts, and more.
- Basic mobile phone services to allow users to make calls and send text messages.
- All GSM phones use a SIM card to allow an account to be swapped among devices. Some CDMA devices also have a similar card called an R-UIM.
- Individual GSM, WCDMA, iDEN and some satellite phone devices are uniquely identified by an International Mobile Equipment Identity (IMEI) number.

Low-end mobile phones are often referred to as feature phones and offer basic telephony. Handsets with more advanced computing ability through the use of native software applications are known as smartphones.

Sound

In sound, smartphones and feature phones vary little.
Some audio-quality enhancing features, such as Voice
over LTE and HD Voice, have appeared and are often
available on newer smartphones. Sound quality can
remain a problem due to the design of the phone, the
quality of the cellular network and compression
algorithms used in long distance calls.[16][17] Audio quality
can be improved using a VoIP application
over WiFi.[18] Cellphones have small speakers so that the
user can use a speakerphone feature and talk to a person
on the phone without holding it to their ear. The small
speakers can also be used to listen to digital audio files of
music or speech or watch videos with an audio
component, without holding the phone close to the ear.

SIM card

Typical mobile phone mini-SIM card.

GSM feature phones require a small microchip called a Subscriber Identity Module or SIM card, in order to function. The SIM card is approximately the size of a small postage stamp and is usually placed underneath the battery in the rear of the unit. The SIM securely stores the service-subscriber key (IMSI) and the K_i used to identify and authenticate the user of the mobile phone. The SIM card allows users to change phones by simply removing the SIM card from one mobile phone and inserting it into another mobile phone or broadband telephony device, provided that this is not prevented by a SIM lock. The first SIM card was made in 1991 by Munich smart card maker Giesecke & Devrient for the Finnish wireless network operator Radiolinja.[citation needed]

A hybrid mobile phone can hold up to four SIM cards. SIM and R-UIM cards may be mixed together to allow both GSM and CDMA networks to be accessed. From 2010 onwards, such phones became popular in emerging markets,[19] and this was attributed to the desire to obtain the lowest on-net calling rate.

Infrastructure

Mobile phones communicate with cell towers that are placed to give coverage across a telephone service area which is divided up into 'cells'. Each cell uses a different set of frequencies from neighboring cells, and will typically be covered by 3 towers placed at different locations. The cell towers are usually interconnected to each other and the phone network and the internet by wired connections. Due to bandwidth limitations each cell will have a maximum number of cell phones it can handle at once. The cells are therefore sized depending on the expected usage density, and may be much smaller in cities. In that case much lower transmitter powers are used to avoid broadcasting beyond the cell.

As a phone moves around, a phone will "hand off"- automatically disconnect and reconnect to the tower that gives the best reception.

Additionally, short-range Wi-Fi infrastructure is often used by smartphones as much as possible as it offloads traffic from cell networks on to local area networks.

Software

Text messaging

A text message (SMS).

A common data application on mobile phones is Short Message Service (SMS) text messaging. The first SMS message was sent from a computer to a mobile phone in 1992 in the UK while the first person-to-person SMS from phone to phone was sent in Finland in 1993. The first mobile news service, delivered via SMS, was launched in Finland in 2000,[citation needed] and subsequently many organizations provided "on-demand" and "instant" news services by SMS. Multimedia Messaging Service (MMS) was introduced in 2001.

Sales

By manufacturer

Market share of top-five worldwide mobile phone vendors, Q2 2016

Rank	Manufacturer	Strategy Analytics report[20]
1	Samsung	22.3%
2	Apple	12.9%
3	Huawei	8.9%
4	Oppo	5.4%
5	Xiaomi	4.5%

Others	46.0%
Note: Vendor shipments are branded shipments and exclude OEM sales for all vendors	

From 1983 to 1998, Motorola was market leader in mobile phones. Nokia was the market leader in mobile phones from 1998 to 2012.[21] In Q1 2012, Samsung surpassed Nokia, selling 93.5 million units as against Nokia's 82.7 million units. Samsung has retained its top position since then. In Q2 2016, the top five manufacturers were Samsung (22.3%), Apple (12.9%), Huawei (8.9%), Oppo (5.4%), and Xiaomi (4.5%).[22]

By mobile phone operator

Growth in mobile phone subscribers per country from 1980 to 2009.

The world's largest individual mobile operator by number of subscribers is China Mobile, which has over 500 million mobile phone subscribers.[23] Over 50 mobile operators have over ten million subscribers each, and over 150 mobile operators had at least one million subscribers by the end of 2009.[24] In 2014, there were more than seven billion mobile phone subscribers worldwide, a number that is expected to keep growing.

Use General

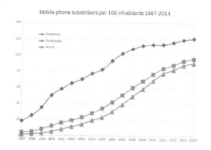

Mobile phone subscribers per 100 inhabitants. 2014 figure is estimated.

Mobile phones are used for a variety of purposes, such as keeping in touch with family members, for conducting business, and in order to have access to a telephone in the event of an emergency. Some people carry more than one mobile phone for different purposes, such as for business and personal use. Multiple SIM cards may be used to take advantage of the benefits of different calling plans. For example, a particular plan might provide for cheaper local calls, long-distance calls, international calls, or roaming.

The mobile phone has been used in a variety of diverse contexts in society. For example:

- A study by Motorola found that one in ten mobile phone subscribers have a second phone that is often kept secret from other family members. These phones may be used to engage in such activities as extramarital affairs or clandestine business dealings.[25]
- Some organizations assist victims of domestic violence by providing mobile phones for use in emergencies. These are often refurbished phones.[26]
- The advent of widespread text-messaging has resulted in the cell phone novel, the first literary genre to emerge from the cellular age, via text messaging to a website that collects the novels as a whole.[27]
- Mobile telephony also facilitates activism and public journalism being explored by Reuters and Yahoo![28] and small independent news companies such as Jasmine News in Sri Lanka.
- The United Nations reported that mobile phones have spread faster than any other form of technology and can improve the livelihood of the poorest people in developing countries, by providing access to information in places where landlines or the Internet are not available, especially in the least developed countries. Use of mobile phones also spawns a wealth of micro-enterprises, by providing such work as selling

airtime on the streets and repairing or refurbishing handsets.[29]

- In Mali and other African countries, people used to travel from village to village to let friends and relatives know about weddings, births, and other events. This can now be avoided in areas with mobile phone coverage, which are usually more extensive than areas with just land-line penetration.
- The TV industry has recently started using mobile phones to drive live TV viewing through mobile apps, advertising, social TV, and mobile TV.[30] It is estimated that 86% of Americans use their mobile phone while watching TV.
- In some parts of the world, mobile phone sharing is common. Cell phone sharing is prevalent in urban India, as families and groups of friends often share one or more mobile phones among their members. There are obvious economic benefits, but often familial customs and traditional gender roles play a part.[31] It is common for a village to have access to only one mobile phone, perhaps owned by a teacher or missionary, which is available to all members of the village for necessary calls.[32]

Content distribution

In 1998, one of the first examples of distributing and selling media content through the mobile phone was the sale of ringtones by Radiolinja in Finland. Soon afterwards, other media content appeared, such as news, video games, jokes, horoscopes, TV content and advertising. Most early content for mobile phones tended to be copies of legacy media, such as banner advertisements or TV news highlight video clips. Recently, unique content for mobile phones has been emerging, from ringtones and ringback tones to mobisodes, video content that has been produced exclusively for mobile phones.

Mobile banking and payment

Mobile payment system.

Main articles: Mobile banking and Mobile payment

See also: Branchless banking and Contactless payment

In many countries, mobile phones are used to provide mobile banking services, which may include the ability to transfer cash payments by secure SMS text message. Kenya's M-PESA mobile banking service, for example, allows customers of the mobile phone operator Safaricomto hold cash balances which are recorded on their SIM cards. Cash can be deposited or withdrawn from M-PESA accounts at Safaricom retail outlets located throughout the country and can be transferred electronically from person to person and used to pay bills to companies.

Branchless banking has also been successful in South Africa and the Philippines. A pilot project in Bali was launched in 2011 by the International Finance Corporation and an Indonesian bank, Bank Mandiri.[33]

Another application of mobile banking technology is Zidisha, a US-based nonprofit micro-lending platform that allows residents of developing countries to raise small business loans from Web users worldwide. Zidisha uses mobile banking for loan disbursements and repayments, transferring funds from lenders in the United States to borrowers in rural Africa who have mobile phones and can use the Internet.[34]

Mobile payments were first trialled in Finland in 1998 when two Coca-Cola vending machines in Espoo were enabled to work with SMS payments. Eventually, the idea spread and in 1999, the Philippines launched the country's first commercial mobile payments systems with mobile operators Globe and Smart.

Some mobile phones can make mobile payments via direct mobile billing schemes, or through contactless payments if the phone and the point of sale support near field communication (NFC).[35] Enabling contactless payments through NFC-equipped mobile phones requires the co-operation of manufacturers, network operators, and retail merchants.[36][37][38]

Mobile tracking

Mobile phones are commonly used to collect location data. While the phone is turned on, the geographical location of a mobile phone can be determined easily (whether it is being used or not) using a technique known as multilateration to calculate the differences in time for a signal to travel from the mobile phone to each

of several cell towers near the owner of the phone.[39][40]

The movements of a mobile phone user can be tracked by their service provider and if desired, by law enforcement agencies and their governments. Both the SIM card and the handset can be tracked.[39]

443

China has proposed using this technology to track the commuting patterns of Beijing city residents.[41] In the UK and US, law enforcement and intelligence services use mobile phones to perform surveillance operations. They possess technology that enables them to activate the microphones in mobile phones remotely in order to listen to conversations which take place near the phone.[42][43]

Hackers are able to track a phone's location, read messages, and record calls, just by knowing the phone number.[44]

While driving

A driver using two hand-held mobile phones at once.

A sign along Bellaire Boulevard in Southside Place, Texas (Greater Houston) states that using mobile phones while driving is prohibited from 7:30 am to 9:00 am and from 2:00 pm to 4:15 pm

Mobile phone use while driving, including talking on the phone, texting, or operating other phone features, is common but controversial. It is widely considered dangerous due to distracted driving. Being distracted while operating a motor vehicle has been shown to increase the risk of accidents. In September 2010, the US National Highway Traffic Safety Administration (NHTSA) reported that 995 people were killed by drivers distracted by cell phones. In March 2011, a U.S. insurance company, State Farm Insurance, announced the results of a study which showed 19% of drivers surveyed accessed the Internet on a smartphone while driving.[45] Many jurisdictions prohibit the use of mobile phones while driving. In Egypt, Israel, Japan, Portugal, and Singapore, both handheld and hands-free use of a mobile phone (which uses a speakerphone) is banned. In other countries, including the UK and France and in many U.S. states, only handheld phone use is banned while hands-free use is permitted.

A 2011 study reported that over 90% of college students surveyed text (initiate, reply or read) while driving.[46] The scientific literature on the dangers of driving while sending a text message from a mobile phone, or *texting while driving*, is limited. A simulation study at the University of Utah found a sixfold increase in distraction-related accidents when texting.[47]

Due to the increasing complexity of mobile phones, they are often more like mobile computers in their available uses. This has introduced additional difficulties for law enforcement officials when attempting to distinguish one usage from another in drivers using their devices. This is more apparent in countries which ban both handheld and hands-free usage, rather than those which ban handheld use only, as officials cannot easily tell which function of the mobile phone is being used simply by looking at the driver. This can lead to drivers being stopped for using their device illegally for a phone call when, in fact, they were using the device legally, for example, when using the phone's incorporated controls for car stereo, GPS or satnav.

A 2010 study reviewed the incidence of mobile phone use while cycling and its effects on behaviour and safety.[48] In 2013, a national survey in the US reported the number of drivers who reported using their cellphones to access the Internet while driving had risen to nearly one of four.[49] A study conducted by the University of Vienna examined approaches for reducing inappropriate and problematic use of mobile phones, such as using mobile phones while driving.[50]

Accidents involving a driver being distracted by talking on a mobile phone have begun to be prosecuted as negligence similar to speeding. In the United Kingdom, from 27 February 2007, motorists who are caught using a hand-held mobile phone while driving will have three penalty points added to their license in addition to the fine of £60.[51] This increase was introduced to try to stem the increase in drivers ignoring the law.[52] Japan prohibits all mobile phone use while driving, including use of hands-free devices. New Zealand has banned hand-held cell phone use since 1 November 2009. Many states in the United States have banned texting on cell phones while driving. Illinois became the 17th American state to enforce this law.[53] As of July 2010, 30 states had banned texting while driving, with Kentucky becoming the most recent addition on July 15.[54]

Public Health Law Research maintains a list of distracted driving laws in the United States. This database of laws provides a comprehensive view of the provisions of laws that restrict the use of mobile communication devices while driving for all 50 states and the District of Columbia between 1992 when first law was passed, through December 1, 2010. The dataset contains information on 22 dichotomous, continuous or categorical variables including, for example, activities regulated (e.g., texting versus talking, hands-free versus handheld), targeted populations, and exemptions.[55]

In 2010, an estimated 1500 pedestrians were injured in the US while using a cellphone and some jurisdictions have attempted to ban pedestrians from using their cellphones.[56][57]

Health effect

The effect of mobile phone radiation on human health is the subject of recentinterest and study, as a result of the enormous increase in mobile phone usage throughout the world. Mobile phones use electromagnetic radiation in the microwave range, which some believe may be harmful to human health. A large body of research exists, both epidemiological and experimental, in non-human animals and in humans. The majority of this research shows no definite causative relationship between exposure to mobile phones and harmful biological effects in humans. This is often paraphrased simply as the balance of evidence showing no harm to humans from mobile phones, although a significant number of individual studies do suggest such a relationship, or are inconclusive. Other digital wireless systems, such as data communication networks, produce similar radiation.

On 31 May 2011, the World Health Organization stated that mobile phone use may possibly represent a long-term health risk,[58][59] classifying mobile phone radiation as "possibly carcinogenic to humans" after a team of scientists reviewed studies on mobile phone safety.[60] The mobile phone is in category 2B, which ranks it alongside coffee and other possibly carcinogenic substances.[61][62]

Some recentstudies have found an association between mobile phone use and certain kinds of brain and salivary gland tumors. Lennart Hardell and other authors of a 2009 meta-analysis of 11 studies from peer-reviewed journals concluded that cell phone usage for at least ten years "approximately doubles the risk of being diagnosed with a brain tumor on the same ('ipsilateral') side of the head as that preferred for cell phone use".[63]

One study of past mobile phone use cited in the report showed a "40% increased risk for gliomas (brain cancer) in the highest category of heavy users (reported average: 30 minutes per day over a 10-year period)".[64] This is a reversal of the study's prior position that cancer was unlikely to be caused by cellular phones or their base stations and that reviews had found no convincing evidence for other health effects.[59][65] However, a study published 24 March 2012, in the *British Medical Journal* questioned these estimates because the increase in brain cancers has not paralleled the increase in mobile phone use.[66] Certain countries, including France, have

449

warned against the use of mobile phones by minors in particular, due to health risk uncertainties.[67] Mobile pollution by transmitting electromagnetic waves can be decreased up to 90% by adopting the circuit as designed in mobile phone and mobile exchange.[68]

In May 2016, preliminary findings of a long-term study by the U.S. government suggested that radio-frequency (RF) radiation, the type emitted by cell phones, can cause cancer.[69][70]

Educational impact

A study by the London School of Economics found that banning mobile phones in schools could increase pupils' academic performance, providing benefits equal to one extra week of schooling per year.[71]

Electronic waste regulation

Scrapped mobile phones.

See also: Mobile phone recycling

Studies have shown that around 40-50% of the environmental impact of mobile phones occurs during the manufacture of their printed wiring boards and integrated circuits.[72]

The average user replaces their mobile phone every 11 to 18 months,[73] and the discarded phones then contribute to electronic waste. Mobile phone manufacturers within Europe are subject to the WEEE directive, and Australia has introduced a mobile phone recycling scheme.[74]

Apple Inc. had an advanced robotic disassembler and sorter called Liam specifically for recycling outdated or broken iPhones. [350]

Theft

According to the Federal Communications Commission, one out of three robberies involve the theft of a cellular phone. Police data in San Francisco show that half of all robberies in 2012 were thefts of cellular phones.An online petition on Change.org, called *Secure our Smartphones*, urged smartphone manufacturers to install kill switches in their devices to make them unusable if stolen. The petition is part of a joint effort by New York Attorney General Eric Schneiderman and San Francisco District Attorney George Gascón and was directed to the CEOs of the major smartphone manufacturers and telecommunication carriers.[75] On Monday, 10 June 2013, Apple announced that it would install a "kill switch" on its next iPhone operating system, due to debut in October 2013.[76]

All mobile phones have a unique identifier called IMEI. Anyone can report their phone as lost or stolen with their Telecom Carrier, and the IMEI would be blacklisted with a central registry.[77] Telecom carriers, depending upon local regulation can or must implement blocking of blacklisted phones in their network. There are, however, a number of ways to circumvent a blacklist. One method is to send the phone to a country where the telecom carriers are not required to implement the blacklisting and sell it there,[78] another involves altering the phone's IMEI number.[79] Even so, blacklisted phones typically have less value on the second-hand market if the phones original IMEI is blacklisted.

Future

5G is a technology and term used in research papers and projects to denote the next major phase in mobile telecommunication standards beyond the 4G/IMT-Advanced standards. The term 5G is not officially used in any specification or official document yet made public by telecommunication companies or standardization bodies such as 3GPP, WiMAX Forum or ITU-R. New standards beyond 4G are currently being developed by standardization bodies, but they are at this time seen as under the 4G umbrella, not for a new mobile generation.

Conflict minerals

Demand for metals used in mobile phones and other electronics fuelled the Second Congo War, which claimed almost 5.5 million lives.[80] In a 2012 news story, *The Guardian* reported: "In unsafe mines deep underground in eastern Congo, children are working to extract minerals essential for the electronics industry. The profits from the minerals finance the bloodiest conflict since the second world war; the war has lasted nearly 20 years and has recently flared up again. ... For the last 15 years, the Democratic Republic of the Congo has been a major source of natural resources for the mobile phone industry."[81] The company Fairphone has worked to develop a mobile phone that does not contain conflict minerals.

CHAPTER ELEVEN

MOBILE DEVICE MANAGEMENT

Mobile device management (MDM) is an industry term for the administration of mobile devices, such as smartphones, tablet computers, laptops and desktop computers. MDM is usually implemented with the use of a third party product that has management features for particular vendors of mobile devices.

Overview

MDM is a way to ensure employees stay productive and do not breach corporate policies. Many organizations control activities of their employees using MDM products/services. MDM primarily deals with corporate data segregation, securing emails, securing corporate documents on devices, enforcing corporate policies, integrating and managing mobile devices including laptops and handhelds of various categories. MDM implementations may be either on-premises or cloud-based.

MDM functionality can include over-the-air distribution of applications, data and configuration settings for all types of mobile devices, including mobile phones, smartphones, tablet computers, ruggedized mobile computers, mobile printers, mobile POS devices, etc. Most recently laptops and desktops have been added to the list of systems supported as Mobile Device Management becomes more about basic device management and less about the mobile platform itself. MDM tools are leveraged for both company-owned and employee-owned (BYOD) devices across the enterprise or mobile devices owned by consumers.[1][2] Consumer Demand for BYOD is now requiring a greater effort for MDM and increased security for both the devices and the enterprise they connect to,[3] especially since employers and employees have different expectations concerning the types of restrictions that should be applied to mobile devices.[4]

By controlling and protecting the data and configuration settings of all mobile devices in a network, MDM can reduce support costs and business risks. The intent of MDM is to optimize the functionality and security of a mobile communications network while minimizing cost and downtime.[5]

With mobile devices becoming ubiquitous and applications flooding the market, mobile monitoring is growing in importance.[6] Numerous vendors help mobile device manufacturers, content portals and developers test and monitor the delivery of their mobile content, applications and services. This testing of content is done in real time by simulating the actions of thousands of customers and detecting and correcting bugs in the applications.

Implementation

Typically solutions include a server component, which sends out the management commands to the mobile devices, and a client component, which runs on the managed device and receives and implements the management commands. In some cases, a single vendor provides both the client and the server, while in other cases the client and server come from different sources.

The management of mobile devices has evolved over time. At first it was necessary to either connect to the handset or install a SIM in order to make changes and updates; scalability was a problem.[7]

One of the next steps was to allow a client-initiated update, similar to when a user requests a Windows Update.

Central remote management, using commands sent over the air, is the next step. An administrator at the mobile operator, an enterprise IT data center or a handset OEM can use an administrative console to update or configure any one handset, group or groups of handsets. This provides scalability benefits particularly useful when the fleet of managed devices is large in size.

Device management software platforms ensure that end-users benefit from plug and play data services for whatever device they are using.[citation needed] Such a platform can automatically detect devices in the network, sending them settings for immediate and continued usability. The process is fully automated, keeps a history of used devices and sends settings only to subscriber devices which were not previously set, sometimes at speeds reaching 50 over-the-air settings update files per second.[citation needed] Device management systems can deliver this function by filtering IMEI/IMSI pairs.[citation needed]

Device management specifications

• The Open Mobile Alliance (OMA) specified a platform-independent device management protocol called OMA Device Management. The specification meets the common definitions of an open standard, meaning the specification is freely available and implementable. It is supported by several mobile devices, such as PDAs and mobile phones.[8]

- Smart message is text SMS-based provisioning protocol (ringtones, calendar entries but service settings also supported like: ftp, telnet, SMSC number, email settings, etc...)
- OMA Client Provisioning is a binary SMS-based service settings provisioning protocol.
- Nokia-Ericsson OTA is binary SMS-based service settings provisioning protocol, designed mainly for older Nokia and Ericsson mobile phones.

Over-the-air programming (OTA) capabilities are considered a main component of mobile network operator and enterprise-grade mobile device management software. These include the ability to remotely configure a single mobile device, an entire fleet of mobile devices or any IT-defined set of mobile devices; send software and OS updates; remotely lock and wipe a device, which protects the data stored on the device when it is lost or stolen; and remote troubleshooting. OTA commands are sent as a binary SMS message. Binary SMS is a message including binary data.[9]

Mobile device management software enables corporate IT departments to manage the many mobile devices used across the enterprise; consequently, over-the-air capabilities are in high demand. Enterprises using OTA SMS as part of their MDM infrastructure demand high quality in the sending of OTA messages, which imposes on SMS gateway providers a requirement to offer a high level of quality and reliability.

Use in the enterprise

As the bring your own device (BYOD) approach becomes increasingly popular across mobile service providers, MDM lets corporations provide employees with access to the internal networks using a device of their choice, whilst these devices are managed remotely with minimal disruption to employees' schedules.[10]

For mobile security

All MDM products are built with an idea of Containerization. The MDM Container is secured using the latest cryptographic techniques (AES-256 or more preferred Corporate data such as email, documents, and enterprise applications are encrypted and processed inside the container. This ensures that corporate data is separated from user's personal data on the device. Additionally, encryption for the entire device and/or SD Card can be enforced depending on MDM product capability.

Secure email: MDM products allow organizations to integrate their existing email setup to be easily integrated with the MDM environment. Almost all MDM products support easy integration with Exchange Server (2003/2007/2010), Office365, Lotus Notes, BlackBerry Enterprise Server (BES) and others. This provides the flexibility of configuring email over the air. Secure Docs:

Employees frequently copy attachments downloaded from corporate email to their personal devices and then misuse it. MDM can restrict or disable clipboard usage into or out of the secure container, restrict forwarding of attachments to external domains, or prevent saving attachments on SD card. This ensures corporate data is secure.

Secure browser: Using a secure browser can avoid many potential security risks. Every MDM solution comes with built-in custom browser. An administrator can disable native browsers to force users to use the secure browser inside the MDM container. URL filtering can be enforced to add additional security measures.

Secure app catalog: Organizations can distribute, manage, and upgrade applications on an employee's device using an App Catalogue. This allows applications to be pushed onto the user's device directly from the App Store or push an enterprise developed private application through the App Catalogue. This provides an option for the organization to deploy devices in Kiosk Mode or Lock-Down Mode.

Additional MDM features

There are plenty of other features depending on which MDM product is chosen:

- Policy Enforcing: There are multiple types of policies which can be enforced on MDM users.
  1. Personal Policy: According to corporate environment, highly customizable
  2. Device Platform specific: policies for advanced management of Android, iOS, Windows and Blackberry devices.
  3. Compliance Policies/Rules
- VPN configuration
- Application Catalogue
- Pre-defined Wi-Fi and Hotspot settings
- Jailbreak/Root detection
- Remote Wipe of corporate data
- Remote Wipe of entire device
- Device remote locking
- Remote messaging/buzz
- Disabling native apps on device
- Some Kiosk software features[11]

SaaS versus on-premises solutions

Present day MDM solutions offer both software as a service (SaaS) and on-premises models. In the rapidly evolving industry such as mobile, SaaS (cloud-based) systems are sometimes quicker to set up, offer easier updates with lower capital costs compared to on-premises solutions which require hardware or virtual machines, need regular software maintenance, and might incur higher capital costs.

For security in cloud computing, the US Government has compliance audits such as Federal Information Security Management Act of 2002 (FISMA) which cloud providers can go through to meet security standards.

The primary policy approach taken by Federal agencies to build relationships with cloud service providers is Federal Risk and Authorization Management Program (FedRAMP) accreditation and certification, designed in part to protect FISMA Low and Moderate systems.[12]

More on MDM, MAM and MEM

Mobile device management (MDM) is like adding an extra layer of security and ensuring a way to monitor device related activities. MDM provides device platform specific features like device encryption, platform specific policies, SD Card encryption. Geo-location tracking, connectivity profiles (VPN, Wi-Fi, Bluetooth) and plenty other features are part of MDM Suite.

Mobile application management (MAM) is done by application wrapping, i.e. injection of arbitrary encryption code in the mobile application source. This is necessary for commercial applications or applications being developed in-house for Enterprise use. Additionally, white-listing/black-listing of application can be done. Features like Application Catalogue allow admin to push applications remotely to the devices for instant install, push remote updates and also remote removal of apps.

Mobile content management (MCM) is a solution that lets enterprise admin to securely push business content to mobile devices used by employees for business use. It lets employees store data on their mobile devices securely using authentication and access files and documents secured by copy/paste restriction policies. MCM provides push-based file distribution, replacement and deleting options.

Mobile email management (MEM) ensures your corporate emails are containerized using advanced proprietary/free encryption algorithms. MEM ensures all emails remain inside the secure container, so that attackers get encrypted data even if they try to compromise the device data using USB cable on a system. Heavy restrictions on clipboard, attachments and trusted domains can be enforced. Nothing can move in-out of the secure container as clipboard is disabled. Even the attachments are downloaded and saved inside the secure container. To view the attachments there is secure document reader as well as secure document editor available in MDM solutions. Adding trusted domains will ensure that data from corporate email is not leaked to malicious/suspicious domains.

CHAPTER TWELVE

MOBILE PAYMENT

 Mobile payment (also referred to as mobile money, mobile money transfer, and mobile wallet) generally refer to payment services operated under financial regulation and performed from or via a mobile device. Instead of paying with cash, cheque, or credit cards, a consumer can use a mobile to pay for a wide range of services and digital or hard goods. Although the concept of using non-coin-based currency systems has a long history,[1] it is only recently that the technology to support such systems has become widely available.

Mobile payment is being adopted all over the world in different ways.[2][3] In 2008, the combined market for all types of mobile payments was projected to reach more than $600 billion globally by 2013,[4] which would be double the figure as of February, 2011.[5] The mobile payment market for goods and services, excluding contactless payments using near field

465

communication (NFC) and money transfers, is expected to exceed $300 billion globally by 2013.[6] Investment on mobile money services is expected to grow by 22.2% during the next two years across the globe. It will result in revenue share of mobile money reaching up to 9% by 2018. Asia and Africa will observe significant growth for mobile money with technological innovation and focus on interoperability emerging as prominent trends by 2018.[7]

In developing countries mobile payment solutions have been deployed as a means of extending financial services to the community known as the "unbanked" or "underbanked," which is estimated to be as much as 50% of the world's adult population, according to Financial Access' 2009 Report "Half the World is Unbanked".[8] These payment networks are often used for micropayments.[9] The use of mobile payments in developing countries has attracted public and private funding by organizations such as the Bill & Melinda Gates Foundation, United States Agency for International Development and Mercy Corps.

Mobile payments are becoming a key instrument for PSPs and other market participants, in order to achieve new growth opportunities, according to the European Payments Council (EPC).[10] The EPC states that "new technology solutions provide a direct improvement to the operations efficiency, ultimately resulting in cost savings and in an increase in business volume".

Models

There are five primary models for mobile payments:[11]

Mobile money outlet in Uganda.

- Mobile wallets
- Card-based payments
- Carrier billing (Premium SMS or direct carrier billing)
- Contactless payments NFC (Near Field Communication)
- Direct transfers between payer and payee bank accounts in near real-time (bank-led model, intra/inter-bank transfers/payments that are both bank and mobile operator agnostic)

There can be combinations:

- Direct carrier/bank co-operation, emerging in Haiti.[citation needed]
- Both bank account and card, like Vipps and MobilePay (users with an account

467

at the right bank can debit their account, while
other users can debit their card)
Financial institutions and credit card companies[12] as well
as Internet companies such as Google[13] and a number
of mobile communication companies, such as mobile
network operators and major telecommunications
infrastructure such as w-HA from Orange and
smartphone multinationals such as Ericsson[14][15] and
BlackBerry have implemented mobile payment solutions.

Mobile wallets

Online companies like PayPal, Amazon Payments,
and Google Wallet also have mobile options.[16]

Generally, this is the process:

First payment:

- User registers, inputs their phone number, and
  the provider sends them an SMS with a PIN
- User enters the received PIN, authenticating the
  number
- User inputs their credit card info or another
  payment method if necessary (not necessary if the
  account has already been added) and validates
  payment

Subsequent payments:

- The user reenters their PIN to authenticate and validates payment

Requesting a PIN is known to lower the success rate (conversion) for payments. These systems can be integrated with directly or can be combined with operator and credit card payments through a unified mobile web payment platform.

Credit card

A simple mobile web payment system can also include a credit card payment flow allowing a consumer to enter their card details to make purchases. This process is familiar but any entry of details on a mobile phone is known to reduce the success rate (conversion) of payments.

In addition, if the payment vendor can automatically and securely identify customers then card details can be recalled for future purchases turning credit card payments into simple single click-to-buy giving higher conversion rates for additional purchases.

Carrier billing

The consumer uses the mobile billing option during checkout at an e-commerce site—such as an online gaming site—to make a payment. After two-factor authentication involving a PIN and One-Time-Password (often abbreviated as *OTP*), the consumer's mobile account is charged for the purchase. It is a true alternative payment method that does not require the use of credit/debit cards or pre-registration at an online payment solution such as PayPal, thus bypassing banks and credit card companies altogether. This type of mobile payment method, which is extremely prevalent and popular in Asia, provides the following benefits:

1. *Security* – Two-factor authentication and a risk management engine prevents fraud.
2. *Convenience* – No pre-registration and no new mobile software is required.
3. *Easy* – It's just another option during the checkout process.
4. *Fast* – Most transactions are completed in less than 10 seconds.
5. *Proven* – 70% of all digital content purchased online in some parts of Asia uses the Direct Mobile Billing method[17]

SMS/USSD-based transactional payments

Premium SMS / Premium MMS

In the predominant model for SMS payments, the consumer sends a payment request via an SMS text message or an USSD to a short code and a premium charge is applied to their phone bill or their online wallet. The merchant involved is informed of the payment success and can then release the paid for goods.[18]

Since a trusted physical delivery address has typically not been given, these goods are most frequently digital with the merchant replying using a Multimedia Messaging Service to deliver the purchased music, ringtones, wallpapers etc.

A Multimedia Messaging Service can also deliver barcodes which can then be scanned for confirmation of payment by a merchant. This is used as an electronic ticket for access to cinemas and events or to collect hard goods.

Transactional payments by SMS have been popular in Asia and Europe and are now accompanied by other mobile payment methods,[citation needed] such as mobile web payments (WAP), mobile payment client (Java ME, Android...) and Direct Mobile Billing.

Inhibiting factors of Premium SMS include:

1. *Poor reliability* – transactional premium SMS payments can easily fail as messages get lost.
2. *Slow speed* – sending messages can be slow and it can take hours for a merchant to get receipt of

payment. Consumers do not want to be kept waiting more than a few seconds.

3. *Security* – The SMS/USSD encryption ends in the radio interface, then the message is a plaintext.

4. *High cost* – There are many high costs associated with this method of payment. The cost of setting up short codes and paying for the delivery of media via a Multimedia Messaging Service and the resulting customer support costs to account for the number of messages that get lost or are delayed.

5. *Low payout rates* – operators also see high costs in running and supporting transactional payments which results in payout rates to the merchant being as low as 30%. Usually around 50%

6. *Low follow-on sales* – once the payment message has been sent and the goods received there is little else the consumer can do. It is difficult for them to remember where something was purchased or how to buy it again. This also makes it difficult to tell a friend.

Some mobile payment services accept "premium SMS payments." Here is the typical end user payment process:

1. User sends SMS with keyword and unique number to a premium short code.
2. User receives a PIN (User billed via the short code on receipt of the PIN)
3. User uses PIN to access content or services.

Remote Payment by SMS and Credit Card Tokenization

 Even as the volume of Premium SMS transactions have flattened, many cloud-based payment systems continue to use SMS for presentment, authorization, and authentication,[19]while the payment itself is processed through existing payment networks such as credit and debit card networks. These solutions combine the ubiquity of the SMS channel,[20] with the security and reliability of existing payment infrastructure. Since SMS lacks end-to-end encryption, such solutions employ a higher-level security strategies known as 'tokenization' and 'target removal' [21] whereby payment occurs without transmitting any sensitive account details, username, password, or PIN.

To date, point-of-sales mobile payment solutions have not relied on SMS-based authentication as a payment mechanism, but remote payments such as bill payments,[22] seat upgrades on flights,[23] and membership or subscription renewals are commonplace.

473

In comparison to premium short code programs which often exist in isolation, relationship marketing and payment systems are often integrated with CRM, ERP, marketing-automation platforms, and reservation systems. Many of the problems inherent with premium SMS have been addressed by solution providers. Remembering keywords is not required since sessions are initiated by the enterprise to establish a transaction specific context. Reply messages are linked to the proper session and authenticated either synchronously through a very short expiry period (every reply is assumed to be to the last message sent) or by tracking session according to varying reply addresses and/or reply options.[24]

Mobile web payments (WAP)

Mobile payment system in Norway.

The consumer uses web pages displayed or additional applications downloaded and installed on the mobile phone to make a payment. It uses WAP (Wireless Application Protocol) as underlying technology and thus inherits all the advantages and disadvantages of WAP. Benefits include:[25][*citation needed*]

1. *Follow-on sales* where the mobile web payment can lead back to a store or to other goods the consumer may like. These pages have a URL and can be bookmarked making it easy to re-visit or share.
2. *High customer satisfaction* from quick and predictable payments
3. *Ease of use* from a familiar set of online payment pages

However, unless the mobile account is directly charged through a mobile network operator, the use of a credit/debit card or pre-registration at online payment solution such as PayPal is still required just as in a desktop environment.

Mobile web payment methods are now being mandated by a number of mobile network operators.

Direct operator billing

Direct operator billing, also known as mobile content billing, WAP billing, and carrier billing, requires integration with the mobile network operator. It provides certain benefits:

1. Mobile network operators already have a billing relationship with consumers, the payment will be added to their bill.
2. Provides instantaneous payment
3. Protects payment details and consumer identity
4. Better conversion rates
5. Reduced customer support costs *for merchants*
6. Alternative monetization option in countries where credit card usage is low

One of the drawbacks is that the payout rate will often be much lower than with other mobile payments options. Examples from a popular provider:

- 92% with PayPal
- 85 to 86% with Credit Card
- 45 to 91.7% with operator billing in the US, UK and some smaller European countries, but usually around 60%[26]

More recently, direct operator billing is being deployed in an in-app environment, where mobile application developers are taking advantage of the one-click payment option that Direct operator billing provides for monetizing mobile applications. This is a logical alternative to credit card and Premium SMS billing.

In 2012, Ericsson and Western Union partnered to expand the direct operator billing market, making it possible for mobile operators to include Western Union Mobile Money Transfers as part of their mobile financial service offerings.[27] Given the international reach of both companies, the partnership is meant to accelerate the interconnection between the m-commerce market and the existing financial world.[28]

Contactless Near Field Communication

Near Field Communication (NFC) is used mostly in paying for purchases made in physical stores or transportation services. A consumer using a special mobile phone equipped with a smartcard waves his/her phone near a reader module. Most transactions do not require authentication, but some require authentication using PIN, before transaction is completed. The payment could be deducted from a pre-paid account or charged to a mobile or bank account directly.

Mobile payment method via NFC faces significant challenges for wide and fast adoption, due to lack of supporting infrastructure, complex ecosystem of stakeholders, and standards.[29] Some phone manufacturers and banks, however, are enthusiastic. Ericsson and Aconite are examples of businesses that make it possible for banks to create consumer mobile payment applications that take advantage of NFC technology.[30]

NFC vendors in Japan are closely related to mass-transit networks, like the Mobile Suica used on the JR East rail network. Osaifu-Keitai system, used for Mobile Suica and many others including Edy and nanaco, has become the *de facto* standard method for mobile payments in Japan. Its core technology, Mobile FeliCa IC, is partially owned by Sony, NTT DoCoMo and JR East. Mobile FeliCa utilize Sony's FeliCa technology, which itself is the de facto standard for contactless smart cards in the country.

Other NFC vendors mostly in Europe use contactless payment over mobile phones to pay for on- and off-street parking in specially demarcated areas. Parking wardens may enforce the parkings by license plate, transponder tags or barcode stickers. First conceptualized in the 1990sthe technology has seen commercial use in this century in both Scandinavia and Estonia. End users benefit from the convenience of being able to pay for parking from the comfort of their car with their mobile phone, and parking operators are not obliged to invest in either existing or new street-based parking infrastructures. Parking wardens maintain order in these systems by license plate, transponder tags or barcode stickers or they read a digital display in the same way as they read a pay and display receipt.

Other vendors use a combination of both NFC and a barcode on the mobile device for mobile payment, for example, Cimbal or DigiMo,[31] making this technique attractive at the point of sale because many mobile devices in the market do not yet support NFC.

Others[edit]

QR code payments

QR Codes 2D barcode are square bar codes. QR codes have been in use since 1994.[32] Originally used to track products in warehouses, QR codes were designed to replace traditional (1D bar codes). Traditional bar codes just represent numbers, which can be looked up in a database and translated into something meaningful. QR, or "Quick Response" bar codes were designed to contain the meaningful info right in the bar code.

QR Codes can be of two main categories:[33]

- The QR Code is presented on the mobile device of the person paying and scanned by a POS or another mobile device of the payee
- The QR Code is presented by the payee, in a static or one time generated fashion and it's scanned by the person executing the payment

Mobile self-checkout allows for one to scan a QR code or barcode of a product inside a brick-and-mortar establishment in order to purchase the product on the spot. This theoretically eliminates reduces the incidence of long checkout lines, even at self-checkout kiosks.

Cloud-based mobile payments

Google, PayPal, GlobalPay and GoPago use a cloud-based approach to in-store mobile payment. The cloud based approach places the mobile payment provider in the middle of the transaction, which involves two separate steps. First, a cloud-linked payment method is selected and payment is authorized via NFC or an alternative method. During this step, the payment provider automatically covers the cost of the purchase with issuer linked funds. Second, in a separate transaction, the payment provider charges the purchaser's selected, cloud-linked account in a card-not-present environment to recoup its losses on the first transaction.[34][35][36]

Audio signal-based payments

The audio channel of the mobile phone is another wireless interface that is used to make payments. Several companies have created technology to use the acoustic features of cell phones to support mobile payments and other applications that are not chip-based. The technologies Near sound data transfer (NSDT), Data Over Voice and NFC 2.0 produce audio signatures that the microphone of the cell phone can pick up to enable electronic transactions.[37]

Direct carrier/bank co-operation

In the T-Cash[38] model, the mobile phone and the phone carrier is the front-end interface to the consumers. The consumer can purchase goods, transfer money to a peer, cash out, and cash in.[39] A 'mini wallet' account can be opened as simply as entering *700# on the mobile phone,[40] presumably by depositing money at a participating local merchant and the mobile phone number. Presumably, other transactions are similarly accomplished by entering special codes and the phone number of the other party on the consumer's mobile phone.

Bank transfer systems

Swish is the name of a system established in Sweden.[41] It was established through a collaboration from major banks in 2012 and has been very successful, with half the population as users in 2016. It's mainly used for peer-to-peer payments between private people, but is also used by street vendors and other small businesses. A person's account is tied to his or her phone number and the connection between the phone number and the actual bank account number is registered in the internet bank. Users with a simple phone or without the app can still receive money if the phone number is registered in the internet bank. Like many other mobile payment system, it's main obstacle is getting people to register and download the app, but it has managed to reach a critical mass and it has become part of everyday life for many Swedes.

Swedish payments company Trustly also enables mobile bank transfers, but is used mainly for business-to-consumer transactions that occur solely online. If an e-tailer integrates with Trustly, its customers can pay directly from their bank account. As opposed to Swish, users don't need to register a Trustly account or download software to pay with it.

Mobile payment service provider model

There are four potential mobile payment models:[42]

1. *Operator-Centric Model*: The mobile operator acts independently to deploy mobile payment service. The operator could provide an independent mobile wallet from the user mobile account(airtime). A large deployment of the Operator-Centric Model is severely challenged

by the lack of connection to existing payment networks. Mobile network operator should handle the interfacing with the banking network to provide advanced mobile payment service in banked and under banked environment. Pilots using this model have been launched in emerging countries but they did not cover most of the mobile payment service use cases. Payments were limited to remittance and airtime top up.

2. *Bank-Centric Model:* A bank deploys mobile payment applications or devices to customers and ensures merchants have the required point-of-sale (POS) acceptance capability. Mobile network operator are used as a simple carrier, they bring their experience to provide Quality of service (QOS) assurance.

3. *Collaboration Model:* This model involves collaboration among banks, mobile operators and a trusted third party.

4. *Peer-to-Peer Model:* The mobile payment service provider acts independently from financial institutions and mobile network operators to provide mobile payment. For example, the MHITS SMS payment service uses a peer-to-peer model.

Unstructured Supplementary Service Data

 USSD on a Sony
Ericsson mobile phone
(2005)

Unstructured Supplementary
Service Data (USSD),
sometimes referred to as
"Quick Codes" or "Feature
codes", is a communications
protocol used
by GSM cellular telephones to communicate with
the mobile network operator's computers. USSD can be
used for WAP browsing, prepaid callback service,
mobile-money services, location-based content services,
menu-based information services, and as part of
configuring the phone on the network.[1]

USSD messages are up to 182 alphanumeric characters
long. Unlike Short Message Service (SMS) messages,
USSD messages create a real-time connection during a
USSD session. The connection remains open, allowing a
two-way exchange of a sequence of data. This makes
USSD more responsive than services that use SMS.[1]

Uses

When a user sends a message to the phone company network, it is received by a computer dedicated to USSD. The computer's response is sent back to the phone, generally in a basic format that can easily be seen on the phone display. Messages sent over USSD are not defined by any standardization body, so each network operator can implement whatever is most suitable for its customers.

USSD can be used to provide independent calling services such as a callback service (to reduce phone charges while roaming), enhance mobile marketing capabilities or interactive data services.

USSD is commonly used by prepaid GSM cellular phones to query the available balance. The vendor's "check balance" application hides the details of the USSD protocol from the user. On some pay as you go networks, such as Tesco Mobile, once a user performs an action that costs money, the user sees a USSD message with his or her new balance. USSD can also be used to refill the balance on the user's SIM card and to deliver one time passwords or PIN codes.

Some operators use USSD to provide access to real-time updates from social-networking websites like Facebook and Twitter.[2]

Wikipedia uses USSD to send articles to some feature phones.[3]

USSD is sometimes used in conjunction with SMS. The user sends a request to the network via USSD, and the network replies with an acknowledgement of receipt:

"Thank you, your message is being processed. A message will be sent to your phone."

Subsequently, one or more mobile terminated SMS messages communicate the status and/or results of the initial request.[4] In such cases, SMS is used to "push" a reply or updates to the handset when the network is ready to send them.[5] In contrast, USSD is used for command-and-control only.

Technical details

Most GSM phones have USSD capability.[6] USSD is generally associated with real-time or instant messaging services. There is no store-and-forward capability, as is typical of other short-message protocols like SMS. In other words, an SMSC is not present in the processing path.

USSD Phase 1, as specified in GSM 02.90, only supports mobile-initiated ("pull") operations.[7] In the core network, the message is delivered over MAP, USSD

Phase 2, as specified in GSM 03.90.[8] After entering a USSD code on a GSM handset, the reply from the GSM operator is displayed within a few seconds.

Format

A typical USSD message starts with an asterisk (*) followed by digits that comprise commands or data. Groups of digits may be separated by additional asterisks. The message is terminated with a number sign (#).[1]

USSD Mode

Mobile-initiated

- USSD/ PULL or USSD/ P2P
- when the user dials a code, e.g. *139# from a GSM mobile handset

Network-initiated

- USSD/ PUSH or USSD/A2P
- when the user receives a push message from the network; primarily used for promotional services

Evolution-Data Optimized

A Kyocera PC Card EV-DO routerwith Wi-Fi

BlackBerry Style (9670 series) smartphone displaying '1XEV' as the service status as highlighted in the upper right corner.

Evolution-Data Optimized (EV-DO, EVDO, etc.) is a telecommunications standard for the wireless transmission of data through radio signals, typically for broadband Internet access. EV-DO is an evolution of the CDMA2000 (IS-2000) standard that supports high data rates and can be deployed alongside a wireless carrier's voice services. It uses advanced multiplexing techniques including code division multiple access (CDMA) as well as time division multiplexing (TDM) to maximize throughput. It is a part of the CDMA2000 family of standards and has been adopted by many mobile phone service providers around the world particularly those previously employing CDMA networks. It is also used on the Globalstar satellite phone network.[1]

EV-DO service has been or will be discontinued in much of Canada in 2015.[2]

An EV-DO channel has a bandwidth of 1.25 MHz, the same bandwidth size that IS-95A (IS-95) and IS-2000 (1xRTT) use.[3] The channel structure, on the other hand, is very different. Additionally, the back-end network is entirely packet-based, and thus is not constrained by the restrictions typically present on a circuit switched network.

The EV-DO feature of CDMA2000 networks provides access to mobile devices with forward link air interface speeds of up to 2.4 Mbit/s with Rel. 0 and up to 3.1 Mbit/s with Rev. A. The reverse link rate for Rel. 0 can operate up to 153 kbit/s, while Rev. A can operate at up to 1.8 Mbit/s. It was designed to be operated end-to-end as an IP based network, and so it can support any application which can operate on such a network and bit rate constraints.

Standard Revisions

Huawei CDMA2000 E V-DO USB wireless modem

Huawei 3G HSPA+ EV-DO USB wireless modem from MovistarColombia

There have been several revisions of the standard, starting with Release 0 (Rel. 0). This was later expanded upon with Revision A (Rev. A) to support Quality of Service (to improve latency) and higher rates on the forward link and reverse link. Later in 2006 Revision B (Rev. B) was published, that among other features includes the ability to bundle multiple carriers to achieve even higher rates and lower latencies (see TIA-856 Rev. B below). The upgrade from EV-DO Rev. A to EV-DO Rev. B involves a software update to the cell site modem, and additional equipment for the new EV-DO carriers. Existing cdma2000 operators may also have to retune some of their existing 1xRTT channels to other frequencies, since Rev. B requires all DO carriers be within 5 MHz.

EV-DO Rel. 0 (TIA-856 Release 0)

The initial design of EV-DO was developed by Qualcomm in 1999 to meet IMT-2000 requirements for a greater-than-2-Mbit/s down link for stationary communications, as opposed to mobile communication such as a moving cellular phone. Initially, the standard was called High Data Rate (HDR), but was renamed to 1xEV-DO after it was ratified by the International Telecommunication Union (ITU) under the designation TIA-856. Originally, 1xEV-DO stood for "1x Evolution-Data Only", referring to its being a direct evolution of the 1x (1xRTT) air interface standard, with its channels carrying only data traffic. The title of the 1xEV-DO standard document is "cdma2000 High Rate Packet Data Air Interface Specification", as cdma2000 (lowercase) is another name for the 1x standard, numerically designated as TIA-2000.

Later, likely due to the possible negative connotations of the word "only", the "DO" part of the standard's name 1xEV-DO was changed to stand for "Data Optimized". So EV-DO now stands for "Evolution-Data Optimized." The 1x prefix has been dropped by many of the major carriers, and is marketed simply as EV-DO.[4] This provides a more marketing-friendly emphasis that the technology was optimized for data.

Forward link channel structure

The primary characteristic that differentiates an EV-DO channel from a 1xRTT channel is that it is time multiplexed on the forward link (from the tower to the mobile). This means that a single mobile has full use of the forward traffic channel within a particular geographic area (a sector) during a given slot of time. Using this technique, EV-DO is able to modulateeach user's time slot independently. This allows the service of users that are in favorable RF conditions with very complex modulation techniques while also serving users in poor RF conditions with simpler and more redundant signals.[5]

The forward channel is divided into slots, each being 1.667 ms long. In addition to user traffic, overhead channels are interlaced into the stream. These include the Pilot which helps the mobile find and identify the channel, the Media Access Channel (MAC) which tells the mobiles when their data is scheduled, and the Control Channel, which contains other information that the network needs the mobiles to know.

The modulation to be used to communicate with a given mobile is determined by the mobile itself. It listens to the traffic on the channel, and depending on the receive signal strength along with the perceived multi-path and fading conditions, makes its best guess as to what data-rate it can sustain while maintaining a reasonable frame error rate of 1-2%. It then communicates this information back to the serving sector in the form of an integer between 1 and 12 on the "Digital Rate Control" (DRC) channel. Alternatively, the mobile can select a "null" rate (DRC 0), indicating that the mobile either cannot decode data at any rate, or that it is attempting to hand off to another serving sector.[5]

Another important aspect of the EV-DO forward link channel is the scheduler. The scheduler most commonly used is called "proportional fair". It's designed to maximize sector throughput while also guaranteeing each user a certain minimum level of service. The idea is to schedule mobiles reporting higher DRC indices more often, with the hope that those reporting worse conditions will improve in time.

The system also incorporates Incremental Redundancy Hybrid ARQ. Each sub-packet of a multi-slot transmission is a turbo-coded replica of the original data bits. This allows mobiles to acknowledge a packet before all of its sub-sections have been transmitted. For example, if a mobile transmits a DRC index of 3 and is scheduled to receive data, it will expect to get data during four time slots. If after decoding the first slot the mobile is able to determine the entire data packet, it can send an early acknowledgement back at that time; the remaining three sub-packets will be cancelled. If however the packet is not acknowledged, the network will proceed with the transmission of the remaining parts until all have been transmitted or the packet is acknowledged.[5]

Reverse link structure

The reverse link (from the mobile back to the Base Transceiver Station) on EV-DO Rel. 0 operates very similar to that of 3G1X CDMA. The channel includes a reverse link pilot (helps with decoding the signal) along with the user data channels. Some additional channels that do not exist in 3G1X include the DRC channel (described above) and the ACK channel (used for HARQ). Only the reverse link has any sort of power control, because the forward link is always transmitted at full power for use by all the mobiles.[6] The reverse link has both open loop and closed loop power control. In the open loop, the reverse link transmission power is set based upon the received power on the forward link. In the closed loop, the reverse link power is adjusted up or down 800 times a second, as indicated by the serving sector (similar to 3G1X).[7]

All of the reverse link channels are combined using code division and transmitted back to the base station using BPSK[8] where they are decoded. The maximum speed available for user data is 153.2 kbit/s, but in real-life conditions this is rarely achieved. Typical speeds achieved are between 20-50 kbit/s.

EV-DO Rev. A (TIA-856 Revision A)

Revision A of EV-DO makes several additions to the protocol while keeping it completely backwards compatible with Release 0.

These changes included the introduction of several new forward link data rates that increase the maximum burst rate from 2.45 Mbit/s to 3.1 Mbit/s. Also included were protocols that would decrease connection establishment time (called enhanced access channel MAC), the ability for more than one mobile to share the same timeslot (multi-user packets) and the introduction of QoS flags.

All of these were put in place to allow for low latency, low bit rate communications such as VoIP.[9]

The additional forward rates for EV-DO Rev. An are:[10]

DRC Index	Data rate in kbit/s	Slots scheduled	Payload size (bits)	Code Rate	Modulation
13	1536	2	5120	5/12	16-QAM
14	3072	1	5120	5/6	16-QAM

In addition to the changes on the forward link, the reverse link was enhanced to support higher complexity modulation (and thus higher bit rates). An optional secondary pilot was added, which is activated by the mobile when it tries to achieve enhanced data rates. To combat reverse link congestion and noise rise, the protocol calls for each mobile to be given an interference allowance which is replenished by the network when the reverse link conditions allow it.[10] The reverse link has a maximum rate of 1.8 Mbit/s, but under normal conditions users experience a rate of approximately 500-1000 kbit/s but with more latency than cable and dsl.

EV-DO Rev. B (TIA-856 Revision B)

EV-DO Rev. B is a multi-carrier evolution of the Rev. A specification. It maintains the capabilities of EV-DO Rev. A, and provides the following enhancements:

- Higher rates per carrier (up to 4.9 Mbit/s on the downlink per carrier). Typical deployments are expected to include 2 or 3 carriers for a peak rate of 14.7 Mbit/s. Higher rates by bundling multiple channels together enhance the user experience and enable new services such as high definition video streaming.
- Reduced latency by using statistical multiplexing across channels—enhances the experience for latency sensitive services such as gaming, video telephony, remote console sessions and web browsing.
- Increased talk-time and standby time
- Reduced interference from the adjacent sectors especially to users at the edge of the cell signal which improves the rates that can be offered by using Hybrid frequency re-use.

- Efficient support for services that have asymmetric download and upload requirements (i.e. different data rates required in each direction) such as file transfers, web browsing, and broadband multimedia content delivery.

EV-DO Rev. C (TIA-856 Revision C) and TIA-1121

Qualcomm early on realized that EV-DO was a stop-gap solution, and foresaw an upcoming format war between LTE and determined that a new standard would be needed. Qualcomm originally called this technology EV-DV (Evolution Data and Voice).[11] As EV-DO became more pervasive, EV-DV evolved into EV-DO Rev C.

The EV-DO Rev. C standard was specified by 3GPP2 to improve the CDMA2000 mobile phone standard for next generation applications and requirements. It was proposed by Qualcomm as the natural evolution path for CDMA2000 and the specifications were published by 3GPP2 (C.S0084-*) and TIA (TIA-1121) in 2007 and 2008 respectively.[12][13]

The brand name UMB (Ultra Mobile Broadband) was introduced in 2006 as a synonym for this standard.[14]

UMB was intended to be a so-called fourth-generation technology. These technologies use a high bandwidth, low latency, underlying TCP/IP network with high level services such as voice built on top. Widespread deployment of 4G networks promises to make applications that were previously not feasible not only possible but ubiquitous. Examples of such applications include mobile high definition video streaming and mobile.

Like LTE, the UMB system was to be based upon Internet networking technologies running over a next generation radio system, with peak rates of up to 280 Mbit/s. Its designers intended for the system to be more efficient and capable of providing more services than the technologies it was intended to replace. To provide compatibility with the systems it was intended to replace, UMB was to support handoffs with other technologies including existing CDMA2000 1X and 1xEV-DO systems.

UMB's use of OFDMA would have eliminated many of the disadvantages of the CDMA technology used by its predecessor, including the "breathing" phenomenon, the difficulty of adding capacity via microcells, the fixed bandwidth sizes that limit the total bandwidth available to handsets, and the near complete control by one company of the required intellectual property.

While capacity of existing Rel. B networks can be increased 1.5-fold by using EVRC-B voice codec and QLIC handset interference cancellation, 1x Advanced and EV-DO Advanced offers up to 4x network capacity increase using BTS interference cancellation (reverse link interference cancellation), multi-carrier links, and smart network management technologies.[15][16]

In November 2008, Qualcomm, UMB's lead sponsor, announced it was ending development of the technology, favoring LTE instead. This followed the announcement that most CDMA carriers chose to adopt either WiMAX or the competing 3GPP Long Term Evolution (LTE) standard as their 4G technology. In fact no carrier had announced plans to adopt UMB.[17]

However, during the ongoing development process of the 4G technology, 3GPP added some functionalities to LTE, allowing it to become a sole upgrade path for all wireless networks.

Features

- OFDMA-based air interface
- Frequency Division Duplex
- Scalable bandwidth between 1.25–20 MHz (OFDMA systems are especially well suited for wider bandwidths larger than 5 MHz)

- Support of mixed cell sizes, e.g., macro-cellular, micro-cellular & pico-cellular.
- IP network architecture
- Support of flat, centralized and mixed topologies
- Data speeds over 275 Mbit/s downstream and over 75 Mbit/s upstream
- Significantly higher data rates & reduced latencies using Forward Link (FL) advanced antenna techniques
- MIMO, SDMA and Beamforming
- Higher Reverse Link (RL) sector capacity with quasi-orthogonal reverse link
- Increased cell edge user data rates using adaptive interference management
- Dynamic fractional frequency reuse
- Distributed RL power control based on other cell interference
- Real time services enabled by fast seamless L1/L2 handoffs
- Independent RL & FL handoffs provide better airlink and handoff performance
- Power optimization through use of quick paging and semi-connected state
- Low-overhead signaling using flexible airlink resource management
- Fast access and request using RL CDMA control channels
- New scalable IP architecture supports inter-technology handoffs

- New handoff mechanisms support real-time services throughout the network and across different airlink technologies
- Fast acquisition and efficient multi-carrier operation through use of beacons
- Multi-carrier configuration supports incremental deployment & mix of low-complexity & wideband devices

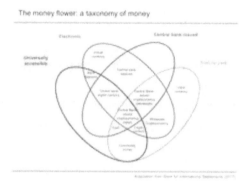

Digital currency

Taxonomy of money, based on "Central bank cryptocurrencies" by Morten Linnemann Bech and Rodney Garratt.

"E-cash" redirects here. For the 20th century brand, see ecash.

Digital currency (digital money or electronic money or electronic currency) is a type of currency available only in digital form, not in physical (such as banknotes and coins). It exhibits properties similar to physical currencies, but allows for instantaneous transactions and borderless transfer-of-ownership. Examples include virtual currencies and cryptocurrencies[1] or even central bank issued "digital base money". Like traditional money, these currencies may be used to buy physical goods and services, but may also be restricted to certain communities such as for use inside an on-line game or social network.[2]

Digital currency is a money balance recorded electronically on a stored-value card or other device. Another form of electronic money is network money, allowing the transfer of value on computer networks, particularly the Internet. Electronic money is also a claim on a private bank or other financial institution such as bank deposits.[3]

Digital money can either be centralized, where there is a central point of control over the money supply, or decentralized, where the control over the money supply can come from various sources.

History

In 1983, a research paper by David Chaum introduced the idea of digital cash.[4] In 1990, he founded DigiCash, an electronic cash company, in Amsterdam to commercialize the ideas in his research.[5] It filed for bankruptcy in 1998.[6][7] In 1999, Chaum left the company.

In 1997, Coca-Cola offered buying from vending machines using mobile payments.[8] After that PayPal emerged in 1998.[9] Other system such as e-gold followed suit, but faced issues because it was used by criminals and was raided by US Feds[who?] in 2005.[5] In 2008, bitcoin was introduced, which marked the start of Digital currencies.[5]

Origins of digital currencies date back to the 1990s Dot-com bubble. One of the first was E-gold, founded in 1996 and backed by gold. Another known digital currency service was Liberty Reserve, founded in 2006; it let users convert dollars or euros to Liberty Reserve Dollars or Euros, and exchange them freely with one another at a 1% fee. Both services were centralized, reputed to be used for money laundering, and inevitably shut down by the US government.[10] Q coins or QQ coins, were used as a type of commodity-based digital currency on Tencent QQ's messaging platform and emerged in early 2005. Q coins were so effective in China that they were said to have had a destabilizing effect on the Chinese Yuan currency due to speculation.[11] Recent interest in cryptocurrencieshas prompted renewed interest in digital currencies, with bitcoin, introduced in 2008, becoming the most widely used and accepted digital currency.

Comparisons

Digital versus virtual currency

According to the European Central Bank's "Virtual currency schemes – a further analysis" report of February 2015, virtual currency is a digital representation of value, not issued by a central bank, credit institution or e-money institution, which, in some circumstances, can be used as an alternative to money. In the previous report of October 2012, the virtual currency was defined as a type of unregulated, digital money, which is issued and usually controlled by its developers, and used and accepted among the members of a specific virtual community.

According to the Bank For International Settlements' "Digital currencies" report of November 2015, digital currency is an asset represented in digital form and having some monetary characteristics. Digital currency can be denominated to a sovereign currency and issued by the issuer responsible to redeem digital money for cash. In that case, digital currency represents electronic money (e-money). Digital currency denominated in its own units of value or with decentralized or automatic issuance will be considered as a virtual currency.

As such, bitcoin is a digital currency but also a type of virtual currency. Bitcoin and its alternatives are based on cryptographic algorithms, so these kinds of virtual currencies are also called cryptocurrencies.

Digital versus traditional currency

Most of the traditional money supply is bank money held on computers. This is also considered digital currency. One could argue that our increasingly cashless society means that all currencies are becoming digital (sometimes referred to as "electronic money"), but they are not presented to us as such.[12]

Types of systems

Centralized systems

Many systems—such as PayPal, eCash, WebMoney, Payoneer, cashU, and Hub Culture's Ven will sell their electronic currency [clarification needed] directly to the end user. Other systems only sell through third party digital currency exchangers. The M-Pesa system is used to transfer money through mobile phones in Africa, India, Afghanistan, and Eastern Europe. Some community currencies, like some local exchange trading systems (LETS) and the Community Exchange System, work with electronic transactions.

Mobile digital wallets

A number of electronic money systems use contactless payment transfer in order to facilitate easy payment and give the payee more confidence in not letting go of their electronic wallet during the transaction.

- In 1994 Mondex and National Westminster Bank provided an 'electronic purse' to residents of Swindon
- In about 2005 Telefónica and BBVA Bank launched a payment system in Spain called Mobipay[13] which used simple short message service facilities of feature phones intended for pay-as you go services including taxis and pre-pay phone recharges via a BBVA current bank account debit.
- In Jan 2010, Venmo launched as a mobile payment system through SMS, which transformed into a social app where friends can pay each other for minor expenses like a cup of coffee, rent and paying your share of the restaurant bill when you forget your wallet.[14] It is popular with college students, but has some security issues.[15] It can be linked to your bank account, credit/debit card or have a loaded value

to limit the amount of loss in case of a security breach. Credit cards and non-major debit cards incur a 3% processing fee.[16]

- On September 19, 2011, Google Wallet was released in the US only, which makes it easy to carry all your credit/debit cards on your phone.[17]
- In 2012 O2 (Ireland) (owned by Telefónica) launched Easytrip[18] to pay road tolls which were charged to the mobile phone account or prepay credit.
- O2 (United Kingdom) invented O2 Wallet[19] at about the same time. The wallet can be charged with regular bank accounts or cards and discharged by participating retailers using a technique known as 'money messages'. The service closed in 2014.
- On September 9, 2014 Apple Pay was announced at the iPhone 6 event. In October 2014 it was released as an update to work on iPhone 6 and Apple Watch. It is very similar to Google Wallet, but for Apple devices only.[20]

Decentralized systems

Unofficial bitcoin logo

508

A cryptocurrency is a type of digital token that relies on cryptography for chaining together digital signatures of token transfers, peer-to-peer networking and decentralization.

In some cases a proof-of-work scheme is used to create and manage the currency.[21][22][23][24]

Cryptocurrencies allow electronic money systems to be decentralized; systems include:

- Bitcoin, the first cryptocurrency, a peer-to-peer electronic monetary system based on cryptography.
- Ethereum[25], an open-source, public, blockchain-based distributed computing platform featuring smart contract (scripting) functionality.
- Bitcoin Cash, a 2017 fork of bitcoin; main differences from bitcoin are larger blocks, different difficulty adjustment algorithm, and lack of Segregated Witness.
- IOTA, an open-source distributed ledger and an electronic monetary system designed for the Internet of Things. It uses a directed acyclic graph (DAG) instead of a blockchain.
- Ripple monetary system, a monetary system based on trust networks.
- Litecoin, originally based on the bitcoin protocol, intended to improve upon its alleged inefficiencies. Faster block times and different mining algorithm compared to bitcoin.

- Dash, originally based on the bitcoin protocol, it offers the option of instant and private transactions. It is a Decentralized Autonomous Organization.
- NEM, a peer-to-peer electronic monetary system and a blockchain platform which allows for storing digital assets.
- NEO[26], an open-source, public, blockchain-based distributed computing platform featuring smart assets contract functionality.
- Divi[27], an open source, Proof Of Stake (POS) and masternode protocol/cryptocurrency and ecosystem, built on a custom blockchain.

Virtual currency

A virtual currency has been defined in 2012 by the European Central Bank as "a type of unregulated, digital money, which is issued and usually controlled by its developers, and used and accepted among the members of a specific virtual community". The US Department of Treasury in 2013 defined it more tersely as "a medium of exchange that operates like a currency in some environments, but does not have all the attributes of real currency". The key attribute a virtual currency does not have according to these definitions, is the status as legal tender.

Law

Since 2001, the European Union has implemented the E-Money Directive "on the taking up, pursuit and prudential supervision of the business of electronic money institutions" last amended in 2009.[28] Doubts on the real nature of EU electronic money have arisen, since calls have been made in connection with the 2007 EU Payment Services Directive in favor of merging payment institutions and electronic money institutions. Such a merger could mean that electronic money is of the same nature as bank money or scriptural money.

In the United States, electronic money is governed by Article 4A of the Uniform Commercial Code for wholesale transactions and the Electronic Fund Transfer Actfor consumer transactions. Provider's responsibility and consumer's liability are regulated under Regulation E.[29][30]

Regulation

Virtual currencies pose challenges for central banks, financial regulators, departments or ministries of finance, as well as fiscal authorities and statistical authorities.

US Treasury guidance

On 20 March 2013, the Financial Crimes Enforcement Network issued a guidance to clarify how the US Bank Secrecy Act applied to persons creating, exchanging and transmitting virtual currencies.[31]

Securities and Exchange Commission guidance

In May 2014 the U.S. Securities and Exchange Commission (SEC) "warned about the hazards of bitcoin and other virtual currencies".[32]

New York state regulation

In July 2014, the New York State Department of Financial Services proposed the most comprehensive regulation of virtual currencies to date, commonly called BitLicense.[33] Unlike the US federal regulators it has gathered input from bitcoin supporters and the financial industry through public hearings and a comment period until 21 October 2014 to customize the rules. The proposal per NY DFS press release "... sought to strike an appropriate balance that helps protect consumers and root out illegal activity".[34] It has been criticized by smaller companies to favor established institutions, and Chinese bitcoin exchanges have complained that the rules are "overly broad in its application outside the United States".[35]

Adoption by governments

As of 2016, over 24 countries are investing in distributed ledger technologies (DLT) with $1.4bn in investments. In addition, over 90 central banks are engaged in DLT discussions, including implications of a central bank issued digital currency.[36]

- Hong Kong's Octopus card system: Launched in 1997 as an electronic purse for public transportation, is the most successful and mature implementation of contactless smart cards used for mass transit payments. After only 5 years, 25 percent of Octopus card transactions are unrelated to transit, and accepted by more than 160 merchants.[37]
- London Transport's Oyster card system: Oyster is a plastic smartcard which can hold pay as you go credit, Travelcards and Bus & Tram season tickets. You can use an Oyster card to travel on bus, Tube, tram, DLR, London Overground and most National Rail services in London.[38]
- Japan's FeliCa: A contactless RFID smart card, used in a variety of ways such as in ticketing

systems for public transportation, e-money, and residence door keys.[39]

- Netherlands' Chipknip: As an electronic cash system used in the Netherlands, all ATM cards issued by the Dutch banks had value that could be loaded via Chipknip loading stations. For people without a bank, pre-paid Chipknip cards could be purchased at various locations in the Netherlands. As of January 1, 2015, you can no longer pay with Chipknip.[40]
- Belgium's Proton: An electronic purse application for debit cards in Belgium. Introduced in February 1995, as a means to replace cash for small transactions. The system was retired in December 31, 2014.[41]

Canada

The Bank of Canada have explored the possibility of creating a version of its currency on the blockchain.[42]

The Bank of Canada teamed up with the nation's five largest banks — and the blockchain consulting firm R3 — for what was known as Project Jasper. In a simulation run in 2016, the central bank issued CAD-Coins onto a blockchain similar Ethereum.[43] The banks used the CAD-Coins to exchange money the way they do at the end of each day to settle their master accounts.[43]

China

A deputy governor at the central bank of China, Fan Yifei, wrote that "the conditions are ripe for digital currencies, which can reduce operating costs, increase efficiency and enable a wide range of new applications."[43] According to Fan Yifei, the best way to take advantage of the situation is for central banks to take the lead, both in supervising private digital currencies and in developing digital legal tender of their own.[44]

Denmark

The Danish government proposed getting rid of the obligation for selected retailers to accept payment in cash, moving the country closer to a "cashless" economy.[45] The Danish Chamber of Commerce is backing the move.[46] Nearly a third of the Danish population uses MobilePay, a smartphone application for transferring money.[45]

Ecuador

A law passed by the National Assembly of Ecuador gives the government permission to make payments in electronic currency and proposes the creation of a national digital currency. "Electronic money will stimulate the economy; it will be possible to attract more Ecuadorian citizens, especially those who do not have checking or savings accounts and credit cards alone. The electronic currency will be backed by the assets of the Central Bank of Ecuador," the National Assembly said in a statement.[47] In December 2015, Sistema de Dinero Electrónico ("electronic money system") was launched, making Ecuador the first country with a state-run electronic payment system.[48]

Germany

The German central bank is testing a functional prototype for the blockchain technology-based settlement of securities and transfer of centrally-issued digital coins.[49][50]

Netherlands

The Dutch central bank is experimenting with a bitcoin-based virtual currency called "DNBCoin".[43][51]

Russia

Government-controlled Sberbank of
Russia owns Yandex.Money - electronic payment service
and digital currency of the same name.[52] Russia's
President Vladimir Putin has signed off on regulation of
ICOs and cryptocurrency mining by July 2018.[53]

South Korea

South Korea plans national digital currency using a
Blockchain.[54] The chairman of South Korea's Financial
Services Commission (FSC), Yim Jong-yong, announced
that his department will "Lay the systemic groundwork
for the spread of digital currency."[54] South Korea has
already announced plans to discontinue coins by the
year 2020.[55]

Sweden

Sweden is in the process of replacing all of its physical
banknotes, and most of its coins by mid 2017. However
the new banknotes and coins of the Swedish krona will
probably be circulating at about half the 2007 peak of
12,494 kronor per capita. The Riksbank is planning to
begin discussions of an electronic currency issued by the
central bank to which "is not to replace cash, but to act
as complement to it."[56] Deputy Governor Cecilia
Skingsley states that cash will continue to spiral out of

use in Sweden, and while it is currently fairly easy to get cash in Sweden, it is often very difficult to deposit it into bank accounts, especially in rural areas. No decision has been currently made about the decision to create "e-krona". In her speech Skingsley states: "The first question is whether e-krona should be booked in accounts or whether the ekrona should be some form of digitally transferable unit that does not need an underlying account structure, roughly like cash." Skingsley also states that: "Another important question is whether the Riksbank should issue e-krona directly to the general public or go via the banks, as we do now with banknotes and coins." Other questions will be addressed like interest rates, should they be positive, negative, or zero?

Switzerland

In 2016, a city government first accepted digital currency in payment of city fees. Zug, Switzerland added bitcoin as a means of paying small amounts, up to 200 SFr., in a test and an attempt to advance Zug as a region that is advancing future technologies. In order to reduce risk, Zug immediately converts any bitcoin received into the Swiss currency.[57]

Swiss Federal Railways, government-owned railway company of Switzerland, sells bitcoins at its ticket machines.[58][58]

UK

The Chief Scientific Adviser to the UK government advised his Prime Minister and Parliament to consider using a blockchain-based digital currency.[59]

The chief economist of Bank of England, the central bank of the United Kingdom, proposed abolition of paper currency. The Bank has also taken an interest in bitcoin.[43][60] In 2016 it has embarked on a multi-year research programme to explore the implications of a central bank issued digital currency.[36] The Bank of England has produced several research papers on the topic. One suggests that the economic benefits of issuing a digital currency on a distributed ledger could add as much as 3 percent to a country's economic output.[43] The Bank said that it wanted the next version of the bank's basic software infrastructure to be compatible with distributed ledgers.[43]

Ukraine

The National Bank of Ukraine is considering a creation of its own issuance/turnover/servicing system for a blockchain-based national cryptocurrency.[61] The regulator also announced that blockchain could be a part of a national project called "Cashless Economy".[61]

Hard vs. soft digital currencies

A *hard electronic currency* is one that does not have services to dispute or reverse charges. In other words, it is akin to cash in that it only supports non-reversible transactions. Reversing transactions, even in case of a legitimate error, unauthorized use, or failure of a vendor to supply goods is difficult, if not impossible. The advantage of this arrangement is that the operating costs of the electronic currency system are greatly reduced by not having to resolve payment disputes. Additionally, it allows the electronic currency transactions to clear instantly, making the funds available immediately to the recipient. This means that using hard electronic currency is more akin to a cash transaction. Examples are Western Union, KlickEx and bitcoin.

A *soft electronic currency* is one that allows for reversal of payments, for example in case of fraud or disputes. Reversible payment methods generally have a "clearing

time" of 72 hours or more. Examples
are PayPal and credit card. A hard currency can
be *softened* by using a trusted third party or
an escrow service.

Criticism

Many of existing digital currencies have not yet seen
widespread usage, and may not be easily used or
exchanged. Banks generally do not accept or offer
services for them.[62] There are concerns that
cryptocurrencies are extremely risky due to their very
high volatility[63] and potential for pump and
dumpschemes.[64] Regulators in several countries have
warned against their use and some have taken concrete
regulatory measures to dissuade users.[65] The non-
cryptocurrencies are all centralized. As such, they may
be shut down or seized by a government at any
time.[66] The more anonymous a currency is, the more
attractive it is to criminals, regardless of the intentions of
its creators.[66] Forbes writer Tim Worstall has written that
the value of bitcoin is largely derived from speculative
trading.[67] Bitcoin has also been criticised for its energy
inefficient SHA-256-based proof of work.[68]

REFERENCES

1. http://www.hindustantimes.com/ tech/five-billion-mobile-phone-users-in-2017-study/story-zXhZeRKHv9u1C5WQ8fkK1K.html accessed 27/09/2017

2. https://www.maximizer.com/blog/4-advantages-of-mobile-technology/ accessed 27/09/2017

3. https://www.forbes.com/sites/johnkoetsier/2017/01/03 /mobile-2017-76-predictions-on-the-future-of-mobile-from-influencers-and-industry-vips/#272329b963bc accessed 27/09/17

4. http://idealog.co.nz/tech/2017/03/future-smartphones-and-mobile-technology accessed 27/09/2017

5. *Jan Koum in Forbes". Forbes. Retrieved 2017-09-28.*
6. Jump up^ *"Why WhatsApp's Founder Hates Being Called An Entrepreneur". Retrieved 2016-07-22.*
7. Jump up^ Forbes Announces Its 33rd Annual Forbes 400 Ranking Of The Richest Americans; 29 September 2014, Forbes.com, accessed 12 November 2014
8. Jump up^ *"WhatsApp Founder Jan Koum's Jewish Rags-to-Riches Tale". The Jewish Daily Forward. Reuters. 20 February 2014. Retrieved 1 March 2014.*
9. Jump up^ *Rowan, David. "WhatsApp: The inside story (Wired UK)". Wired.co.uk. Retrieved 2014-02-20.*
10. ^Jump up to:[a][b][c][d][e][f] *Parmy Olson (February 19, 2014). "Exclusive: The Rags-To-Riches Tale Of How Jan Koum Built WhatsApp Into Facebook's New $19 Billion Baby". Forbes. Retrieved February 20, 2014..*
11. Jump up^ WhatsApp: Jan Koum – The Story Of A Man Who Kept It Simple, Jewish Business News, Feb 20th, 2014
12. Jump up^ *De Jong, David (2014-10-20). "Facebook's Jan Koum Apologizes for Past Restraining Order". Bloomberg.*
13. Jump up^ *"The Memories from Rags-to-Riches by Jan Koum". Eyerys. Retrieved May 15, 2015.*
14. Jump up^ *Olson, Parmy (2009-02-24). "Exclusive: The Rags-To-Riches Tale Of How Jan Koum Built WhatsApp Into Facebook's New $19 Billion Baby". Forbes. Retrieved 2014-02-20.*
15. Jump up^ *"Facebook acquires WhatsApp in massive deal worth $19 billion - ABC News (Australian Broadcasting Corporation)". Abc.net.au. Retrieved 2014-02-20.*
16. Jump up^ *"WhatsApp Founders Are Low Key — And Now Very Rich". Mashable.com. 2013-10-26. Retrieved 2014-02-20.*

17. Jump up^ "WhatsApp's Founder Goes From Food Stamps to Billionaire". *Bloomberg News*. Retrieved February 20, 2014.

18. Jump up^ Wood, Zoe (February 20, 2014). "Facebook turned down WhatsApp co-founder Brian Acton for job in 2009". *The Guardian*. Retrieved 21 February 2014.

19. Jump up^ "Jan Koum Insider Trading Overview". *www.insidermole.com*. Retrieved 2017-09-28.

20. Jump up^ "January Kum: communist Ukraine to 19 billion Whatsapp | Network 2". 2014-06-15. Archived from the original on 2014-06-15. Retrieved 2017-09-28.

21. Jump up^ "No. 4: Jan Koum - Philanthropy". *Philanthropy.com*. 8 February 2015.

22. Pilkington, Ed (March 10, 2011). "Forbes rich list: Facebook six stake their claims". *The Guardian*. UK. Retrieved March 30, 2011.

23. ^Jump up to:[a][b] "Facebook, Inc. Proxy Statement". *United States Security and Exchange Commission*. April 26, 2013. p. 31. Retrieved March 30, 2014. On January 1, 2013, Mr. Zuckerberg's annual base salary was reduced to $1 and he will no longer receive annual bonus compensation under our Bonus Plan.

24. ^Jump up to:[a][b][c] "Mark Zuckerberg". *Forbes*. Retrieved May 19, 2012.

25. Jump up^ Napach, Bernice (July 26, 2013). "Facebook Surges and Mark Zuckerberg Pockets $3.8 Billion". *Yahoo! Finance*.

26. Jump up^ Hiltzik, Michael (May 20, 2012). "Facebook shareholders are wedded to the whims of Mark Zuckerberg". *Los Angeles Times*.

27. Jump up^ "The World's Billionaires List". *Forbes*. Retrieved December 12, 2016.

28. Jump up^ Carlson, Nicholas (March 5, 2010). "At Last – The Full Story Of How Facebook Was Founded". *Business Insider*.

29. Jump up^ "They sued Mark Zuckerberg for $65m. But it was not enough". *The Independent*. December 10, 2010. Retrieved October 10, 2017.

30. Jump up^ The Giving Pledge website, retrieved December 3, 2015

31. Jump up^ BBC News. The great Facebook giveaway - how will it work?, December 2, 2015

32. Jump up^ https://www.bbc.com/news/world-us-canada-34978249

33. ^Jump up to:[a][b] Grossman, Lev (December 15, 2010). "Person of the Year 2010: Mark Zuckerberg". *Time*.

34. Jump up^ *"The All-Time TIME 100 of All Time"*. *Time*. April 18, 2012. Retrieved April 20, 2012.

35. Jump up^ *"The World's Most Powerful People"*. *Forbes*. December 2016. Retrieved December 14,2016.

36. Jump up^ *"Mark Zuckerberg's career in 90 seconds"*. *The Daily Telegraph*. Retrieved March 3,2017.

37. Jump up^ Malone, Jasmine (Dec 15, 2010). *"Mark Zuckerberg wins Time person of the year: profile"*. *The Daily Telegraph*. London.

38. Jump up^ *"The Zuckerbergs of Dobbs Ferry"*, *New York, no. May 14, 2012*, retrieved May 21,2012

39. Jump up^ Zuckerberg, Mark (Jan 27, 2017). *"My great grandparents came from Germany, Austria, and Poland"*. *Facebook*. PaloAlto.

40. ^Jump up to:^a b c d^ Vargas, Jose Antonio (September 20, 2010). *"The Face of Facebook"*. *The New Yorker*. Retrieved September 22, 2010.

41. Jump up^ Burrell, Ian (July 24, 2010). *"Mark Zuckerberg: He's got the whole world on his site"*. *The Independent*. UK. Retrieved November 6, 2010.

42. ^Jump up to:^a b^ Kirkpatrick, David (2010). *The Facebook Effect: The Inside Story of the Company That Is Connecting the World*. New York: Simon & Schuster. pp. 20–21. ISBN 978-1-4391-0211-4. Retrieved November 9, 2010.

43. Jump up^ McDevitt, Caitlin (March 5, 2010). *"What We Learned About Mark Zuckerberg This Week"*. *The Big Money*. Retrieved March 5, 2010.

44. Jump up^ Grynbaum, Michael M. (June 10, 2004). *"Mark E. Zuckerberg '06: The whiz behind thefacebook.com"*. *The Harvard Crimson*.

45. Jump up^ *"4-thing-mark-zuckerberg"*. Retrieved April 21, 2016.

46. Jump up^ *"facebook-founder-mark-zuckerberg-child-prodigy"*. Retrieved April 21, 2016.

47. Jump up^ Hemos/Dan Moore (April 21, 2003). *"Machine Learning and MP3s"*. *Slashdot*. Retrieved September 3, 2010.

48. Jump up^ Dreier, Troy (February 8, 2005). *"Synapse Media Player Review"*. *PCMag.com*. Retrieved September 3, 2010.

49. Jump up^ Larson, Chase (March 25, 2011), *Mark Zuckerberg speaks at BYU, calls Facebook "as much psychology and sociology as it is technology"*, Deseret News, retrieved May 21,2012

50. ^ Jump up to:[a][b] *"Facebook founder's roommate recounts creation of Internet giant"*. Haaretz. Oct 5, 2009.

51. Jump up^ Hoffman, Claire (June 28, 2008). *"The Battle for Facebook"*. Rolling Stone. New York. Archived from the original on July 3, 2008. Retrieved February 5, 2009.

52. Jump up^ Seward, Zachary M. (July 25, 2007). *"Judge Expresses Skepticism About Facebook Lawsuit"*. The Wall Street Journal. New York. Retrieved April 30, 2008.

53. Jump up^ Carlson, Nicolas (March 5, 2010). *"In 2004, Mark Zuckerberg Broke Into A Facebook User's Private Email Account"*. Business Insider. Retrieved March 5, 2010.

54. Jump up^ Stone, Brad (June 28, 2008). *"Judge Ends Facebook's Feud With ConnectU"*. New York Times blog.

55. Jump up^ Rushe, Dominic (February 2, 2012). *"Facebook IPO sees Winklevoss twins heading for $300m fortune"*. The Guardian. London.

56. Jump up^ *"Mark Zuckerberg, Harvard dropout, returns to open arms"*. CS Monitor. November 9, 2011.

57. Jump up^ Fell, Jason (14 May 2014). *"As Mark Zuckerberg Turns 30, His 10 Best Quotes as CEO"*. Entrepreneur. Entrepreneur Media, Inc. Retrieved 16 May 2014.

58. Jump up^ Steinbock, Anna (May 25, 2017). *"Harvard awards 10 honorary degrees"*. Harvard Gazette. Retrieved May 25, 2017.

59. Jump up^ *"13 YEARS AFTER QUITTING, FACEBOOK CEO MARK ZUCKERBERG GETS HONORARY HARVARD DEGREE"*. PPP Focus. May 28, 2017.

60. ^ Jump up to:[a][b] Antonas, Steffan (May 10, 2009). *"Did Mark Zuckerberg's Inspiration for Facebook Come Before Harvard?"*. ReadWrite Social. SAY Media, Inc. Archived from the originalon February 1, 2012. Retrieved March 26, 2013.

61. ^ Jump up to:[a][b] *"Face-to-Face with Mark Zuckerberg '02"*. Phillips Exeter Academy. Phillips Exeter Academy. January 24, 2007. Retrieved March 26, 2013.

62. Jump up^

a. Holt, Chris (March 10, 2004). *"Thefacebook.com's darker side"*. The Stanford Daily.

b. Nguyen, Lananh (April 12, 2004). "Online network created by Harvard students flourishes". The Tufts Daily. College Media Network. Archived from the original on October 15, 2013. Retrieved March 26, 2013.

c. Rotberg, Emily (April 14, 2004). "Thefacebook.com opens to Duke students". The Chronicle. Duke Student Publishing Company. Retrieved March 26, 2013.

d. "Students flock to join college online facebook". The Daily Pennsylvanian. Archived from the original on August 25, 2011.

63. Jump up^ Alice Speri (August 7, 2012). "Zuckerberg's Roomie Aims to Win for Haiti". The Wall Street Journal. Retrieved March 26, 2013.

64. Jump up^ Teller, Sam (November 1, 2005). "Zuckerberg To Leave Harvard Indefinitely". The Harvard Crimson. The Harvard Crimson, Inc. Retrieved March 26, 2013.

65. Jump up^ Kevin J. Feeney (February 24, 2005). "Business, Casual". The Harvard Crimson. The Harvard Crimson, Inc. Retrieved March 26, 2013.

66. ^Jump up to:[a][b][c] Singel, Ryan (May 28, 2010). "Epicenter: Mark Zuckerberg: I Donated to Open Source, Facebook Competitor". Wired News. Condé Nast Publishing. Retrieved May 29,2010.

67. Jump up^ MacMillan, Robert (April 1, 2009). "Yu, Zuckerberg and the Facebook fallout". Reuters. Retrieved March 26, 2013. In a back-to-the-future move, former Netscape CFO Peter Currie will be the key adviser to Facebook about financial matters, until a new search for a CFO is found, sources said.

68. Jump up^ Zuckerberg, Mark (July 22, 2010), 500 Million Stories, The Facebook Blog, retrieved May 21, 2012

69. ^Jump up to:[a][b][c] Levy, Steven (April 19, 2010). "Geek Power: Steven Levy Revisits Tech Titans, Hackers, Idealists". Wired. Retrieved September 23, 2010.

70. ^Jump up to:[a][b] McGirt, Ellen (February 17, 2010). "The World's Most Innovative Companies 2010". Fast Company. Retrieved September 24, 2010.

71. Jump up^ "The Vanity Fair 100". Vanity Fair. October 2010. Retrieved September 23, 2010.

72. Jump up^ "The Vanity Fair 100". Vanity Fair. September 1, 2010. Retrieved September 23, 2010.

73. Jump up^ "Mark Zuckerberg – 50 People who matter 2010". New Statesman. UK. Retrieved September 27, 2010.

74. Jump up^ *"Facebook's Zuckerberg says Steve Jobs advised on company focus, management". Bloomberg. November 7, 2011. Retrieved November 12, 2011.*

75. Jump up^ *"Zuckerberg in Moscow to boost Facebook's presence". France24.com. October 1, 2012. Archived from the original on October 3, 2012.*

76. Jump up^ *"Russia pushes Facebook to open research center". FoxNews. October 1, 2012.*

77. Jump up^ *Delo, Cotton (April 16, 2013). "Facebook Practices What It Preaches for 'Home' Ad Blitz". Ad Age digital. Crain Communications. Retrieved April 18, 2013.*

78. Jump up^ *Caitlin Dewey (August 19, 2013). "Mark Zuckerberg's Facebook page was hacked by an unemployed web developer". The Washington Post. Retrieved August 19, 2013.*

79. ^ Jump up to:[a][b] *Edwards, Victoria (September 21, 2013). "6 Things We Learned From Marissa Mayer and Mark Zuckerberg at TechCrunch Disrupt 2013". TechCrunch. AOL Inc. Retrieved September 23, 2013.*

80. ^ Jump up to:[a][b] *Stevenson, Alastair (August 22, 2013). "Mark Zuckerberg Creates Tech Justice League to Bring Internet to the Masses". Search Engine Watch. Incisive Media Incisive Interactive Marketing LLC. Retrieved September 23, 2013.*

81. Jump up^

a. *Samuel Gibbs (February 23, 2014). "Mark Zuckerberg goes to Barcelona to make mobile friends". The Guardian. Retrieved February 24, 2014.*

b. *Sven Grundberg (January 16, 2014). "Facebook's Zuckerberg to Speak at Mobile World Congress". Wall Street Journal. Retrieved February 24, 2014.*

c. *Meyer, David (January 16, 2014). "Facebook's Zuckerberg to headline Mobile World Congress this year". Gigaom. Gigaom, Inc. Retrieved February 24, 2014.*

82. Jump up^ *Mark Gregory (February 22, 2014). "Mobile World Congress: What to expect from Barcelona". BBC News. Retrieved February 24, 2014.*

83. Jump up^ Alex Hern, Jonathan Kaiman (October 23, 2014). "Mark Zuckerberg addresses Chinese university in Mandarin". *The Guardian*. Retrieved December 14, 2014.

84. Jump up^ Maria Tadeo (December 12, 2014). "Mark Zuckerberg Q&A: What we learnt about the Facebook founder". *The Independent*. Retrieved December 14, 2014.

85. Jump up^ Sam Colt (December 12, 2014). "Facebook May Be Adding a 'Dislike' Button". *Inc. Monsueto Ventures*. Retrieved December 14, 2014.

86. Jump up^ "The top 10 business visionaries creating value for the world". *Business Insider. Business Insider Inc*.

87. Jump up^ Martey Dodoo (August 16, 2004). "Wirehog?". *Martey Dodoo*.

88. Jump up^ Alan J. Tabak (August 13, 2004). "Zuckerberg Programs New Website". *Harvard Crimson*.

89. Jump up^ "80000 developers". Retrieved April 21, 2016.

90. Jump up^ "The Facebook Blog | Facebook". *Blog.facebook.com*. Retrieved June 26, 2010.

91. Jump up^ "2007 Young Innovators Under 35: Mark Zuckerberg, 23". *MIT Technology Review*. 2007. Retrieved August 14, 2011.

92. Jump up^ "Meet at the Silicon Valley among the tech leaders and Indian Prime Minister-Narendra Modi". Retrieved October 9, 2015.

93. Jump up^ "Mark Zuckerberg supports Digital India". Retrieved October 9, 2015.

94. Jump up^ Carlson, Nicholas. "In 2004, Mark Zuckerberg Broke Into A Facebook User's Private Email Account". *Silicon Alley Insider*. Retrieved March 5, 2010.

95. Jump up^ Logged in as click here to log out (February 12, 2009). "Facebook paid up to $65m to founder Mark Zuckerberg's ex-classmates". *Guardian. UK*. Retrieved August 21, 2009.

96. Jump up^ McCarthy, Caroline (November 30, 2007). "article about 02138". *News.com*. Retrieved June 26, 2010.

97. Jump up^ Hempel, Jessi (July 25, 2009). "The book that Facebook doesn't want you to read". *CNN Money*. Archived from the original on September 14, 2010. Retrieved May 21, 2011.

98. Jump up^ West, Jackson. "Facebook CEO Named in Pakistan Criminal Investigation". *NBC Bay Area*. Retrieved June 26, 2010.

99. Jump up^ "Zuckerberg faces criminal investigation in Pakistan".

100. Jump up^ Anderson, John (July 29, 2010). "Facebook does not have a like button for Ceglia". WellsvilleDaily.com. Retrieved August 29, 2010.

101. Jump up^ "Venture beat coverage of Ceglia lawsuit".

102. Jump up^ "Feds Collar Would-Be Facebook Fraudster". E-Commerce News. October 29, 2012.

103. Jump up^ "A Dubious Case Found Lawyers Eager to Make Some Money". New York Times. October 29, 2012.

104. Jump up^ "Paul Ceglia's lawyer drops out of Facebook suit after arrest". San Jose Mercury News. October 30, 2012.

105. Jump up^ "Israeli minister accused facebook and its founder". Newsweek. Retrieved July 4, 2016.

106. Jump up^ "Mark Zuckerberg is facing claims that Facebook is not helping Israel crack down on terror". Express. Retrieved July 3, 2016.

107. Jump up^ "Mark Zuckerberg has terror victim's 'blood on his hands', Israeli minister says". International Business Times. Retrieved July 4, 2016.

108. Jump up^ Mark Zuckerberg hits back at 'misleading' claims he is suing Hawaiian landowners, Wired, January 20, 2017

109. Jump up^ "Facebook's Zuckerberg officially drops Hawaii 'quiet title' actions", Pacific Business News, February 26, 2017

110. Jump up^ Fried, Ina (June 2, 2010). "Zuckerberg in the hot seat at D8". CNET. Retrieved June 26,2010.

111. Jump up^ Harlow, John (May 16, 2010). "Movie depicts seamy life of Facebook boss". The Times Online. London. Retrieved July 18, 2010.

112. Jump up^ Cieply, Michael & Helft, Miguel (August 20, 2010). "Facebook Feels Unfriendly Toward Film It Inspired". The New York Times. Retrieved September 22, 2010.

113. Jump up^ Harris, Mark (September 17, 2010). "Inventing Facebook". New York. Retrieved September 22, 2010.

114. Jump up^ "The Social Network Filmmakers Thank Zuckerberg During Golden Globes". Techland. Time. January 17, 2011.

115. Jump up^ "Last Night, Aaron Sorkin Demonstrated How to Apologize Without Accepting Responsibility". NYMag. January 17, 2011.

116. Jump up^ "Mark Zuckerberg Meets Jesse Eisenberg on Saturday Night Live". People. January 30, 2011. Retrieved January 30, 2011.

117. Jump up^ "Jesse Eisenberg meets the real Mark Zuckerberg on SNL". Digital Trends. January 31, 2011.

118. Jump up^ "Jesse Eisenberg Calls Mark Zuckerberg "Sweet" and "Generous" in His Funny Oscar Nominees Lunch Interview" *Popsugar*, February 7, 2011

119. Jump up^ "Mark Zuckerberg Meets Jesse Eisenberg On The 'Saturday Night Live' Stage" *NPR*, January 30, 2011

120. ^ Jump up to:^*a b c* Rohrer, Finlo. "Is the Facebook movie the truth about Mark Zuckerberg" BBC, September 30, 2010

121. Jump up^ "The Facebook Effect: The Inside Story of the Company That Is Connecting the World", release date February 1, 2011

122. Jump up^ *"Facebook Creator Mark Zuckerberg to Get Yellow on The Simpsons". New York. July 21, 2010. Retrieved September 22, 2010.*

123. Jump up^ *Griggs, Brandon (October 11, 2010). "Facebook, Zuckerberg spoofed on 'SNL'". CNN. Retrieved October 11, 2010.*

124. Jump up^ *"Mark Zuckerberg 'Liked' SNL's Facebook Skit". New York. October 12, 2010. Retrieved January 28, 2011.*

125. Jump up^ *Lerer, Lisa & McMillan, Traci (October 30, 2010). "Comedy Central's Stewart Says Press, Politicians Are Creating Extremism". Bloomberg. Retrieved November 4, 2010.*

126. Jump up^ *Nina Metz Chicago Closeup 9:00 a.m. CDT, July 18, 2013 (July 18, 2013). "Terms and Conditions May Apply". chicagotribune.com. Retrieved May 25, 2014.*

127. Jump up^ *"'Terms and Conditions May Apply' Details Digital-Age Loss of Privacy". New York Times. Retrieved May 25, 2014.* (paid)

128. Jump up^ *Hoback, Cullen. "Our data is our digital identity - and we need to reclaim control | Technology". theguardian.com. Retrieved May 25, 2014.*

129. Jump up^ *"Mayor Says Newark Is 40% There in Matching Facebook Founder's Grant". The Chronicle of Philanthropy. September 27, 2010.*

130. Jump up^ *Ng, Philiana (September 24, 2010). "Mark Zuckerberg: 'The Social Network' is 'fun'". The Hollywood Reporter.*

131. Jump up^ *Tracy, Ryan (November 23, 2010). "Can Mark Zuckerberg's Money Save Newark's Schools?". Newsweek.*

132. Jump up^ *Reidel, David (September 22, 2010). "Facebook CEO to Gift $100M to Newark Schools". CBS News.com. Retrieved September 23, 2010.*

133. Jump up^ *"Mark Zuckerberg's Well-Timed $100 million Donation to Newark Public Schools"*. *New York Magazine*. September 22, 2010. Retrieved September 28, 2010.

134. ^ Jump up to: [a] [b] *Isaac, Mike (September 24, 2010). "Zuckerberg Pressured To Announce $100 million Donation To Newark"*. *Forbes*. Retrieved Sep 28, 2010.

135. Jump up^ https://finance.yahoo.com/news/mark-zuckerbergs-100-million-donation-155608055.html

136. Jump up^ https://www.nytimes.com/2015/08/23/books/review/the-prize-by-dale-russakoff.html

137. Jump up^
a. *Gonzales, Sandra (December 8, 2010). "Zuckerberg to donate wealth"*. *San Jose Mercury News*.
b. *"US billionaires pledge 50% of their wealth to charity"*. *BBC. August 4, 2010. Retrieved September 6, 2010.*
c. *Moss, Rosabeth (December 14, 2010). "Four Strategic Generosity Lessons"*. *Business Week. Retrieved March 9, 2011.*

138. Jump up^
a. *Bailey, Brandon (December 19, 2013). "Facebook's Mark Zuckerberg makes $1 billion donation"*. *San Jose Mercury News. Retrieved December 20, 2013.*
b. *Sparkes, Matthew (December 19, 2013). "Mark Zuckerberg donates $1bn to charity"*. *The Daily Telegraph. London. Retrieved December 20, 2013.*
c. *Wagner, Kurt (January 3, 2014). "Zuckerberg's Other Billion-Dollar Idea: 2013's Biggest Charitable Gift"*. *Mashable. Mashable. Retrieved January 3, 2014.*

139. Jump up^ *"Facebook's Mark Zuckerberg biggest giver in 2013"*. *USA Today. February 10, 2014.*

140. Jump up^ *Phillip, Abby (October 14, 2014). "Facebook's Mark Zuckerberg and wife Priscilla Chan donate $25 million to Ebola fight"*. *The Washington Post. Retrieved October 25, 2014.*

141. Jump up^ *Kroll, Luisa (October 14, 2014). "Mark Zuckerberg Is Giving $25 Million To Fight Ebola"*. *Forbes. Retrieved October 25, 2014.*

142. Jump up^ *"Mark Zuckerberg Vows to Donate 99% of His Facebook Shares for Charity"*. *The New York Times. December 1, 2015.*

143. Jump up^ *"Facebook's Mark Zuckerberg to give away 99% of shares"*. *BBC News Online*. December 1, 2015. Retrieved December 1, 2015.

144. Jump up^ *"How Mark Zuckerberg's Altruism Helps Himself"*. *The New York Times*. December 3, 2015.

145. Jump up^ *"Mark Zuckerberg and the Rise of Philanthrocapitalism"*. *The New Yorker*. December 2, 2015.

146. Jump up^ *"Mark Zuckerberg's Philanthropy Uses L.L.C. for More Control"*. *The New York Times*. December 2, 2015.

147. Jump up^ *"Why Mark Zuckerberg's huge new donation is going to an LLC rather than a charity"*. *Vox*. December 2, 2015.

148. Jump up^ givingpledge.org/

149. Jump up^ https://www.facebook.com/4/posts/10103996712572761/

150. Jump up^ *Katharine Mieszkowski (April 19, 2011)*. *"President Obama's Facebook appearance aimed at young voters; Bay Area visit targets big donors"*. *The Bay Citizen*. Retrieved December 23, 2013.

151. Jump up^ *David Cohen (February 14, 2013)*. *"Protestors Target Mark Zuckerberg's Fundraiser For N.J. Gov. Chris Christie"*. *AllFacebook*. Retrieved December 23, 2013.

152. Jump up^ *Ben Branstetter (October 21, 2013)*. *"Conservatives including Mark Zuckerberg, Grover Norquist urge House to pass immigration reform"*. *UPI*. Retrieved December 23, 2013.

153. Jump up^ *"Why Mark Zuckerberg is a conservative (and why that matters)"*. *The Daily Dot*. October 30, 2013. Retrieved December 23, 2013.

154. Jump up^ *"2013: Year of the Liberal Billionaires"*. *Politico*. November 1, 2013.

155. Jump up^ *Julia Boorstin (February 13, 2013)*. *"Mark Zuckerberg 'Likes' Governor Chris Christie"*. *CNBC*. Retrieved June 20, 2013.

156. Jump up^ *Kate Zernike (January 24, 2013)*. *"Facebook Chief to Hold Fund-Raiser for Christie"*. *The New York Times*. Retrieved June 20, 2013.

157. Jump up^ *Young, Elise (June 8, 2013)*. *"Zuckerberg Plans Fundraiser for Cory Booker's Senate Run"*. *Bloomberg*. Retrieved October 18, 2013.

158. Jump up^ Christine Richard, "Ackman Cash for Booker Brings $240 Million Aid From Wall Street", *Bloomberg*, October 28, 2010

159. Jump up^ *"Education"*. *Silicon valley Community Foundation*.

160. Jump up^ Cassidy, Mike (February 15, 2013). *"Cassidy: Silicon Valley needs to harness its innovative spirit to level the playing field for blacks and Hispanics"*. *The Mercury News. Retrieved April 23, 2013.*

161. Jump up^ Constine, Josh (April 11, 2013). *"Zuckerberg And A Team Of Tech All-Stars Launch Political Advocacy Group FWD.us"*. *TechCrunch. Retrieved April 17, 2013.*

162. Jump up^ Ferenstein, Gregory (April 11, 2013). *"Zuckerberg Launches A Tech Lobby, But What Will It Do Differently?"*. *TechCrunch. Retrieved April 17, 2013.*

163. Jump up^ Malik, Om (April 11, 2013). *"Why I have issues with Mark Zuckerberg's FWD.us"*. *Gigaom. Retrieved April 17, 2013.*

164. Jump up^ Brian, Matt (April 11, 2013). *"Mark Zuckerberg launches FWD.us with notable Silicon Valley execs in fight for immigration reform"*. *The Verge. Retrieved April 17, 2013.*

165. Jump up^ Zuckerberg, Mark (April 11, 2013). *"Facebook's Mark Zuckerberg: Immigration and the knowledge economy"*. *The Washington Post. Retrieved April 17, 2013.*

166. Jump up^ *"About Us"*. *FWD.us. Retrieved April 17, 2013.*

167. Jump up^ Handley, Meg (April 30, 2013). *"Facebook's Zuckerberg Takes Heat Over Keystone, Drilling Ads"*. *U.S. News & World Report. Archived from the original on May 3, 2013. Retrieved May 3, 2013.*

168. Jump up^ Weiner, Rachel. *"Liberal groups boycotting Facebook over immigration push"*. *The Washington Post. Retrieved August 7, 2013.*

169. Jump up^ Constine, Josh (June 20, 2013). *"Zuckerberg Replies To His Facebook Commenters' Questions On Immigration"*. *TechCrunch. Aol Tech. Retrieved June 20, 2013.*

170. Jump up^ Gallagher, Billy (June 30, 2013). *"Mark Zuckerberg 'Likes' SF LGBT Pride As Tech Companies Publicly Celebrate Equal Rights"*. *TechCrunch. AOL Inc. Retrieved July 2, 2013.*

171. Jump up^ Evelyn M. Rusli (June 30, 2013). *"Mark Zuckerberg Leads 700 Facebook Employees in SF Gay Pride"*. *Wall Street Journal. Retrieved July 2, 2013.*

172. Jump up^ Emery, Debbie (December 9, 2015). *"Mark Zuckerberg Vows to 'Fight to Protect' Muslim Rights on Facebook"*. *The Wrap. Retrieved December 10, 2015.*

173. Jump up^ *White, Daniel (December 9, 2015). "Mark Zuckerberg Offers Support to Muslims in Facebook Post". Time Magazine. Retrieved December 10, 2015.*

174. Jump up^ *Griffin, Andrew (December 9, 2015). "Mark Zuckerberg speaks in support of Muslims after week of 'hate'". The Guardian. Retrieved December 10, 2015.*

175. Jump up^ *Cenk Uygur (December 10, 2015). "Mark Zuckerberg Stands With Muslims". The Young Turks. Retrieved December 11, 2015.*

176. Jump up^ *"Zuckerberg Invokes Jewish Heritage in Facebook Post Supporting Muslims". Haaretz. December 10, 2015. Retrieved December 10, 2015.*

177. Jump up^ *Tait, Robert (December 9, 2015). "Mark Zuckerberg voices support for Muslims amid Donald Trump ban row". The Daily Telegraph. Retrieved December 10, 2015.*

178. ^Jump up to:[a][b] *King, Shaun (February 25, 2016). "Mark Zuckerberg forced to address racism among Facebook staff after vandals target Black Lives Matter phrases". New York Daily News. Retrieved February 26, 2016.*

179. Jump up^ *Jessica, Guynn (February 25, 2016). "Zuckerberg reprimands Facebook staff defacing 'Black Lives Matter' slogan". USA Today. Retrieved February 26, 2016.*

180. Jump up^ *Snyder, Benjamin (February 25, 2016). "Mark Zuckerberg Takes Facebook Workers to Task Over "All Lives Matter" Graffiti". Fortune (magazine). Retrieved February 26, 2016.*

181. Jump up^ theguardian.com January 28, 2017: *Mark Zuckerberg challenges Trump on immigration and 'extreme vetting' order*

182. Jump up^ *O'Connor, Clare (May 20, 2012), Mark Zuckerberg's Wife Priscilla Chan: A New Brand of Billionaire Bride, Forbes, retrieved May 21, 2012*

183. Jump up^ *Status Update: Mark Zuckerberg is married to Priscilla Chan, Techstroke, May 20, 2012, retrieved May 21, 2012*

184. Jump up^ "White Coats on a Rainbow of Students", *Spotlight*, UCSF School of Medicine. Cf. Priscilla Chan, 23.

185. Jump up^ *Spiegel, Rob (December 20, 2010). "Zuckerberg Goes Searching in China".*

186. Jump up^ *"Facebook founder Mark Zuckerberg learn chinese every morning". ChineseTime.cn. September 29, 2010.*

187. Jump up^ *Stein, Joel. "Facebook's Mark Zuckerberg marries sweetheart". Archived from the original on May 24, 2012. Retrieved May 19, 2012.*

188. Jump up^ *"Facebook's Mark Zuckerberg marries Priscilla Chan". cbsnews.com. Retrieved May 20,2012.*

189. Jump up^ *Wohlsen, Marcus (May 19, 2012). "Facebook's Mark Zuckerberg marries longtime girlfriend, Priscilla Chan: Palo Alto, Calif., ceremony caps busy week after company goes public". msnbc.com. Associated Press. Retrieved May 20, 2012.*

190. Jump up^ *"Facebook founder Mark Zuckerberg to become a father". BBC News. BBC. July 31, 2015. Retrieved August 1, 2015.*

191. Jump up^ *"The Switch Mark Zuckerberg and Priscilla Chan to give away 99 percent of their Facebook stock, worth $45 billion".*

192. Jump up^ *"A letter to our daughter". www.facebook.com. Retrieved December 1, 2015.*

193. Jump up^ *Kell, John (February 8, 2016). "Mark Zuckerberg Reveals Daughter's Chinese Name". Fortune.com. Retrieved February 29, 2016. In a pretty adorable video shared by the tech executive over the weekend, Zuckerberg and his wife Priscilla Chan said their daughter Max's Chinese name is Chen Mingyu.*

194. Jump up^ *"Mark Zuckerberg and his wife just unveiled their new baby girl to the world". Fox News. August 28, 2017. Retrieved August 28, 2017.*

195. Jump up^ *"Mark Zuckerberg is back in China as Facebook eyes opportunity to finally enter the country". Business Insider. October 28, 2017.*

196. Jump up^ *Vara, Vauhini (November 28, 2007). "Just How Much Do We Want to Share On Social Networks?". The Wall Street Journal. Retrieved December 30, 2016.*

197. Jump up^ *Daniel Alef (October 17, 2010). Mark Zuckerberg: The Face Behind Facebook and Social Networking. Titans of Fortune Publishing. ISBN 9781608043118. Retrieved December 30,2016.*

198. ^Jump up to:[a][b] *Julie Zauzmer (December 30, 2016). "Mark Zuckerberg says he's no longer an atheist, believes 'religion is very important'". The Washington Post. Retrieved December 30,2016.*

199. Jump up^ *"Facebook Is Injecting Buddhism Into Its Core Business So It Can Be More Compassionate"*. Retrieved June 25, 2013.

200. Jump up^ *"Mark Zuckerberg says "Buddhism is an amazing religion"*. Retrieved October 27, 2015.

201. Jump up^ Zauzmer, Julie (August 29, 2016). *"Pope Francis and Facebook's Mark Zuckerberg had a meeting today - The Washington Post"*. The Washington Post. Retrieved January 7, 2017.

202. Jump up^ Fox, Emily Jane (August 29, 2016). *"Mark Zuckerberg Gives the Pope an Unusual Gift"*. Vanity Fair. Retrieved January 7, 2017.

203. Jump up^ Esteves, Junno Arocho (August 29, 2016). *"Pope meets with Facebook founder Mark Zuckerberg"*. America. Retrieved January 7, 2017.

204. Jump up^ Bailey, Sarah Pulliam (May 25, 2017). *"Mark Zuckerberg shares the prayer he says to his daughter every night -"*. The Washington Post. Retrieved June 6, 2017. Facebook founder Mark Zuckerberg gave the commencement address at Harvard University on Thursday, closing his speech by sharing a Jewish prayer called the "Mi Shebeirach," which he said he recites whenever he faces a big challenge and which he sings to his daughter, thinking of her future, when he tucks her in at night.

205. Jump up^ Hallowell, Billy (May 26, 2017). *"After Abandoning Atheism, Facebook Founder Mark Zuckerberg Reveals the Prayer He Sings to His Daughter Every Night Before Bed"*. Faithwire. Retrieved June 6, 2017. It was during Zuckerberg's commencement address at Harvard University that he shared a Jewish prayer called the "Mi Shebeirach"— an invocation that he said he recites as he copes with major challenges in life and also when he tucks his child in at night, the Washington Post reported.

206. *"Here's everything Laurene Powell Jobs inherited from the late Steve Jobs, including a superyacht and a colossal stake in Disney"*. Business Insider. April 2016. Retrieved December 22, 2017.

207. Jump up^ *"The Walt Disney Company and Affiliated Companies – board of directors"*. The Walt Disney Company. Retrieved October 2, 2009.

208. Jump up^ D'Onfro, Jillian (March 22, 2015). *"Why execs from other companies wanted to meet with Steve Jobs on Fridays"*. Business Insider. Retrieved September 11, 2015.

209. Jump up^ Foremski, Tom. "The Steve Jobs way: Exploring the intersection of psychedelics and technology | ZDNet". ZDNet. Retrieved February 24, 2016.

210. Jump up^ "The Steve Jobs Nobody Knew". Rolling Stone. Retrieved February 24, 2016.

211. Jump up^ "Here's How Zen Meditation Changed Steve Jobs's Life And Sparked A Design Revolution". Business Insider. Retrieved February 24, 2016.

212. Jump up^ Tsukayama, Hayley (February 9, 2012). "Steve Jobs's unflattering FBI file mentions drug use, 2.65 GPA". The Washington Post. ISSN 0190-8286. Retrieved February 26, 2016.

213. Jump up^ Palmer, Brian (October 6, 2011). "Did Dropping Acid Make Steve Jobs More Creative?". Slate. ISSN 1091-2339. Retrieved February 24, 2016.

214. Jump up^ Swaine, Michael and Paul Frieberger. Fire in the Valley: The Birth and Death of the Personal Computer, 3rd Edition, Dallas: Pragmatic Bookshelf, 2014: 310

215. ^Jump up to:$^{a\ b}$ Smith, Alvy Ray. "Pixar Founding Documents". Alvy Ray Smith Homepage. Archived from the original on April 27, 2005. Retrieved January 11, 2011.

216. ^Jump up to:$^{a\ b\ c\ d\ e\ f\ g\ h}$ "The 'father of invention'". Saudi Gazette. January 18, 2011. Archived from the original on July 1, 2015. Retrieved June 27, 2015.

217. ^Jump up to:$^{a\ b\ c\ d\ e\ f\ g\ h\ i\ j\ k\ l\ m\ n\ o\ p\ q\ r\ s\ t\ u\ v\ w\ x\ y\ z\ aa\ ab\ ac\ ad\ ae\ af\ ag\ ah\ ai\ aj\ ak\ al\ am\ an\ ao\ a\ p\ aq\ ar\ asat\ au\ av\ aw\ ax\ ay}$ Isaacson, Walter (2011). Steve Jobs. Simon & Schuster.[pages needed]

218. Jump up^ Graff, Amy (November 18, 2015). "Social media reminds us Steve Jobs was the son of a Syrian migrant". SFGate. Hearst Communications. Retrieved May 19, 2016.

219. ^Jump up to:$^{a\ b}$ Meer, Ameena (Summer 1987). "Artists in Conversation: Mona Simpson". Bomb(20). Retrieved July 7, 2015.

220. ^Jump up to:$^{a\ b\ c\ d\ e\ f\ g\ h\ i\ j\ k\ l\ m\ n\ o\ p\ q\ r\ s\ t\ u\ v\ w\ x\ y\ z\ aa\ ab\ ac\ ad}$ Young, Jeffrey S. (1987). "Steve Jobs: The Journey Is the Reward". Amazon Digital Services, 2011 ebook edition (originally Scott Foresman).[pages needed]

221. Jump up^ "The Lost Interview: Steve Jobs Tells Us What Really Matters". Forbes. November 17, 2011. Retrieved July 12, 2015.

222. ^ Jump up to:[a][b][c] Staff (August 27, 2011). "Dad waits for Jobs to iPhone". New York Post. Retrieved June 27, 2015.

223. ^ Jump up to:[a][b][c][d][e][f][g][h][i][j][k][l][m][n][o][p][q][r][s][t][u][v][w][x][y][z][aa][ab] Brennan, Chrisann. THE BITE IN THE APPLE:A Memoir of My Life with Steve Jobs. St. Martin's Griffin. p. ebook.[pages needed]

224. ^ Jump up to:[a][b][c][d][e][f][g] Schlender, Brent; Tetzeli, Rick (2015). "Becoming Steve Jobs: The Evolution of a Reckless Upstart into a Visionary Leader". Crown (ebook).

225. ^ Jump up to:[a][b] "Steve Jobs' childhood home becomes a landmark". mercurynews.com.

226. ^ Jump up to:[a][b][c][d] "Steve Jobs' old garage about to become a piece of history". mercurynews.com.

227. Jump up^ Brennan, Chrisann (October 19, 2011). "Jobs at 17: Nerd, Poet, Romantic". Rolling Stone Magazine. Archived from the original on April 25, 2012. Retrieved February 9,2015.

228. Jump up^ John Naughton (October 8, 2011). "Steve Jobs: Stanford commencement address, June 2005". The Guardian. London. Archived from the original on February 11, 2012.

229. Jump up^ Schlender, Brent (November 9, 1998). "The Three Faces of Steve in this exclusive, personal conversation, Apple's CEO reflects on the turnaround, and on how a wunderkind became an old pro". Fortune. Retrieved June 27, 2015.

230. Jump up^ "How Steve Wozniak's Breakout Defined Apple's Future". Gameinformer. June 27, 2013. Archived from the original on November 1, 2013. Retrieved February 13, 2014.

231. ^ Jump up to:[a][b][c][d] "An exclusive interview with Daniel Kottke". India Today. September 13, 2011. Archived from the original on May 18, 2012. Retrieved October 27, 2011.

232. Jump up^ "Cassidy on Nolan Bushnell: 'Steve was difficult,' says man who first hired Steve Jobs". Mercury News. March 29, 2013. Archived from the original on December 6, 2013. Retrieved April 2, 2013.

233. Jump up^ "The morning of the day Steve left for India he came to my house to say good-bye and to give me a $100 bill. He had made a bit of money at Atari and he just wanted to give me this gift. I hadn't seen

him in a while and was standing with my new boyfriend at the entrance to the apartment when Steve walked up. Steve touched my forehead to indicate that I was his, which I found outrageous. When I objected to the money, Steve demanded I not play the game of rejecting it. Steve was nothing if not ceremonial in his passages and this money was about him, not me, so I took it and thanked him."
In *Brennan, Chrisann. The Bite in the Apple: A Memoir of My Life with Steve Jobs. St. Martin's Griffin. p. ebook.*

234. Jump up^ *"What really shaped Steve Jobs's view of India – Realms of intuition or the pains of Delhi belly?". Economic Times. India. September 25, 2011. Archived from the original on May 11, 2012. Retrieved October 27, 2011.*

235. Jump up^ *"Il santone della Silicon Valley che ha conquistato i tecno-boss" (in Italian). Repubblica.it. June 9, 2008. Archived from the original on June 24, 2012. Retrieved August 30, 2011.*

236. Jump up^ *"Wandering in India for 7 months: Steve Jobs". Yahoo News. October 24, 2011. Archived from the original on June 24, 2012. Retrieved October 27, 2011.*

237. Jump up^ *Andrews, Amanda (January 14, 2009). "Steve Jobs, Apple's iGod: Profile". The Daily Telegraph. UK. Archived from the original on May 11, 2012. Retrieved October 29, 2009.*

238. Jump up^ *"Steve Jobs profile: Apple's hard core". Edinburgh: News scotsman. January 11, 2009. Archived from the original on September 26, 2011. Retrieved October 29, 2009.*

239. ^ Jump up to:[a][b] *John Markoff (2005). What the Dormouse Said: How the Sixties Counterculture Shaped the Personal Computer Industry. Penguin. p. preface xix. ISBN 978-0-14-303676-0. Retrieved October 5, 2011.*

240. Jump up^ *"Jobs's Pentagon papers: kidnap fears, drug use and a speeding ticket". The Sydney Morning Herald. Archived from the original on June 24, 2012. Retrieved June 12, 2012.*

241. Jump up^ *Silberman, Steve (October 28, 2011). "What Kind of Buddhist was Steve Jobs, Really?". NeuroTribes. Archived from the original on June 24, 2012. Retrieved December 29, 2011.*

242. Jump up^ *Burke, Daniel (November 2, 2011). "Steve Jobs' private spirituality now an open book". USA Today. Retrieved December 29, 2011.*

243. Jump up^ *Murphy, Conor. "The History of Breakout". Big Fish. Big Fish Games, Inc. Retrieved April 22, 2015.*

244. Jump up^ *"Letters – General Questions Answered"*. *Archived from the original on June 12, 2011. Retrieved June 20, 2016.*, Woz.org
Wozniak, Steven: "iWoz", a: pp. 147–48, b: p. 180. W. W. Norton, 2006. ISBN 978-0-393-06143-7
Kent, Stevn: "The Ultimate History of Video Games", pp. 71–3. Three Rivers, 2001. ISBN 978-0-7615-3643-7
"Breakout". Arcade History. June 25, 2002. Retrieved April 19, 2010.
"Classic Gaming: A Complete History of Breakout". GameSpy.
Archived from the original on June 23, 2014. Retrieved April 19, 2010.

245. Jump up^ Isaacson. 2011. Chapter Four – "Atari and India" pp. 104–107.

246. Jump up^ *"Steve Jobs and the Early Apple Years". The PC Is Born. Joomla. Archived from the original on June 24, 2012. Retrieved March 27, 2012.*

247. Jump up^ *McBurney, Sally (Director) (2013). Steve Jobs 1994 Uncut Interview with English Subtitles(Video). Menlo Park, California: Silicon Valley Historical Association.*

248. Jump up^ Silicon Valley Historical Association official YouTube Channel, *Steve Jobs Interview about the Blue Box Story* on YouTube *"Archived copy". Archived from the original on April 2, 2013. Retrieved June 14, 2015.*

249. ^ Jump up to:[a][b] *McBurney, Sally (Director) (2013). Steve Jobs: Visionary Entrepreneur (Video). Menlo Park, California: Silicon Valley Historical Association.*

250. ^ Jump up to:[a][b] *Markoff, John (October 5, 2011). "Steven P. Jobs, 1955–2011: Apple's Visionary Redefined Digital Age". The New York Times.*

251. Jump up^ *Linzmayer, Owen W. "Apple Confidential: The Real Story of Apple Computer, Inc". The Denver Post. Archived from the original on March 20, 2012.*

252. Jump up^ *Simon, Dan (June 24, 2010). "The gambling man who co-founded Apple and left for $800". CNN. Archived from the original on April 10, 2014. Retrieved June 24, 2010.*

253. Jump up^ *"How Did Apple Computer Get Its Brand Name?". Branding Strategy Insider. November 17, 2011. Retrieved November 6, 2017.*

254. Jump up^ *Markoff, John (September 1, 1997). "An 'Unknown' Co-Founder Leaves After 20 Years of Glory and Turmoil". The New York Times. Retrieved August 24, 2011.*

255. ^ Jump up to:*a b* Reimer, Jeremy (December 15, 2005). "Total share: 30 years of personal computer market share figures". Ars Technica. Condé Nast. Retrieved May 25, 2010.

256. ^ Jump up to:*a b* Wozniak, Steve. "woz.org: Comment From e-mail: Why didn't the early Apple II's use Fans?". woz.org. Retrieved May 10, 2015.

257. ^ Jump up to:*a b* "Steve Jobs' black turtleneck reportedly explained in biography". The Los Angeles Times. October 11, 2011. Archived from the original on October 26, 2011. Retrieved October 14, 2011.

258. Jump up^ "Wear the Exact Outfit of Steve Jobs for $458". Gizmodo. February 28, 2006. Archived from the original on February 4, 2012. Retrieved April 19, 2010.

259. Jump up^ Edwards, Jim (December 26, 2013). "These Pictures of Apple's First Employees Are Absolutely Wonderful". Business Insider. Retrieved January 19, 2015.

260. Jump up^ Metz, Rachel (October 15, 2013). "Steve Jobs' ex-girlfriend pens memoir on life with 'vicious' Apple founder". The Guardian. Retrieved January 17, 2015.

261. Jump up^ Bullock, Diane (August 31, 2010). "The Kids of Business Icons: Lisa Brennan-Jobs". Minyanville. Retrieved October 6, 2011.

262. Jump up^ Isaacson, Walter (2011). Steve Jobs. Simon & Schuster. p. 93. ISBN 1-4516-4853-7.

263. Jump up^ "Machine of the Year: The Computer Moves in". Time, January 3, 1983

264. ^ Jump up to:*a b c* Cocks Jay. Reported by Michael Moritz. "The Updated Book of Jobs" in Machine of the Year: The Computer Moves in. Time, January 3, 1983:27.

265. Jump up^ John Sculley is quoted is saying this to official biographer Walter Isaacson, on page 386-387 of Steve Jobs

266. Jump up^ "Photos: The Historic House Steve Jobs Demolished". Wired. February 17, 2011.

267. Jump up^ Lee, Henry K. (February 15, 2011). "Steve Jobs' historic Woodside mansion is torn down". The San Francisco Chronicle.

268. Jump up^ Kahney, Leander (January 6, 2004). "Wired News: We're All Mac Users Now". Wired News. Archived from the original on January 4, 2014. Retrieved September 20, 2006.

269. Jump up^ "America's Most Admired Companies: Jobs' journey timeline". Fortune. Archived from the original on April 10, 2014. Retrieved May 24, 2010. Jobs and a team of engineers visit Xerox PARC, where they see a demo of mouse and graphical user interface

270. Jump up^ Hertzfeld, Andy. "The Times They Are A-Changin'". folklore.org. Archived from the original on February 4, 2012.

271. Jump up^ Swaine, Michael and Paul Frieberger. Fire in the Valley: The Birth and Death of the Personal Computer, 3rd Edition, Dallas: Pragmatic Bookshelf, 2014: 308–309

272. ^ Jump up to:[a b] Swaine, Michael and Paul Frieberger. Fire in the Valley: The Birth and Death of the Personal Computer, 3rd Edition, Dallas: Pragmatic Bookshelf, 2014: 321

273. ^ Jump up to:[a b c] Swaine, Michael and Paul Frieberger. Fire in the Valley: The Birth and Death of the Personal Computer, 3rd Edition, Dallas: Pragmatic Bookshelf, 2014: 322

274. Jump up^ "Machine That Changed The World, The; Paperback Computer, The; Interview with Steve Jobs, 1990". Open Vault. WGBH Media Library & Archives. May 14, 1990. Retrieved September 15, 2016.

275. Jump up^ Robbeloth, DeWitt (Oct–Nov 1985). "Whither Apple?". II Computing. p. 8. Retrieved January 28, 2015.

276. Jump up^ Rice, Valerie (April 15, 1985). "Unrecognized Apple II Employees Exit". InfoWorld. p. 35. Retrieved February 4, 2015.

277. Jump up^ Spector, G (September 24, 1985). "Apple's Jobs Starts New Firm, Targets Education Market". PC Week. p. 109.

278. ^ Jump up to:[a b c d] Linzmayer, Owen W. (2004). Apple Confidential 2.0: The Definitive History of the World's Most Colorful Company. No Starch Press. ISBN 978-1-59327-010-0. Retrieved April 15, 2014. [pages needed]

279. Jump up^ Schwartz, John (October 24, 1988). "Steve Jobs Comes Back". Newsweek. Palo Alto, California. p. Business. Retrieved October 20, 2014.

280. Jump up^ "NeXT Timeline". Retrieved January 21, 2015.

281. Jump up^ Schlender, Brenton R. (October 13, 1988). "Next Project: Apple Era Behind Him, Steve Jobs Tries Again, Using a New System". The Wall Street Journal (Western ed.). Palo Alto,

California: Dow Jones & Company Inc. p. Front Page Leader. Retrieved October 20, 2014.

282. ^ Jump up to:*a b* "Steve Wozniak on Newton, Tesla, and why the original Macintosh was a 'lousy' product". Archived from the original on March 12, 2016. Retrieved June 28, 2013.

283. Jump up^ Rose, F. (April 23, 2009). *Rose, Frank (August 24, 2011). "The End of Innocence at Apple: What Happened After Steve Jobs was Fired". Wired. Archived from the original on October 7, 2011.. Wired.*

284. Jump up^ *"Welcome to info.cern.ch: The website of the world's first-ever web server". CERN (European Organization for Nuclear Research). 2008. Archived from the original on January 18, 2010. Retrieved November 1, 2011.*

285. Jump up^ *Computimes.* (May 31, 1990). Interpersonal computing – the third revolution?. *New Straits Times.* (230), 20; Schlender, B. R., Alpert, M. (February 12, 1990). *Schlender, Brenton R. (February 12, 1990). "Who's ahead in the computer wars". CNN.. Fortune.*

286. Jump up^ Stross, R. E. (1993). *Steve Jobs and the NeXT Big Thing.* Atheneum. ISBN 978-0-689-12135-7. pp. 117, 120, 246.

287. ^ Jump up to:*a b* O'Grady, J. (2008). *Apple Inc.* Greenwood Press. ISBN 978-0-313-36244-6.[*pages needed*]

288. Jump up^ *""Toy Story" Credits". IMDB. Archived from the original on June 24, 2012.*

289. Jump up^ *Hill, Jim (February 5, 2012).* "Steve Jobs bio reveals how Michael Eisner actively tried to derail Disney's 2006 acquisition of Pixar". *Jim Hill Media. Archived from the original on June 24, 2012. Retrieved February 10, 2012.*

290. Jump up^ Wolff, Michael, *"iPod, Therefore I am". Archived from the original on March 28, 2014.,* Vanity Fair, April 2006. Retrieved September 3, 2010.

291. ^ Jump up to:*a b* January 25, 2006 *"Disney buys Pixar for $7.4 bn". Archived from the original on November 9, 2013.,* rediff.com

292. Jump up^ *"The Walt Disney Company – Steve Jobs Biography". Holson, Laura M. (January 25, 2006). "Disney Agrees to Acquire Pixar in a $7.4 Billion Deal". The New York Times. Retrieved January 17, 2010.*
   "Pixar Becomes Unit of Disney". The New York Times. Associated Press. May 6, 2006. Retrieved January 17, 2010.

293. Jump up^ *"Steve Jobs, 1955–2011"*. *Splashnogly*. October 6, 2011. *Archived from the originalon April 7, 2012. Retrieved January 15, 2012.*

294. Jump up^ *"Jobs's 7.7% Disney Stake Transfers to Trust Led by Widow Laurene"*. *Bloomberg. Archived from the original on April 10, 2014.*

295. Jump up^ Floyd Norman (January 19, 2009). *"Steve Jobs: A Tough Act to Follow"*. *Jim Hill Media. Archived from the original on May 8, 2010. Retrieved January 19, 2009.*

296. Jump up^ Julie Bort (June 5, 2014). *"Steve Jobs Taught This Man How To Win Arguments With Really Stubborn People"*. *Inc. Monsueto Ventures. Retrieved June 8, 2014.*

297. ^ Jump up to:*[a][b]* *"Steve Jobs dead: Birth mother Joanne Simpson does not know son has died – Daily Mail Online"*. *Mail Online.*

298. ^ Jump up to:*[a][b][c]* Simpson, Mona (October 30, 2011). *"A Sister's Eulogy for Steve Jobs"*. *The New York Times. Retrieved October 30, 2011.*

299. Jump up^ *"Laurene Powell Jobs – PARSA"*. *PARSA Community Foundation. 2006. Archived from the original on September 14, 2010. Retrieved July 8, 2008.*

300. Jump up^ Kadifa, Margaret. *"Halloween at Steve Jobs' house"*. *Houston Chronicle. Retrieved December 2, 2015.*

301. Jump up^ Apple Computer, Inc. Finalizes Acquisition of NeXT Software Inc. at the Wayback Machine (archive index), *Apple Inc.*, February 7, 1997. Retrieved June 25, 2006.

302. Jump up^ *"Apple Formally Names Jobs as Interim Chief"*. *The New York Times. September 17, 1997. Retrieved June 27, 2011.*

303. Jump up^ *"The once and future Steve Jobs"*. *Salon.com. October 11, 2000. Archived from the original on April 16, 2009.*

304. Jump up^ Norr, Henry (January 6, 2000). *"MacWorld Expo/Permanent Jobs/Apple CEO finally drops 'interim' from title"*. *San Francisco Chronicle. Archived from the original on November 2, 2011. Retrieved June 27, 2011.*

305. Jump up^ *"Jobs announces new MacOS, becomes 'iCEO'"*. *CNN. January 5, 2000. Archived from the original on August 20, 2013.*

306. Jump up^ Levy, Steven (1995). Insanely great: the life and times of Macintosh, the computer that changed everything. Penguin Books. p. 312. ISBN 978-0-14-023237-0.

307. Jump up^ "If Apple can go home again, why not Dell?". Archived from the original on October 10, 2011. CNET News. May 19, 2008.

308. Jump up^ "Dell: Apple should close shop". CNET. Archived from the original on May 17, 2008.

309. Jump up^ Markoff, John (January 16, 2006). "Michael Dell Should Eat His Words, Apple Chief Suggests". The New York Times. Retrieved May 24, 2010.

310. Jump up^ "11 Presentation Lessons You Can Still Learn From Steve Jobs". Forbes. May 28, 2014. Retrieved June 16, 2014.

311. Jump up^ Liedtke, Michael (October 5, 2002). "Steve Jobs resigns from Gap's board". The Berkeley Daily Planet. Archived from the original on April 19, 2012. Retrieved December 23, 2011.

312. Jump up^ "New questions raised about Steve Jobs's role in Apple stock options scandal". December 28, 2006. Archived from the original on May 9, 2007.

313. Jump up^ "Apple restates, acknowledges faked documents". EE Times. December 29, 2006. Archived from the original on May 21, 2013. Retrieved January 1, 2007.

314. Jump up^ "Apple Improves Recycling Plan". PC Magazine. April 21, 2006. Archived from the original on October 20, 2008.

315. Jump up^ Nick Bilton, Bilton, Nick (August 9, 2011). "Apple Is the Most Valuable Company". The New York Times., New York Times, August 9, 2011

316. Jump up^ "7.30". ABCnet.au. Archived from the original on October 9, 2011. Retrieved November 12, 2011.

317. Jump up^ "Lateline: "Visionary Steve Jobs succumbs to cancer"". ABCnet.au. October 6, 2011. Archived from the original on October 9, 2011. Retrieved November 12, 2011.

318. Jump up^ "Live from Macworld 2007: Steve Jobs keynote". 2007. Archived from the original on June 24, 2012. Retrieved April 19, 2010.

319. Jump up^ "Group Wants $7B USD From Apple, Steve Jobs, Executives Over Securities Fraud". Archived from the original on February 4, 2012.

320. Jump up^ *"Apple, Steve Jobs, Executives, Board, Sued For Securities Fraud"*. Archived from the original on May 19, 2009.

321. ^ Jump up to:[a][b] *Andrew S. Ross (November 1, 2011). "Steve Jobs bio sheds light on Obama relationship"*. San Francisco Chronicle. Archived from the original on November 4, 2011. Retrieved November 12, 2011.

322. ^ Jump up to:[a][b] Graham Smith. *"Smith, Graham (October 14, 2011). "Steve Jobs doomed himself by shunning conventional medicine until too late, claims Harvard expert"*. Daily Mail. London. Archived from the original on October 16, 2011.." *Daily Mail* October 14, 2011.

323. ^ Jump up to:[a][b][c][d] *Evangelista, Benny (August 2, 2004). "Apple's Jobs has cancerous tumor removed"*. San Francisco Chronicle. p. A1. Archived from the original on August 18, 2006. Retrieved August 9, 2006.

324. Jump up^ *"Steve Jobs and the Celebrity Diagnosis Complete Guide to Tumors of the Pancreas"*. Celebrity Diagnosis. Archived from the original on June 24, 2012. Retrieved November 12, 2011.

325. Jump up^ *Elkind, Peter (March 5, 2008). "The trouble with Steve Jobs"*. Fortune. Archived from the original on May 18, 2010. Retrieved March 5, 2008.

326. Jump up^ *Fiore, Kristina (December 28, 2012). "Jobs Leaves Lessons for Cancer Care"*. MedPage Today. Archived from the original on April 10, 2014. Retrieved July 14, 2013.

327. Jump up^ Physician Biography for Barrie R. Cassileth. Archived November 13, 2011, at the Wayback Machine.

328. Jump up^ *Liz Szabo (June 18, 2013). "Book raises alarms about alternative medicine"*. USA Today. Retrieved June 19, 2013.

329. Jump up^ Ned Potter. *"Steve Jobs Regretted Delaying Cancer Surgery 9 Months, Biographer Says"*. Archived from the original on April 10, 2014. ABC News October 20, 2011

330. Jump up^ *"Bio Sheds Light on Steve Jobs' Decision to Delay Cancer Surgery, Pursue Herbal Remedies"*. Fox News. October 20, 2011. Archived from the original on June 26, 2012.Associated Press October 20, 2011

331. Jump up^ *"Pancreatic Cancer Treatment"*. Mayo Clinic. Archived from the original on February 4, 2012. Retrieved April 19, 2010.

332. Jump up^ *Markoff, John (July 23, 2008). "Talk of Chief's Health Weighs on Apple's Share Price"*. The New York Times.

333. ^ Jump up to:[a][b] *Elmer, Philip (June 13, 2008). "Steve Jobs and Whipple". Fortune. Archived from the original on June 24, 2012. Retrieved April 19, 2010.*

334. Jump up^ *Kahney, Leander (August 8, 2006). "Has Steve Jobs Lost His Magic?". Cult of Mac. Wired News. Archived from the original on February 4, 2012. Retrieved August 8, 2006. Looking very thin, almost gaunt, Jobs used the 90-minute presentation to introduce a new desktop Mac and preview the next version of Apple's operating system, code-named Leopard.*

335. Jump up^ *Meyers, Michelle. "Jobs speech wasn't very Jobs-like". BLOGMA. CNET News.com. Archived from the original on December 25, 2007. Retrieved August 8, 2006. [The audience was] uninspired (and concerned) by Jobs's relatively listless delivery*

336. Jump up^ *Saracevic, Al (August 9, 2006). "Where's Jobs' Mojo?". San Francisco Chronicle. p. C1. Archived from the original on January 28, 2012. Retrieved August 9, 2006.*

337. Jump up^ *Cheng, Jacqui. "What happened to The Steve we know and love?". Ars Technica. Archived from the original on February 4, 2012. Retrieved August 8, 2006.*

338. Jump up^ *Claburn, Thomas (August 11, 2006). "Steve Jobs Lives!". InformationWeek. Archived from the original on February 4, 2012. Retrieved October 9, 2007.*

339. Jump up^ *"Business Technology: Steve Jobs's Appearance Grabs Notice, Not Just the IPhone". The Wall Street Journal. Archived from the original on April 26, 2009. Retrieved April 19,2010.*

340. Jump up^ *"Apple says Steve Jobs feeling a little under the weather". Archived from the original on April 10, 2014. in AppleInsider.*

341. Jump up^ *"Steve Jobs and Apple". Archived from the original on April 10, 2014.* Marketing Doctor Blog. July 24, 2008.

342. Jump up^ *"Steve Jobs Did Not Have 'Pancreatic Cancer'". Medpagetoday.com. Archived from the original on June 24, 2012. Retrieved November 12, 2011.*

343. Jump up^ *Joe Nocera (July 26, 2008). "Apple's Culture of Secrecy". The New York Times. While his health problems amounted*

to a good deal more than 'a common bug,' they weren't life-threatening and he doesn't have a recurrence of cancer.

344. Jump up^ "Steve Jobs's Obituary, As Run By Bloomberg". Gawker Media. August 27, 2008. Archived from the original on February 4, 2012. Retrieved August 28, 2008.

345. Jump up^ "Bloomberg publishes Jobs obit but why?". Zdnet Blogs. ZDnet. August 28, 2008. Archived from the original on August 31, 2008. Retrieved August 29, 2008.

346. Jump up^ Mikkelson, Barbara (September 26, 2007). "And Never The Twain Shall Tweet". Snopes.com. Archived from the original on August 22, 2011. Retrieved November 2,2012.

347. Jump up^ "Apple posts 'Lets Rock' event video". Macworld. September 10, 2008. Archived from the original on February 4, 2012. Retrieved September 11, 2008.

348. Jump up^ "Live from Apple's "spotlight turns to notebooks" event". Engadget. October 14, 2008. Archived from the original on June 24, 2012. Retrieved October 14, 2008.

349. Jump up^ Stone, Brad (December 17, 2008). "Apple's Chief to Skip Macworld, Fueling Speculation". The New York Times. Retrieved May 24, 2010.

350. Jump up^ "Steve Jobs' Health Declining Rapidly, Reason for Macworld Cancellation". Gizmodo. December 30, 2008. Archived from the original on June 24, 2012. Retrieved April 19,2010.

351. Jump up^ "Apple's Jobs admits poor health". BBC News. January 5, 2009. Archived from the original on August 25, 2011. Retrieved January 5, 2009.

352. Jump up^ Jobs, Steve (January 5, 2009). "Letter from Apple CEO Steve Jobs" (Press release). Apple Inc. Archived from the original on February 4, 2012. Retrieved January 20, 2009.

353. ^ Jump up to:^a ^b "Apple Media Advisory" (Press release). Apple Inc. January 14, 2009. Archived from the original on February 4, 2012. Retrieved January 14, 2009.

354. Jump up^ I BEG YOU, mighty Jobs, TAKE MY LIVER, Cook told Apple's dying co-founder, The Register, March 13, 2015

355. ^ Jump up to:^a ^b "Steve Jobs recovering after liver transplant". CNN. June 23, 2009. Archived from the original on March 31, 2014. Retrieved April 19, 2010.

356. Jump up^ "Liver Transplant in Memphis: Jobs' was Sickest Patient on Waiting List". Celebrity Diagnosis. June 24, 2009. Archived from the original on June 24, 2012.

357. Jump up^ Grady, Denise; Meier, Barry (June 22, 2009). "A Transplant That Is Raising Many Questions". New York Times.

358. Jump up^ Helft, Miguel (January 17, 2010). "Apple Says Steve Jobs Will Take a New Medical Leave". The New York Times. Retrieved January 17, 2010.

359. Jump up^ "Steve Jobs to take medical leave of absence but remain Apple CEO". Archived from the original on February 4, 2012.

360. Jump up^ Abell, John (June 8, 2011). "Video: Jobs Pitches New 'Mothership' to Approving Cupertino City Council". Wired. Archived from the original on February 4, 2012. Retrieved June 9, 2011.

361. Jump up^ Letter from Steve Jobs To the Apple Board of Directors and the Apple Community(resignation letter August 24, 2011) Archived April 15, 2012, at WebCite

362. Jump up^ "Apple Resignation Letter" (Press release). Apple Inc. Archived from the original on April 15, 2012. Retrieved August 29, 2011.

363. Jump up^ "Steve Jobs Resigns as CEO of Apple" (Press release). Apple Inc. August 24, 2011. Archived from the original on April 15, 2012. Retrieved August 24, 2011.

364. Jump up^ Biddle, Sam (October 19, 2011). "Steve Jobs Worked the Day Before He Died". Gizmodo. Archived from the original on June 24, 2012. Retrieved October 21, 2011.

365. Jump up^ Gupta, Poornima (August 18, 2011). "Steve Jobs Quits". Reuters. Archived from the original on February 4, 2012. Retrieved August 25, 2011.

366. Jump up^ Siegler, M.G. "Steve Jobs Resigns As CEO of Apple". TechCrunch. Archived from the original on August 25, 2011. Retrieved August 25, 2011.

367. Jump up^ "Rare Pancreatic Cancer Caused Steve Jobs' Death" (Press release). Voice of America. October 7, 2011. Archived from the original on January 24, 2012. Retrieved October 7, 2011.

368. Jump up^ Rushe, Dominic (October 6, 2011). "Steve Jobs, Apple co-founder, dies at 56". The Guardian. UK. Archived from the original on June 19, 2013.

369. Jump up^ Gullo, Karen (October 10, 2011). "Steve Jobs Died at Home of Respiratory Arrest Related to Pancreatic Cancer". Bloomberg L.P. Archived from the original on February 10, 2012. Retrieved February 10, 2012.

370. Jump up^ Ian Sherr; Geoffrey A. Fowler (October 7, 2011). "Steve Jobs Funeral Is Friday". The Wall Street Journal. Archived from the original on August 13, 2013.

371. Jump up^ Tim Cook (October 5, 2011). "Statement by Apple's Board of Directors" (Press release). Apple Inc. Archived from the original on April 25, 2012. Retrieved October 5, 2011.

372. Jump up^ "Pixar Animation Studios". Pixar. Archived from the original on June 8, 2012. Retrieved April 18, 2013.

373. Jump up^ "Remembering Steve Jobs". Apple Inc. Archived from the original on June 24, 2012. Retrieved October 10, 2011.

374. Jump up^ "Apple flies flags at half staff for Steve Jobs". KOKI-TV. October 6, 2011. Archived from the original on August 13, 2013. Retrieved October 29, 2011.

375. Jump up^ "Microsoft lowers flags to half staff in tribute to Steve Jobs". Network World. October 6, 2011. Archived from the original on November 9, 2013. Retrieved October 29, 2011.

376. Jump up^ "Disney World flags at half-staff in memory of Steve Jobs". Bay News 9. October 6, 2011. Archived from the original on December 13, 2011. Retrieved October 29, 2011.

377. Jump up^ Pepitone, Julianne (October 6, 2011). "Steve Jobs: The homepage tributes". CNN. Archived from the original on April 25, 2012. Retrieved January 10, 2012.

378. Jump up^ "Apple website pays tribute to Steve Jobs". The Times of India. India. October 5, 2011. Archived from the original on April 25, 2012. Retrieved October 7, 2011.

379. Jump up^ "Remembering Steve Jobs". Apple Inc. Archived from the original on June 24, 2012. Retrieved October 6, 2011.

380. ^ Jump up to:[a][b] "A Celebration of Steve's Life". Archived from the original on December 29, 2013.Apple.com Retrieved October 26, 2011

381. Jump up^ Fernandez, Sofia M. (October 14, 2011). "Private Steve Jobs Memorial Set for Oct. 16 – The Hollywood Reporter". The Hollywood Reporter. Archived from the original on December 31, 2013. Retrieved November 12, 2011.

382. Jump up^ "Steve Jobs Memorial Service To Be Held Oct. 16". The Wall Street Journal. October 15, 2011. Archived from the original on August 13, 2013. Retrieved November 12, 2011.

383. Jump up^ Vascellaro, Jessica E. (October 17, 2011). "Steve Jobs's Family Gave Moving Words at Sunday Memorial – Digits – WSJ". The Wall Street Journal. Archived from the original on April 10, 2014. Retrieved November 12, 2011.

384. Jump up^ Wadhwa, Hitendra (June 21, 2015). "Steve Jobs's Secret to Greatness: Yogananda". Inc. Retrieved June 23, 2015.

385. Jump up^ Wozniak Tearfully Remembers His Friend Steve Jobs. YouTube. October 6, 2011.

386. Jump up^ Patricia Sellers (October 6, 2011). "George Lucas on Steve Jobs". Fortune. Archived from the original on January 28, 2012. Retrieved October 6, 2011.

387. Jump up^ "Steve Jobs". Thegatesnotes.com. October 5, 2011. Archived from the original on January 27, 2012. Retrieved November 12, 2011.

388. Jump up^ "Statement by the President on the Passing of Steve Jobs" (Press release). The White House. October 5, 2011. Archived from the original on April 25, 2012.

389. Jump up^ "Steve Jobs Died of Respiratory Arrest Amid Pancreatic Tumor". ABC News. October 10, 2011. Archived from the original on April 25, 2012. Retrieved November 12, 2011.

390. Jump up^ Gupta, Poornima (October 10, 2011). "Steve Jobs died of respiratory arrest, tumor". Reuters. Archived from the original on April 10, 2014. Retrieved September 21, 2012.

391. ^ Jump up to:[a][b] "Steve Jobs' autobiography: a chronicle of a complex genius". The Hindu. Chennai, India. October 24, 2011. Archived from the original on November 9, 2013.

392. Jump up^ "What Made Steve Jobs So Great?". Archived from the original on April 10, 2014. Retrieved August 21, 2012.

393. ^ Jump up to:[a][b] "Does Steve Jobs know how to code?". Archived from the original on October 31, 2013. Retrieved August 21, 2012.

394. Jump up^ "Searching for Magic in India and Silicon Valley: An Interview with Daniel Kottke, Apple Employee #12". Archived from the original on January 11, 2014. Retrieved August 30, 2012.

395. Jump up^ "Portfolio of over 300 patents underscores Steve Jobs' attention to detail". Archived from the original on April 10, 2014. Retrieved September 26, 2012.

396. ^ Jump up to:^{a b} *"U.S. Government patent database". Archived from the original on June 24, 2012. Retrieved August 29, 2011.*

397. Jump up^ *"U.S. Government patent application database". Archived from the original on April 20, 2012. Retrieved August 29, 2011.*

398. Jump up^ *"United States Patent 8,032,843, Ording, et al., October 4, 2011, "User interface for providing consolidation and access"". Archived from the original on June 24, 2012.*

399. Jump up^ *"Steve Jobs Told Me Why He Loved Being A CEO". Business Insider. Archived from the original on August 6, 2011. Retrieved February 2, 2013. He told me once that part of the reason he wanted to be CEO was so that nobody could tell him that he wasn't allowed to participate in the nitty-gritty of product design", Reid writes. "He was right there in the middle of it. All of it. As a team member, not as CEO. He quietly left his CEO hat by the door, and collaborated with us.*

400. Jump up^ *Kachka, Boris (August 26, 2015). "How Kate Winslet Won a Role in Steve Jobs and Managed All That Sorkin Dialogue". Vulture. Archived from the original on June 18, 2016. Retrieved December 28, 2017.*

401. Jump up^ *Simpson, Mona (October 30, 2011). "A Sister's Eulogy for Steve Jobs". The New York Times. Retrieved September 16, 2012.*

402. Jump up^ *Rosenwald, Michael S. (October 24, 2011). "Walter Isaacson's 'Steve Jobs' biography shows Apple co-founder's genius, flaws". The Washington Post. Retrieved September 16,2012.*

403. Jump up^ *"Steve Jobs Still Wins Plenty of Patents – MIT Technology Review". MIT Technology Review. Retrieved January 21, 2015.*

404. Jump up^ *Christoph Dernbach (October 12, 2007). "Apple Lisa". Mac History. Retrieved November 15, 2012.*

405. Jump up^ Apple Lisa computer, http://oldcomputers.net/lisa.html

406. Jump up^ *Simon, Jeffrey S. Young, William L. (April 14, 2006). iCon : Steve Jobs, the greatest second act in the history of business (Newly updated. ed.). Hoboken, NJ: Wiley (retrieved via Google Books). ISBN 978-0471787846. Retrieved January 6, 2014.*

407. Jump up^ *Linzmayer, Owen W. (2004). Apple confidential 2.0 : the definitive history of the world's most colorful company (2nd ed.). San Francisco, Calif.: No Starch Press (retrieved via Google Books). p. 79. ISBN 978-1593270100. Retrieved January 6, 2014.*

408. Jump up^ Polsson, Ken (July 29, 2009). "Chronology of Apple Computer Personal Computers". Archived from the original on August 21, 2009. Retrieved August 27, 2009. See May 3, 1984.

409. Jump up^ Linzmayer, Owen W. (2004). Apple Confidential 2.0. No Starch Press. p. 113. ISBN 1-59327-010-0.

410. Jump up^ Maney, Kevin (January 28, 2004). "Apple's '1984' Super Bowl commercial still stands as watershed event". USA Today. Retrieved April 11, 2010.

411. Jump up^ Leopold, Todd (February 3, 2006). "Why 2006 isn't like '1984'". CNN. Retrieved May 10,2008.

412. Jump up^ Creamer, Matthew (March 1, 2012). "Apple's First Marketing Guru on Why '1984' Is Overrated". Ad Age. Retrieved April 19, 2015.

413. Jump up^ Cellini, Adelia (January 2004). "The Story Behind Apple's '1984' TV commercial: Big Brother at 20". MacWorld. 1 (21). p. 18. Archived from the original on June 28, 2009. Retrieved May 9, 2008.

414. Jump up^ Long, Tony (January 22, 2007). "Jan. 22, 1984: Dawn of the Mac". Wired. Retrieved April 11, 2010.

415. Jump up^ Reimer, Jeremy (December 14, 2005). "Total share: 30 years of personal computer market share figures". Ars Technica. Retrieved April 16, 2015.

416. Jump up^ Carter, Mia. "Steve Jobs: 10 Products that Define this Tech Legend". Inventions and Discoveries. Archived from the original on April 4, 2012. Retrieved March 27, 2012.

417. Jump up^ "Steve Jobs Introduces NeXTComputer". Archived from the original on April 7, 2013. Retrieved April 7, 2013. Steve Jobs unveiled the NeXT, the computer he designed after moving on from Apple Computer Inc...

418. Jump up^ Hoppel, Adrian. "Magical Inventions of Steve Jobs". Best Inventions of Steve Jobs. Magical Inventions of Steve Jobs. Archived from the original on April 10, 2014. Retrieved March 27, 2012.

419. Jump up^ Paola Antonelli, Paola. "iMac – 1998". MetropolisMag. Archived from the original on May 11, 2013. Retrieved March 28, 2012.

420. Jump up^ Michael (August 7, 2007). "Apple History: Evolution of the iMac". Apple Gazette. Apple Gazette. Archived from the original on June 24, 2012. Retrieved March 28, 2012.

421. Jump up^ "iPod First Generation". iPod History. iPod History. Archived from the original on June 24, 2012. Retrieved March 28, 2012.

422. ^ Jump up to:[a][b] Block, Ryan. "The iPod family cemetery". iPods. EndGadget. Archived from the original on June 24, 2012. Retrieved March 28, 2012.

423. Jump up^ Asiado, Tel (August 24, 2011). "Steve Jobs: 10 Products that Define this Tech Legend". Inventions and Discoveries. Archived from the original on April 4, 2012. Retrieved March 27, 2012.

424. ^ Jump up to:[a][b] "iPhone History – Read About The iPhone Story Here". The Apple Biter's Blog. November 4, 2011. Archived from the original on June 24, 2012. Retrieved October 15,2014.

425. Jump up^ "iPhone History and Development". iPhone apps, tricks, tips, and hacks. Apple iPhone Blog. Archived from the original on June 24, 2012. Retrieved March 28, 2012.

426. Jump up^ "iPhone 3GS". iPhone News. iPhoneHistory. Archived from the original on June 24, 2012. Retrieved March 28, 2012.

427. Jump up^ "iPhone 4 Tech Specs". Apple. Archived from the original on June 24, 2012. Retrieved March 28, 2012.

428. Jump up^ "The iPad's 5th anniversary: a timeline of Apple's category-defining tablet". The Verge. Retrieved April 17, 2015.

429. Jump up^ "Steve Jobs statue unveiled in Hungary science park". GlobalPost. December 21, 2011. Archived from the original on January 10, 2012. Retrieved December 28, 2011.

430. Jump up^ "Apple Park's Steve Jobs Theater opens to host 2017 keynote". Dezeen. 2017-09-12. Retrieved 2018-01-04.

431. Jump up^ Ford, Rebecca (July 10, 2013). "Steve Jobs, Billy Crystal to Receive Disney Legends Awards". The Hollywood Reporter. Archived from the original on April 4, 2014. Retrieved July 18, 2013.

432. Jump up^ Arico, Joe (December 22, 2011). "Steve Jobs Wins Special Grammy". Mobiledia.com. Archived from the original on September 6, 2012. Retrieved December 28, 2011.

433. Jump up^ "Jobs inducted into California Hall of Fame". Archived from the original on January 10, 2008., California Museum. Retrieved 2007.

434. Jump up^ "25 most powerful people in business – #1: Steve Jobs". Fortune. Archived from the original on April 10, 2014. Retrieved April 19, 2010.

435. Jump up^ *"Reed College Convocation"*. *Apple iTunes*. Portland, Oregon, USA: Reed College. August 27, 1991. Retrieved December 6, 2016.

436. Jump up^ Bo Burlingham and George Gendron (April 1, 1989). *"The Entrepreneur of the Decade"*. *Inc. magazine*. Archived from the original on June 24, 2012. Retrieved October 8, 2011.

437. Jump up^ *"National Winners / public service awards"*. Jefferson Awards.org. Archived from the original on February 4, 2012. Retrieved April 19, 2010.

438. Jump up^ *"The National Medal of Technology Recipients 1985 Laureates"*. *Uspto.gov*. Archived from the original on February 4, 2012. Retrieved April 19, 2010.

439. *"Bill Gates"*. *Forbes*. Retrieved September 9, 2017.

440. Jump up^ Manes 1994, p. 11.

441. Jump up^ *"Bill Gates (American computer programmer, businessman, and philanthropist)"*. Retrieved March 20, 2013.

442. Jump up^ Sheridan, Patrick (May 2, 2014). *"Bill Gates no longer Microsoft's biggest shareholder"*. *CNN Money*. Retrieved August 22, 2014.

443. Jump up^ *MSFT (Holdings)*, NASDAQ, retrieved April 10, 2016

444. Jump up^ *MSFT (Symbol)*, NASDAQ, retrieved April 10, 2016

445. Jump up^ Einstein, David (January 13, 2000). *"Gates steps down as Microsoft CEO"*. *forbes.com*. Retrieved January 21, 2016.

446. Jump up^ *"Microsoft Chairman Gates to leave day-to-day role. – Jun. 16, 2006"*. *money.cnn.com*. Retrieved January 21, 2016.

447. Jump up^ *"Bill Gates / Development of Information and Knowledge Management"*. *tlu.ee*. Retrieved January 21, 2016.

448. ^ Jump up to:[a][b] *"Bill Gates steps down as chairman, will assist new CEO as 'technology advisor'"*. *The Verge*. Retrieved February 4, 2014.

449. Jump up^ Lesinski 2006, p. 96; Manes 1994, p. 459.

450. Jump up^ *"Why Putin Isn't on 'Forbes' Billionaires List"*. *Newsweek*.

451. ^ Jump up to:[a][b] Thibault, Marie (January 19, 2010). *"The Next Bill Gates"*. *Forbes*. Archived from the original on July 19, 2012. Retrieved December 20, 2010.

452. ^ Jump up to:[a][b] *"Amazon CEO Jeff Bezos Is The Richest Perosn In The World-Again"*. *Forbes*.

453. ^ Jump up to:[a][b] *"The $600 billion challenge"*. *Fortune*. Retrieved April 16, 2017.

454. Jump up^ *"Bill Gates Cofounder, Bill & Melinda Gates Foundation"*. Forbes. Retrieved September 1, 2017.

455. Jump up^ *"Ancestry of Bill Gates"*. Wargs. Archived from the original on September 16, 2012. Retrieved June 9, 2010.

456. Jump up^ *"Scottish Americans"*. Alba West. Archived from the original on May 11, 2008. Retrieved April 29, 2009.

457. Jump up^ Manes 1994, p. 15.

458. Jump up^ Manes 1994, p. 47.

459. Jump up^ *Lesinski, Jeanne M (September 1, 2008). Bill Gates: Entrepreneur and Philanthropist. Twenty First Century Books. ISBN 978-1-58013-570-2. Retrieved March 10, 2011. The Gates family regularly went to services at the University Congregational Church.*

460. Jump up^ *Lowe, Janet (January 5, 2001). Bill Gates Speaks: Insight from the World's Greatest Entrepreneur. Wiley. ISBN 978-0-471-40169-8. Retrieved March 10, 2011. The Gates family attended the University Congregational Church, where the Reverend Dale Turner was pastor.*

461. Jump up^ *Berkowitz, Edward D (2006). Something Happened: A Political and Cultural Overview of the Seventies. Columbia University Press. ISBN 978-0-231-12494-2. Retrieved March 10, 2011. Bill Gates was a member of the baby boom, born in 1955 into an upper-middle-class family near Seattle." He attended the Congregational Church, participated in the Boy Scouts, and went to a fancy private school.*

462. Jump up^ *Cringely, Robert X. (June 1996). "Part II". Triumph of the Nerds: The Rise of Accidental Empires. Season 1. PBS.*

463. Jump up^ Manes 1994, p. 24.

464. Jump up^ Manes 1994, p. 27.

465. ^Jump up to:[a] [b] Gates 1996, p. 12.

466. Jump up^ Manes 1994, p. 34.

467. Jump up^ *Paul Allen spills the beans on Gates' criminal past, UK, V3*

468. Jump up^ *"Remarks by Bill Gates, co-chair", Bill & Melinda Gates Foundation – Press Room, Speeches, retrieved July 13, 2013*

469. Jump up^ Gates 1996, p. 14.

470. Jump up^ *Congressional Page History, The United States House Page Association of America, archived from the original on May 1, 2015, The Page Program has produced many politicians, Members of Congress, as well as other famous men and women. Some of these include: the Honorable John Dingell, the longest serving Member of*

Congress, Bill Gates, founder and CEO of the Microsoft Corporation, and Donnald K. Anderson, former Clerk of the House.

471. Jump up^ *"National Merit Scholarship Corporation – Scholars You May Know". nationalmerit.org. Retrieved October 25, 2015.*

472. Jump up^ *"The new—and improved?—SAT". The Week Magazine. Archived from the originalon May 10, 2006. Retrieved May 23, 2006.*

473. Jump up^ Gates 1996, p. 15.

474. Jump up^ *"Timeline : Bill Gates : 1973; from google (bill gates major in harvard) result 3".*

475. Jump up^ *Michael Hitt; R. Duane Ireland; Robert Hoskisson. Strategic Management: Concepts and Cases: Competitiveness and Globalization. p. 263. ISBN 978-1-111-82587-4. Retrieved October 25, 2015.*

476. ^Jump up to:[a b c] *Kestenbaum, David (July 4, 2008). "Before Microsoft, Gates Solved A Pancake Problem". National Public Radio. Archived from the original on September 16, 2012.*

477. Jump up^ *"UT Dallas Team Bests Young Bill Gates With Improved Answer to So-Called Pancake Problem in Mathematics". University of Texas at Dallas. September 17, 2008. Archived from the original on August 26, 2010.*

478. Jump up^ *Gates, William; Papadimitriou, Christos (1979). "Bounds for sorting by prefix reversal". Discrete Mathematics. 27: 47–57. doi:10.1016/0012-365X(79)90068-2.*

479. ^Jump up to:[a b] Gates 1996, p. 19.

480. Jump up^ Wallace 1993, p. 59.

481. Jump up^ Gates 1996, p. 18.

482. Jump up^ The History of Microsoft – 1976: Bill Gates explaining that his departure from Harvard was reversible if Microsoft had failed.

483. ^Jump up to:[a b c] *"Microsoft Visitor Center Student Information: Key Events in Microsoft History". Microsoft. Archived from the original (.DOC) on February 26, 2008. Retrieved February 18,2008.*

484. ^Jump up to:[a b c d] *"Microsoft history". The History of Computing Project. Archived from the original on May 14, 2008. Retrieved March 31, 2008.*

485. Jump up^ Manes 1994, p. 81.

486. Jump up^ *Gates, William 'Bill' (October 13, 2005). Remarks (Speech). Waterloo, ON. Archived from the original on April 6, 2008. Retrieved March 31, 2008.*

487. ^ Jump up to:[a][b] Bunnell, David (Feb–Mar 1982). "The Man Behind The Machine?". PC Magazine(interview). p. 16. Retrieved February 17, 2012.

488. Jump up^ Gordon, John Steele; Maiello, Michael (December 23, 2002). "Pioneers Die Broke". Forbes. Archived from the original on September 16, 2012. Retrieved March 31, 2008.

489. ^ Jump up to:[a][b] Gates 1996, p. 54.

490. Jump up^ Manes 1994, p. 193.

491. Jump up^ Freiberger, Paul (August 23, 1982). "Bill Gates, Microsoft and the IBM Personal Computer". InfoWorld. p. 22. Retrieved January 29, 2015.

492. Jump up^ "Challenges and Strategy" (PDF). Groklaw. Retrieved November 17, 2011.

493. Jump up^ Freiberger, Paul (August 31, 1981). "Bugs in Radio Shack TRS-80 Model III: How Bad Are They?". InfoWorld. p. 49. Retrieved February 28, 2011.

494. Jump up^ Thorlin, Fred (April 2000). "Fred Thorlin: The Big Boss at Atari Program Exchange"(Interview). Interview with Kevin Savetz. Atari archives. Retrieved December 6, 2012.

495. Jump up^ Rensin, David (1994). "The Bill Gates Interview". Playboy.

496. Jump up^ Ballmer, Steve (October 9, 1997). "Steve Ballmer Speech Transcript – Church Hill Club". Microsoft. Archived from the original on April 20, 2008. Retrieved March 31,2008.

497. ^ Jump up to:[a][b] Isaacson, Walter (January 13, 1997). "The Gates Operating System". Time. Archived from the original on June 19, 2000. Retrieved March 31, 2008.

498. Jump up^ Bank, David (February 1, 1999). "Breaking Windows". The Wall Street Journal. Archived from the original on April 16, 2016. Retrieved March 31, 2008.

499. Jump up^ Chapman, Glenn (June 27, 2008). "Bill Gates Signs Off". Agence France-Presse. Archived from the original on June 30, 2008.

500. ^ Jump up to:[a][b] Gates, Bill (September 26, 1997). Remarks by Bill Gates (Speech). San Diego. Archived from the original on April 20, 2008. Retrieved March 31, 2008.

501. Jump up^ Herbold, Robert (2004). The Fiefdom Syndrome: The Turf Battles That Undermine Careers and Companies – And How to Overcome Them. ISBN 0-385-51067-5.

502. Jump up^ Gates, Bill. "Bill Gates Interview". Transcript of a Video History Interview / Computer History Collection (Interview). Interview with David Allison. National Museum of American History, Smithsonian Institution. Retrieved April 10, 2013.

503. Jump up^ Pournelle, Jerry (September 1985). "PCs, Peripherals, Programs, and People". BYTE. p. 347. Retrieved March 20, 2016.

504. Jump up^ "Microsoft Announces Plans for July 2008 Transition for Bill Gates". Microsoft. June 15, 2006. Archived from the original on June 19, 2006.

505. Jump up^ Wasserman, Elizabeth (November 17, 1998). "Gates deposition makes judge laugh in court". CNN. Retrieved April 10, 2013.

506. Jump up^ "Microsoft's Teflon Bill". BusinessWeek. November 30, 1998. Archived from the original on April 7, 2008. Retrieved March 30, 2008.

507. ^Jump up to:ᵃ ᵇ Heilemann, John (November 1, 2000). "The Truth, The Whole Truth, and Nothing But The Truth". Wired (8.11). Archived from the original on May 28, 2014. Retrieved March 31, 2008.

508. Jump up^ "Mugshots". The Smoking Gun. Archived from the original on July 24, 2010. Retrieved June 9, 2010.

509. Jump up^ "Adblog". MSNBC. September 8, 2008. Retrieved May 23, 2014.

510. Jump up^ Ina Fried (September 11, 2008). "Seinfeld and Gates Hit the Road for Vista". CNET. Retrieved July 26, 2015.

511. Jump up^ Matthew G. Miller; Peter Newcomb (January 2, 2014). "Billionaires Worth $3.7 Trillion Surge as Gates Wins 2013". Bloomberg Businessweek. Retrieved January 3, 2014.

512. Jump up^ "Microsoft names Satya Nadella to replace Steve Ballmer". BBC News. February 4, 2014. Retrieved February 4, 2014.

513. Jump up^ Jeff Goodell (March 13, 2014). "Bill Gates: The Rolling Stone Interview". Rolling Stone. Jann S. Wenner. Retrieved March 28, 2014.

514. Jump up^ Mack, Eric (January 28, 2015). "Bill Gates Says You Should Worry About Artificial Intelligence". Forbes. Retrieved February 19, 2015.

515. Jump up^ Lumby, Andrew (January 28, 2015). "Bill Gates Is Worried About the Rise of the Machines". The Fiscal Times. Retrieved February 19, 2015.

516. Jump up^ Holley, Peter (March 24, 2015). "Apple co-founder on artificial intelligence: 'The future is scary and very bad for people'". *The Washington Post*. Retrieved April 8, 2015.

517. Jump up^ "Permalink to an answer from "Hi Reddit, I'm Bill Gates and I'm back for my third AMA. Ask me anything. • /r/IAmA"". *reddit*. Retrieved June 10, 2015.

518. Jump up^ "Baidu CEO Robin Li interviews Bill Gates and Elon Musk at the Boao Forum, March 29, 2015". *YouTube*. Retrieved April 8, 2015.

519. Jump up^ Mary Riddell (October 21, 2016). "Bill Gates: He eats Big Macs for lunch and schedules every minute of his day – meet the man worth $80 billion". *The Telegraph*. Retrieved October 24, 2016.

520. Jump up^ "coverage of the Gates' Medina, Washington estate". *Forbes*. May 22, 2002. Archived from the original on September 6, 2012. Retrieved June 9, 2010.

521. ^ Jump up to:^a ^b Goodell, Jeff (March 27, 2014). "Bill Gates: The Rolling Stone Interview". *Rolling Stone*. Retrieved April 14, 2014.

522. Jump up^ Lesinski 2006, p. 74

523. Jump up^ Paterson, Thane (June 13, 2000). ""He had come a long way to this blue lawn and his dream must have seemed so close he could hardly fail to grasp it"-FSF (Advice for Bill Gates: A Little Culture Wouldn't Hurt)". *Business Week*. Archived from the original on May 1, 2008. Retrieved April 28, 2008.

524. Jump up^ "Bill Gates: Chairman". *Microsoft Corporation*. 2008. Archived from the original on August 28, 2008.

525. Jump up^ "Profile: Bill Gates". *BBC news*. January 26, 2004. Archived from the original on July 21, 2012. Retrieved January 1, 2010.

526. Jump up^ Fridson 2001, p. 113

527. Jump up^ Zuckerman, Laurence (October 27, 1997). "New Jet Eases Travel Hassles For Bill Gates". *The New York Times*. Archived from the original on September 16, 2012. Retrieved September 2, 2012.

528. Jump up^ Bolger, Joe (May 5, 2006). "I wish I was not the richest man in the world, says Bill Gates". *The Times*. UK. Archived from the original on July 10, 2012. Retrieved March 31, 2008.

529. Jump up^ Cuadros, Alex; Harrison, Crayton (May 17, 2013). "Bill Gates Retakes World's Richest Title From Carlos Slim". *Forbes*. Retrieved May 30, 2013.

530. Jump up^ *"Bill Gates regains world's richest man title: Forbes"*. The *Times of India*. March 3, 2014.

531. Jump up^ *"Forbes Billionaires list"*. Archived from the original on May 25, 2012.

532. Jump up^ Estevez, Dolia (June 7, 2014). *"Mexico's Carlos Slim Reclaims World's Richest Man Title From Bill Gates"*. *Forbes*. Retrieved September 1, 2014.

533. Jump up^ *"The World's Billionaires"*. *Forbes*. Retrieved November 30, 2014.

534. Jump up^ *"Bill Gates"*. *Forbes*. Retrieved 2017-08-25.

535. Jump up^ *"Microsoft 2006 Proxy Statement"*. *Microsoft*. October 6, 2007. Archived from the original on February 19, 2008. Retrieved February 14, 2008.

536. Jump up^ Fried, Ina (December 14, 2004). *"Gates joins board of Buffett's Berkshire Hathaway"*. *CNET*. Archived from the original on September 8, 2012. Retrieved March 31, 2008.

537. Jump up^ Alex Osborn (February 18, 2016). *"This Was Bill Gates' Favorite XBLA Game"*. *IGN*. Ziff Davis.

538. Jump up^ *"Newsnight Interview"*. *BBC*. January 24, 2014. Retrieved August 23, 2017.

539. Jump up^ *"US Should Pay More Tax"*. *ABC*. May 28, 2013. Retrieved August 23, 2017.

540. Jump up^ *"Gates foundation"*. Archived from the original on May 23, 2012.[dead link]

541. Jump up^ Robin Toal (September 16, 2013). *"The Top Ten US Charitable Foundations"*. *Funds For NGOs*. Funds For NGOs, LLC. Retrieved April 6, 2014.

542. Jump up^ Cronin, Jon (January 25, 2005). *"Bill Gates: billionaire philanthropist"*. *BBC News*. Archived from the original on July 31, 2012. Retrieved April 1, 2008.

543. Jump up^ *"Our Approach to Giving"*. *Bill & Melinda Gates Foundation*. Archived from the original on April 4, 2008. Retrieved April 1, 2008.

544. Jump up^ *"2005 Annual Report"* (PDF). *Rockefeller Brothers Fund*. January 1, 2006. Archived from the original (PDF) on February 16, 2008. Retrieved February 14, 2008.

545. Jump up^ *"The 50 most generous Americans"*. Archived from the original on February 22, 2012.

546. Jump up^ "Bill and Melinda Gates give 95% of wealth to charity". BBC News. October 18, 2010. Archived from the original on July 19, 2012.

547. Jump up^ "What We Do". Bill and Melinda Gates Foundation. Bill and Melinda Gates Foundation. 2014. Retrieved April 6, 2014.

548. Jump up^ "Agricultural Development Golden Rice". Archived from the original on February 3, 2016. Retrieved February 3, 2016.

549. Jump up^ Bina Abraham (October 1, 2010). "They half it in them". Gulf News. Archived from the original on January 21, 2011. Retrieved March 17, 2011.

550. Jump up^ Moss, Rosabeth (December 14, 2010). "Four Strategic Generosity Lessons". Business Week. Archived from the original on February 25, 2011. Retrieved March 9, 2011.

551. Jump up^ "40 billionaires pledge to give away half of wealth". Archived from the original on November 4, 2012. Retrieved August 8, 2010.

552. Jump up^ Robyn Griggs Lawrence (February 22, 2011). "A Rich Gift: Homemade Jelly for Bill and Melinda Gates". Mother Earth News. Archived from the original on February 24, 2011. Retrieved March 10, 2011.

553. Jump up^ Matthew G.H. Chun (April 14, 1999). "Bill Gates Donates $20 million to MIT". The Harvard Crimson. The Harvard Crimson, Inc. Retrieved April 6, 2014.

554. Jump up^ "Our Campus TEACHING, RESEARCH, AND ADMINISTRATIVE SPACES". Harvard School of Engineering and Applied Sciences. President and Fellows of Harvard College. 2014. Retrieved April 6, 2014.

555. Jump up^ "Gates Computer Science Building". Stanford Engineering. Stanford University. 2014. Archived from the original on April 1, 2014. Retrieved April 6, 2014.

556. Jump up^ "Bill Gates". Facebook. Retrieved August 15, 2014.

557. Jump up^ Kass, Jason (November 18, 2013). "Bill Gates Can't Build a Toilet". New York Times Opinion Pages. New York Times. Retrieved March 24, 2015.

558. Jump up^ "BBC news article "Bill Gates drinks water distilled from human faeces"". Retrieved January 11, 2015.

559. Jump up^ "From poop to portable, This Ingenious Machine Turns Feces into Drinking Water". gatesnotes, The Blog of Bill Gates. January 5, 2015. Retrieved January 13, 2015.

560. Jump up^ "Bill Gates and Jimmy Drink Poop Water". Youtube Channel of The Tonight Show Starring Jimmy Fallon. January 22, 2015.

561. Jump up^ "Bill Gates makes $100 million personal investment to fight Alzheimer's". www.reuters.com. Retrieved November 13, 2017.

562. Jump up^ "Briefly Noted / Excellence in Philanthropy / The Philanthropy Roundtable". www.philanthropyroundtable.org. Retrieved March 10, 2016.

563. Jump up^ "Dark butt over good works of Gates Foundation". Los Angeles Times. January 7, 2007. Archived from the original on September 16, 2012., Los Angeles Times, January 7, 2006.

564. Jump up^ Heim, Kristi (January 10, 2007). "Gates Foundation to review investments". The Seattle Times. Archived from the original on May 16, 2007., The Seattle Times, January 10, 2007.

565. Jump up^ Gates Foundation to maintain its investment plan, The Austin Statesman, January 14, 2007.[dead link]

566. Jump up^ "Lefever, Ernest W. (November 1, 1999). "Bill Gates' 'Diversity' Subverts Merit". Los Angeles Times. Archived from the original on July 10, 2012.", Los Angeles Times, November 1, 1999

567. Jump up^ " "The Gates Millennium Scholars program". Archived from the original on January 15, 2013."

568. Jump up^ "Bill Gates faces circumcision protest". Vancouver 24 hrs. Retrieved March 29, 2016.

569. Jump up^ Andy Coghlan. "Bill Gates helps fund mass circumcision programme". New Scientist. Retrieved March 29, 2016.

570. Jump up^ "Live blog: Bill Gates and Roger Federer play tennis for charity in Seattle". April 30, 2017.

571. Jump up^ see Forbes World's Richest People 1996, 1997, and 1998

572. Jump up^ Wahba, Phil (September 17, 2008). "Bill Gates tops US wealth list 15 years continuously". Reuters. Archived from the original on September 16, 2012. Retrieved November 6, 2008.

573. Jump up^ Kirsch, Noah. "Here's Why Jeff Bezos Is Not Truly The Richest Person In History". Forbes. Retrieved 2018-01-11.

574. Jump up^ Lesinski 2006, p. 102

575. Jump up^ Cowley, Jason (June 22, 2006). "Heroes of our time – the top 50". New Statesman. UK. Archived from the original on December 31, 2007. Retrieved February 17, 2008.

576. Jump up^ *"Gates 'second only to Blair'"*. *BBC News. September 26, 1999. Archived from the original on July 11, 2012. Retrieved March 30, 2008.*

577. Jump up^ *"The World's Most Powerful People". Forbes. December 5, 2012. Archived from the original on December 30, 2012. Retrieved June 30, 2013.*

578. Jump up^ *"The World's Most Powerful People". Forbes. November 2, 2011. Archived from the original on November 3, 2011. Retrieved June 30, 2013.*

579. Jump up^ *"Bill Gates Speaks of Opportunities and Challenges Facing "Generation I"". News Center. Microsoft. Retrieved October 25, 2015.*

580. Jump up^ *"Eredoctoraat Universiteit Nyenrode voor Wim Kok" (Press release) (in Dutch). Nyenrode Business Universiteit. August 13, 2003. Archived from the original on February 18, 2008. Retrieved February 18, 2008.*

581. Jump up^ *"Honorary doctors at KTH". About KTH. Stockholm: KTH Royal Institute of Technology. Retrieved January 19, 2015.*

582. Jump up^ *"Bill Gates Awarded Honorary Doctorate of Tsinghua". Tsinghua University. April 19, 2007. Archived from the original on July 7, 2011. Retrieved June 9, 2010.*

583. Jump up^ *Hughes, Gina (June 8, 2007). "Bill Gates Gets Degree After 30 Years". Yahoo!. Archived from the original on December 27, 2007. Retrieved February 18, 2008.*

584. Jump up^ *"Karolinska Institutet Medicine hedersdoktorer 1910-2013" [Honorary doctors of medicine at the Karolinska Institute 1910–2013] (PDF) (in Swedish). Karolinska Institutet. May 22, 2013. Retrieved January 19, 2015.*

585. Jump up^ *University of Cambridge (June 12, 2009). "The Chancellor in Cambridge to confer Honorary Degrees". University of Cambridge. Archived from the original on August 17, 2009. Retrieved August 20, 2009.*

586. Jump up^ *Blakely, Rhys (July 18, 2007). "Gates how piracy worked for me in China". The Times. London. Archived from the original on July 7, 2012. Retrieved April 26, 2010.*

587. Jump up^ *"Knighthood for Microsoft's Gates". BBC News. March 2, 2005. Archived from the original on July 11, 2012. Retrieved February 18, 2008.*

588. Jump up^ *"Proclamation of the Award"*. *Diario Oficial de la Federación*. Archived from the original on March 6, 2008. Retrieved March 30, 2008.

589. Jump up^ *"Bower Award for Business Leadership"*. *The Franklin Institute*. 2010. Retrieved June 30, 2013.

590. Jump up^ *"2010 Silver Buffalo Recipients"*. *Scouting: 39*. September–October 2010.

591. Jump up^ Thompson, F. Christian (August 19, 1999). *"Bill Gates' Flower Fly Eristalis gatesiThompson"*. *The Diptera Site*. Archived from the original on February 12, 2008. Retrieved February 18, 2008.

592. Jump up^ National Winners | public service awards. Jefferson Awards.org. Retrieved on September 4, 2013.

593. Jump up^ *"The 2006 James C. Morgan Global Humanitarian Award"*. *The Tech Museum of Innovation*. Retrieved April 2, 2014.

594. Jump up^ *"Padma Awards – Press Information Board of India"*. *Ministry of Home Affairs, India*. Archived from the original on January 26, 2015.

595. Jump up^ *"Padma awards 2015 announced: Advani, Amitabh among 104 awardees"*. *Zee News*.

596. Jump up^ *"President Obama Names Recipients of the Presidential Medal of Freedom"*. *whitehouse.gov*. *The White House*. November 16, 2016. Retrieved November 16, 2016.

597. Jump up^ *"Bill and Melinda Gates receive Légion d'Honneur medals"*.

598. Jump up^ Levy, Jared Ari (June 4, 2013). *"Bill Gates Joins $35 Million Funding in Startup ResearchGate"*. *Bloomberg*. Retrieved January 28, 2015.

599. Jump up^ *"Machine That Changed The World, The; Interview with Bill Gates, 1990 (raw video)"*. *WGBH Open Vault*. 1990. Retrieved September 19, 2016.

600. Jump up^ *"Bill Gates Goes to Sundance, Offers an Education"*. *ABC News*. January 23, 2010. Archived from the original on July 1, 2012.

601. Jump up^ *"'Bogus Bill' has a blast playing billionaire in 'The Social Network'"*. *KVAL 13*. Archived from the original on July 30, 2015. Retrieved October 25, 2015.

602. Jump up^ *"American Genius"*. *American Genius*. Retrieved September 10, 2015.

603. Jump up^ Wills, Amanda. "Bill Gates Joins LinkedIn", *Mashable*, New York, June 13, 2013. Retrieved on July 30, 2013.

604. Jump up^ *"BBC Radio 4 – Desert Island Discs, Bill Gates"*. BBC. *Retrieved March 29, 2016*.

605. *"Ma Huateng"*. *Forbes*.

606. Jump up^ *"Tencent posts 69 percent jump in quarterly net profit; becomes the most valuable company in Asia"*. *Tech2*.

607. Jump up^ Investing in China: The Emerging Venture Capital Industry Jonsson Yinya Li, *Google Book Search*

608. ^Jump up to:[a][b][c] Tencent Tencent official site

609. Jump up^ *"The 100 Most Influential People in the World"*. *Time. April 24, 2014*.

610. Jump up^ Biographical Dictionary of New Chinese Entrepreneurs and Business Leaders, Pg. 111 Ilan Alon and Wenxian Zhang. Edward Elgar Publishing, 2009. Google Book Search.

611. Jump up^ *"Businessperson of the Year"*. *Fortune. 16 November 2017*.

612. Jump up^ Schuman, Michael. *"Ma Huateng - pg.49"*. *Forbes*.

613. Jump up^ *"Tencent's Pony Ma is Asian tech spaces' new Warren Buffett"*. *www.dealstreetasia.com*.

614. Jump up^ *"Huateng "Pony" Ma"*. *Fortune. 24 March 2016*.

615. Jump up^ *"Internet mogul Pony Ma named most generous Chinese philanthropist"*. *South China Morning Post*.

616. Jump up^ Flannery, Russell. *"Tencent Rally Adds Billions to Chairman's Philanthropy Pile, Highlights China Influence"*. *Forbes*.

617. Jump up^ Flannery, Russell. *"China Billionaire Horse Race: Tencent's Ma Huateng Is Asia's Richest Again"*. *Forbes*.

618. Jump up^ *"Asia's Tech Scene Gets a New Warren Buffett"*. *Bloomberg Quint*.

619. Jump up^ Chanchani, Madhav (7 August 2015). *"After Alibaba Holdings, Tencent makes first investment in Indian firm"*. *The Economic Times*.

620. Jump up^ Walters, Natalie (17 August 2017). *"Asia's Richest Man Jack Ma Has Become Much Wealthier This Year - See The Number"*. *TheStreet*.

621. Jump up^ *"Tencent Chief Overtakes Wanda's Wang as China's Second-Richest Person"*. *Bloomberg.com. 20 July 2017*.

622. Jump up^ *"Ma Huateng"*. *Forbes*.

623. Jump up^ *"Ma Huateng became one of the top 10 richest men in the world, surpassing Larry Page and Sergey Brin"*. *Forbes*.

624. Jump up^ *"Tencent's Ma Huateng is China's second-richest man on WeChat mania". www.livemint.com/. Retrieved 2016-01-12.*

625. Jump up^ *"Pony Ma - Founder, Executive Director & CEO @ Tencent Holdings | CrunchBase". www.crunchbase.com. Retrieved 2016-01-12.*

626. Jump up^ *"Tencent's Ma becomes China's second-richest man". www.businessspectator.com.au. Retrieved 2016-01-12.*

627. ^Jump up to:[a][b][c][d][e] *"A mysterious message millionaire". www.chinadaily.com.cn. Retrieved 2016-01-12.*

628. Jump up^ *"Ma Huateng | Chinese entrepreneur". Encyclopædia Britannica. Retrieved 2016-01-12.*

629. ^Jump up to:[a][b][c] *"Tencent: The Secretive, Chinese Tech Giant That Can Rival Facebook and Amazon". Fast Company. Retrieved 2016-01-12.*

630. ^Jump up to:[a][b][c][d] *"Pony Ma Biography - life, family, name, young, born, time, year, Career, Sidelights - Newsmakers Cumulation". www.notablebiographies.com. Retrieved 2016-01-12.*

631. Jump up^ *"Ten Years of Tencent – Beijing Review". www.bjreview.com. Retrieved 2016-01-12.*

632. Jump up^ *"Language Log » A New Morpheme in Mandarin". languagelog.ldc.upenn.edu. Retrieved 2016-01-12.*

633. Jump up^ *"Tech in Asia - Connecting Asia's startup ecosystem". www.techinasia.com. Retrieved 2016-01-12.*

634. ^Jump up to:[a][b] *M, Swathi R. "Internet Users In Malaysia Are More Active On WhatsApp And Facebook Than Those In US, UK And China [REPORT]". Dazeinfo. Retrieved 2016-01-12.*

635. Jump up^ *"What are the next big things in the world of high technology? Let China's internet giants tell you". South China Morning Post. Retrieved 2016-01-12.*

636. Jump up^ *Fuchs, Christian (2015-01-09). Culture and Economy in the Age of Social Media. Routledge. ISBN 9781317558194.*

637. Jump up^ *"Pony Ma and his Tencent". Luxatic. Retrieved 2016-01-12.*

638. ^Jump up to:[a][b] *"Ma vs. Ma: The most expensive house in Hong Kong belongs to one of China's internet kings - but is it Jack or Pony?". South China Morning Post. Retrieved 2016-01-12.*

639. Jump up^ *"Ma Huateng". Forbes. Retrieved 2017-05-07.*

640. https://www.forbes.com/profile/michael-dell/

641. Jump up^ *"Michael Dell Profile". Forbes. Retrieved February 20, 2017.*

642. Jump up^ Brown, Joshua (2011-03-20). "Michael Dell's Very Big Stock Purchase". The Reformed Broker. Retrieved 2011-10-15.

643. Jump up^ Calnan, Christopher (2010-02-07). "Managing Michael Dell's multibillions". BizJournals. Retrieved 2011-10-15.

644. Jump up^ Guglielmo, Connie (October 30, 2013). "Dell Officially Goes Private: Inside The Nastiest Tech Buyout Ever". Forbes.

645. ^Jump up to:[a][b] "Dell agrees $67bn EMC takeover". BBC News. 2015-10-12. Retrieved 2017-01-11.

646. ^Jump up to:[a][b] "Dell to Buy EMC in Deal Worth About $67 Billion". Bloomberg.com. 2015-10-12. Retrieved 2017-01-11.

647. ^Jump up to:[a][b] "Historic Dell and EMC Merger Complete; Forms World's Largest Privately-Controlled Tech Company | Business Wire". www.businesswire.com. Retrieved 2017-01-11.

648. Jump up^ Lone stars of David: the Jews of Texas, By Hollace Ava Weiner, Kenneth Roseman, page 257, UPNE, 2007

649. Jump up^ Biography of Michael Dell. businessweek.com (From The Associated Press; 2007-01-31).

650. Jump up^ History of Our School. Es.houstonisd.org. Retrieved on 2012-07-12.

651. Jump up^ "Biography: Michael Dell Founder & Chairman, Dell Inc". American Academy of Achievement. Retrieved April 15, 2010.

652. Jump up^ Dell, Michael; Catherine Fredman (1999). Direct from Dell: Strategies that Revolutionized an Industry. HarperBusiness. pp. 6–7. ISBN 0-88730-914-3.

653. Jump up^ http://www.nbcnews.com/id/38168029/ns/business-careers/t/lowest-paying-jobs-america/#.WMHJUBLyvaY

654. Jump up^ Dell, Michael; Catherine Fredman (1999). Direct from Dell: Strategies that Revolutionized an Industry. HarperBusiness. pp. 4–5. ISBN 0-88730-914-3.

655. Jump up^ Kirk Ladendorf. "Dell remembers his beginning while looking toward the future" Austin American-Statesman. November 27, 2011, pp. E1, E2.

656. Jump up^ Dell, Michael; Catherine Fredman (1999). Direct from Dell: Strategies that Revolutionized an Industry. HarperBusiness. pp. 9–10. ISBN 0-88730-914-3.

657. Jump up^ Larry Faulkner, President, University of Texas at Austin (2003). Michael Dell Remarks. dell.com

658. Jump up^ Buchholz, Jan (2014-04-29). "UT's famed high-rise dorm where Dell launched to get $4 million makeover". Statesman.com. Retrieved 2017-01-05.

659. Jump up^ Dell, Michael; Catherine Fredman (1999). Direct from Dell: Strategies that Revolutionized an Industry. HarperBusiness. pp. 12–13. ISBN 0-88730-914-3.

660. Jump up^ Kessler, Michelle (March 4, 2004). "Dell founder passes torch to new CEO". USA Today. Retrieved January 6, 2010.

661. Jump up^ "Michael Dell". National Press Club Summary. National Public Radio. June 8, 2008. Retrieved April 16, 2010.

662. Jump up^ Dell, Michael; Catherine Fredman (1999). Direct from Dell: Strategies that Revolutionized an Industry. HarperBusiness. p. xiv. ISBN 0-88730-914-3.

663. Jump up^ Kanellos, Michael (April 1, 2001). "Dell beats Compaq for No. 1 ranking". CNET News. Retrieved April 16, 2010.

664. Jump up^ "MSC Capital – About Us". Retrieved April 17, 2010.

665. Jump up^ "Dell Chief Replaced by Founder", New York Times.

666. Jump up^ Guglielmo, Connie. "Dell Officially Goes Private: Inside the Nastiest Tech Buyout Ever". Forbes. Retrieved 23 October 2016.

667. ^ Jump up to:[a][b] "Dell Inc., Michael S. Dell, Kevin B. Rollins, James M. Schneider, Leslie L. Jackson, Nicholas A.R. Dunning". Sec.gov. 2010-07-22. Retrieved 2011-01-26.

668. Jump up^ Richman, Tom (January 1, 1990). "The Entrepreneur of the Year". Inc. Retrieved April 16, 2010.

669. Jump up^ "MICHAEL S. DELL". Franklin Institute. Retrieved 2016-12-19.

670. Jump up^ "Michael Dell". Dell Inc. Retrieved 28 April 2017.

671. Jump up^ Dell, Michael; Catherine Fredman (1999). Direct from Dell: Strategies that Revolutionized an Industry. HarperBusiness. ISBN 0-88730-914-3.

672. Jump up^ "Forbes - Michael Dell". www.forbes.com. March 2013. Retrieved December 9, 2014.

673. Jump up^ Fishman, Charles (2001-02-28). "Face Time With Michael Dell". Fast Company. Archived from the original on 2016-10-20. Retrieved 2016-10-20.

674. Jump up^ Schwinn, Elizabeth (2006-04-06). "A Focus on Efficiency". The Chronicle of Philanthropy. Retrieved 2016-10-20. (Subscription required (help)).

675. Jump up^ COLLOFF, PAMELA (2000-07-31). "Suddenly Susan". Texas Monthly. Archived from the original on 2016-10-20. Retrieved 2016-10-20.

676. Jump up^ Foundation, Michael & Susan Dell. "Michael & Susan Dell Foundation Grants $50 Million to University of Texas to Bring Excellence in Children's Health and Education to Austin". www.prnewswire.com. Retrieved 2017-01-31.

677. Jump up^ "Michael & Susan Dell Foundation Invests $50 million to Establish the Dell Medical School at The University of Texas at Austin". UT News | The University of Texas at Austin. 2013-01-30. Retrieved 2017-01-31.

678. Jump up^ "Michael & Susan Dell Foundation". Michael & Susan Dell Foundation. Retrieved 2017-01-31.

679. Jump up^ Gwynne, S.C. (February 7, 2013). "Dell's Great Success Story". Texas Monthly. Retrieved 1 October 2017.

680. Jump up^ Foundation, Michael & Susan Dell. "Michael & Susan Dell Foundation Applauds the First Lady's 'Let's Move!' Campaign to End Childhood Obesity". Retrieved September 13,2016.

681. Jump up^ "The Michael and Susan Dell Foundation: Private Company Information - Businessweek". Retrieved September 13, 2016.

682. Jump up^ Annette Condon (2002-05-29), Michael Dell Conferred with Honorary Doctorate from the University of Limerick. University of Limerick Press Release

683. Jump up^ Ralph K.M. Haurwitz (January 30, 2013). "Dell family foundation to donate $60 million for UT medical school, local health care". Austin American-Statesman.

684. Jump up^ "Hollywood gala raises a record $33 million for IDF". TIMES OF ISRAEL. November 8, 2014. Retrieved November 17, 2014.

685. Jump up^ "Tech billionaire Michael Dell pledges $36 million to Harvey relief efforts". CNN. September 1, 2017. Retrieved September 1, 2017.

686. Anthony, Scott D.; Johnson, Mark W.; Sinfield, Joseph V.; Altman, Elizabeth J. (2008). Innovator's Guide to Growth - Putting Disruptive Innovation to Work. Harvard Business School Press. ISBN 978-1-59139-846-2.

687. Daniele Archibugi, Blade Runner Economics: Will Innovation Lead the Economic Recovery?, Social Science Research Network, January 29, 2015.

688. *Archibugi, Daniele; Filippetti, Andrea; Frenz, Marion (2013). "Economic crisis and innovation: Is destruction prevailing over accumulation?". Research Policy. 42 (2): 303–314. doi:10.1016/j.respol.2012.07.002.*

689. How to Identify and Build Disruptive New Businesses, *MIT Sloan Management Review* Spring 2002

690. *Christensen, Clayton M. (1997), The innovator's dilemma: when new technologies cause great firms to fail, Boston, Massachusetts, USA: Harvard Business School Press, ISBN 978-0-87584-585-2.* (edit)

691. Christensen, Clayton M. & Overdorf, Michael. (2000). "Meeting the Challenge of Disruptive Change" *Harvard Business Review*, March–April 2000.

692. Christensen, Clayton M., Bohmer, Richard, & Kenagy, John. (2000). "Will Disruptive Innovations Cure Health Care?" *Harvard Business Review*, September 2000.

693. *Christensen, Clayton M. (2003). The innovator's solution : creating and sustaining successful growth. Harvard Business Press. ISBN 978-1-57851-852-4.*

694. *Christensen, Clayton M.; Scott, Anthony D.; Roth, Erik A. (2004). Seeing What's Next. Harvard Business School Press. ISBN 978-1-59139-185-2.*

695. Christensen, Clayton M., Baumann, Heiner, Ruggles, Rudy, & Sadtler, Thomas M. (2006). "Disruptive Innovation for Social Change" *Harvard Business Review*, December 2006.

696. Mountain, Darryl R., Could New Technologies Cause Great Law Firms to Fail?

697. *Mountain, Darryl R (2006). "Disrupting conventional law firm business models using document assembly". International Journal of Law and Information Technology. 15: 170–191. doi:10.1093/ijlit/eal019.*

698. *Tushman, M.L.; Anderson, P. (1986). "Technological Discontinuities and Organizational Environments". Administrative Science Quarterly. 31: 439–465. doi:10.2307/2392832.*

699. Eric Chaniot (2007). "The Red Pill of Technology Innovation" *Red Pill*, October 2007.

700.

701. ITU-R, Report M.2134, Requirements related to technical performance for IMT-Advanced radio interface(s), Approved in November 2008

702. ∧ Jump up to:[a] [b] "ITU World Radiocommunication Seminar highlights future communication technologies". International Telecommunication Union.

703. Jump up∧ 62 commercial networks support DC-HSPA+, drives HSPA investments LteWorld February 7, 2012

704. ∧ Jump up to:[a] [b] Vilches, J. (April 29, 2010). "Everything You Need To Know About 4G Wireless Technology". TechSpot. Retrieved January 11, 2016.

705. Jump up∧ "2009-12: The way of LTE towards 4G". Nomor Research. Retrieved January 11, 2016.

706. Jump up∧ "3GPP specification: Requirements for further advancements for E-UTRA (LTE Advanced)". 3GPP. Retrieved August 21, 2013.

707. Jump up∧ "3GPP Technical Report: Feasibility study for Further Advancements for E-UTRA (LTE Advanced)". 3GPP. Retrieved August 21, 2013.

708. Jump up∧ "ITU paves way for next-generation 4G mobile technologies" (press release). ITU. 21 October 2010

709. Jump up∧ Parkvall, Stefan; Dahlman, Erik; Furuskär, Anders; Jading, Ylva; Olsson, Magnus; Wänstedt, Stefan; Zangi, Kambiz (21–24 September 2008). LTE Advanced – Evolving LTE towards IMT-Advanced (PDF). Vehicular Technology Conference Fall 2008. Ericsson Research. Stockholm. Retrieved November 26, 2010.

710. Jump up∧ Parkvall, Stefan; Astely, David (April 2009). "The evolution of LTE toward LTE Advanced". Journal of Communications. 4 (3): 146–54. doi:10.4304/jcm.4.3.146-154. Archived from the original on August 10, 2011.

711. Jump up∧ "The Draft IEEE 802.16m System Description Document" (PDF). ieee802.org. April 4, 2008.

712. Jump up∧ "Light Reading Mobile – 4G/LTE – Ericsson, Samsung Make LTE Connection – Telecom News Analysis". Unstrung.com. Retrieved March 24, 2010.[permanent dead link]

713. Jump up∧ "MetroPCS Launches First 4G LTE Services in the United States and Unveils World's First Commercially Available 4G LTE Phone". MetroPCS IR. 21 September 2010. Archived from the original on 2010-09-24. Retrieved April 8, 2011.

714. Jump up∧ Jason Hiner (12 January 2011). "How AT&T and T-Mobile conjured 4G networks out of thin air". TechRepublic. Retrieved April 5, 2011.

715. Jump up^ Brian Bennet (5 April 2012). "Meet U.S. Cellular's first 4G LTE phone: Samsung Galaxy S Aviator". CNet. Retrieved April 11, 2012.

716. Jump up^ "Sprint 4G LTE Launching in 5 Cities July 15". PC Magazine. 27 June 2012. Retrieved November 3, 2012.

717. Jump up^ "We have you covered like nobody else". T-Mobile USA. April 6, 2013. Archived from the original on March 29, 2013. Retrieved April 6, 2013.

718. Jump up^ "SK Telecom and LG U+ launch LTE in Seoul, fellow South Koreans seethe with envy". 5 July 2011. Retrieved July 13, 2011.

719. Jump up^ "EE launches Superfast 4G and Fibre for UK consumers and businesses today". EE. October 30, 2012. Retrieved August 29, 2013.

720. Jump up^ Miller, Joe (August 29, 2013). "Vodafone and O2 begin limited roll-out of 4G networks". BBC News. Retrieved August 29, 2013.

721. Jump up^ Shukla, Anuradha (October 10, 2011). "Super-Fast 4G Wireless Service Launching in South Korea". Asia-Pacific Business and Technology Report. Retrieved November 24, 2011.

722. Jump up^ "Sprint announces seven new WiMAX markets, says 'Let AT&T and Verizon yak about maps and 3G coverage'". Engadget. March 23, 2010. Archived from the original on March 25, 2010. Retrieved April 8, 2010.

723. Jump up^ "UPDATE 1-Russia's Yota drops WiMax in favour of LTE". May 21, 2010 – via Reuters.

724. Jump up^ Qualcomm halts UMB project, Reuters, November 13th, 2008

725. Jump up^ G. Fettweis; E. Zimmermann; H. Bonneville; W. Schott; K. Gosse; M. de Courville (2004). "High Throughput WLAN/WPAN" (PDF). WWRF. Archived from the original (PDF) on 2008-02-16.

726. Jump up^ "4G standards that lack cooperative relaying".

727. Jump up^ For details, see the article on IPv4 address exhaustion

728. Jump up^ Morr, Derek (June 9, 2009). "Verizon mandates IPv6 support for next-gen cell phones". Retrieved June 10, 2009.

729. Jump up^ Zheng, P; Peterson, L; Davie, B; Farrel, A (2009). "Wireless Networking Complete". Morgan Kaufmann

730. Jump up^ Alabaster, Jay (20 August 2012). "Japan's NTT DoCoMo signs up 1 million LTE users in a month, hits 5 million total". Network

574

World. IDG. Archived from the original on December 3, 2013. Retrieved 29 October 2013.

731. Jump up^ *"KT Launches Commercial WiBro Services in Korea". WiMAX Forum. November 15, 2005. Archived from the original on May 29, 2010. Retrieved June 23, 2010.*

732. Jump up^ *"KT's Experience In Development Projects". March 2011.*

733. Jump up^ *"4G Mobile Broadband". Sprint. Archived from the original on February 22, 2008. Retrieved March 12, 2008.*

734. Jump up^ *Federal Reserve Bank of Minneapolis Community Development Project. "Consumer Price Index (estimate) 1800–". Federal Reserve Bank of Minneapolis. Retrieved January 2,2018.*

735. Jump up^ *"DoCoMo Achieves 5 Gbit/s Data Speed". NTT DoCoMo Press. February 9, 2007.*

736. Jump up^ *Reynolds, Melanie (September 14, 2007). "NTT DoCoMo develops low power chip for 3G LTE handsets". Electronics Weekly. Archived from the original on September 27, 2011. Retrieved April 8, 2010.*

737. Jump up^ *"Auctions Schedule". FCC. Archived from the original on January 24, 2008. Retrieved January 8, 2008.*

738. Jump up^ *"European Commission proposes TV spectrum for WiMax". zdnetasia.com. Archivedfrom the original on December 14, 2007. Retrieved January 8, 2008.*

739. Jump up^ *"Skyworks Rolls Out Front-End Module for 3.9G Wireless Applications. (Skyworks Solutions Inc.)" (free registration required). Wireless News. February 14, 2008. Retrieved September 14, 2008.*

740. Jump up^ *"Wireless News Briefs — February 15, 2008". WirelessWeek. February 15, 2008. Archived from the original on August 19, 2015. Retrieved September 14, 2008.*

741. Jump up^ *"Skyworks Introduces Industry's First Front-End Module for 3.9G Wireless Applications". Skyworks press release. 11 February 2008. Retrieved September 14, 2008.*

742. Jump up^ ITU-R Report M.2134, "Requirements related to technical performance for IMT-Advanced radio interface(s)," November 2008.

743. Jump up^ *"Nortel and LG Electronics Demo LTE at CTIA and with High Vehicle Speeds :: Wireless-Watch Community". Archived from the original on 2008-06-06.*

744. Jump up^ "Scartel and HTC Launch World's First Integrated GSM/WiMAX Handset" (Press release). HTC Corporation. 12 November 2008. Archived from the original on 2008-11-22. Retrieved March 1, 2011.

745. Jump up^ "San Miguel and Qatar Telecom Sign MOU". Archived from the original on February 18, 2009. Retrieved 2009-02-18. San Miguel Corporation, December 15, 2008

746. Jump up^ "LRTC to Launch Lithuania's First Mobile WiMAX 4G Internet Service" (Press release). WiMAX Forum. 3 March 2009. Archived from the original on 2010-06-12. Retrieved November 26, 2010.

747. Jump up^ "4G Coverage and Speeds". Sprint. Archived from the original on April 5, 2010. Retrieved November 26, 2010.

748. Jump up^ "Teliasonera First To Offer 4G Mobile Services". The Wall Street Journal. December 14, 2009. Archived from the original on 2010-01-14.

749. Jump up^ NetCom.no – NetCom 4G (in English)

750. Jump up^ "TeliaSonera´s 4G Speed Test – looking good". Daily Mobile. Retrieved January 11,2016.

751. Jump up^ Anand Lal Shimpi (June 28, 2010). "The Sprint HTC EVO 4G Review". AnandTech. Retrieved March 19, 2011.

752. Jump up^ [1][permanent dead link].

753. Jump up^ "Verizon launches its first LTE handset". Telegeography.com. March 16, 2011. Retrieved July 31, 2012.

754. Jump up^ "HTC ThunderBolt is officially Verizon's first LTE handset, come March 17th". Phonearena.com. 2011. Retrieved July 31, 2012.

755. Jump up^ "demonstrates Broadcast Video/TV over LTE". Ericsson. Retrieved July 31, 2012.

756. Jump up^ IT R&D program of MKE/IITA: 2008-F-004-01 "5G mobile communication systems based on beam-division multiple access and relays with group cooperation".

OTHER BOOKS BY STEPHEN AKINTAYO

1. HOW TO EARN 7 FIGURES FROM BULK SMS BUSINESS:
Secrets of Building a Successful Mobile Marketing Empire

2. HOW TO MAKE MONEY FAST FROM SOCIAL MEDIA
    MARKETING:
The Ultimate Guide to Social Media Marketing

3. QUICKEST WAYS TO EARN MONEY BLOGGING:
How to Make Money Fast As a Blogger

4. MILLIONAIRE FREELANCER:
Best Ways to Make Money from Freelance Jobs

5. SCHOLARSHIP MADE EASY:
Fastest Ways to Get Scholarships & Study Abroad

6.   SURVIVAL INSTINCTS:
Becoming a Success in a Third World Country

8. TURNING YOUR MESS INTO YOUR MESSAGE

5. HOW TO EARN 6 FIGURES FROM DIGITAL MARKETING:
Understanding, Monetizing and Consultancy in Digital Marketing

6. SOUL MATE:
Becoming and Finding the Perfect Mate

Made in the USA
Middletown, DE
19 September 2024